Armageddon in Waco

Armageddon

Edited by
STUART A. WRIGHT

The University of Chicago Press • Chicago and London

in Waco

Critical

Perspectives

on the

Branch

Davidian

Conflict

STUART A. WRIGHT is associate professor of
sociology at Lamar University in Texas.

The University of Chicago Press, Chicago 60637
The University of Chicago Press, Ltd., London
© 1995 by The University of Chicago
All rights reserved. Published 1995
Printed in the United States of America

04 03 02 01 00 99 98 97 96 95   1 2 3 4 5

ISBN: 0-226-90844-5 (cloth)
    0-226-90845-3 (paper)

Library of Congress Cataloging-in-Publication Data

Armageddon in Waco: critical perspectives on the Branch Davidian
    conflict/edited by Stuart A. Wright.
        p. cm.
    Includes bibliographical references and index.
    1. Branch Davidians. 2. Waco Branch Davidian Disaster, Tex.,
    1993. 3. Psychology, Religious. 4. Cults—United States—
    Psychology. 5. United States—Religion—1960– 6. Psychology and
    religion. I. Wright, Stuart A.
    BP605.B72A76 1995
    299'.93—dc20   95-8872
                                                    CIP

Contents

Preface

As this manuscript entered the first stages of production in December, the Treasury Department announced the reinstatement of two BATF agents previously dismissed for their roles in the Waco Branch Davidian fiasco. The records of Phil Chojnacki, special agent in charge of the Bureau's Houston division who supervised the raid, and Charles Sarabyn, assistant special agent in the Houston division, were expunged and each was reassigned—with full back pay and benefits—according to settlements negotiated by attorneys for the BATF and the agents (*Houston Chronicle*, December 22, 1994). The actions by the Treasury Department were both disturbing and perplexing given that the department's own report castigated the two agents for proceeding with the raid despite specific instructions from their superior (Ron Noble) to abort if the element of surprise was lost. Setting aside legal and ethical questions about the defensibility of the planned raid, the Treasury Department report states unequivocally that agent Robert Rodriguez, who covertly joined the sect as part of an intelligence gathering operation, warned agent Sarabyn through an intermediary that the raid had been compromised only minutes before the command was given to commence. Curiously, Sarabyn's reaction was to accelerate, rather than abandon, the raid. Later, the report indicates that agents Chojnacki and Sarabyn lied about Rodriguez's disclosure and attempted to conceal their own misjudgments about the entire episode.

While some critics observed that the actions of these government agents were deserving of criminal charges, Treasury moved quickly to quell public criticism by initiating a disciplinary review culminating in dismissal. BATF Deputy Director Daniel Black concluded in October that the agents (1) made gross errors in judgment (read: should never have carried through with the assault), (2) issued false and misleading statements to authorities, and (3) in Chojnacki's case, attempted to shift blame to subordinates. Yet, in the end, two federal officials whose "errors" are linked directly to the deaths of six people in the initial assault (and indirectly to the deaths of seventy-four people in the April 19 fire), walked away with their jobs intact, their incomes and benefits secured, and their legal fees paid by BATF. By any measure, the most recent decisions by this federal agency add another puzzling chapter to the debacle at Waco.

This turn of events provides evidence for two predominant themes of the book: first, that marginal religions and their members are accorded diminished human and social value, largely tied to disparaging stigmas and widespread stereotypes ("brainwashed cultists") that recall some of the most vicious racial, ethnic, and religious prejudices of our nation's past; and second, that minority religions are more likely to be victimized by extreme efforts of social control, most notably by government, but hastened and incited by selected interest groups. These themes help to explain the seemingly inexplicable attitude of callous "expendability" shown toward the Branch Davidians, demonstrated by BATF officials who orchestrated the raid, as well as the calculated, "noose tightening" strategies of the FBI during the standoff that escalated the conflict, and the tepid response of federal authorities to the various excesses and face-saving machinations of their own personnel.

The Branch Davidian melee is a tragic page in history and clearly deserves close scrutiny on its own merits. The congressional investigation called for by civil and religious rights groups may yet materialize; however such an effort may also be rendered impotent by special interests or partisan politics. All the more reason that the events at Mt. Carmel not be pushed aside, but instead dutifully exhumed, carefully recorded, and frankly analyzed for public consumption, disentangled from self-serving political agendas, official deceit, and government secrecy in the conveniently redacted reports, particularly the one issued by the Justice Department. Pulitzer prize winning columnist William Safire echoed the sentiments of many informed observers when he referred to the Justice report as a "whitewash" (*Houston Chronicle*, October 16, 1993). Special investigator Edward Dennis's conclusion that there was "no place in the evaluation for blame" blatantly contradicts the accompanying reports of social and behavioral science experts Ammerman, Sullivan, Cancro, and Stone, whose evaluations of FBI actions were damning. In effect, Ammerman and colleagues suggested that federal agents were largely responsible for the explosive outcome at the Davidian settlement.

At the same time, while a case for the culpability of law enforcement can be made in the Waco affair, an explanation of the problem cannot be reduced simply to government malfeasance. Clearly other social actors—both collective and individual—played significant roles. It is precisely this larger configuration of social forces that needs to be addressed. In this regard, Waco has much broader implications. There is substantial hostility directed toward new or unconventional religions, built on unsupported fears, perpetuated by misguided or reactionary interests, and quietly but thoroughly woven into the very fabric of society. Against this backdrop of peculiar weave, the debacle at Waco was made possible, perhaps probable.

Through this collective work, it is our hope that readers will discover both the particular and the general, a critical link between the ostensibly isolated case of the Branch Davidians and the larger cultural ethos of antagonism surrounding sectarian religious expression. Sociologically, these two variables are inseparable. The Mt. Carmel events were as predictable as they were avoidable. But one suspects that other Wacos may lie ahead if we fail to understand the forces that shaped and ignited the violent confrontation between sect and state.

More recently, in the wake of the shocking Oklahoma City bombing, new questions have been raised about the disturbing, antigovernment sentiments that run through some marginalized portions of the population. While no direct link exists between Branch Davidians and the perpetrators of the Oklahoma City disaster (Davidian survivors I spoke to were horrified), it is possible that Waco has contributed to an increased polarization between impenitent federal officials and disenfranchised social groups (e.g., bankrupt farmers and ranchers, a dislocated working class). Besieged groups in the throes of economic difficulties, political turmoil, and heated "culture wars" may be more agitated by an excessive show of force on the part of big government. One common thread that ties the two events together is the shared outrage at federal government's failure to acknowledge the full extent of their responsibility for Waco. Of course, this does not excuse the actions of extremists in Oklahoma City, but it does shed light on how deep these rifts have become. Perhaps not until the Waco matter is satisfactorily resolved can a regenerative process begin to repair the damaged trust between some disaffected citizens and their government.

This project could not have been completed without the encouragement and support of a number of individuals. I owe a debt of gratitude to Philip Arnold, David Bromley, Donna Birdwell-Pheasant, Chris Ellison, Gordon Melton, and James Tabor, all of whom shared with me, at various times and places, engaging and compelling explorations of the Waco tragedy. Out of these conversations and dialogues came the principal ideas and directions for this book.

I am deeply indebted to the Davidian survivors who opened up their lives to me, however painful a recounting of the past may have been. I found them to be selfless and caring people characterized by conviction and courage, a pattern I have come to realize is quite typical in my study of new religious movements over the past fifteen years. I am often struck by the gross disparity between my own first-hand impressions, drawn through fieldwork, and the absurd, cartoonlike images of so-called cultists portrayed by media and anticult organizations. I concede that in more recent years, I have become less patient with these prejudices and the people who promote them.

I am especially grateful to Davidian survivor Rita Riddle, who endured countless hours of inquiries. Rita enabled me to gain a much richer understanding of the Mt. Carmel community and their religious worldview.

I must also mention the contribution of members of another sect I have been studying. In my research on a religious movement called "The Family," I was intrigued by their reaction to the Waco incident. They expressed similar concerns about government raids (for good reason: they have experienced raids on their homes in other countries) and hostile attitudes by authorities. Their obvious trepidations informed a comparative perspective on sectarian tensions and helped to confirm my observations about wider social implications.

I wish to acknowledge the support of Lamar University through the Graduate Studies Division, which supplied funding for travel and research. Special thanks to Dr. Robert Moulton, who recognized the significance of the project during the early stages.

I also want to acknowledge the enthusiastic support of my editor, Doug Mitchell, and his very competent staff, especially Matt Howard. Carol Saller was the manuscript editor, and her relentless attention to detail was matched only by her equanimity and dedication. Helen Ebaugh and Phillip Hammond were reviewers for the manuscript and offered constructive insights and suggestions.

Finally, apologies to my family—Nancy, Kate, Jenna, and Jared—for all those long hours away from home. Their patience and support was crucial, as always.

STUART A. WRIGHT

Introduction

Another View of the
Mt. Carmel Standoff

One year after the April 19 fire that killed seventy-four Branch Davidians1 outside Waco, Texas, a few hundred people gathered at the ruins of Mt. Carmel to offer eulogies for families and friends, to listen to a few sympathetic scholars try to make sense of the tragedy, and to hear Davidian survivors recount their experiences and console each other in a memorial service. A handful of the survivors and their families still appeared stunned at the events that had destroyed their community the previous year. They struggled visibly for answers to explain how this tragedy could have taken place in a nation that extols the principle of religious freedom as a fundamental right. As both an invited speaker and observer, I shared their bewilderment and frustration, and I wondered to myself: how could this have happened? Why was it allowed to go this far? Standing over the debris and rubble that was once the home of the Branch Davidians, I felt the crushing loss of human lives. I also felt a deep sense of rage. Although this was a very complex and difficult problem for federal authorities to manage, particularly after the disastrous assault by the Bureau of Alcohol, Tobacco, and Firearms (BATF), the truth is that efforts at damage control took precedence over factual candor and accuracy as officials scrambled to erect legitimations for their actions. In the aftermath of these gatekeeping activities, it would be an arduous task to clear up the misconceptions and bring the matter to some reasonable conclusion. But the tragedy would be far greater if the death of the Mt. Carmel community were allowed to fade quietly into the back pages of yesterday's news; not so much for the few remaining Davidians, but for those who still embrace the promise of a just society. Predictably, the survivors had arrived at a shared meaning of the Waco siege and conflagration as part of the unfolding apocalyptic drama foretold in the book of Revelation. The saints had been martyred, the prophet slain, their property destroyed, their families divided and killed. They had been persecuted for their faith; they would await the resurrection of the believers at the sound of the Trump. While consoling to the survivors, however, the explanation was sorely inadequate for many scholars and critical observers who witnessed the events at Mt. Carmel between February 28 and April 19, 1993.

The entire Mt. Carmel episode was replete with ambiguities and perplexities—rumors of friendly fire, allegations of miscalculations and confusion surrounding the ill-fated raid, accusations of media interference and heated exchanges between reporters and federal agents, contradictory statements made by BATF and FBI spokespersons, puzzling strategies of pressure deployed by the FBI such as the "psychological warfare" tactic, and mounting frustration by fatigued federal agents over the protracted negotiations with the sect. Attorney General Janet Reno and the FBI repeatedly claimed to have consulted with "cult experts" but refused to identify any of these individuals. At the same time, scholars of new or marginal religious movements complained loudly and in near unison that they were not consulted, myself included (Wright 1993, 11A). Indeed, many troublesome questions about the siege and standoff remain unanswered, and many more have yet to be asked. In light of these questions and events, there is a compelling intellectual and public interest in providing a forum for inquiry and dialogue, sorting out the details, exploring the implications, and generally gaining a better understanding of this fatal affair.

Thematically, the volume rejects as simplistic many of the popular images and attitudes that have arisen about the Waco confrontation. It seeks to answer hard, penetrating, and incisive questions from many different perspectives—sociological, legal, historical, and ethical. The result is a mutual and deep-seated dissatisfaction with the official treatment of, and response to, the religious sect known as the Branch Davidians. Official reports have accepted only a small portion of the blame for the destruction of the Mt. Carmel community. Media accounts adopted wholesale the stigmatization of the Davidians as a "cult" and conveyed, uncritically for the most part, the government's version of events during the siege and standoff. Not surprisingly, a CNN/Gallup poll taken after the fiery holocaust found that 73 percent of Americans thought the decision to teargas (for seven hours) the men, women, and children (including infants and toddlers) at Mt. Carmel was "responsible," and 93 percent believed that Koresh was to blame for their deaths (Mayfield 1993, 1A). The few criticisms that did surface eventually in the media came too late and too piecemeal to undercut the general impression that the federal agents acted properly. As indicated by numerous comments on talk shows and college campuses, Waco has become a second "Jonestown" in the collective memory of American culture—the duped minions of a maniacal cult leader were essentially victims of their own self-destruction.

The present volume challenges the reader to entertain *another* view of the Waco tragedy, one that runs counter to popular opinion and media accounts. Few citizens, even the most skilled and curious, have the motivation, time, or energy to pore over thousands of pages of government documents, newspaper clippings, professional reports, and transcripts of hearings, trials, interviews, and various other sources of information in order to form an independent and impartial assessment of the Branch Davidian conflict. But this is the luxury (and for some, the bane) of ambitious scholars and venturesome academics. In an increasingly secular and bureaucratic state, it is an essential function of a free society that such skeptical inquiry make government actions accountable. And, as the title suggests, the distinguished contributors to this work offer conclusions very different from those found in the official reports or in popular consciousness.

The inquisitive reader will find a number of important questions addressed and—I believe—satisfactorily answered. I am deeply gratified that what began as a project to sort out some of the key issues and problems in this calamitous sect-state conflict has yielded significant insights and explanations. Considerable clarity has been given to the history, beliefs, traditions, and controversial practices of the Branch Davidians, and placed in a dispassionate, historical context. Queries about the initial BATF investigation and the rationale for the raid have produced meaningful explanations firmly grounded in sociological theory. Media controversies, such as the "demonization" of Koresh and the FBI's centralized control of information to the public, have been documented and analyzed. The use and misuse of consultants or self-styled experts have been detailed by those who worked with the federal agencies. Constitutional issues have been raised and explored alongside policy implications for future law enforcement actions involving religious sects.

Yet there are other questions that have not been answered within these pages. Evidence for mass suicide adduced in the government reports and at the trial of the eleven Davidians in San Antonio was inconclusive. According to the coroner's report (U.S. Department of Justice 1993, 311–28), eighteen sect members died of gunshot wounds that appeared to be indicative of suicide, or perhaps more accurately, mercy killings. But most of the others in Mt. Carmel died of smoke and carbon monoxide inhalation, while a few others suffocated (buried alive) or died of blunt trauma (from collapsing structures). In a remarkable videotape made by the Davidians during the fifty-one-day standoff, and released by the FBI only after the trial, it was clearly evident from comments made by sect members who were interviewed that *they anticipated coming out in the near future and rejoining their families and friends*—not what one would expect from a group preparing for mass suicide. Dr. Rodney Crow, the chief medical examiner for Tarrant County who conducted the coroner's investigation, candidly stated in a television interview that the conditions at Mt. Carmel during the fire were so intolerable that if he were inside the compound he might have shot his own child as an act of compassion rather than let him or her suffer.[2] Dr. Crow also noted that the remains of a number of women's and children's bodies were found huddled together under wet blankets attempting to escape the heat and smoke. It is unlikely that the questions about the cause of the fires and relatedly, mass suicides, will ever be answered. But it is not insignificant that the actions of the federal government—bulldozing the remains of the crime scene, removing evidence en masse to take to Washington, withholding redacted information in the official reports—helped to obscure public access and scrutiny with regard to these questions. Though this book is not intended to be a forum for conspiracy theories, the government did little to curb suspicions of more wrongdoings in the wake of disclosures about the BATF cover-up and disinformation campaign to hide the bungled siege, as detailed in the Treasury Department report (1993).

The holocaust at Mt. Carmel represents a tragic episode in the history of sectarian religion in America. It belies some of our deepest and most sacred convictions about the sanctity of religious freedom and tolerance for individual differences and beliefs. We should find it odd that a nation founded by religious sectarians (Puritans attempting to escape religious persecution at the hands of the state) should itself so easily forget the lessons of history. Much of what American culture can claim in the way of democratic ideas and civic virtues—lay-directed, participatory political activism; voluntary association; moral obligation of service to community; opposition and reform; expression of discontent; radical ideology and revolution; and the politics of perfection written into town and church covenant—derive from sectarian religion (Miller 1954; Walzer 1965). Sectarian or non-traditional religion (once called "heresies," now called "cults" by their detractors), Weber (1963, 1968) reminds us, is a critical source of cultural innovation, revitalization, and social change. Though these forces may appear disruptive to the status quo, they are typically expressions of a growing state of tension, social strain, and deep-seated disillusionment with the hardened and unresponsive institutional fabric of society fostered by secular rationalization processes. Within the charismatic forces of history, one finds the unpredictable, the spontaneous, the creative forms of social activity that enervate life and infuse the truly revolutionary visions of change that shape the future. In effect, Weber saw sectarian movements as an indispensable driving force for reform and change. Such forces are likely to be unstable, volatile, even explosive, at least until tempered by the processes of institutionalization and routinization of charisma.

Similarly, Tracy (1987) argues that sectarian religions function as important intermediate groups in society curbing majoritarian tyranny by dividing allegiances of citizens and proffering views that are often radically different from the preferences of the state. In other words, they serve society best as "resistance groups," refusing to be domesticated sacred canopies for dominant elites. According to Yale law professor Stephen Carter (1993, 41), "A religion is, at its heart, a way of denying the authority of the rest of the world; it is a way of saying to fellow human beings and to the state those fellow humans have erected, 'No I will *not* accede to your will.'" As the very term "Protestant" implies, it is an expression of dissent.

Given what is known about the importance of sectarian religions as indicators of social tension, agents of resistance, and vehicles for change, it is essential that a greater understanding of this phenomenon serve as the template for future responses by authorities. Such an understanding would have undoubtedly engendered greater toleration, appreciation, and patience in Waco, likely resulting in the preservation of precious human lives. Instead, the propensity for armed confrontation and destruction prevailed. It is clear now that any chance of understanding the Branch Davidians was seriously impeded by the various forces of deviance amplification, rumor transmission, anticult stereotyping, and brutal ignorance. The paramilitary tactics displayed by federal agents in the execution of warrants at Mt. Carmel, the premature abandonment of conciliatory negotiations by the FBI and the subsequent deployment of psychological warfare, and the final assault by armored tanks and CS gas all point to the official predisposition to consider the use of force necessary in resolving the conflict. Since the application of extreme deadly force should, in theory, always be the last resort taken by law enforcement, the failure of federal agents to seek the least dangerous means is in need of explanation. Tragically, that explanation is firmly embedded in the morass of misunderstanding that is described and documented in the following pages.

The volume begins by deconstructing the pop-psychology, ahistorical renderings of marginal religions typically conveyed by the media and reflected in mass public opinion after the Waco siege. In part I, the Branch Davidians are shown to be part of a long-standing, sectarian, millennial tradition rich in imagination, colorful in character, and always provocative in the eyes of majoritarian religionists and conventional society. Robert Fogarty surveys millennial sects and charismatic leaders over the last three centuries, each outrageous and controversial in its own right. From the Quaker enthusiast James Naylor, to the Shaker mystic Mother Ann Lee, to the polygamous Benjamin Purnell and the "House of David," Fogarty skillfully weaves his way through this distinct religious history linking together varied remote, disparate, and little-known groups in a common heritage and tradition. These millennial expectations and prophetic utterances have been assimilated and transmitted generationally and form the basis of a distinguishable subculture that is wholly and unabashedly American. Moreover, Fogarty observes, mainstream societal reactions to these sectarian expressions—persecution, recriminations, allegations of subversion, bewitchment, seduction, legal harassment, and even mob violence—have also been quite American.

Historian William Pitts follows, in chapter 2, with a chronology of the genesis and growth of the Davidian sect up to the emergence of David Koresh. Drawing on original documents, including interviews with members and accounts by visitors drawn from the Oral History archive at Baylor University in Waco, he traces its origins to a small splinter group of Seventh-Day Adventists that began in Los Angeles in 1929. Victor Houteff, the founder and prophet of the Davidians, reformulated Adventist beliefs and infused them with personal claims of divine inspiration, visions, and revelations. Pitts details the migration of the group to Texas and the formation and organization of the communal settlement at Mt. Carmel. The history of the sect is divided into two distinct periods, the Houteff era and the Roden era. Extensive use of Houteff's original writings are made, demonstrating the linkage between Adventist and Davidian beliefs, and laying a groundwork for contextualizing the teachings of the Rodens (Ben and Lois) and later, Koresh.

In chapter 3, David Bromley and Edward Silver furnish an analysis of Davidian history and development in terms of two discrete organizational forms, the patronal clan and the prophetic movement. The "patronal clan" refers to a network of families clustered around a single family unit or head, joined by a spiritual (rather than consanguinal) lineage, and through whom the identity of members derives from ties to the sacralized family. The patronal clan emphasizes the received spiritual tradition and experiences moderate tension with the surrounding culture. The "prophetic movement," on the other hand, refers to a network of individuals, tightly organized into a communal group which emphasizes its role in creating a "new" tradition and an imminent transformative event. The prophetic movement experiences high levels of tension with the surrounding culture, promotes social distance, and affixes individual identity to one's relation with the charismatic figure. It is argued that the Houteff and Roden eras were largely characterized by elements of the patronal clan, while the Koresh era assumed primary features of the prophetic movement, though some overlapping is evident. The authors make a convincing case for the transformation of the Davidian community under Koresh's charismatic leadership, describing innovative but controversial changes.

In part II, the sources and origins of the Branch Davidian conflict are examined. I begin chapter 4 with the "constructionist" theoretical perspective (Spector and Kitsuse 1981) that social problems are not always self-evident. It is axiomatic that many problems in society never get the serious attention they deserve from authorities, while others get more than their share. Thus the likelihood or degree of recognition of a problem may have no clear relationship to the actual danger or threat posed to society by a particular group or individual. In some instances, the threat may be exaggerated or embellished by antagonists in order to catalyze the attention of authorities. Drawing on the research literature on deviance amplification and moral panics, or what Hall et al. (1978) call the "politics of signification," I examine the processes by which the Branch Davidians came to be defined by officials as a special problem deserving such extraordinary attention. These processes may be understood as a symbolic campaign wherein selected interest groups sought to define the sect, lodged and pressed claims to authorities, publicized their concerns to the media, and lobbied to formulate the issue and gain support for their cause. The interest groups in question (disgruntled apostates, anticultists, selected media) are analyzed as "moral entrepreneurs" involved in organized claims-making activities designed to promote recognition of the Davidian sect as a problem, eventually creating moral panic and overreaction by law enforcement officials.

In chapter 5, James Lewis focuses on the evolution and entrenchment of the cult stereotype in American society in recent decades promulgated by organized anticultism. Less concerned with direct influences by the anticult interest groups in Waco, Lewis analyzes the powerful yet indirect effects of the meaning and construction of the term "cult" as a disparaging label which imposes a crippling stigma on any religious group unfortunate enough to be so maligned. Traditionally linked to racial, ethnic, or sexual minorities, the usage of a stereotype can incite deep-seated prejudices and function as a scapegoating mechanism for societal fears and anxieties. Prejudicial treatment of disenfranchised groups in the past (African Americans, Jews, Mormons) may be seen as emanating from stereotypes that justified such actions. Lewis notes pointedly that the "long-term effectiveness of anticult propaganda was evident from the very beginning of the crisis, when the media immediately, unreflectively, and irresponsibly began referring to them [Davidians] as a 'cult.'" Pregnant with demonic imagery, the cult stereotype allowed authorities to treat the religious sect as less than human, providing a rationale for intolerance and ill-considered decisions that resulted in the massive, violent assault at Mt. Carmel.

In chapter 6, Christopher Ellison and John Bartkowski examine the role of child abuse allegations in the Branch Davidian conflict. Though largely unsubstantiated (the Texas Department of Child Protective Services failed to turn up evidence of abuse and dropped the case), these allegations became a touchstone in the initial government investigation, appearing in the affidavit accompanying the warrants, and later in the Treasury Department report's account of how the BATF investigation materialized. Ellison and Bartkowski observe that similar allegations have been lodged against other new or unconventional religions (the Northeast Kingdom Community, the Family) which have also led to government raids yielding embarrassingly inconsequential evidence and resulting in the dismissal of charges against the targeted groups. The authors turn to larger social and historical forces to explain the recent development of "endangered children" as a pervasive theme in American culture, giving impetus to well-intentioned but often unnecessary and excessive child-saving efforts; for instance, a contemporary moral panic about child welfare issues. In this context, they address three types of child abuse allegations faced by Koresh: (1) severe corporal punishment, (2) sexual abuse, and (3) psychological abuse and material deprivation. They conclude that the evidence is far more limited and ambiguous than media accounts and government reports indicated, and they suggest that allegations were treated uncritically by authorities.

Part III of the book focuses attention on the role of the media in Waco. James Richardson offers an analysis of mass media structures that helps to explain marked patterns of sensationalism and frequently distorted news coverage involving nontraditional religions in general, and the Branch Davidians in particular. Employing a model of news construction developed by Herman and Chomsky (1988), he examines five "filters" that determine the frequency and quality of news coverage. These filters are said to impede objective news reporting and force media outlets to promote culturally edited or "politically correct" renditions. In a more sympathetic tone, Richardson also describes the precarious position of reporters and journalists in Waco under the government-mandated restrictions that cut off all direct communication with the sect and imposed a three-mile perimeter around the Mt. Carmel site, virtually eliminating access by a free press.

In chapter 8, Anson Shupe and Jeffrey Hadden invoke a sociology-of-knowledge approach to newsmaking in order to explain how information becomes hostage to interpreters or "players" with their own interests and agendas. Expanding their analysis beyond simple media culpability, the authors identify five emergent and competing narratives (mass media, public agent, anticult, Branch Davidian, contrarian) in the Waco standoff. The authors then demonstrate how the players developed narratives that sought to legitimize and validate their own roles and, in turn, attempted to influence the formation of public opinion.

Part IV of the book is devoted to exploring the relation between violence and apocalyptic sects. John Hall, in a provocative work, conducts a comparative analysis of Jonestown and Mt. Carmel by examining the constructed narratives of the groups' antagonists. Hall finds that in each circumstance the tragic endings were fueled by adversaries (family members of converts, apostates) through increasing levels of pressure and agitation. In the case of Mt. Carmel, he concludes that the sect's adversaries attempted to exploit the theme of mass suicide, which inadvertently heightened tensions and helped propel the standoff toward the very end authorities sought to avoid: "The cultural opponents of David Koresh reinvoked and reworked narratives about mass suicide in ways that shaped the escalating trajectory of conflict at Mt. Carmel." Hall's thesis provides a strong complementary perspective to the arguments found in the chapters by Shupe and Hadden, Lewis, James Tabor, and myself.

Tom Robbins and Dick Anthony extend the focus on violence in marginal religious movements beyond Waco and Jonestown to determine the existence of common variables or patterns that can be identified in a larger sociological context. The authors suggest that sources of violence may generally fall into two categories, *endogenous* and *exogenous*. Endogenous variables refer to select features within the religious group (organizational, social-psychological) that may increase the risk of violence, while exogenous variables refer to those external to the group (religious, political, ethnic, legal). Noting the preponderance of attention devoted to exogenous variables by contributors to this volume (and rightfully so, as a corrective to popular psychologizing), Robbins and Anthony concentrate largely on endogenous factors enhancing the volatility of marginal sects or "cults." The analysis of endogenous factors is developed around three characteristics: (1) apocalyptic beliefs, (2) charismatic leadership, and (3) communal-ideological systems posing "boundary" problems with society.

Part V turns to the role of experts or consultants in the siege and standoff at Mt. Carmel. Both contributors to this section of the book had an active part as scholarly experts either during or after the siege at Waco. In chapter 11, James Tabor details his frustrating involvement with FBI officials and suggests that the violent deaths of the Branch Davidians could have been avoided if good advice had been heeded. Tabor combines descriptive and analytical materials to marshal a persuasive argument that another outcome to the standoff was both accessible and feasible had not federal agents dismissed Koresh's religion as incoherent "Bible-babble." Law enforcement officials unfamiliar with the religious discourse of fundamentalism and apocalyptic beliefs failed to appreciate the biblical symbolism and metaphor, and quickly responded with tactics designed to deal with a terrorist-hostage crisis.

Nancy Ammerman, who was asked by the Justice and Treasury Departments to serve on a panel of behavioral science experts in evaluating the actions of federal law enforcement in Waco, comes to similar conclusions in chapter 12. Ammerman, echoing the criticisms of other experts on the panel, contends that federal law enforcement officials erred in not taking Koresh's religion seriously, treating him as a "con man" who used religion as a pretext for criminal activities. Strengthening arguments made by Tabor, Ammerman documents that FBI agents in charge at Waco actually received reliable advice from two behavioral scientists at Quantico, who urged their superiors against abandoning negotiations with Koresh. The advisors also warned against the strategy of increasing psychological and tactical pressure for fear that it would backfire. Ammerman offers a number of insightful observations about the internal culture of the FBI which made the use of deadly force more likely. She concludes with recommendations for future law enforcement actions involving confrontations with religious groups.

In the final section of the book, constitutional and policy issues are explored. Rhys Williams, a sociologist specializing in church-state issues, analyzes the events at Mt. Carmel in light of the First Amendment to determine whether authorities acted within proper legal and constitutional boundaries. Williams raises numerous critical questions challenging governmental actions, though noting through historical analysis and case studies that such responses are not unprecedented. The federal enforcement action against the Branch Davidians is said to illustrate the precarious tension in the "free exercise" clause, demonstrating the uneven treatment of marginal groups (religious outsiders), compared to mainstream or traditional religious organizations.

In chapter 14, law professor and dean Edward Gaffney offers a critical but even-handed legal analysis of enforcement actions in relation to the First, Second, and Fourth Amendments. Gaffney argues that limitations of governmental power set forth by the Bill of Rights did not inform the decisions of the federal agencies involved in the Mt. Carmel affair. While giving the government its due (there *was* probable cause for the warrants, he contends), Gaffney identifies several key violations of constitutional protections that federal agents— sworn to uphold the law—should have known beforehand, particularly in the execution of the warrants, but in the planned CS gas assault on the compound on April 19 as well. He concludes by exploring policy implications, advancing a credible defense of "second-guessing" as an essential function of administrative review.

Finally, Dean Kelley, a leading church-state scholar, offers an analysis of high-energy religious movements and their essential role in the religious enterprise of culture-building. Kelley then suggests that a critical misunderstanding of these groups was the central error of the government agencies involved, serving as a fallacious model or prototype for strategies and decision-making. He cautions against the "danger of implosion" in such groups, and contends that "religious communities that pose no clear and present danger to others should be left alone." Of course, the potential for danger or harm was clearly judged to be more serious by some than others, an issue addressed by this author (chapter 5). And for the very reasons that marginal religious groups may be subject to stigmatization and exaggerated fears leading to repression, Kelley advocates restraint. In making this argument, he does not propose that religious groups are above the law. Rather, he states, they are "in it"—inextricably woven into the Constitution—and as such, they should be afforded the legal protections intended them.

The value in this collaborative effort lies in its ability to make us think reflectively about how the events at Mt. Carmel could have been shaped and directed differently. Perhaps the most important question we should ask ourselves as a society is, "What did we learn from Waco?" The contributors to this volume have been brought together by a discrete historical event. But the issues raised transcend Mt. Carmel. The Branch Davidians represent a disenfranchised religious sect in high tension with its host society, regardless of place and time. There are no strikingly unique or idiosyncratic features which separate this particular group from many other millenarian or sectarian movements, both in the present and in the past, despite such inferences by some. The successful but unfortunate convergence of oppositional forces, while not unprecedented, helps to explain in large part the peculiar development of the conflict. To the dismay of many scholars, there are some disturbing signs that these forces of anticultism have already gained control, or ownership, of the putative problem and will make their imprint on future altercations, making the likelihood of another Mt. Carmel greater. No doubt, millenarian and apocalyptic fervor will increase as we move toward the end of the second millennium. The question remains, will we be able to apply the lessons learned from Waco (if any) to future sect-state confrontations? Or can we expect more of the same? The day after the fiery holocaust claimed the lives of the seventy-four sect members inside the Davidian structure, President Clinton asked, in a press conference, several piercing questions. "Is there something else we should have done? . . . Is there some other question we should have asked? . . . Can I say for sure . . . we could have done nothing else to make the outcome different?" Those questions deserve serious attention and it is to that end that this volume is dedicated.

Notes

1. There was some confusion over the number of Davidians who died in the fire. Newspaper accounts consistently reported the figure to be eighty. The coroner's report, included in the Justice Department's official report (1993), set the figure at seventy-five, but this figure included the six sect members killed in the shoot-out. Subsequent DNA tests and other evidence concluded that the actual death toll from the fire was seventy-four bodies (and two fetuses). The total figure for all Branch Davidians who died, including the six killed in the raid (but not the two fetuses) is eighty. This information was obtained by cross-checking lists separately compiled by Rita Riddle and James Tabor and confirmed in an interview with Dr. Rodney Crow, the chief medical examiner of Tarrant County in charge of the coroner's investigation (January 12, 1995).

2. The comments were made during an interview on the Maury Povich show which aired in October 1993. Detailed information was later corroborated in a telephone interview with Dr. Crow (January 4, 1994).

References

Carter, Stephen L. 1993. *The Culture of Disbelief: How American Law and Politics Trivialize Religious Devotion.* New York: Basic Books.

Hall, Stuart, Chris Critcher, Tony Jefferson, John Clarke, and Brian Roberts. 1978. *Policing the Crisis: Mugging, the State, and Law and Order.* London: Macmillan.

Herman, Edward S., and Noam Chomsky. 1988. *Manufacturing Consent: The Political Economy of the Mass Media.* New York: Pantheon Books.

Mayfield, Mark. 1993. "Poll: 93% Blame Koresh." *USA Today,* April 21, p. 2A.

Miller, Perry. 1954. *The New England Mind: The Seventeenth Century.* Cambridge: Harvard University.

Spector, Malcolm, and John I. Kitsuse. 1987. *Constructing Social Problems.* Hawthorne, NY: Walter de Gruyter.

Tracy, David. 1987. *Plurality and Ambiguity: Hermeneutics, Religion, Hope.* Chicago: University of Chicago.

U.S. Department of Justice. 1993. *Report to the Deputy Attorney General on the Events at Waco, Texas: February 28 to April 19, 1993.* Redacted Version, October 8. Washington, DC: U.S. Government Printing Office.

U.S. Department of Treasury. 1993. *Report of the Department of Trea-*

sury on the Bureau of Alcohol, Tobacco, and Firearms Investigation of Vernon Wayne Howell, Also Known as David Koresh. Washington, DC: U.S. Government Printing Office.

Walzer, Michael. 1965. *The Revolution of the Saints.* Cambridge: Harvard University.

Weber, Max. 1963. *The Sociology of Religion.* Translated by Ephraim Fischoff. Boston: Beacon.

————. 1968. *Max Weber on Charisma and Institution Building.* Edited by S. N. Eisenstadt. Chicago: University of Chicago.

Wright, Stuart A. 1993. "Before We Write off Cult, Society Needs Answers." *Houston Chronicle,* April 27, p. 11A.

Part One

1

ROBERT S. FOGARTY

An Age of Wisdom, An Age of Foolishness

The Davidians, Some Forerunners, and Our Age

The extent to which cultic or marginal religious groups have entered the heart of the American consciousness can be grasped only by avid viewers of *Hard Copy* and listeners to the daily hot-line talk shows. Such shows feed on tales of exploitation, seduction, and fraud and often feature discussions about the latest "odd" religion. The media frenzy surrounding the Waco case reached epic proportions during the standoff, and the fallout still continues. For example, a respected and award-winning television drama, *Law and Order*, recently devoted a full episode to a tale about a sect leader, the bombing of a federal building by an ardent devotee, and a subsequent pact suicide by members after their leader was jailed, prosecuted, found guilty, and sentenced for brainwashing his young follower into planting an explosive device that killed her (Fogarty 1993).[1] Such is the stuff of contemporary understanding.

Writing in *Religious Outsiders and the Making of Americans* (1986, 126), R. Laurence Moore has noted: "In one form or another, the present charges against religious 'cults,' including that of brainwashing, were hurled against every new religious group organized in this country, and usually with some measure of justification. Religious enthusiasm has always been a dangerous thing. It sometimes inspires people to do noble things. With equal frequency, it does not. The religious prophet trying to lead people in a new direction is not likely to be without blemish."

Popular interest and concern about religious sects are nothing new. When Dickens published his *Tale of Two Cities* in 1859 he opened it with his now famous line: "It was the best of times, it was the worst of times, it was an age of wisdom, it was an age of foolishness," and went on to note that "spiritual revelations were conceded to England at that favored period . . . Mrs. Southcott [a prophetess] had recently attained her five and twentieth blessed birthday, . . . a prophetic guard in the Life Guards had heralded the sublime appearance by announcing arrangements were made for the swallowing up of London and Westminster" (Dickens 1859, 1). Dickens thought the Southcottians "foolish" but worthy of a place in his grand chronicle of English social life since such groups were part of the culture, not something separate from it. Later, in his *In Search of White Crows* (1977), Moore argued that nineteenth-century American spiritualism should be placed at the center of the American experience from 1860 to 1900 rather than on the "table-rapping" margins where historians had formerly placed it (Braude 1989). Such "extreme" or alternative groups must be seen as reflecting aspects of the universe and society they live in rather than viewed merely as a thing apart, something alien. They may be in opposition to certain trends, or they may reiterate them, but they are rarely irrelevant to mainstream concerns about values and ethics.

For the record, there has been a long history of millennial expectations, prophetic utterances, and outlandish activities that have resulted in both confrontations and destructive behavior. You pick your century and you can pick your "crazed" prophet. Let's start with James Naylor, that seventeenth-century Quaker enthusiast, who thought he was Jesus Christ and rode through Bristol to the hosannas of many women. Parliament (and George Fox) took a dim view of all this and the authorities branded him with the letter "B" (for blasphemer) as a punishment and bored a hole through his tongue. Naylor's career can serve as a touchstone for an ongoing debate about the nature of the English Revolution and the relation of Quaker enthusiasm to the "world turned upside down" by Cromwellian politics. Naylor became, to quote Christopher Hill, "a black shadow across memory" because of his meteoric rise and fall and because of the role he played within the history of Quaker enthusiasm (Hill 1972, 206). This prophet, who had fallen under the ideas of either Boehme or the Familists, suffered from what Fox called "imaginations," and he became a Quaker leader who had "run out," or exhausted himself.

Naylor's emergence in the 1650s as a prophetic leader, his scandalous behavior, his cruel punishment, and his subsequent recanting of errors have been the subject of a long and intense historical debate. George Fox tried to put distance between Naylor's actions and "true" Quaker belief, and Naylor plays in Fox's journal (again according to Hill) "a part only slightly greater than that of Trotsky in official Soviet histories of the Russian Revolution" (1970, 186). Born at Ardsley near Wakefield in 1617, he was married in 1638 and served as a soldier for the Independents under Fairfax in 1643. Between 1646 and 1651 he was a quartermaster, emerging in 1651 as a prominent Quaker preacher second only to Fox in bringing in converts to the new sect. During 1656 he preached in the west of England and while in Bristol became the center of the controversy that marked him for life. For it was in Bristol that he declared his messianic character by riding into the city on an ass in imitation of Jesus' entry into Jerusalem. As he entered the city his supporters threw garments in his path and shouted "Holy, holy, holy Lord God of Israel." Because of his actions—his "imaginations" to use Fox's words—he was charged with blasphemy and became a cause celebre in the heat of the revolution. Naylor defended his actions by saying that all he had done was to allow his followers to "worship the appearance of God in him, as a sign of Christ's second coming and being revealed in his Saints" (Fox 1890, 243).

Worshiping signs and symbols and having millenarian expectations (Naylor would sadly learn) was not, in Cromwell's day, a passive activity. Narrowly he escaped the death penalty. His punishment was a strong signal given by the authorities that they would no longer tolerate Quaker enthusiasm. Both the event and the sentence shocked Fox and he began, from that point forward, to exert greater control over the believers. For over three centuries a pictorial hagiography surrounded James Naylor as he was portrayed by admirers as the "Quaker Jesus," a benign and humble man (his earliest portrait is, in fact, a direct copy of Rembrandt's "A Bearded Man"), and by his detractors as a false prophet akin to Sabbati Sevi. In a 1661 edition of Ephraim Paggit's *Heresiography,* an account of how "Hereticks and Sectaries Sprang Upp in these latter times...," he appears along with other eminent "sectaries" like the Jesuits and Seekers. Naylor was both an early Quaker martyr and an apostate from the true Quaker spirit (Paggitt 1661).

Or consider another British martyr, the Shaker mystic Ann Lee, who came to the United States on the eve of the American Revolution. The Shakers were reported to be acting as spies for the British crown when they first came to America; Mother Ann Lee was presumed to be deranged because of her visions, her assertions of spiritual line and authority. On the Ohio frontier the Shakers were mobbed because some believed they kidnaped children. When one looks at charges brought against them by former members, one finds a catalog of willful acts of deception, fraud, coercion, and wrongdoing. Furthermore, Stephen Stein, a modern historian of Shakerism, believes that testimony against them by dissidents may actually have contained some truths rather than a mere list of calumnies.[2] One apostate, Valentine Rathbun, noted in 1780 that the Shakers were "Europeans," dangers to the state, duplicitous in their recruiting practices, going so far as to gather around any potential convert and "touch him here and there, and give him a sly cross, and in a very loving way, put their hands on his head and then begin to preach the doctrine to him" (Stein 1993, 16). Not quite "flirty fishing," as practiced by a contemporary group, the Children of God (now called The Family), but clearly directed at creating an aura of intimacy.

The famous mobbing of the Shakers at Union Village, Ohio, in 1810 had been preceded by a campaign against them depicting them as murderers, wolves in sheep's clothes who "castrated all their males, ... stripped and danced naked in the night meetings, blew out the candles and went into promiscuous debauch" (Stein 1993, 77) (possibly true at least on one occasion, but not a widespread practice). When the mobs appeared at Union Village they usually came to take away a female relative or a child brought into the Shaker "family" (their term) by a parent. In 1800 fifty citizens of New Lebanon submitted a petition to the New York State legislature on behalf of the young people in the Shaker community because the Shakers "threatened them, kept them in ignorance," and treated them like chattel slaves, while Pleasant Hill, Kentucky, was visited by a mob in 1825 to free a teenage girl from "bondage." For Americans in the first two decades of the nineteenth century, the abolishment of white servitude was a major issue. In the late 1830s and early 1840s, the Shakers experienced a "spiritual revival" coinciding with the first great wave of spiritualism that swept through America and, in fact, they invited the famous and wildly popular Fox sisters to visit them in the 1850s. On the eve of the Civil War, there were Shaker communities charged with harboring sympathetic attitudes toward blacks by their Southern neighbors and, in effect, asked to choose sides. Although opposed to slavery in principle, the communities in Kentucky walked a fine line and compromised their beliefs on some occasions—such as at Pleasant Hill, where they established a separate black family. The Shakers were, in a sense, at the heart of the first phase of the American industrial revolution, utilizing labor-saving devices at every turn. Shaker furniture was sold to average Americans who needed chairs for their parlors, not to museum directors in pursuit of beautiful objects. Mother Ann Lee's theology found a place on the American frontier and a distinguished place in religious history.

For a community closer to David Koresh and the Branch Davidians both in spirit and theology one has only to turn to the history of Benjamin Purnell, an illiterate itinerant preacher, who founded the "House of David" at Benton Harbor, Michigan, in 1903 to establish an "in-gathering" of the elect 144,000 who were preparing for the end. Purnell was a lecher extraordinaire who seduced and attacked young women, amassing a fortune for himself and bringing in converts from England and Australia. For most Americans the "House of David" is an obscure reference, and even those who remember it think of the group as some odd semiprofessional baseball and basketball team with a vaguely Jewish background (actually quite Protestant, English, and Southcottian) who wore beards. Yet it is the most obvious parallel to the Davidic group, since Purnell was a "corrupter," did establish a separate kingdom, and viewed the outside world with considerable hostility. When the state of Michigan (in the form of the state police) moved in on him—after over twenty years of surveillance—his community of about 700 people not only hid him in an attic room over a number of years, but flocked to his defense in court, claiming he was the Shiloh, or Jesus Christ in spiritual form.

The origins of the House of David can be found in the obscure mists of late eighteenth-century England, when figures like Richard Brothers appeared on the scene to promote the cause of a Polish count, Tadeusz Grabianka, who would, according to his promoters "conquer Palestine at the head of the Polish armies, transfer his capital to Jerusalem, and extend his sway, till every king surrender his crown to him. But first, since the old Israel was apostate, he had to gather a new tribe whom he grouped into twelve tribes with old Biblical names" (Roth 1933, 20). Among the new messiah's supporters was Jacob Duche, former chaplain to the Continental Congress, a major salon figure and a religious enthusiast. Although the Polish count failed to gain an audience, his admirer Richard Brothers did so, particularly after the publication of his 1794 tract "A Revealed Knowledge of the Prophecies and Times, Wrote under the Direction of God by the Man Who Will Be Revealed to the Hebrews As Their Prince." Popularly known as "Mad" Brothers (a former lieutenant in the British Navy), he issued another pamphlet to the powerful—and mad—king of England: "The Lord commands me to say to you, George III King of England, that immediately upon my being revealed to the Hebrews as their Prince, and to all nations as their Governor, your crown must be delivered up to me, that your power and authority may cease" (Roth 1933, 31).

With that proclamation Brothers became a threat and was duly questioned by the Privy Council and committed to an asylum in Islington. Yet he commanded a certain respect in some circles, with Nathaniel Halhead, M.P. and author of *The Grammar of the Bengal Language*, his major backer. Thomas Foley of Jesus College, Cambridge, and John Finlayson, a wealthy Scottish lawyer, were both converts to the beliefs of this "Prince of the Hebrews." Others, of course, ridiculed him, as did the famous engraver James Gillray, who depicted him, in 1795, carrying a "bundle of the elect" in a bag over his shoulders and leading a pack of Semites to the "Gates of Jerusalem."

While Brothers was still under care, the cult of Joanna Southcott took hold. Southcott was an illiterate domestic who in 1792 began (when she was forty-two) receiving and transcribing messages about her special prophetic role. In 1802 she came to London from Exeter with her box of prophecies and a belief that she was, according to Clarke Garrett (1975, 221), "the woman promised in Revelation to free the world from the burden of sin and to give the faithful the assurance that they would be preserved after the Second Coming." She began to travel about and "seal" her followers by giving them little slips of paper. On each slip there was a circle with the following words inside: "The sealed of the Lord, the elect and precious, man's redemption to inherit the tree of life, to be made heirs of God and joint heirs with Jesus Christ." By 1807 she had sealed 14,000 out of a possible 144,000. Her supporters grew in numbers and included former followers of Brothers and a new group of admirers (many wealthy) who saw in her the fulfillment of the scriptures. The apogee of her fame came in 1814 when she announced that in her sixty-fifth year she was going to give birth to the Shiloh, or Jesus Christ. Newspapers attacked this "deluded virgin" while her admirers presented her with a crib made of satinwood and gold. In Southcottian chapels, a new hymn (to the tune of "Rule Britannia") was sung: "Rule King Shiloh! King Shiloh, Rule Alone with Glory Crowned on David's Throne." She married a steward of the Earl of Darnley after spurning other suitors and the event came to a tragic end when she announced that her pregnancy had been "all delusion." Some of her faithful refused to accept her statement and instead spread the word that she was indeed the "Woman of the Sun" foretold in the book of Revelation and that the divine child had been taken up into heaven to escape the dragon. She died shortly after that, though a terse notice of her death stated that she was dead "to all appearances." The refusal to accept the death of a prophet is found throughout human history, and David Koresh's death (confirmed through the identification of dental remains) was questioned by some followers.

The Southcottian mantle fell on no single figure, but there were many eager to take it up over the years and to become her aborted Shiloh child. The line of prophets from Southcott to Benjamin Purnell included the megalomaniac George Turner, who demanded a palace from his followers; and the hunchbacked John Wroe, who had himself publicly circumcised in 1824 and had his followers adhere to the Mosaic Law and wear special garments. In 1827 he was acquitted of a rape charge, but later three members confessed to having practiced "idiotic indecencies" with him. Wroe traveled to America on four occasions and visited Australia four times in the belief that it was an important spot for the coming millennium. "Christian Israelite" communities were established in England, Australia, and the United States. John Wroe may have been, as one detractor commented, "half saint, half satyr," but he did head a religious body of believers molded from an evolving historical tradition with certain recurring characteristics such as prophetic prerogatives and power (sexual and social), separation from the world, and continuous biblical exegesis as a way to truth. This broad religious triangular trade continued to flourish between the countries, with the Mormons—as outlined in John F. C. Harrison's *The Second Coming: Popular Millenarianism, 1750-1850*—reaping the largest body of travelers. In all of these cases there was a social critique of the broader society as being corrupt, an emphasis on the incoming kingdom and the ingathering work that would save the righteous remnant, and a growing sense of the need to both convert and bring members into a special community of saints.

Benjamin Purnell was, like David Koresh, marginally educated, yet it did not prevent him from issuing numerous pamphlets, memorizing large sections of the Bible, preparing a place for the elect 144,000, and writing that "the mysterious mysteries must be unsealed and revealed to them; and they must gather for the work and fulfill the scriptures" (Roth 1933, 31). He was the Ishi-husband, the creator husband, the seventh messenger who had come to open the seventh seal and prepare the ingathering for the Israelites. Purnell was an unsuccessful prophet until 1903, when he chanced on a body of Anglo-Israelite believers living near Grand Rapids, Michigan, who accepted him as their leader. Prior to that date he had been an itinerant preacher traveling in a bigamous relationship with a companion, Mary Stollard, who was to become "Queen Mary" when he became "King Ben." From his base in Benton Harbor, Purnell launched out on missionary trips and succeeded in bringing in eighty-five from a Wroeite church in Australia and a group from England who believed that the Ark was located in America. Similarly when David Koresh went to Australia in search of converts he preached (as reported by the apostate Marc Breault) that "the Passover was coming quickly. Something big was about to happen. They must go to America, or die" (Breault and King 1993, 53). In short, both prophets tapped into older Adventist-oriented churches for whom the Shiloh was the potent and prophetic figure long awaited.

Like Koresh, Purnell always made good use of music in his services, and when firmly established at Benton Harbor (where he opened an amusement park), he organized two colony bands that played for visitors from the booming city of Chicago. On one level, the House of David was a thriving religious and commercial enterprise with industries, a growing body of followers brought together both by an Israelite past and a prophetic unfolding in the present. Their cold-storage warehouses in Benton Harbor served a growing fruit industry in western Michigan; their members worked as day laborers and ticket takers on the Benton Harbor trolley lines. Yet it was a community that had a leader who was an alleged rapist and encouraged fraud. In addition, he could be quite charming and was thought to be charismatic. In 1923 Benjamin Purnell went into hiding just before a grand jury began its investigations and a nationwide search was begun for him. Wanted posters were sent throughout the country, but he was not caught until late 1926. Stupendous rumors circulated in the press concerning his whereabouts. In fact, Purnell had not fled to Australia but had hidden in a secret room in the attic of his main residence, "Diamond House," suffering from tuberculosis and diabetes. On the evening of November 26, 1926, the Michigan State Police, acting on a tip from a former member (a "scorpion" to the House of David) smashed into the colony accompanied by a contingent of photographers and reporters and caught "King Ben" in his nightgown, shawl, and slippers and surrounded by a bevy of female attendants. The community leaders told the press that the young women were there on a "jelly-making" project.

The State of Michigan then conducted the largest and most expensive trial in its history, with 225 witnesses sworn and 15,000 pages of testimony taken. Newspapers all over the country, including the *New York Times*, followed the four-month trial on a daily basis. It was a sensational case with astounding, contradictory claims made by all parties and with daughters testifying against their mothers. Purnell was dying and died shortly after his guilty verdict came in late 1927. Following his death there were the inevitable fights over leadership, with Mary Purnell and lawyer Thomas Dewhirst vying for control. Eventually Mary set up a colony—the City of David—across the street and drifted into the "I Am" movement of St. Germaine. The colony's baseball team thrived under attorney Dewhirst's leadership, and its House of David motel—the "Grande Vista Tourist Court"—was called by *Motor News* "one of the most beautiful motels in America." By the 1970s the colony was a mere shadow of itself, a few aging members living with their memories of the ingathering of the elect 144,000. As head of the House of David at Benton Harbor, Benjamin Purnell established a virtual harem, enjoying sexual relations with many of the young women under a theology that assured them that sexual intercourse with the Shiloh would move them along the path to perfection; he did all this with the knowledge of his regal partner, Mary Purnell, who reportedly carried on an affair with the colony treasurer. Central to the success of the House of David was the work of attorney Dewhirst, who joined in 1919 and whose legal talents and prior political connections (with California Senator Hiram Johnson) helped keep federal and state investigators at bay.

In both the Branch Davidian and Jonestown groups lawyers played key roles in advising and defending vital community interests. Jim Jones employed the notorious Mark Lane at one juncture, with Lane playing up and into the group's paranoia about the role of the government. At Waco, Wayne Martin, a Harvard Law graduate, was not only a trusted lieutenant (a member of the "Mighty Men" group) but a key intermediary between the group and law enforcement agencies. Dewhirst, Lane, and Martin all had legal authority in the Weberian sense, but more to the point is that lawyers play an essential role in our contemporary litigious society, and no group should be without a house attorney, even if it is predicting the imminent destruction of the world.

When the State of Michigan finally caught up with Purnell and prosecuted him there was a parade of colony women and men who continued to defend him under oath. Of the sixteen charges brought against him in 1927 Purnell may have been guilty of all except one: the charge that he was a "religious impostor." He was not, because he was being true to a long history that sanctioned kingly behavior and that gave the "Lamb" special rights (including better food and clothing), and because the scriptures were being fulfilled.

Others have drawn a comparison between an earlier group and the Branch Davidians based on the common use of the name Koresh by the leaders. In 1887 an obscure eclectic physician, Cyrus Teed, mounted a stage in Chicago to address the National Association of Mental Health. His address was a mixture of mind-cure philosophy and self-help that led to the establishment of communes in Chicago and, later, Florida. He took on another name—"Koresh"—and promulgated a theory that stated that the universe was a closed system and that we lived on the inside of the earth. His theory of "cellular cosmogony" took him to the west coast of Florida, where he established, at Ft. Meyers, a community that was to be the "vitellus of the great cosmological egg." At one point the colonists (decent enough sorts—no real corruption) backed the Socialist party organization in Lee County, Florida, and organized the Progressive Liberty party, which ran on a platform that emphasized public ownership of utilities, free schools, equalization of wealth, protection of the environment, and conservation of natural resources. When he died—in a boating accident—his followers thought he would rise from the dead. The site of their colony is now a lovely Florida State Park.

When the story first broke about the confrontation at Waco, J. Philip Arnold of the Reunion Institute in Houston suggested a possible parallel with an earlier "Koresh" who had started a group in Florida in the 1890s (Claiborne 1993). According to Arnold, both took the name of Koresh, both were obsessed with the book of Revelation, both had a violent confrontation with the law, and both had followers who believed in their immortality. But Arnold was wrong on several counts: the Florida Koresh made very little of Revelation and made a great deal of Emmanuel Swedenborg, the eighteenth-century Swedish philosopher, to mold his bizarre cosmology; Cyrus Teed adopted the celibate state as the highest state and denounced sexual congress in sharp contrast to David Koresh, who spread his seed; and although the Florida Koresh did sustain injuries in a fight over politics, he died in a boating accident. According to the *Washington Post* account, "Koresh either had read some of at least six books that Cyrus Teed Koresh wrote or had come under the influence of someone who had been a student of Teed" (Claiborne 1993). But most of Teed's works are about "cellular cosmogony," and his theology is certainly tainted by many other sources far removed from classic dispensationalism, as outlined by Paul Boyer in his *When Time Shall Be No More* (1992). Cyrus Teed's worldview was shaped by a number of forces that included a denial of the Copernican hypothesis and a conservative reaction to the challenge of science in late-nineteenth-century America. His message also included faith healing just as modern medicine was organizing itself and when the fastest growing religion, both in the United States and Great Britain, was Mary Baker Eddy's Christian Science, which denied the material world its power. Eddy's followers turned inward; so did the followers of Teed.

From the very start of the Adventist movement in the 1840s there have been contentious forces at work that were muted when it emerged from "sect" to "church" status in the late 1880s, but splits did emerge that were marked by a shifting religious power struggle between male and female prophets. When Victor Houteff founded his Davidian Seventh Day Adventist sect in 1929 and published *The Shepherd's Rod*, he proclaimed himself the true messenger and began the ingathering of the elect 144,000. At its height it never had more than 125 members, and on his death in 1955 he was succeeded by his wife, Florence. She proclaimed that on April 22, 1959, God would establish the kingdom in Palestine, and her followers prepared to move there. When that event failed there was a further splintering of the sect.

In a similar move, Lois Roden assumed messenger status when her mate, Ben, died. George Roden, their son, was both in and out of his mother's favor and opposed David Koresh's rise in the organization as the prophetess's consort; Koresh not only allegedly slept with the 69-year-old "Queen" (my term) of the Branch Davidians, but married the fourteen-year-old daughter of the group's executive director, Perry Jones. Such power shifts within the Davidian family may seem primitive, outlandish, or bizarre, but can help explain why a parent might let a young daughter marry or have sex with a potential "king," and why the "Lamb" both presumed upon his followers and demanded their sexual favors (see Bromley and Silver, this volume). Prophetic families may tend toward incest (see Fogarty 1994). David Koresh had a lot of history to work with and there was no easy telling which part of the tradition he would turn toward in the end, although Tabor's analysis (this volume) of Koresh's final efforts at hermeneutics suggests that an alternative and peaceful ending was possible.

What does distinguish both the standoff at Waco and the current batch of retreat communes is their willingness sometimes to rely on weaponry (like the Mormons) rather than pamphlets to protect their vital interests. Most of these historic groups have had a mission to the world, with millennial expectations, and they too retreated when the pressures got too great. These sects are—as they have been in the past—simply *representative of tendencies and trends in the present.* As a scholar of such groups, Gordon Melton writes: "They (merely) represent more radical and religious innovations within the culture" (1986, 2). Not necessarily everyone's innovation, but one that needs to be understood, not simply labeled.

If the Davidians (who preferred to be called Koreshans) were rightfully called a religious "sect," we could then focus on legal issues and the simple fact that they were defending their holy turf with guns, protecting their messiah with an arsenal. They seem to have stockpiled their weapons with as much ease as they stockpiled feed for their animals (that right to "bear arms" enabled the Mormons to have their own militia) and Texas gun laws did make this all possible once again, but the Koreshans are not merely the product of some Texas tendency to shoot things out. Rather they reflect our national preference for force over persuasion, our belief that bullets should be as free as words. If guns were under control, the confrontation at Waco might have been waged by a prophet forced to throw verses from Revelation against his detractors rather than the 8,000 pounds of ammunition, 260 magazines, 90 pounds of powdered aluminum, and the parts needed to assemble hundreds of automatic and semi-automatic weapons Koresh putatively possessed. Just think of all the pamphlets Koresh could have issued and the great debates the citizens of Waco could have had with him over texts and interpretations. Instead we all waited to see which side had the greatest fire power and who might get killed. It does not take a prophet, or a psychologist, or even a cult deprogrammer, to see that a little gun control might have gone a long way toward preventing this pending apocalyptic confrontation.

Not all historical analogies yield the same conclusions. Cyrus Teed and David Koresh shared some nomenclature but little theology or philosophy. Teed used the ballot box, Koresh the bullet and the ballad. Benjamin Purnell provides us with more clues to the nature of the prophetic mind, to the bond that holds community and prophet together, to the belief in the "ingathering," to the hope that the end may justify the means and that the "end of time" may be within one's grasp, as promised by the Lord and his messengers.

When in 1884 Albert Shaw (under the direction of Richard Ely of

Johns Hopkins) wrote his study of the Icarian community, he hoped to take a "scientific" approach to the study of a utopian society and "picture its inner life as a miniature social and political organization" (Shaw 1884, 175). His pioneering sociological work emphasized conflicting goals within the group, ideological disputes, and contending personalities vying for authority, power, and control. Shaw's approach showed great sensitivity to the interior lives of such communities, but did not go far enough in placing them within a wider cultural and social framework.

The controversy surrounding the allegations of child abuse, fraud, the destruction of families, violence, and cultic activity by David Koresh and the Branch Davidians can, for example, best be understood within a broader and contemporary context that includes the royal family, Michael Jackson, Mia Farrow, Woody Allen, The Family, Hugh Hefner, the Amish and their dogs, and the Shakers. Normally we fail to associate Michael Jackson with the Shakers, or the royal family with the Branch Davidians, or Mia Farrow and Woody Allen with the Children of God, but taken separately, they are all icons of some belief system, either as validators or wreckers of societal values. By the way they arrange their private lives and conduct themselves in public, they have all become a curious litmus test for questions about family values and social arrangements. Margaret Thatcher once argued that there is no such thing as "society," that there are only individuals and families, and with that observation she hit a commonsensical and popular chord with the British public, who turned their back on the abstract notion of society and dumped her political target—her Labour opponents—who represented the state as both society and family.

The royal family, for one, seems to be engaged in a curious form of public hari-kari, with marriages dissolving, mistresses and misters maintained on the side, and public dissatisfaction with their behavior at an all-time high. Michael Jackson, that celibate male/female figure and leading icon for the Pepsi-Cola international "Children's Crusade," has had his lifestyle scrutinized, his infantile obsessions laid bare, and his feud with his sister Latoya made the subject of gossip columns. That family story has been enhanced by the sight of the many-times married Elizabeth Taylor rushing across the world to offer him succor in a dark hour. Mia Farrow and Woody Allen once epitomized the postmodern family with acres of adopted children, two separate households, two separate careers, two enormous talents operating within a redefined notion of what a family means. Then there were charges of abuse, incest once-removed, and other allegations. The Children of God, founded in the 1960s by Moses David

Berg ("Mo"), is an archetypal cult with strange practices, multiple wives in the Mormon tradition, and dubious recruitment practices called "flirty fishing." They faced new charges in Argentina of child abuse in late 1993, which resulted in 268 children being taken into care (and subsequently released). Hefner and Mo were both sexual radicals and came to prominence in the sixties when the sexual revolution was roiling in America. At the crudest level, one could say that the royal family is dysfunctional in every way; Michael Jackson is a cultural freak distorted by his Jehovah's Witness upbringing and show business; Farrow and Allen are egomaniacs driven by privilege; the Children of God the product of a disordered mind and sex-driven habits. Regrettably, such shorthand and demonizing analyses get us nowhere in understanding them as institutions, as the products of history, as personalities of our time and age.

In *The Shaker Experience in America* (1993), Stephen Stein brought Mother Ann Lee's followers down to earth by reminding historians that they had been canonized just as sects and pop singers were demonized. In the late twentieth century, they were transformed into a company of "aesthetically inclined" saints, forerunners of the Bauhaus, singers of sacred songs and dancers of native American hymns, almost obliterating their history from 1870 to the present. Recently the Amish, who have also been canonized, broke into the news not with just another report concerning their quaint ways but one that related their thriving dog-breeding business. Certain Amish farmers were raising dogs (pit bulls, rottweilers) for the commercial market just as they raise cattle for sale. Animal lovers and activists were outraged, but were hesitant to take on the sainted Amish because of their powerful image in American society as embodiments of religious piety and simplicity. How could they be Amish and do such a thing; how could they be both traditional and hideously modern?

After Waco, a student of mine learned of my interest in the Branch Davidians, and supplied me with the latest news from his network (he is an avid hacker). He had learned about new allegations of a BATF cover-up; he had read reports from gun proponents who knew that the Davidians could not have converted their semiautomatic weapons to fully automatic weapons; and he had received the address of a John Birch like group in Indiana that could supply the latest video of the final minutes at Mt. Carmel. Such pieces of instantaneous data tended to overwhelm any historic view of such religious groups and let conspiratorial interpretations emerge: for instance, that a law enforcement network opposed to religious groups not only existed but stretched around the globe; that David Koresh had escaped from the fire alive; that Attorney General Janet Reno was engineering a massive cover-up. There was good reason why my student decided to hook into a conspiracy theory that blamed the events of Waco on malevolent forces such as the BATF; they did have a large hand in the proceedings. It was if they were on one computer terminal processing data, and he on another with similar facts. All this speculating, all this instant analyzing, all this deconstructing about groups and tendencies should give us pause about finding a simple answer to the tragedy, since the facts of the case remain (and will for some time remain) in dispute.

It is inconceivable for many secular-minded Americans that anyone could accept the teachings of David Koresh or Sheik Rahman, and follow a set of religious principles that might lead them to death, or at least toward a commitment beyond rational expectations. It is as inconceivable as someone becoming a Scientologist (despite their use of a method akin to Freudian analyses), or becoming a member of the Rajneesh colony (where a large number had advanced degrees in psychology). Actually, it is quite American to believe in prophecy, as Paul Boyer (1992) has carefully outlined in his recent work. To be fearful about the future, to hope that by placing faith in some guitar-strumming leader, the past will be eradicated, our future secured, and our lives protected from elements unknown and unseen has a solid foundation—almost a denominational character—in our history.

There are at least two ways to view groups like the Davidians: first, that they developed out of a limited (and often local) set of historical circumstances that frame their leadership patterns, their interactions with the world, and the dynamics of their growth. Clarke Garrett, in writing about religious life in eighteenth-century France, has emphasized the religious revivals of the period and has questioned the use of broad sociopolitical or psychological theories to explain millenarianism in both France and England, attributing such disturbances to local circumstances and conditions. Certainly one has to look at both Adventist history and the peculiar religious atmosphere of Waco, which is home to over 100 denominations. A second perspective, and one most clearly enunciated by Bryan Wilson in numerous works, argues that such groups are part of larger processes such as modernization, value shifts in the society, and redefined notions of religiosity and community. In *Contemporary Transformations of Religion*, Wilson argues:

> The sources of secularization and the appeal of the new cults are themselves to be found in the contemporary social situation. These phenomena are related to other aspects of social change. Secularization is intimately related to the decline of community, to

increased social mobility, and to the impersonality of role-rela-
tionships. The new cults and the eclecticism that is indebted to
them stand in direct continuity with the protest against all these
developments misleadingly called the "counter culture." That
protest exists in many forms. . . . Behind all these diverse phenomena are the demands for authentic experience, for immediacy,
spontaneity, and instantaneity. (1976, 99)

These approaches are not mutually exclusive and should, in fact,
be seen in tandem. To comprehend David Koresh we must understand the eschatology of millennialism and the dynamic power that
charismatic figures have and how they relate it to popular culture
with its demands for stardom; to understand the Branch Davidians
we must comprehend the growth of evangelicalism and the intense
longing for "community" that the contemporary secular communi-
tarians espouse; to appreciate the tragedy of Waco we need to see it
as part of a long history of communal formation based on biblical
prophecy and belief and the failure of law enforcement officials to
know about that heavenly science.

Notes

1. Parts of this essay have appeared (in altered form) in "Cults, Guns,
and the Kingdom," *Nation* (April 12): 1993; and in my study *The Righteous Remnant: The House of David* (Kent, OH: Kent State University
Press, 1981). It was also presented to the Friends of the Bracken Library,
Ball State University, in March 1994.

2. With his revisionist approach, Stein has altered the interpretive
landscape for Shaker studies.

References

Boyer, Paul. 1992. *When Time Shall Be No More: Prophecy Belief in
    Modern America.* Cambridge: Harvard University Press, Belknap
    Press.
Braude, Anne. 1989. *Radical Spirits: Spiritualism and Women's Rights
    in Nineteenth Century America.* Boston: Beacon.
Breault, Mark, and Martin King. 1993. *Inside the Cult.* New York: Signet.
Claiborne, William. 1993. "Is Waco Cultist Emulating Turn of the Cen-
    tury Messiah?" *Washington Post,* April 18.
Dickens, Charles. 1859. *Tale of Two Cities.* Reprint. New York: Oxford
    University, 1967.
Fogarty, Robert S. 1975. Introduction to *The Cellular Cosmology,* by
    Cyrus Teed. Philadelphia: Porcupine. Originally published 1899.
———. 1981. *The Righteous Remnant: The House of David.* Kent, OH:
    Kent State University.

———. 1990. *All Things New: American Communes and Utopian Movements, 1860-1914.* Chicago: University of Chicago.

———, ed. 1994. *Special Love/Special Sex: An Oneida Community Diary,* by Victor Hawley. Syracuse, NY: Syracuse University Press.

Fox, George. 1890. *A Journal or Historical Account of the Life, Travels, Sufferings, Christian Experiences, and Labour of Love, in the Work of the Ministry, of That Ancient, Eminent, and Faithful Servant of Jesus Christ, George Fox.* Philadelphia: Friends Book Shop.

Garrett, Clarke. 1975. *Respectable Folly: Millenarians in France and England.* Baltimore: Johns Hopkins.

Hill, Christopher. 1972. *The World Turned Upside Down.* London: Viking.

Melton, J. Gordon. 1986. *Biographical Dictionary of American Cult and Sect Leaders.* New York: Garland.

Moore, Laurence. 1977. *In Search of White Crows.* New York: Oxford University.

———. 1986. *Religious Outsiders and the Making of Americans.* New York: Oxford University.

Paggitt, Ephraim. 1661. *Heresiography.* London: Cranford.

Roth, Cecil. 1933. *The Nephew of the Almighty.* London: E. Goldston.

Shaw, Albert. 1884. *Icaria.* Reprint. Philadelphia: Porcupine, 1975.

Stein, Stephen. 1993. *The Shaker Experience in America.* New Haven: Yale University.

Wilson, Bryan. 1976. *Contemporary Transformations of Religion.* New York: Oxford University.

2

WILLIAM L. PITTS, JR.

Davidians
and Branch
Davidians

1929–1987

Introduction

In 1929 the Davidians emerged in Los Angeles
as a movement calling for reform within the
Seventh-Day Adventist Church. They moved
to central Texas in 1935 under the leadership
of Victor T. Houteff and established a community of about seventy followers. Houteff firmly
believed that the end of time was near and that his mission in life was to prepare the church for the second
advent of Christ. The community suffered a great disappointment when the Kingdom was not established
in 1959 as predicted. They divided almost immediately into several splinter groups of two major families—

Davidians and Branch Davidians. Davidians scattered and Branch Davidians occupied the Mt. Carmel property under the leadership of Ben Roden and his family. The Roden era lasted until 1987. At that point leadership passed to Vernon Howell, who later called himself David Koresh. The purpose of this paper is to examine key elements in Davidian heritage through 1987. The story centers inevitably on two traditions, two leaders, and two eras: Davidians led by Houteff, 1929–59, and Branch Davidians led by the Rodens, 1959–87.

Houteff and the Seventh-Day Adventists

Victor Tasho Houteff, who founded the movement known as the Davidian Seventh-Day Adventists (Davidians), was born in Raikovo, Bulgaria, on March 2, 1885, and was brought up in the Orthodox Church. In 1907, Houteff emigrated to the United States at the age of twenty-two (Saether 1975).[1] Here he found work in restaurants and hotels, and after a brief stay in Milwaukee, moved to Rockford, Illinois, where in 1918 he heard Seventh-Day Adventist teaching at a revivalist tent meeting.

Houteff studied the Adventist message and soon embraced the millennial denomination with passion (Saether 1975, 197). By this time Houteff owned a small hotel and he demonstrated commitment to his new faith by helping to finance a new building for the Seventh-Day Adventists of Rockford. For reasons not clear, Houteff later left Rockford for Los Angeles, where he became quite active in the life of the local church. He eventually assumed the position of assistant superintendent of Sabbath School at the Olympic Exposition Park Seventh-Day Adventist Church. His weekly task was to review the Sabbath School lesson. Houteff's meditations and ponderings of faith during this time apparently inspired a visionary calling when, in 1929, he made public his personal interpretation of scripture. He called this new teaching "Shepherd's Rod," a reference to Micah 6:9, which admonishes, "Hear ye the rod."[2] Houteff identified the rod with the true teaching or interpretation of the Bible and thereby implied that the Seventh-Day Adventist doctrines and teachings were deficient. Laying claim to the prophetic role, he declared that Moses's rod was an instrument of deliverance.

Local church leaders were quick to isolate Houteff and to charge him with heresy and disruption, denying him permission to teach in the church. Houteff responded by moving the venue of his teaching to the nearby home of a sympathetic hearer, and continued to attract a significant following of Adventist adherents. In retaliation, church leaders then threatened that anyone who listened to his teaching or read his literature would be disfellowshipped. Houteff cites numerous incidents of his followers being barred from churches, labeled as heretics, and at least on one occasion, physically accosted.

The connection between the Davidians and the Seventh-Day Adventists was conflict-ridden and ambivalent from the beginning. Davidian thought is based on a general Seventh-Day Adventist frame of reference. Houteff affirmed the teaching of Christ's imminent return, and he revered particularly the writings of Ellen G. White. At the same time, the Seventh-Day Adventist denomination was highly apprehensive about the Davidian reformers. Adventists rejected their message unequivocally from the outset and periodically warned members of Davidian activity.[3] The Davidians responded initially by refusing to leave the Seventh-Day Adventist church and by calling for substantial reform within the denomination. Davidians argued that they were a legitimate extension of the Adventist message because Houteff was the divinely selected prophet who succeeded White.

Houteff's Message

The Leviticus of the Davidians (1992e), the constitution of the group, clearly states that Davidians embrace the core teachings of the Seventh-Day Adventists. The central teaching of the group, as the name implies, rests on the firm belief in the imminent return of Christ. This message was set forth in the 1830s and 1840s by William Miller, who unsuccessfully predicted the second coming in 1844 (Cross 1950), and was popularized by Joshua V. Himes. The expectation of the second advent is the cornerstone on which the new Seventh-Day Adventist denomination was created (Butler 1986). In the millenarian tradition, the Davidians eagerly anticipated prophetic voices and apocalyptic visions, a pattern that would persist throughout their history. Further linkages to Seventh-Day Adventists can be found in the Adventist name, which affirms the significance of the Sabbath, or Saturday. Drawing on the teaching of Seventh-Day Baptists, the Adventists declared that Sabbath day observance, though widely abandoned in Christendom, had nowhere been abrogated in scripture and was still as binding as the other nine commandments. Another linkage is evident with regard to the Adventists' strong emphasis on health (Numbers 1992). This aspect of their thought focused primarily on diet, and specifically on vegetarianism. Finally, Davidians followed the tradition of Seventh-Day Adventists as conscientious objectors in military service. They were traditionally patriotic, but refused to bear arms against others.[4] Davidians thus adopted much of the teachings of Seventh-Day Adventists. However, as has been the case with the leaders of countless other sectarian movements in the history of the church, Houteff did not initially want to start a new denomination. Rather, he wanted to reform an old one; but the old one did not welcome his reform.

Houteff's message of the imminent establishment of the Kingdom of God was predicated on his reading of apocalyptic biblical literature. He believed that these passages provided the clues to the future of the church and humankind. The recently published index of his publications (Adair 1993) shows that Houteff drew widely from scriptural texts, but the books cited most frequently are Isaiah, Ezekiel, Daniel, Zechariah, Matthew, John, and Revelation. Houteff interpreted the Bible in terms of prophecy and fulfillment, hence his extensive use of the Old Testament prophets and of the book of Revelation. In typical millenarian hermeneutic, he reconstructed a history on the basis of mysterious and arcane passages recorded in Daniel, and interpreted signs in current events which suggested fulfillment of the end of time.

For Houteff, as for many other sectarian prophets, numerics provided a large part of the fascination with millenarian teaching. Standard millenarian interpretation adopted the position that a day equals a year, and thus Daniel's 2,300 "days" found their consummation in the hands of modern interpreters in the nineteenth or twentieth centuries. Houteff was also deeply influenced by the so-called "theory of correspondence" in scripture in which he uncovered the various types and antitypes throughout the sacred text and history. He argued that "every letter, word, and phrase of a sentence has its appointed part to play in giving coherent expression to the thought intended . . . in unfolding Bible truths. The Bible marvelously builds its richly varied materials (types, symbols, parables, allegories, numerics, etc.) into a towering revelation foreordained, of perfectly co-ordinated, life-saving truth" (1992a, 36). Essentially, he viewed the Bible as a vast repository of secret and inviolable truths wherein typology and numerology offered keys to its hidden meanings.

In the pattern of many millennial prophets, Houteff believed strongly that truth was revealed progressively. He often used the image of a scroll being unrolled, in reference to his own work, and referred repeatedly to his teaching as "Present Truth." Thus he could argue that he accepted traditional Seventh-Day Adventist teaching, but that he was presenting a new message for his age. In effect, the "Present Truth" he proclaimed was that Christ could not return and the Kingdom could not be established because his church—the Seventh-Day Adventist denomination—had grown worldly and apathetic. Hence, the apocalyptic events were forestalled until the Adventist church could be reformed and spiritually mobilized.

Interestingly, then, Houteff addressed neither all people nor even all Christian denominations. He spoke exclusively to the Seventh Day Adventists because only they were allegedly prepared to understand the implications of his teachings, and if they heeded the new message, the forces to bring history to a conclusion could be set in motion. Houteff compared the Seventh-Day Adventist denomination to the church of Laodicea described in Revelation: it was "lukewarm." Houteff envisioned an "absolute match" between description and condition, and he appealed to biblical imagery to make his point. The church was often likened to unfaithful Gomer or the prodigal son. Similarly, he invoked the parable of the wheat and tares to convey the putative corruption of the church (Houteff 1992d, 5, 24). Periodically, Houteff appealed to Ellen White, who, in her *Testimonies*, wrote of "sleeping preachers, preaching to a sleeping people" (Houteff 1992c, 7).

Houteff provided more specific detail, when during the mid-1930s he charged: "Some of our schools discredit the spirit of prophecy; some students adopt a style of dress which shows their preoccupation with worldly fashion, many Seventh-day Adventists, including leaders, adhere to worldly pleasures such as beach parties and moving picture shows. Just how far can we go in the matter of worldly conformity?" (Houteff 1992i, 52–53). And again: "The course being pursued by the church is taking her with the drift of the world . . . Her institutions—schools, sanitariums, etc.—have compromised with the institutions of the world [and] continued backsliding has separated us from God" (Houteff 1992b, 66).

The Davidian prophet also directed attacks on Adventist ministers who relied on formal college training, intellect, and talent (Houteff 1992h, 43). He found them to be "blind leaders who cannot bring their people to God" (1992i, 38–39). Like other religious sects, the Davidians did not subscribe to formal seminary training; instead they relied entirely on Houteff's writings as the sure guide to true Christianity. The Davidians offered a modest but systematic introduction to Houteff's thought in their ministerial training program, and registered many of their number as ministers or student licentiates (Houteff 1992g, 17–18).

The Seventh-Day Adventists responded neither to Houteff's attack on worldliness nor to his criticism of the established institutions, but rather sought to rebut his prophetic claims and teachings. Houteff believed that the Seventh-Day Adventists correctly understood the message of Christ's imminent return, but that they had more to learn—a new truth—delineated by Houteff in a two-stage judgment. According to Houteff, an invisible remnant of 144,000 believers must arise to form the true church (this number represent-ed about half of the Seventh-Day Adventists in 1930). Lifelong Davidian Sidney Smith stated that the Davidian church "is trying to warn the Seventh-day Adventists of the impending doom . . . They don't believe it. . . . That's what I'm doing" (Green, Smith, and Smith 1989, 12). Thus, according to Davidian beliefs, the Seventh-Day Adventists had become a worldly, lethargic church, while Houteff's followers were touted as the true remnant called to proclaim divine judgment (the "rod"). Houteff believed that the kingdom of God would be established in Palestine in the near future and that the 144,000 would make their way there as the harbingers of a new day that would attract multitudes to God (Houteff 1992h, 54; 1992d, 32; F. Houteff 1961, 17, 31–32).

In his own way, Houteff understood the psychological and social problems associated with embracing new religious ideas. He acknowledged that biblical figures had their messages rejected—notably, Noah and Jesus. Similarly, sectarian, charismatic leaders such as Luther, Knox, Wesley, Campbell, Miller, and Sister White met with vehement resistance (1992d, 7). Houteff therefore warned adherents of the "costs" of membership and urged his readers to be like Nathaniel and make their own independent decisions to partic-ipate (1992b, 12).

Houteff gave unique symbolic expression to his conviction that the end was near. He designed a clock to be set in the floor of the main building at Mt. Carmel, its hands set near 11:00.[5] The end-time clock visually reminded the Davidian faithful that the last stage of the world's history was at hand. It was his life's work to unlock the biblical secrets and to show how the end would come.

Institutional Structures: Davidian Life at Mt. Carmel

Mt. Carmel, near Waco, Texas, became the headquarters for the Davidians in 1935, and they would be identified with that place throughout the remainder of the century. Houteff and two followers left Los Angeles in January 1935 to find a desirable location. They initially investigated Texas sites near Dallas, San Antonio, Houston, and Waco. They purchased three hundred and seventy-seven acres located two and a half miles from the Waco city limits (Power 1940, 18–19).[6] Twelve Davidians volunteered to occupy the new site and they arrived May 24, 1935, to begin the new venture (Green, Smith, and Smith 1989, 17). By August their number had grown to thirty-seven (Power 1940, 54). Houteff thought they would be at Mt. Carmel less than a year (Saether 1975, 215), but the parousia was

delayed, and they eventually carved out a fascinating quasi-commu-
nal life. By 1940 the community had reached its capacity of sixty
four and had built ten buildings, created a water supply and sewage
system, and installed electricity.

Leadership and Authority

Houteff was the undisputed leader and patriarch of the group. The
Davidian constitution provided for four offices and a council, but all
decisions were subject to Houteff's approval (Houteff 1992e, 6–7;
Power 1940, 85; Saether 1975, 214). Bonnie Smith recalled that Houteff shared all of the hardships of the community (Green 1989, 11). In
this aspect, Houteff exhibited characteristics of what Max Weber
(1963, 55) called the "exemplary" prophet—one who leads others
down the same difficult path that he or she sojourns. On occasions,
this path could be hard and demanding. Saether remembered Houteff's domineering personality: "He could be pretty rough with people,
and they resented that" (Saether 1975, 172).

Houteff's power was enhanced by the fact that family members
held key offices. His wife, Florence, was secretary, and his mother-
in-law, Mrs. Hermanson, was treasurer. The convergence of kinship
and religious devotion provided powerful support for the Davidian
leader, no doubt enabling him to persevere more effectively in his
mission (see Bromley and Silver, this volume).[7] Of course, the most
important source of Houteff's authority was his religious leadership
and his ability to inspire in his followers a deep sense of sacrifice and
devotion. In the words of those who knew him: "We believe . . . with
all our heart . . . that Brother Houteff is a prophet of God" (Green,
Smith, and Smith 1989, 6, 58). This belief goes far to explain the self-
sacrifice, commitment, and cohesiveness which helped the community succeed. It also set an enormously important precedent for the
community. Houteff himself was the first of many Davidian leaders
who assumed the role of prophet.

Economic Organization

The Davidians aimed at expanding self-sufficiency, using their land
to produce as much food, lumber, and fuel as possible. They created
a rational economy of need, designed to produce only enough sur-
plus—canned food, fuel reserves—to ensure the security and survival
of the group (Power 1940, 70; Saether 1975, 164). This reduced their
dependency on the outside world and focused energies on sustaining
the practical life of the community. Houteff also believed that physical labor built character and contributed to sharing and enrichment
of communal life (Green 1989, 10). He required everyone to work,

including children, and he paid wages to all of them. However, some Davidians also took jobs in nearby communities. Though the Davidians were separatists in many ways, they were also realistic about economic necessities. The farming operation could not support entirely a community of sixty or seventy, and thus, they were willing to work for wages to help the community succeed. Their flexibility and diverse work skills paid significant dividends in the 1930s. Although Houteff established the community in the midst of the Depression, Bonnie Smith recalls that "all our needs were taken care of" (Green, Smith, and Smith 1989, 49). The Davidians' emphasis on such values as frugality and a plain lifestyle undoubtedly increased their survival ability during these difficult times.

The Davidians also produced their own money system, including green paper bills of different denominations and round cardboard currency. It could be used only at Mt. Carmel, of course, but it gave symbolic significance to the kind of independence from secular society they sought to establish. All of the money carried two logos: the lion of Judah, representing the Davidic kingdom, and the eleventh-hour clock, a reminder of the impending end-time. The Davidian currency also anticipated the triumph of the second coming and the new world order under Christ.

In an effort to increase the economic viability of the community, as well as test the faith of Davidian adherents, Houteff instituted the "second tithe" in 1936. The second tithe was an innovative policy introduced to address concerns like health care and education. After members donated a first tithe to promote religious work, they were asked to contribute a second tithe (10% of the remaining 90%) for such practical community needs as health insurance, the school, and old-age care (Green, Smith, and Smith 1989, 47).

Education

Like many contemporary religious sects, the Davidians created a separate educational system in order to control socialization of the young, instill religious beliefs, and transmit their own culture. The school was named the Mt. Carmel Academy and was designed to train children in moral and religious subjects as well as in the basic academic subjects. Children were required to learn the fundamentals of the Davidian faith, which were rooted primarily in the Bible and the writings of Ellen White (Power 1940, 42–48). Davidian children were also required to cultivate and acquire a practical skill. This objective was accomplished by alternating activities of work and study throughout the eight-hour day, suggesting that transition between these spheres of activity was accomplished with considerable ease in the routines of daily life (Green, Smith, and Smith 1989, 11). The integration of religion, work, and schooling prepared children adequately for the kinds of knowledge useful in the communal organization.

Second tithe and tuition, however, could not cover all expenses. The Mt. Carmel Academy was eventually forced to close for financial reasons, and students were moved reluctantly to public schools (Power 1940, 19).

Worship, Ritual, and Practice

One of the chief purposes of Shepherd's Rod was to live as the true church in preparation for the great ingathering of saints. Although the believers worked regular hours either at Mt. Carmel or in town, the focus of their corporate life was centered on religious rituals and worship. Religious worship services were held routinely on Friday evenings and Saturday afternoons, and instructional classes were held each evening. Houteff, the prophet and teacher, always led the sessions, preaching, prophesying, and inveighing against the corruption of the world, inspiring Davidian Glen Green to declare many years later, "We were spellbound" (Green, Smith, and Smith 1987, 32). Houteff's method of teaching and preaching was expository—a chapter-by-chapter Bible study or exposition of a topic. His messages were typically recorded, transcribed, and printed in the form of tracts for dissemination. Since Houteff was expected to enlighten believers with progressive revelation, the recordings of his preachments were carefully preserved for potential converts, providing very thorough documentation for historians of religion. Houteff spent literally hundreds of hours poring over scripture and attempting to link biblical passages and predictions with the teachings of Ellen White and current events. The Davidian faith emphasized separation from the world, giving rise to specific community practices. One such practice involved religious endogamy. Members were not permitted to intermarry with nonbelievers (Power 1940, 50). In fact, Saether (1975, 168, 248) reports that many Davidians divorced when they joined the group. Marriages were carefully supervised and familial lines were held to be sacred (see Bromley and Silver, this volume). Another set of practices focused on norms of attire. In typical sectarian tradition, the Davidians rejected display in their dress. Women's dresses were required to fall at least halfway between the knee and the ground. Exposure of the female anatomy was generally discouraged altogether; even elbows were expected to be covered. Davidian women eschewed cosmetics, wore their hair long, and donned prayer caps. Other practices were implemented to insulate members from various corrupting influences of secular society. Like other communal organizations (Kanter 1972), the Davidians regulated information coming into the community: only selected newspaper articles were read at mealtimes (Power 1940, 46). They permitted no ball games (even miniature golf) or any form of competition (Green, Smith, and Smith 1989, 13–15, 21–22).

Transition and Change

After the Rod followers moved to Mt. Carmel they were preoccupied in the mid-1930s with building the necessary physical facilities of their new home, establishing the printing press, and creating the tracts that contained their message. Just prior to World War II, Houteff left for Bulgaria to visit his mother. He appointed C. I. Wilson to supervise Mt. Carmel, but a rival leader, M. J. Bingham, challenged his authority. Houteff returned and resumed control, but factional strife remained.

World War II created special problems for the group; they wanted to demonstrate appropriate compliance with the state, but their first allegiance was to God. The Davidians took seriously the command not to kill, and objected to serving as combatants in war. Consequently, they appealed for conscientious objector status,[8] but the government initially refused their request. This episode prompted Houteff to change the name of his Shepherd's Rod to the Davidian Seventh-Day Adventists in 1942, thus coming under the protective umbrella of a well-established conscientious objector tradition which was already recognized by the draft boards. Houteff's young men would thereby be spared the possibility of killing another Christian, a prospect which appalled them. Davidians proposed to fulfill their military obligations by aiding the wounded (Houteff 1992f, 2).

In the years following the war, the tension between the Seventh-Day Adventists and the Davidians remained high. The Davidian method of evangelizing was to visit local Seventh-Day Adventist churches and Adventist camps, where they distributed literature and took names of supporters and sympathizers for future mailings. Seventh-Day Adventist conferences consistently warned members about Davidian teaching, and the number of converts apparently remained small. In 1952–53 Houteff engaged in an accelerated evangelization campaign. Twenty to thirty workers were sent out with the mission of contacting every Seventh-Day Adventist family in North America, England, India, the West Indies, and Australia. The Davidian movement still did not increase significantly, but it planted roots firmly in these areas and became international in scope.

These areas were chosen, in part, because the Davidian tracts had been produced principally in English. Houteff believed that the stage was set for the great ingathering and fully anticipated expanded growth in the immediate future.

The Davidian movement was struck a sudden and unexpected blow, however, when the prophet died in 1955. Houteff's death shocked his followers because they had come to believe that Houteff was the new Elijah who would help usher in the reign of God. His mission was incomplete and his prophetic claims were unfulfilled. After some internecine conflict, Houteff's wife, Florence, assumed leadership of the movement. Splinter groups remained, however, the most notable of which was the Branch Davidians, led by Ben Roden. Though failing to forge a significant following from which effectively to challenge Florence Houteff's leadership in 1955, the Roden family would reappear later to take charge of the Davidian movement.

The (Second) Great Disappointment

William Miller's failed prophecy is often referred to as "the Great Disappointment" (Melton 1986, 181). In the Millerite tradition, the Davidians experienced a second great disappointment, though on a smaller scale, in 1959. Victor Houteff had refused to predict the exact time of God's judgment on the church, but Florence Houteff's single most notable act as Davidian leader was to take that step. She published her revelatory message on November 5, 1955, stating that the kingdom would be established 1,260 days later: it would fall on April 22, the Jewish Passover in 1959. She called on the Davidians to report to Mt. Carmel, and many resolved to come. Some nine hundred people gathered at New Mt. Carmel just prior to April 22, 1959, suggesting something of Davidian numerical strength.

Florence Houteff's invested authority as a Davidian leader hinged largely on the millennial expectation she created, the fruits of which she enjoyed for a period of four years. In turn, the community also drew considerable solidarity and energy from the anticipation of the ingathering. The excitement and shared enthusiasm of believers served to crystallize Florence Houteff's reign and stabilize the community in the wake of Victor Houteff's death. But the period of great anticipation was soon to turn into a great disappointment.

In the weeks leading up to the prophesied event, activity was frenzied. Reporters conducted many interviews during the week of April 22. The recurrent theme was that members had sold their homes and businesses and had come in response to Florence Houteff's call to report to Mt. Carmel (Turner 1962a). George Walton and his wife led thirty-five members from California. "We burned all our bridges behind us," he reported (*Waco Times Herald*, April 21, 1959). Tommy Thompson from Narco, California, sold his house, furniture, and trenching business and made the pilgrimage as well (*Waco Times Herald*, April 21, 1959). Mr. and Mrs. C. C. Lyons sold their home and most of their worldly possessions in Portland, Oregon, just prior to coming to Texas (*Waco News Tribune*, n.d.). The stories were sensational and numerous. The elect came from all over the United States and Canada in expectation of the second coming. The Davidian faithful pitched seventy-five tents for temporary shelter and waited in the rainy weather of central Texas that spring.

The Davidians expected a sign of divine intervention, such as purification of the Seventh-Day Adventist Church, establishment of God's kingdom in Israel, or outbreak of war in the Middle East. One of these events would be for them a sure indication of the beginning of a new age (Saether 1975, 404–5; *Waco Tribune Herald*, April 21, 1959). Davidians believed that they would escape the terrible slaughter promised in Ezekiel 9 and would emerge as "firstfruits" of the living (Houteff 1992i, 23). But as they waited, no such sign appeared. In the following days, confusion and disappointment gave way to despair, and by May 5, half of the hopeful had departed in bitter dejection (*Waco News Tribune*, May 4, 1959). A year later a remnant of only about fifty remained at Mt. Carmel, where they continued operating a dairy farm (Turner 1962a).

The Seventh-Day Adventists responded to the Davidian sect by issuing two of the most compelling critiques that they published during the Florence Houteff era. The Committee on Defense Literature of the General Conference produced a detailed criticism of Houteff's work in March 1956—four months after Florence's prediction. And four months after the disappointment, they criticized Davidians for time-setting and misusing Ellen White's teachings (Committee on Defense Literature 1956; Research Committee 1960). In the summer of 1959, Adventist A. V. Olson led a series of discussions at Mt. Carmel. The principal aim of the discussions was to bring the Davidians back into the Adventist fold, but the effort failed.

On December 12, 1961, and January 16, 1962, the Rod leaders notified their followers that the Rod literature was at variance with the Bible regarding the correct interpretation of Ezekiel 4 and 5. They called for a special session of the association, held March 11, 1962, at which time Florence and the other officers resigned, dissolved the Davidian Association, and placed their assets in the hands of the court for disposal (Odom 1962, 6–8). Despite formal dissolution of the Houteff reign, however, the movement did not die. Eight Davidian splinter groups were identified within the next four years, and court battles over assets and property continued for years (Court of Civil Appeals, no. 4533, 1966).

The Roden–Branch Davidian Era

In the generation following, the Roden family emerged as the most visible Davidian leaders. Tarling (1981, 131) suggests that the reason for Roden's success was that in the wake of the disastrous leadership of Florence Houteff, the Davidians needed a strong and compelling figure. No single individual was able to command the loyalty that Victor Houteff had generated. When Florence eventually left Texas for California—apparently with $20,000 of Davidian money (Green 1989, 44), the Branch Davidians reclaimed Mt. Carmel, while other groups settled in Missouri, South Carolina, New York, and Washington.

Ben Roden's Message

Ben Roden established an alternative tradition in the Davidian camp as early as 1955, and adopted the name "Branch" to designate this splinter group within the movement. The account of his call asserts that the Lord instructed him to write a letter to the Davidians. The letter included an appeal to the believers to acknowledge him as the new leader of the Davidians. When he finished writing, he hesitated to sign it simply "Ben Roden," asking for divine guidance regarding an appropriate signature. He reported that the message came to him to sign it simply "Branch" (Tarling 1981, 131–32), a biblical reference in the prophetic tradition of Davidians to Isaiah 11:1: "a shoot shall come out from the stump of Jesse and a branch shall grow out of his roots." Since Jesse was father of David in the Old Testament, the allusion kept the Branch clearly associated with the Davidian movement while at the same time introducing a separate identity. The Branch was the name for Jesus Christ which the Davidians commonly preferred. Ben Roden was fond of quoting Zechariah 6:2, which states that "a man whose name is the Branch shall build the Temple of the Lord." The Branch Davidians under Roden created a logo that symbolized key ideas and beliefs. The logo was a circular field filled with a large star of David and twelve perimeter stars. The word "Ensign" was written across the center, and the reference "Isaiah 11:1" was placed under it. A plant was superimposed upon the design with three final designations: Jesse the Stem, David the Rod, and Christ the Branch (Roden 1978, 2).

Roden clearly built on the ideas of those who came before him.

The writings of White and Houteff figured prominently in his publications. He envisioned his role primarily as the leader of the third and final phase of the movement. According to Roden, in the first stage the Adventists unraveled the mysteries of the gospel, laid claim to the true church, and established the Sabbath as the divinely appointed day of worship. In the second phase Houteff stressed the notions of progressive revelation, the impending millennium, and the gathered remnant. In the final era led by Roden, the goal was to reproduce the character of Christ perfectly in the lives of the elect 144,000 in preparation for the second advent (Tarling 1981, 132). Tarling (1981, 132) observes that Roden focused largely on developing Adventist *perfectionism*, a doctrine commonly associated with millennial movements.

Though the Roden literature was not as extensive as Houteff's, there were distinctive themes in his writings: the significance of Israel, General Conference reform, anti-Catholicism, and a concern for recovery of Israelite festivals. Ben Roden gave special emphasis to the restored state of Israel and to the religious opportunities it offered. He intended to create a Branch Davidian center in Israel and made contact with Israeli officials, obtaining permission to move followers there in the late 1950s. Roden recorded his success with evident pleasure: "For the first time in the history of Zionist colonization, an organized Christian group has been granted official status in Israel as recognized immigrants and land settlers" (Roden 1968, 4). He reported that six families had settled in the Galilee village of Amirim and made special note that "like their Jewish neighbors, the Adventist settlers observe Saturday as their Sabbath" (Roden 1968, 4). But Roden's initial optimism soured when his prophetic claims were rejected by native Israelis. Tarling (1981, 133) also suggests that this experiment failed because numbers were simply too small. Roden wanted to promote emigration to Israel. In *The Star and the Trumpet* he wrote that the 1967 Israeli-Arab war had opened a new chapter in Bible prophecy. He often quoted Isaiah 2:3: "In the last days all nations shall flow to the mountain of the Lord's house and the word of the Lord from Jerusalem." "Are you ready to help fulfill this prophecy?" he asked. "You will have to change your residence to Jerusalem!" (Roden 1968, 2).

Millennialists often find in political change in Israel signs of the end-time. For Roden the Arab-Israeli war of June 1967 was a fulfillment of prophecy, invoking Isaiah 31:5: "As birds flying so will the Lord of hosts defend Jerusalem." Roden alleged that the flying birds were Israeli jets which rendered the Arab air force inoperable and thereby paved the way to an abrupt and decisive victory. But for

Roden the greater significance was that it made possible fulfillment of many conditions for the end: the law must go out from Jerusalem (Isa. 2:3); the 144,000 will be gathered at Mount Zion (Rev. 14: 1); and a man whose name is the Branch shall build the Temple of the Lord (Zech. 6: 12) (Roden 1969, 4). Without question, the Israeli-Arab War of 1967 gave him much encouragement. In 1970 he called on the General Conference to move its headquarters to Jerusalem (1970b, 1), and in a 1973 publication Roden depicted the earth as the domain of the beast, but Israel as the ark of safety where some Adventists had already migrated (Roden 1973, 3).

In 1970, when the General Conference of Adventists was meeting in Dallas, Roden took the opportunity to call on them to hear his message. Though not allowed to speak to the conferees, the Branch Davidians distributed literature proclaiming Roden's message: "Sunday, June 14, 1970 is Pentecost," he noted, "and the General Conference meeting is June 7–20. Pentecostal power fell on the 120; will it happen now? In order to receive power, the church must be receptive to truth" (Roden 1970a, 2–3). Roden was unusually productive in preparing informational literature for this meeting. He wrote *The Urgent Need of the Church* (1970d), a call for reform; *Pentecostal Fire* (1970c), with counsel about bringing new life into the church; *Crowned in the Wilderness* (1970a), an appeal to recognize him as Adventist leader; and a broadside declaring, *Move the General Conference to Israel* (1970b).

During the mid-seventies, the aging Roden produced a virulent strand of anti-Catholic attacks, peppered with epithets aimed at papal authority and accusing Rome of subversion and conspiracy. The allegations were not without some precedent. Early Adventism generally blamed the Roman Catholic Church for distorting the faith, as well as promoting and establishing Sunday rather than Sabbath worship. Roden believed that Nixon's impeachment was due to an insidious Catholic plot to elect Ted Kennedy, who would enforce Sunday laws. He therefore called for excisement of Kennedy, removal of Catholics from the president's staff, and resistance to the Vatican conspiracy to take over the United States (Roden 1974).

Roden also believed that ceremonial law of the Old Testament should continue to be observed. Standard Christian interpretation argued that the ethical law epitomized by the Ten Commandments were still binding, but that ceremonial and sacrificial features of ancient Israel need no longer be observed. Roden stressed the keeping not only of the Sabbath but of other festival days as well. Just as the Sabbath was meant to be kept literally, so were yearly festivals such as Passover and Pentecost. They were not mere types which passed away with the coming of Christ, but were still binding: "It is time for the church to recognize the *entire* system-of-worship of the Levitical law . . . [we must] include not only the weekly sabbath, but the yearly sabbath as well" (Roden 1971, 3–4). According to Roden, the reason to observe the Jewish festivals was that "the ceremonial Law sets the *time* for the important events in the last days . . . [and] ceremonial law points to blood atonement which purifies the church" (Roden 1978, 1–8).

Leadership and Organization

Roden thought of himself as king and patriarch of the community of saints, just as the biblical David had been king. Although he may have despaired privately at the modest numbers drawn to Mt. Carmel, he did not lack for a sense of his own authority and place in the scheme of things. He told the General Conference to "spread the news quickly that God is calling us to New Mount Carmel Center, Waco, Texas, to appoint ourselves one head . . . on June 14, 1970" (Roden 1970a, 4). E. A. Shaw, the leader of the Branch Davidians in Australia, said in 1977, "Ben Roden is the King. He is King David. . . . Brother Roden is the viceregent of God. . . . I'm subject to Ben Roden" (Tarling 1981, 141).

The basis of authority in the Davidian tradition, as was made evident by Houteff, was the claim to prophetic interpretation and revelation, and of course, the acceptance of that claim as legitimate by others in the community. The rationale for deferring to prophets for collective direction was their special power of interpretation, as one Davidian attested: "Anybody who goes direct to the Bible and thinks that they can interpret is just deceiving themselves. . . . It's written by inspiration and it must be understood by inspiration" (Tarling 1981, 141).

Organizationally, the new Mt. Carmel offered little in the way of structural changes. The farming operation remained the central focus of work; some adherents held part-time jobs to supplement the Davidian mission; tithing remained a strict requirement of all members; and Roden carried on the various administrative duties, training ministers, writing religious tracts, and directing the publishing center just as Houteff had in old Mt. Carmel.

The Emergence of Lois Roden

The Roden family worked together as a unit, each contributing his or her own efforts to the success of the new Mt. Carmel community.

Lois Roden, Ben's wife, was often described by both adherents and detractors as a strong, stubborn, and persevering woman. Her zeal for the faith was equal to her husband's, and when later she became locked in a power struggle with her son, George, for leadership of the movement, she would prevail in impressive style.

A critical event for the emergence of Lois Roden's reign at Mt. Carmel occurred in 1977 when she experienced a vision. By her own account, she was visited by an angel who was said to represent the Holy Spirit Mother. Introducing an innovative and revolutionary modification of Davidian beliefs, Lois Roden began to teach that the Holy Spirit was feminine. In the prophetic tradition of the Davidians, she laid claim to her own divine message and calling, articulating her beliefs in a series of pamphlets called *The Holy Spirit, She,* and later, a magazine entitled *SHEkinah.* Among other things, Lois Roden proclaimed that when the Lord returned at the second advent, the messiah would appear in female form. She envisioned her own mission as an effort to make known to all believers the femininity of God (Barrineau 1980, 1, 3).

It is unclear to what extent Ben Roden accepted the prophetic claims of his wife. There is no indication that he ever rejected her message, though by 1977 Ben Roden's health was declining rapidly and at least some have suggested that physical debilitation prevented him from challenging his partner. Ben Roden died the following year and Lois Roden, effectively fighting off the efforts of her son to assume leadership, inherited the mantel of the prophet. She wasted no time in exercising her new powers. Immediately following the death of her husband, Lois declared the event to have apocalyptic significance, as its timing was strategically placed between two key Old Testament ceremonial days. She announced that the seventh seal in the book of Revelation had been opened on the day of Ben Roden's death.

Lois Roden's reign over Mt. Carmel was characterized by frequent mission trips to spread the word about her new revelation. Her publications chronicled the successes and exploits of these numerous sojourns all over the world. She claimed to have thousands of followers on several continents and was curiously popular in Canada. However, troubles continued to brew back home as George, insistent on his divine appointment as the true prophet, engaged in endless legal maneuverings to wrest control of Mt. Carmel from his mother. The bitter struggle between mother and son only alienated George further and set the stage for Lois's alliance with young Vernon Howell, whom she attempted to groom as her replacement.

The Struggle for Succession

Howell, who had arrived at Mt. Carmel in 1981, impressed the prophetess with his consuming hunger for the faith and considerable abilities to repair equipment and buildings. He also demonstrated an aptitude for memorizing and quoting scripture and showed promise as a teacher. Apparently, the relationship was not merely platonic; it was rumored that Howell was the prophetess's consort. If true, Lois, who was sixty-seven years old, may have been seeking to control the destiny of the movement by empowering Howell as her successor.

On October 18, 1985, control of Mt. Carmel passed to George after he successfully lobbied and campaigned for election using monopolized mailing lists. Roden promptly purged Howell loyalists and other detractors (at gunpoint, according to some) and changed the name of Mt. Carmel to Rodenville. Lois Roden, in ill health, died the following year.

On November 3, 1987, Roden and eight men led by Vernon Howell exchanged gunfire as part of a battle for control of the property and leadership of the Branch Davidian movement. The Howell group sought to discredit Roden by arguing (1) that they had been expelled at gunpoint when Roden took over the seventy-seven acres by force in 1985 (Smith 1987, 5A) and (2) that Roden had desecrated a grave by exhuming a corpse, which he proposed to resurrect. The Howell group was trying to secure a picture of it as evidence of corpse abuse to present to authorities (Parma 1987, n.p.). Roden responded that Howell had written threatening letters and had come to execute the slaughter predicted by the Davidians—to wage holy war (Smith 1987, 5A). He said that the casket was placed in the church out of respect while the community moved its cemetery to the back of the property.

Two issues tipped the scales in Howell's favor. One critical issue for the Branch Davidians was taxes. Roden's position was that they were a religious community and should be granted exemption from taxes. On the other hand, the county argued that taxes were owed and were delinquent in the amount of $68,000. Howell strengthened his position by paying these back taxes (Nelson and Gines 1988, 1A). Secondly, Roden produced two wills claiming ownership, but neither was properly authenticated. Roden became angry with the judges, filing expletive-laden motions and threatening them with a plague of herpes and AIDS and seven plagues from God. He ignored judges' warnings and was sentenced to six months in jail (Witherspoon 1988, 1B).

On March 23, 1988, the day after Roden was jailed, the Howell Branch Davidians occupied Mt. Carmel. They wandered over the land, near barbed wire fences and community buildings. "It's beautiful," said Perry Jones, spokesman for the Howell group; "it has all been worked out by the will of God" (Nelson 1988).

Postscript

In the 1980s Davidians were scattered throughout the United States, with centers in Mountaindale, New York; Spokane, Washington; Yuciape, California; South Carolina; Missouri; and Texas. Salem, South Carolina, was a major center by virtue of the fact that its leader, Don Adair, was intent on reprinting the entire Houteff corpus. He also has produced a major study of his own, *The Fall of the Protestant Nations* (1986).

M. J. Bingham, a close associate of Houteff and editor of many Davidian tracts, founded another group in the late 1960s called Bashan, located on 542 acres near Exeter, Missouri. About thirty-five members took up residence on this property. The current leaders are Jimmy and Jeriel Bingham, relatives of the founder. The Bashan group has also been very active in publishing and mailing (Cattau 1993).

In 1989 Davidians who had moved to New York from Jamaica visited Waco to investigate the possibility of purchasing part of the old Mt. Carmel site. In the following year they bought the available Mt. Carmel land and have established an impressive printing operation, making Houteff's publications available in their original tract format. They have also established a Davidian training center. George Archer leads this group, and for the New York Davidians, old Mt. Carmel holds a special significance: "It is not just a name on a sign [but is] the location that God has chosen." They believe that God intended his headquarters to be "in the midst of the land for the gathering of the 144,000" ("Blessing in the Midst of the Land," n d , 23, 30). Thus Mt. Carmel retains a significance in Davidic tradition.

Tarling has recorded the presence of international groups of Davidians. He has identified E. A. Shaw and Fred Steed as major leaders of the movement in Australia, with its headquarters in Melbourne (Tarling 1981, 138, 141). Davidians have also remained active in Canada, the Caribbean, and Great Britain since Houteff's days. In the 1980s the Branch had established new missions in Australia, New Zealand, England, and Canada as well as in California and Texas.

Notes

1. Saether's five hundred pages of memoirs are a highly useful source of information. Saether was part of the original community from 1937 until its demise. He served on the executive council and was thoroughly familiar with the leadership, structure, and teachings of the movement. In 1989 Baylor University interviewed three additional former members of the Houteff community: Sidney Smith, Bonnie Smith, and Glen Green, whose recollections added valuable insights into the Davidian community.

2. The Shepherd's Rod movement changed its name to Davidian Seventh-day Adventists in 1942. The symbol of the shepherd's rod was placed in Davidian buildings and appeared regularly in Davidian literature. The more familiar name "Davidian" is used in this essay.

3. See especially the Committee on Defense Literature (1956); and the Research Committee (1960). These sources set forth the Adventist position in Houteff's teachings.

4. Although Seventh-Day Adventists have long resisted adopting a formal creed, in 1980 the General Conference issued a summary guideline titled "Fundamental Beliefs of Seventh-day Adventists." A convenient exposition of these doctrines is available in *Seventh-day Adventists Believe,* ed. Ministerial Association of the General Conference of Seventh-day Adventists (1988). For a reliable history of the denomination, consult Schwarz (1979).

5. In his oral memoirs Glen Green describes Houteff's role in designing the clock. The clock survives in its original setting, now in a building owned by Vanguard school. For years it has been the best-known Davidian icon in central Texas.

6. The legacy of the Davidians persists. On the original Davidian site are Waco's Mt. Carmel water treatment plant and streets named for Davidians (Hermanson, Charboneau, Wilson, Deeter, Berlinger). One of the original Davidian buildings stands on Vanguard school property, and Mt. Carmel Center, a redundant Presbyterian church, has housed a small active group of Davidians since 1991.

7. The Hermansons bought the original Mt. Carmel property for $10,000 and sold it to Houteff for $10; he married their daughter Florence when he was fifty-one and she was seventeen (Saether 1975).

8. Their argument is spelled out in Houteff 1992f.

References

Adair, Don. 1986. *The Fall of the Protestant Nations.* Salem, SC: Expose Publications.

———, comp. 1993. *A Complete Scriptural Index to the Original Writings of V. T. Houteff.* Salem, SC: General Association of Seventh-day Adventists.

Arthur, David T. 1993. "Joshua V. Himes and the Cause of Adventism." In *The Disappointed*, edited by Ronald L. Numbers and Jonathan M. Butler, pp. 36–58. Knoxville: University of Tennessee Press.

Barrineau, Mary. 1980. "Female Deity." *SHEkinah*, 1 (1): 1, 3.

"Blessing in the Midst of the Land: Location of Headquarters." N.d. Waco: Universal Publishing Association.

Butler, Jonathan. 1986. "From Millerism to Seventh-day Adventism: Boundlessness to Consolidation." *Church History* 3: 50–64.

Cattau, Daniel. 1993. "Davidians in Missouri Disavow Waco-Area Cult." *Dallas Morning News*, 14 March.

Committee on Defense Literature of the General Conference of Seventh-day Adventists. 1956. *Some Teachings of the Shepherd's Rod Examined*. N.p.

A Complete Scriptural Index to the Writings of V. T. Houteff. 1993. Salem, S.C.: General Association of Davidian Seventh-day Adventists.

Court of Civil Appeals for the Tenth Supreme Judicial District of Texas at Waco. 1966. No. 4533.

Cross, Whitney R. 1950. *The Burned-Over District: The Social and Intellectual History of Enthusiastic Religion in Western New York, 1800–1850*. Ithaca, NY: Cornell.

Green, Glen. 1989. "Oral Memoirs." Institute for Oral History, Baylor University, Waco, TX.

Green, Glen, Sidney Smith, and Bonnie Smith. 1989. "Oral Memoirs." Institute for Oral History, Baylor University, Waco, TX.

Houteff, Florence. 1961. *Christianity from Retreat to Triumph*. Waco, TX: Universal Publishing Association.

Houteff, Victor T. 1992a [1935]. *Final Warning*. Waco, TX: Universal Publishing Association.

_____. 1992b. *The Great Controversy over Shepherd's Rod*. Waco, TX: Universal Publishing Association.

_____. 1992c. *The Judgment and the Harvest*. Waco, TX: Universal Publishing Association.

_____. 1992d [1934]. *The Latest News for "Mother."* Waco, TX: Universal Publishing Association.

_____. 1992e. *The Leviticus of the Davidians*. Waco, TX: Universal Publishing Association.

_____. 1992f. *Military Stand of Davidian Seventh-day Adventists*. Waco, TX: Universal Publishing Association.

_____. 1992g [1943]. *Mount Carmel Training Center*. Waco, TX: Universal Publishing Association.

_____. 1992h [1933]. *Pre-Eleventh Hour Extra: Mystery of Mysteries Exposed*. Waco, TX: Universal Publishing Association.

_____. 1992i [1930]. *The Shepherd's Rod*. Waco, TX: Universal Publishing Association.

_____. 1992j. *The Symbolic Code Series*. Salem, S.C.: General Association of Davidian Seventh-day Adventists.

_____. 1992k. *Timely Greetings*. Vol. 1, nos. 17–20. Waco, TX: Universal Publishing Association.

_____. 1992l. *The Warning Paradox*. Waco, TX: Universal Publishing Association.

———. 1993 [1932]. *The Breaking of the Seven Seals*. Waco, TX: Universal Publishing Association.

Judd, Wayne R. 1993. "William Miller: Disappointed Prophet." In *The Disappointed*, edited by Ronald L. Numbers and Jonathan M. Butler, pp. 17–35. Knoxville: University of Tennessee Press.

Kanter, Rosabeth Moss. 1972. *Commitment and Community*. Cambridge: Harvard.

Land, Gary, ed. 1986. *Adventism in America*. Grand Rapids, MI: Eerdmans.

_____. 1990. "Seventh-day Adventism." In *Dictionary of Christianity in America*, edited by Daniel G. Reid. Downer's Grove, IL: Intervarsity Press.

Melton, J. Gordon. 1986. *Biographical Dictionary of American Cult and Sect Leaders*. New York: Garland.

Ministerial Association of the General Conference of Seventh-day Adventists, ed. 1988. *Seventh-day Adventists Believe*. Hagerstown, MD: Review and Herald Publishing Association.

Nelson, Alan. 1988. "Religious Group Returns 'Home.'" *Waco Tribune-Herald*, March 24, p. 1B.

Nelson, Alan, and Sandra Gines. 1988. "Crying in the Wilderness." *Waco Tribune-Herald*, 17 January, pp. 1A, 8A.

Numbers, Ronald L. 1992. *Prophetess of Health: Ellen G. White and the Origins of Seventh-day Adventist Health Reform*. Knoxville: University of Tennessee Press.

Odom, Robert L. 1962. "The Shepherd's Rod Organization Disbands." *Review and Herald*, 17 May, pp. 6–8.

Parma, Drew. 1987. "Officers Investigate Rodenville Shooting." *Waco Tribune Herald*, November 5.

Power, Mary Elizabeth. 1940. "A Study of the Seventh-day Adventist Community, Mount Carmel Center, Waco, Texas." M.A. Thesis, Baylor University.

Research Committee of the General Conference of Seventh-day Adventists. 1960. *Report of a Meeting between a Group of Shepherd's Rod Leaders and a Group of General Conference Ministers*. Washington, DC.

Roden, Ben. 1968. *The Stars and the Trumpet*. Waco, TX: Branch.

_____. 1969. *As Birds Flying*. Waco, TX: Branch.

_____. 1970a. *Crowned in the Wilderness*. Waco, TX: Branch.

_____. 1970b. *Move General Conference to Jerusalem*. Waco, TX: Branch.

_____. 1970c. *The Pentecost Fire*. Waco, TX: Branch.

_____. 1970d. *The Urgent Need of the Church*. Waco, TX: Branch.

_____. 1971. *The Scroll and the Stone.* Waco, TX: Branch.

_____. 1973. *Marvelous Prophecies of Jerusalem Fulfilled.* Waco, TX: Branch.

_____. 1974. *We're Fed Up: Catholics Crucifying Nixon.* Waco, TX: Universal Publishing Association.

_____. 1978. *The Daily, Part II: Eden Lost to Eden Restored.* Waco, TX: Universal Publishing Association.

Saether, George William. 1975. "Oral Memoirs." Institute for Oral History. Baylor University. Waco, TX.

Sandeen, Ernest. 1974. "Millennialism." In *The Rise of Adventism*, edited by Edwin S. Gaustad, pp. 104–18. New York: Harper and Row.

Schwarz, Richard W. 1979. *Lightbearers to the Remnant.* Mountainview, CA: PPPA.

Smith, LaMarriol. 1987. "Eight Arrested in Connection with Rodenville Shooting." *Waco Tribune-Herald,* November 4.

Tarling, Lowell. 1981. "The Edge of Seventh-day Adventism." Bermagui South, New South Wales, Australia. Typescript.

Turner, Tommy. 1962a. *Dallas Morning News,* April 15.

_____. 1962b. *Dallas Morning News,* April 25.

Weber, Max. 1963. *The Sociology of Religion.* Translated by Ephraim Fischoff. Boston: Beacon.

Weber, Timothy. 1987. *Living in the Shadow of the Second Coming: American Premillennialism, 1875–1982.* Chicago: University of Chicago Press.

Witherspoon, Tommy. 1988. "Rodenville Charges Dismissal to Be Sought." *Waco Tribune-Herald,* January 22, p. 8D.

3

DAVID G. BROMLEY AND
EDWARD D. SILVER

The Davidian

Tradition

*From Patronal Clan to
Prophetic Movement*

The Branch Davidian community outside
Waco, Texas, became the focus of intense
national attention as a protracted confrontation between the Branch Davidians
and federal law enforcement agents ultimately resulted in the tragic destruction of the Mt.
Carmel community.[1] Consistent with news construction priorities during the standoff between federal
agents and the Branch Davidians, electronic and print
media reports emphasized action, simplicity, drama,
the unusual, and personalization (Carey 1988). In the
aftermath of the second federal assault on Mt. Carmel,
the focal concern has been establishing grounds for
assigning legal culpability. As a result, throughout this
entire episode there has been remarkably little effort to

understand the religious tradition out of which the contemporary Branch Davidians evolved, the theological system through which the group symbolically constructed its identity and purpose, the organizational structure of the community, the motivations of ordinary Branch Davidians for affiliating with and participating in the community, and the context in which David Koresh and his followers understood his leadership and authority.

The Davidians' roots in the Millerite movement and Seventh-Day Adventist Church (SDA) are critical to understanding both Davidian history and organization. When the Millerites' premillennial prophecies failed in the "Great Disappointment" of 1844, one of the splinter groups ultimately evolved into the SDA. The SDA reaffirmed the expectation of an imminent second coming of Christ but also gradually lowered its expectation of imminent divine intervention in the world and developed major church, educational, and medical complexes that created an increasingly more denominational character. It was the tension between these transformative and preservative impulses upon which the Davidian tradition was founded. Davidian theology instructed that the SDA indeed was the authentic Christian tradition but had departed from its divinely appointed mission; its organization constituted an attempt to create a more committed spiritual life, and Davidian membership was largely drawn from the ranks of current and former SDA adherents. As time went on, however, the Davidian tradition itself came to incorporate this same tension. We describe the more settled and transformative organizational forms that the Davidians exhibited during each of the three major periods of Davidian history (the Houteff, Roden, and Koresh eras) typologically, as *patronal clans* and *prophetic movements* (Bromley and Shupe 1993; Eisenstadt 1968, 1984; Fiske 1991; Ouichi 1980; Wolff 1963). We argue that patronal clan organization was the predominant form during the first two eras, with temporary moments of prophetic movement organization. In the Koresh era the Branch Davidians moved toward prophetic movement organization, although elements of patronal clan organization remained visible even at the end of the Koresh era.

The typology is constructed along four dimensions: (1) source of legitimation, (2) form of leadership, (3) type of organizational structure, and (4) tension with the larger society. Neither type is expressed only in religious form, but in this instance both clan and movement organization were shaped by religious goals. Patronal clans legitimate themselves as the most recent successors to an authentic spiritual lineage. The strongest temporal link thus is constructed between present and past as legitimation derives from tradition.

Prophetic movements, by contrast, create legitimacy through stressing their role as creators of a new tradition. The temporal emphasis thus is on linking present and future. In both patronal clans and prophetic movements leader-follower relationships are highly asymmetrical. The power of leaders derives from controlling access to the key source of value created within the social formation.

In patronal-client relationships, control typically is exercised over access to various material resources or markets, while in prophet-disciple relationships there is control over direct access to a spiritual source or location. Leaders are accountable for insuring the material/spiritual well-being of followers, and followers reciprocate with acknowledgment of the leader's authority. The result is a highly ritualized system of mutual pledges of well-being and exchange (Bromley and Busching 1988; Cheal 1988).

Patronal leaders offer various goods and services and receive loyalty in return; prophetic leaders offer spiritual resources. Patronal leaders legitimate their positions by identifying themselves as the contemporary successors to a historic lineage; their charisma therefore derives from embodying the continuity of a tradition that often is delineated in sacred texts. Prophetic leaders find legitimacy as initiators of a future lineage that will be born in an imminent transformative moment; their charisma derives from embodying the new tradition that is being discovered through ongoing revelation.

Patronal clans are organized as networks of semiautonomous families, frequently with a single family unit as the center around which others cluster or the head beneath which others are arrayed. In religiously based clans, the connection between family units is spiritual rather than consanguinal as families are linked into a spiritual lineage through a common religious heritage. Individual identity derives from family identity, and families in turn trace their lineage through the patronal figure to a sacralized family tradition. By comparison, prophetic movements are organized as networks of individuals who are tightly integrated into a communal group, with the entire group often described in familial terms. Individual identity derives from one's relationship to the group and the prophetic leader. Finally, the degree of social distancing from and tension with the larger society is moderate for patronal clans and high for prophetic movements (Shils 1965).

The Houteff Era

The group that gave birth to the Branch Davidians was founded in 1929 by Victor Houteff.[2] Born in Bulgaria in 1885, Houteff emigrated to the United States in 1907. He had been brought up in the Eastern Orthodox tradition but converted to Seventh Day Adventism in 1919, threw himself enthusiastically into the SDA cause, and subsequently became an assistant superintendent in an SDA school in California. However, within a few years he had become disillusioned with the church. In 1929 Houteff openly challenged SDA theology in a manifesto, "The Shepherd's Rod." In his manifesto Houteff did not contest the SDA's identity as the authentic church of the remnant, but rather claimed that the church and its ministerial leadership had abandoned scriptural teachings and become overly materialistic and worldly. In fact, he declared that it was SDA worldliness that now prevented the second coming, and that therefore the SDA's paramount mission must be its own spiritual purification.

Houteff claimed prophetic status for himself, announcing that he had been selected as a messenger from God to reveal these new spiritual truths and to lead the purification process. Houteff based his prophetic claims on the assertion that the Bible is a cryptogram containing hidden messages. The present truths of any era therefore can be supplanted by new spiritual revelations, such as those that he now pronounced. Convinced that the end of time was imminent, Houteff assumed two related spiritual missions. The first was to unlock the secrets of the seven seals (contained in the book of Revelation), which held the key to understanding the chronology of events during the end time. The second was to gather the 144,000 faithful who would renounce sin and attract others to true faith. This remnant would be delivered at the second coming of Christ when sinners would be destroyed and the Kingdom of David would be erected in Palestine. Houteff clearly expected that the purification process could be accomplished rapidly, opening the way for Christ's return.

Houteff's call for revitalization of the "true" SDA tradition found a receptive audience to his message within SDA ranks. Church leaders initially responded to his growing popularity by attempting to isolate and sanction him, and the SDA issued a number of theological rejoinders designed to discredit his teachings. When these measures failed to deter Houteff, he was formally disfellowshipped in 1934 and left the church with a small coterie of followers. A year later Houteff established his own group, informally named the Shepherd's Rod after his manifesto. He purchased nearly two hundred acres of land (subsequently expanded to about four hundred acres) on the Brazos river outside Waco and established a farm community, called the Mt. Carmel Center. A small group of families responded to his call to join him at Mt. Carmel, and others offered financial support for the venture through pledges and tithing. There was a brief moment during which the group took on prophetic movement character as Houteff predicted that the community at Mt. Carmel was but a temporary encampment that they would occupy for only a year. The saved remnant were soon to be transported to Palestine to establish a theocratic Kingdom of David, herald the true gospel to the world, and then ascend to heaven with the return of Christ. During this time the group remained in a holding pattern, avoiding long-term commitments while they awaited divine intervention in human history.

There was some consternation among believers when the eagerly anticipated migration to Palestine did not transpire. However, the Shepherd's Rod moved quickly beyond this prophetic crisis and created a more settled pattern of life in which the group linked itself to the past as the true representative of the Adventist tradition rather than live in imminent expectation of world transformation. Over the next two decades the first settlers cleared the land, erected buildings, and constructed a community infrastructure (electrical, water, street, and sewage systems). The organizational structure replicated important SDA characteristics, as it included a rest home, dispensary, publication center, and ministerial school. Important elements of the lifestyle—vegetarianism, evangelism, and intense devotionalism—likewise had SDA roots. The centrality of spirituality to community life is evidenced in the fact that there were Bible study sessions every evening and formal worship services on Fridays and Saturdays. The group also effectively cloistered itself by raising its own food, creating a community-run school, limiting external sources of news, and even printing its own internal currency. While the Shepherd's Rod occasionally attracted some local press coverage, for the most part any tension with the surrounding community was a product of distancing by Shepherd's Rod adherents rather than community hostility.

Because the Shepherd's Rod accepted the spiritual legitimacy of SDA theology, evangelizers sought converts almost exclusively from the ranks of Seventh-Day Adventists, both through direct witnessing activity and through the publication of tracts proclaiming Houteff's theology to SDAs all over the world. At the same time, of course, Shepherd's Rod theology appealed only to current or former SDA adherents. As a result, even with intensive evangelizing the group achieved a membership of fewer than a hundred by the late 1930s, with as many as one third of those children. Shepherd's Rod's challenges to the SDA meant that affiliating with the group often came at the cost of being disfellowshipped by the SDA. Until the beginning of World War II, Houteff tried to remain connected to the Seventh-

Day Adventist Church despite his disfellowshipping. However, in 1942 he was compelled to create a separate formal organization, the Davidian Seventh-Day Adventists (DSDA) in order to gain conscientious objector status and ministerial credentials for his adherents. As the Davidians moved further away from the SDA, their mission became to preserve the pure Adventist tradition in the hope that the SDA would rejoin them on the path to salvation.

Elements of the Patronal Clan

Patronal clan organization emerged as DSDA developed. In the eyes of his followers Houteff embodied the true Adventist tradition to which he had given collective expression in founding the Mt. Carmel community. Houteff ruled Mt. Carmel in authoritarian style. Although the group's constitution stipulated governance by four administrative officers and an executive council, Houteff possessed veto power over all decisions. He used his power, for example, to institute a system of double tithing to support the community's religious mission and the various social services that were then dispensed to adherents. During the early 1950s he launched an ambitious campaign seeking to spread the Shepherd's Rod message everywhere in the world that the SDA had taken root, with the result that the Shepherd's Rod developed a small but committed international membership. His control over community finances and decision making, material needs of adherents, and evangelizing activities located power firmly in his hands. Personal power was transformed into family power when the fifty-two-year-old Houteff, long separated from his first wife, married seventeen-year-old Florence Hermanson, daughter of Oliver and Sophia Hermanson.

This family alliance exemplifies the clan-style organization of the DSDA. The most powerful families clustered around Houteff, providing critical resources to the group and at the same time forming a countervailing powerbase. The Charboneau-Hermanson family was the most prominent example during this era. Charter members of the Shepherd's Rod, the Charboneaus loaned Houteff money for the down payment on the Mt. Carmel property. Oliver Hermanson and his wife, Sophia (Charboneau) Hermanson, then financially underwrote the formation of the Mt. Carmel community by purchasing the original tract of land and selling it to the group for a nominal price. Sophia Hermanson was appointed to the DSDA Executive Council as treasurer, and following her marriage to Houteff, Florence (Hermanson) Houteff served as secretary of the council (Pitts, this volume). The independent power of families was also preserved by the fact that most adherents never took up residence at Mt. Carmel but rather simply offered financial support. This pattern of a more tightly organized core community with a loosely integrated network of supporting families, having varying degrees of commitment to the cause, prevailed up through the beginning years of the Koresh era. Houteff did attempt to exert control over families to the extent of issuing a decree that members must dissolve marriages with spouses who would not adopt the faith, a policy which strengthened group boundaries by uniting spiritual and biological/legal lineage.

Houteff's health began declining by the mid-1940s, and he died in 1955. His death was surprising and unsettling to the group, as believers had expected him to reign over the imminent establishment of the Kingdom of God that he had predicted. His death may have eroded the strength of the prophetic leadership base, but clearly continuity in leadership was preserved at this moment through the strength of the Houteff-Hermanson family coalition. Florence Houteff immediately announced that her husband had selected her to succeed him. Although there was a brief succession struggle among a number of factions, the Hermanson family arranged to have Florence (Hermanson) Houteff installed as Victor Houteff's successor (Bailey and Darden 1993, 37). There was a further consolidation of power when Oliver Hermanson subsequently assumed a position on the DSDA Executive Council.

Florence Houteff attempted to consolidate both prophetic and patronal authority. She continued an initiative begun by her husband to develop Mt. Carmel's land for residential use that shored up the group's tenuous financial position. She then used proceeds from the sale of Mt. Carmel property to purchase a new, much less expensive nine-hundred acre tract of land several miles outside the city. In addition to the financial benefit, the move also allowed the residents of the (New) Mt. Carmel community to maintain its distance from an expanding urban center. Under her leadership, the DSDAs proceeded to build a new church and administrative center, residences, and various farm buildings, but again they constructed temporary structures, since they expected to occupy the property only briefly.

As the new leader of the DSDAs, Florence Houteff also sought to solidify her prophetic leadership with a spiritual revelation, a step that was ultimately to lead to her downfall. In 1955 she announced that through insight gained from her reading of the Bible she had unlocked the biblical code contained in the book of Revelation, by which the timing of the second coming could be known. Based on a numerological analysis, she proclaimed 1959 "The Year of the Kingdom," prophesying that God's earthly kingdom would be established on April 22. The DSDAs expected war to break out in the Middle

East, a purification of the SDA, and the establishment of the Kingdom of God in Jerusalem shortly thereafter. All but God's chosen
faithful, including SDAs who were not following God's true path,
were to be destroyed at the time the new kingdom was established.
There was also considerable speculation that these events would be
accompanied by Victor Houteff's resurrection and ascension to leadership of the city of God. These prophecies created a transformative
moment in Davidian history as members expected imminent world
transformation. Group membership may have grown to as many as
1,500 during this period. Between 500 and 1,000 believers cut their
ties with the past by selling their homes and possessions and committed themselves to the future by moving to Waco in anticipation of
the impending divine intervention.

When April 22 passed uneventfully, the result was a collapse that
resembled the "Great Disappointment" of the Millerite era. Most of
the faithful ultimately drifted away or formed splinter groups; only
about fifty members remained at Mt. Carmel a year later. With the
DSDAs now in great disarray, there was even an abortive attempt to
rejoin the Davidian and SDA traditions through a reconciliation with
the Seventh-Day Adventist Church. Three years later the new
prophet stunned the faithful with the announcement that her
prophecies contained errors; thereupon she closed the new center,
moved away, and finally sold all but a hundred acres of the Mt.
Carmel property. This was one of the few times that the outside
world paid heed to the DSDAs, as predictions of the end of the world
generated substantial local media coverage. However, the media and
public reaction was more one of curiosity than hostility.

Roden Era: A New Patronal Clan

Florence Houteff's relinquishment of leadership left a power void
that immediately triggered another succession struggle among
Davidian families. One of the contenders for DSDA leadership at the
time of Victor Houteff's death had been Benjamin Roden, himself a
disfellowshipped SDA member. Roden and his wife and son had visited Mt. Carmel briefly in 1945 and again in 1953. Working as a team,
the Rodens returned to Mt. Carmel in 1955, claiming that Benjamin
Roden had received a spiritual revelation that he had been divinely
ordained to assume the mantle of DSDA leadership. Benjamin Roden
admonished the DSDAs to "Get off the dead Rod, and move onto a
living Branch" (Linedecker 1993, 57), thereby anticipating the Branch
Davidian tradition. Roden even predicted divine destruction of the
community if his claim to authority went unheeded. Upon the col-

lapse of Florence Houteff's leadership, he immediately launched a new bid for power. Now fifty-seven years old, Benjamin Roden soon won the loyalty of most of the remaining Davidians. The Roden family also contested Florence Houteff's attempt to disband the DSDA. Beginning in 1962 the Rodens commenced a protracted period of litigation, which was finally successful, to gain control of the remaining seventy-seven acres of Mt. Carmel. The group renamed itself the General Association of Davidian Seventh-Day Adventists (GADSA).

Roden enunciated his spiritual mission as creating moral rectitude under biblical law by instilling a Christ-like moral character in each member of the faithful. Once this mission had been fulfilled, he predicted, the second coming would be imminent. In 1970 Roden further enhanced his prophetic authority, announcing a spiritual vision which his followers came to view as the beginning of the rule of God on earth. Once his prophetic status had been solidified, Roden appears to have organized the group predominantly as a patronal clan. He legitimated his authority largely through locating himself in a lineage that could be traced back to the biblical King David. Further, he governed the group in the same authoritative patronal fashion as Houteff had. His followers accepted his claim to be the successor of King David quite literally. Indeed, Pitts (this volume) quotes one adherent who consciously located his own identity in this framework: "Ben Roden is the King. He is King David. . . . I'm subject to Ben Roden." The continued maneuvering for family position within the clan appeared once again when Roden sought to begin the establishment of the Davidic Kingdom in Israel. In 1958 the Rodens visited Israel, established a commune, occupied the site briefly, and urged followers to consider relocating there. The new settlement was very much Roden-controlled as Roden delegated responsibility for overseeing its maintenance and development to his wife and his son, George. Other families were not appreciative of the Roden family monopoly of this initiative; Roden made reference to the fact that "there are murmurings in our ranks that say this movement to Israel by the Adventists is just an affair fostered and controlled by one family" (Bailey and Darden 1993, 63).

Toward the end of Benjamin Roden's life maneuvering for control of GADSA began despite his efforts to institutionalize the succession process and then use that procedure to insure continuity in Roden rule. He incorporated into the group's bylaws a provision that constituted an attempt to link patronal and prophetic authority: "The chairman of the executive council, at the command of Heaven by the Lord Himself, transfers the office of the president to the One . . . that God so names" (Bailey and Darden 1993, 60-61). Thus, the chairman of the Executive Council, Roden himself in this case, would name the group's successor, and he appears to have been attempting to designate his successor when he installed his son, George, as GADSA's vice president. However, the situation became more complex in 1977 when Lois Roden announced her own spiritual vision that the Holy Spirit was female, a view that her husband appears to have tolerated with considerable reservation. She continued to elaborate on this vision, asserting that God is both male and female and that at the second coming the messiah would assume female form. Later she founded a magazine, *SHEkinah*, to disseminate her theological views. Soon after her vision she began intensive scriptural study and subsequently was conferred GADSA ministerial credentials.

What was to become the most bitter succession struggle in Davidian history began on October 22, 1978, when Benjamin Roden died. GADSA members initially attempted to use Roden's death to initiate a transformative moment, announcing that the seventh seal had been opened on the day of his passing. But the date proved to have greater political than spiritual significance. Lois Roden immediately asserted her prophetic and family authority as the basis for laying claim to the mantle of GADSA leadership. However, as a result of political infighting accompanying the transition and her controversial doctrines, as many as half of the Mt. Carmel adherents defected. Further, George Roden was incensed at what he regarded as his mother's usurping of his birthright: "I never took the leadership of the work of the Lord until the death of my Father and I did not do that until I understood what my Father told me one month before he died, that I was the Man Whose Name is the *Branch* and that it was my responsibility to rebuild the temple in Jerusalem just like Solomon was to do so at the death of his father. . . . I was the heir to my father's crown of the House of David" (Bailey and Darden 1993, 68-69).

George Roden next attempted to regain his rightful position, first with an appeal to the membership and then through the courts. When these strategies did not prove successful, he moved out of Mt. Carmel but continued to challenge his mother's leadership. The feud between mother and son became so bitter that Lois Roden ultimately obtained a court order barring George from the Mt. Carmel property. It was into this contentious political situation that David Koresh arrived.

The Koresh Era: Emergence of a Prophetic Movement

In 1979 when he was twenty years old, David Koresh began attending an SDA church in Tyler, Texas, and it was through a friend in that congregation that he first learned of the Branch Davidian community. In 1981 he accepted a job as a handyman at Mt. Carmel, contributing valuable carpentry and mechanical skills to the community. For a time Koresh participated in both groups, but he was disfellowshipped from the SDA congregation in 1983 after a succession of conflicts that precipitated when he announced that God intended him to marry the pastor's daughter, incessantly witnessed to other church members, and on one occasion took over the pulpit to propound his own theological views. Four years after his SDA disfellowshipping Koresh had ascended to undisputed leadership of the Branch Davidian community.

Koresh began building his power base in the Branch Davidian community at a time when Lois Roden's spiritual authority had been seriously challenged and her political power had been eroded by defections. Koresh's rise to leadership was very much a product of patronal clan politics. He almost immediately linked himself to the Rodens and the Joneses, two of the most important Branch Davidian families. Koresh quickly won the favor of Lois Roden, then sixty-seven years old, and rumors soon began circulating that the two were lovers, rumors which Koresh used to his advantage at the time but later disavowed.[3] The alliance served the interests of both parties, since Koresh's status was significantly elevated and Lois Roden gained an ally in her struggle with her son. In 1983 Lois Roden formally allied herself with Koresh by announcing that Koresh was to be her successor and inviting Branch Davidian adherents to come to Mt. Carmel to listen to his teachings and prophecies. A year later Koresh created another important family alliance by marrying Rachel Jones, the daughter of Perry and Mary Bell Jones. Perry Jones was one of the most senior and respected members of the Davidian community, having been one of the earliest and most devoted followers of Benjamin Roden as well as serving as a journalist for *SHEkinah*. The Joneses gave their blessing to the union, and Perry Jones presided at the wedding of his daughter, who at the time was fourteen years old.

Koresh suffered a major, if temporary, setback when in 1985 George Roden, who was now forty-seven years old, finally was able to organize an election for the presidency of the Branch Davidians in which he emerged victorious. Roden quickly sought to consolidate his power by ousting Koresh and his followers at gunpoint from Mt. Carmel, reasserting his family's dominance by renaming the community Rodenville, and passing a new governing code for the community. After being displaced from Mt. Carmel, Koresh and his few dozen followers eked out a primitive existence in nearby Palestine by living in crude shelters that they constructed. Koresh suffered a further setback in 1986 when his ally Lois Roden died. George Roden's victory proved short-lived, however, as the viability of his leadership was eroding rapidly. The population of Mt. Carmel dwindled to probably no more than two or three dozen, and in the struggle for control over the Branch Davidians Koresh now enjoyed the loyalty of the majority of the community. Further, George Roden was unable to sustain the economic viability of the Mt. Carmel community, since the Davidians owed over $65,000 in back school district and county property taxes. Finally, prior to her death Lois Roden had sought enforcement of the earlier 1979 injunction against George, an initiative later renewed by Koresh's faction. The practical effect of the injunction would be that the courts would intervene in the power struggle on Koresh's side by finding George Roden in contempt of court and displace him once again from Mt. Carmel.

The succession of events that led to Roden's downfall began with his seeking to counter judicial actions against him by filing a series of legal motions and suits filled with such vituperation and profanity that the justices threatened contempt citations against him. Then, in a desperate effort to assert spiritual supremacy, Roden challenged Koresh to a spiritual contest to raise from the dead an eighty-five-year-old Davidian, Anna Hughes, who had been buried twenty years earlier at Mt. Carmel. Koresh declined the challenge and instead seized the opportunity to seek criminal prosecution of Roden for disturbing the grave site. On November 3, 1987, Koresh and a group of armed followers invaded the Mt. Carmel center seeking a photograph of Hughes's remains that would serve as evidence to prosecute Roden. A gun battle ensued between Roden and the Koresh group in which Roden was slightly wounded. In the subsequent legal proceedings attempted murder charges against Koresh and his followers were dismissed. Roden, however, was incarcerated for violating earlier restraining orders and for continuing to file profanity-filled legal suits and motions. The following day Koresh and his followers reoccupied Mt. Carmel. Koresh had now physically vanquished his rival and laid undisputed claim to Branch Davidian clan leadership.

Once he was clearly in control of Mt. Carmel, Koresh began rebuilding the community and restoring its financial base; in the process he gained complete control over all important community functions. During the Roden era the property at Mt. Carmel had fallen into disrepair, and Koresh now organized a major cleanup campaign and a construction project that considerably improved the quality of life and expanded living quarters. Rebuilding the community required that members live relatively disciplined lives. On an average day members rose around 6:00 A.M. and then congregated in the dining room for breakfast. During the day men and women devoted their energy to community-building, occupational pursuits, and child-rearing activities necessary to sustain the community. As they had been in the past, members of the Mt. Carmel community attempted to be as self-sufficient as possible by producing a considerable portion of their own food and some of their own clothing. In addition, during some periods children were home-schooled within the community, and the group apparently maintained no bank accounts, as members frequently paid even for large purchases in cash. Despite the major improvements in the community infrastructure, however, life at Mt. Carmel remained arduous in a number of respects. Even the new buildings lacked central heating, air conditioning, and most indoor plumbing; as a result, members were forced to pump water from a well on the grounds and remove waste from the buildings on a daily basis.

In the early stages of Koresh's leadership, economic arrangements at Mt. Carmel reflected patronal organization. Families were important units in maintaining the community's economic base. Indeed, Koresh was able to gain fiscal solvency upon assuming Branch Davidian leadership only after convincing a Branch Davidian family in Hawaii to donate the $68,000 needed to pay back taxes on the property. There were numerous cases of this kind. Some relatively well-to-do members gave substantial sums of money, and sometimes property, to the group. In one prominent example, the Bunds family, which had belonged to the Davidians since the Roden era, gave Koresh $10,000 to purchase a van and spent $100,000 to purchase a home in Pomona, California, which served as a residence for Branch Davidian members (England and McCormick 1993, 8A). In another instance, an elderly Branch Davidian couple donated between $250,000 and $500,000 to the group (McCormick 1993, 5A).

Koresh attempted to expand and diversify the economic resource base by organizing and coordinating several small businesses. The community operated an automobile repair and renovation enterprise, Mag Bag, and a gun and gun-accessory business. Based primarily on Koresh's mechanical skills, the group established an automobile restoration business that rebuilt high-performance cars for sale in California (Pinkerton 1993, A-23). Through the weapons business, which was primarily operated by Paul Fatta, Davidians purchased gun and hunting-related products through the mail and sold them at gun shows. These products included military-style food pouches, guns, ammunition, gun accessories, camouflage jackets and pants, backpacks, knives, and hand-grenade casings mounted on plaques for display (Mahlburg 1993, A-17). As a result of such initiatives, Koresh was thus able to concentrate both political and economic power in his own hands, even though for a time families were an important source of economic resources and political support.

Charisma and Innovation

Several interrelated developments moved the Branch Davidians away from patronal clan toward prophetic movement organization. First, Koresh began actively building a prophetic leadership base through evangelization of new converts and elevation of his charisma claims. Second, Koresh guided the Branch Davidian community toward a more transformative orientation, creating a compelling sense of living in the end time. Third, life at Mt. Carmel became distinctly more communal as family autonomy declined and the individual with personal loyalty to Koresh became the basic building-block unit of the community. Finally, tension with the larger society mounted, primarily as a result Koresh's New Light doctrine and its implementation in the House of David.

One important way in which Koresh built his prophetic leadership base was through converting a new cohort of adherents who were attracted by his spiritual revelations. The ranks of the Branch Davidians had been seriously depleted by the ongoing conflicts within the group since 1960. Upon assuming group leadership, Koresh therefore launched several domestic (in Texas, California, and Hawaii) and international (to Canada, England, and Australia) recruitment campaigns to rebuild the membership base. He and members of his inner circle carried out these campaigns, which almost exclusively targeted current or former Seventh-Day Adventists. In 1987 a Koresh-led evangelizing team proselytized the membership of the SDA Diamond Head Church in Hawaii, with the result that fourteen members returned to Texas with Koresh; two recruiting trips to England and Australia in 1988 yielded about three dozen new adherents (Breault and King 1993, 122). These gains were significant, given the small size of the group when Koresh assumed leadership. Over a several-year period the various recruitment campaigns expanded the number of Branch Davidians living at or near Mt. Carmel to around a hundred adherents.[4]

Converts point to Koresh's prophetic qualities, rooted in biblical interpretation, more than any other single factor in explaining their own attraction to the Branch Davidians. Branch Davidian survivor Rita Riddle recalls meeting Koresh in North Carolina and then engaging in an all-night Bible study session that convinced her of his unique spiritual insight:

I just saw that he had the ability to do what nobody else had ever done. I learned more with him in one night than I had learned in a lifetime of going to church. And that's when I became interested because then I saw that whether we like it or whether we don't like it, God is going to do what He said, as far as what's written in the Bible. From there I just began digging. I started going out and asking people questions and they couldn't answer me, so I kept going back to David, getting more stuff. (Wright 1993b, 2)

Likewise, Paul Fatta, who ran the Davidians weapons business, traces his commitment to Koresh to his prophetic prowess: "I believe David is the Messiah. . . . He has shown me over and over that he knows the book, and he presented Scriptures showing how the last day's events would happen" (Hinds 1993b, A-6). Oliver Gyarfas, a former Australian SDA member whose young daughter became one of Koresh's spiritual wives, evidences the emotional bond Koresh was able to create with his disciples: "David Koresh has a beautiful message, like a silver thread running through the scripture. . . . I believe he is an inspired modern-day prophet. . . . He has a message for us, his brethren, but also for the whole world. . . . I love David Koresh above all" (Sullivan 1993, A-4).

These conversions demonstrated Koresh's charisma, built a nucleus of new converts who spiritually energized the group and were personally devoted to Koresh, recommitted long-standing members who were convinced either by Koresh's message or its impact on others, and bolstered Koresh's claim to be building the ranks of the faithful remnant who would usher in the new age.

The second means through which Koresh built his prophetic leadership base was elevation of his charismatic claims over followers. Upon assuming group leadership, David Koresh sought to establish his prophetic authority in much the same fashion as his predecessors. By linking his personal biography to a historical spiritual lineage, he laid claim to leadership of the Adventist tradition. He went further in this regard than his predecessors, however, in symbolizing his spiritual status by legally changing his name from Vernon Howell to David Koresh in 1990. "Koresh" is the Hebrew for "Cyrus," the Persian king who defeated the Babylonians five hundred years before the birth of Jesus. In biblical language Koresh is *a* (as opposed to *the*) messiah, one appointed to carry out a special mission for God. His first name, David, asserts a lineage directly to the biblical King David, from whom the new messiah will be descended. By taking this name, David Koresh was thereby professing himself to be the spiritual descendent of King David, a messianic figure carrying out a divinely commissioned errand.

In his preaching to followers, Koresh constructed a mission that placed him and his followers in control of humankind's destiny. He taught that his messianic role was crucial to human salvation because Christ had died only for those who lived prior to his crucifixion. This formulation made his mission necessary to permit the salvation of all subsequent generations. Further, in contrast to Christ, who was sinless and therefore embodied an impossible standard for inherently sinful humans to achieve, Koresh was a "sinful messiah." By personally experiencing sin like all other humans, Koresh asserted, he could judge sinners more fairly. However, in contrast to Benjamin Roden, who preached the importance of moral rectitude for achieving salvation, Koresh taught that human sinfulness does not prevent humans from attaining salvation. Koresh offered an alternative route to salvation, by following him as he carried out the opening of the seven seals (Tabor 1993, 27). Koresh believed that it was his special mission to open the seven seals, cryptically described in the New Testament book of Revelation, which is the prelude to the end of the world (which Branch Davidians referred to as the downfall of Babylon).[5] His disciples regarded themselves as the "wavesheaf," God's most faithful servants who would ascend to heaven even prior to the 144,000 exemplary souls selected to reign with the messiah during the millennium (Linedecker 1993, 88).

This mission now assumed paramount importance because world transformation was imminent. Koresh believed that the world had already entered the period of tribulation (preceding the second coming of Jesus Christ and the period of the millennium) that was a prelude to the final cleansing of the earth. Following this process, the earth would be transformed into an eternal, divinely ruled abode for humankind. In his early prophecy, Koresh instructed that the Branch Davidians would migrate to Israel, where they would begin converting the Jews; this would trigger international tumult and a war that would eventuate in an invasion by the American army. These events would signal the beginning of Armageddon, and Koresh would be the cleansing angel who would prepare the earth to receive the New Jerusalem.

Koresh's proclaiming himself to be the bearer of the true Adventist tradition, adopting a messianic role essential to human salvation, and ordaining the end time were not particularly novel in Davidian history. It was in his New Light doctrine that Koresh departed most dramatically from the Davidian tradition and elevated his prophetic status. Drawing on the book of Revelation, Koresh asserted that in his role as a messiah he became the perfect mate of all the female adherents. Central to his messianic mission, Koresh taught, was the creation of a new lineage of God's children from his own seed. The children created through these unions would erect the House of David and ultimately rule the world. As one female Davidian, Alisa Shaw, explained it:

> A central part of the message (of Revelation) is the marriage of the Lamb. That's the way to salvation. There are a few (women) who are worthy to be sown with the seed of God and produce children. It's considered an honor to have a baby for Christ. Not every woman is worthy of Koresh's loins. . . . A woman who becomes "sown with the light" might be worthy, but that doesn't mean she will be selected to bear the leader's seed. He's just given the inspiration and that's how he knows who's worthy. (Fair 1993, 22A)

The implication of the New Light doctrine was that all of the female Branch Davidians potentially became spiritual wives to Koresh. Male adherents would also be united with their perfect mates, but in heaven. In fact, the future mates of male members were already part of them physically, just as Eve was physically a part of Adam before her creation. It was therefore the duty of male adherents to await the bestowal of their perfect mates in heaven (England and McCormick 1993, 8A). Koresh thus placed himself at the center of the spiritual project to restore humanity to divine purpose.

The implementation of this claim, through the establishment of what Koresh named the House of David, produced the single most significant restructuring of the Davidian community during the Koresh era. About three years after marrying Rachel Jones in 1984, Koresh began taking "spiritual wives" from among the young, unmarried women in the group. It appears that in most cases Koresh received the blessing of the parents either before or after the relationship commenced.[6] For example, one of his earliest relationships began with teenager Robyn Bunds in 1987. The Bunds had been members of the Davidians since the 1960s, and Robyn's brother, David, had been one of Koresh's first converts. Robyn's mother, Jeannine, recalls that when her daughter informed her that she had begun a sexual relationship with Koresh, "my husband and I were really upset," but that Koresh "just kept talking to us and he convinced us that this was the way it was supposed to be." It was Koresh's assertion that the relationship was spiritually based that convinced the Bunds: "This is the House of David; she's going to have a baby for God. . . . They're God's children. They're going to be in the kingdom" (Oprah 1993, 5-6). The following year while on a trip to Australia Koresh received permission from Australian Branch Davidians, Bruce and Lisa Gent, to begin a sexual relationship with their nineteen-year-old daughter, Nicole. Bruce Gent acknowledges that "at that point in time, yes I was very influenced. . . . Nicole had spent four days with him being convinced of the message. It wasn't for me to say yes or no . . . she was going to have children for the Lord" (England and McCormick, 1993, 5A).[7]

Koresh later expanded these relationships to include the wives of male Branch Davidian adherents. In the Bunds and Gent families Koresh requested permission to initiate sexual relations with the wives, Jeannine Bunds and Lisa Gent, for the purpose of creating the new spiritual lineage, and in both cases the husbands and wives assented after considerable deliberation. Linedecker reports that Jeannine Bunds and her husband, who had been married for twenty-five years at the time, "were troubled by the command and talked earnestly about the implications, but ultimately they concluded that they had to obey" (1993, 128; Oprah 1993, 8). Jeannine Bunds clearly felt at the time that being selected was an honor: "I wanted to be in the House of David. . . . He made it sound so wonderful. I did. I did believe" (England and McCormick 1993, 9A). Although he was troubled, Bruce Gent asserts that he gave his wife to Koresh because of "what they were going to accomplish in the kingdom" (England and McCormick 1993, 9A).[8]

Koresh's creation of the House of David represented an extreme charisma claim—the way to salvation was the creation of a new spiritual lineage which could be initiated only by Koresh acting in his messianic role.[9] Establishing the House of David thus was an important move in the direction of prophetic movement organization. These were not family alliances in the patronal clan tradition. Rather than bolster a network of families, family organization and autonomy were sacrificed in order to support Koresh's prophetic role. For example, women putatively were selected on spiritual grounds; the spiritual relationships took precedence over the legal and prior kinship ties; legally sanctioned marriages were not performed; children from these spiritual relationships were not regarded as members of the wives' familial units; and the spiritual unions had meaning only in a world that had yet to be reborn. There were other ways in which Koresh asserted his prophetic status as well. For example, he announced new revelations, sometimes in contradiction to earlier pronouncements; this meant that a close, personal connection to him was the only means by which followers could determine that they were engaging in spiritually correct behavior. In addition, Koresh decreed a series of dietary restrictions for followers that he publicly violated, thereby symbolically placing himself above the law.

Koresh also progressively guided the Branch Davidians toward a more transformative orientation, linking the group's activities more closely to an imminent future than to past tradition. The Koresh era resembled previous eras in the intense devotionalism within the community. Following dinner most evenings there were Bible study periods that sometimes lasted long into the night, and morning and afternoon study sessions might be held as well. Indeed, portraits of daily life by Branch Davidians who lived at Mt. Carmel during the Koresh era suggest that devotional activity was at the center of community life. Apostate Branch Davidian Marc Breault recalls that "we lived, ate, and breathed the Bible. . . . It was the whole center of our being. We would have these long studies" (England and McCormick 1993, 9A). Davidian survivor Catherine Matteson describes a community in which adherents had an almost insatiable craving for Bible study.

> He [Koresh] gave prolonged Bible studies, yes. But I'll tell you something, lots of times, maybe he would say, I am tired of giving Bible studies to you guys. I wish you would learn Bible studies. So everybody would hang around. And he'd say, "What is it that you want? More Bible study?" And everybody would run and get their Bibles and come down. We might sit there for 15, 19 hours, 10 hours, 6 hours, it would depend. It was never a bore. (Wright 1993a, 1)

What distinguished the Koresh era was that in these Bible study sessions Koresh was engaged in the process of revealing the secrets of the seven seals, which created in the community a real sense of living in the end times. The group conceived of itself as literally scripting and living in the end time, a process that intensified dramatically once the confrontation with federal authorities commenced. As Koresh began to prepare for an apocalypse that he increasingly thought might occur in America rather than Israel, the group began adopting survivalist tactics such as stockpiling large amounts of dried food and MREs (meals ready to eat) used by the military, weapons and ammunition, and a large storage tank of propane gas. Koresh purportedly informed his followers that the Great Tribulation might begin in the United States with an attack on the Branch Davidians (Linedecker 1993, 151). In fact, Koresh renamed the Mt. Carmel community "Ranch Apocalypse" in 1992.[10]

During the Koresh era the Branch Davidians adopted a much more communal form of organization in which individuals became the basic unit of group membership. One of the most important factors in this restructuring was Koresh's recruitment of young adults. Most often they were members of Branch Davidian families recruited from SDA ranks, but their conversions were independent of family affiliation. In this sense the pre-existing family network became the vehicle for individual conversions that in turn undermined the power of families in the community. In part these conversions were attributable to Koresh's youthful, countercultural demeanor and his musical and automotive interests. For example, one media account of Koresh's recruitment trip to Hawaii notes that several dozen young followers were "attracted to his earring, and long, white, flowing robes" (Cockerham 1993, 5). Branch Davidian survivor Wally Kennett, who described himself as very suspicious of "the system," and as having concluded that "modern-day Christianity was completely lost and completely off track," recollects being duly impressed with David Koresh. He recalls that Koresh "gave me some [Bible] studies, and I was very, very fascinated." After losing touch with the Branch Davidians for an extended period, Kennett resumed his Bible study with them and regained his sense of excitement. He recalls, "I was like 'man, this is serious business here.' So I pretty much dropped everything" to participate in the group (Wright 1993c). In another case, during one of his Australian trips Koresh converted Bruce and Lisa Gent and also their son and daughter, Peter and Nicole. Lisa Gent recalls that "Peter pretty well got impressed right away. . . . The change in Peter seemed almost miraculous. He quit smoking, drinking and doing drugs" (Tate 1993, 1A, 4A).

In addition, various aspects of community organization became more communal. Koresh emphasized to new converts the importance of living at Mt. Carmel. He even arranged marriages between foreign and domestic members to make community residence possible. Koresh moved the residents at Mt. Carmel beyond tithing and self-sufficiency toward an economic system in which members who worked outside the community regularly contributed their wages and older members turned over their food stamps and Social Security checks. Following the establishment of the House of David, Koresh began separating residential quarters for male and female adherents. Finally, he created a coterie of "Mighty Men" (based on the biblical story of guards of King Solomon's bed), trusted lieutenants to whom Koresh delegated various responsibilities within the community (Coser 1964). Membership in both groups was a function of personal closeness and loyalty to Koresh and took precedence over family membership.[11] In the case of one adherent, Steve Schneider, Koresh apparently made public declarations of love to Schneider's wife as a kind of loyalty test. Former Davidian Bruce Gent reports that "when Steve was in earshot, Vernon [Koresh] would say, 'And I love you, too, Judy'" (England 1993b, 10A). Koresh's own family also was less central in community life than in prior eras. Although his mother and other members of his family resided at Mt. Carmel for a time, neither they nor his wife, Rachel, provided central group leadership.

Finally, the level of tension with the larger society dramatically escalated as the Branch Davidians moved toward prophetic movement organization. Historically the Davidians had been in conflict with the SDA as a result of recruitment campaigns directed at SDA membership, a tension that continued during the Koresh era. The Branch Davidians sometimes were willing to be aggressive in promoting their message, even disrupting church services on occasion to gain a hearing. For example, the Branch Davidians proselytized at nearby Southwestern Adventist College and local churches, where on some occasions "Branch Davidians would come to church, begin passing out literature, then begin shouting, quarreling, and trying to take over the services" (Linedecker 1993, 111). Similarly, in 1986 when Koresh was recruiting at a San Diego Seventh-Day Adventist church, he stood up during the service and began professing his own interpretation of the scriptures until he was physically removed from the building by parishioners (Breault and King 1993, 66–67). Although the numbers involved were not large, the Branch Davidians demonstrated the capacity to recruit from the ranks of active SDAs despite SDA warnings and sanctions. For example, in 1987, a Koresh-led evangelizing team proselytized the membership of the SDA Diamond Head Church in Hawaii. Church leaders finally forced parishioners to choose between the church and Koresh's movement, with the result that fourteen members returned to Texas with Koresh and were promptly disfellowshipped by the church. The 1988 campaign in England was successful in winning several converts from SDA-affiliated Newbold College and from the congregations of a number of local SDA churches. So although SDA–Branch Davidian friction remained high, it did not broaden into conflict with other societal institutions. The tension with larger society might have grown had the Branch Davidians' recruitment efforts proved more successful. During the Koresh era the Branch Davidians did attempt to broaden their recruitment campaigns to attract non-SDAs. Koresh visited Israel in 1985 and in 1990 but was unable to convert Israelis, and efforts at general street proselytization also proved unsuccessful.

The increase in tension with larger society can be traced to the development of prophetic movement organization. For example, recruitment of individuals rather than families precipitated intrafamily conflicts when some members defected while others remained loyal. Disaffected family members constituted a pool of potential allies for anticult groups and federal agencies. Emerging communal organization, based on arranged marriages of domestic and foreign adherents, created grounds for investigation of the immigration status of Mt. Carmel residents. Again, however, it was the New Light doctrine and House of David that were most damaging.

Koresh's sexual innovations created a highly volatile issue both inside and outside the group, resulted in a series of defections, and created the basis for legal action against the group. To the extent that David Koresh defined his messianic mission in terms of initiating a new spiritual lineage, the children embodied the group's spiritual mission, legitimated his prophetic status, and constituted the community's future. Disputes over the community's rights with respect to these children were almost certain to produce conflict escalation. At the same time, the practice created conflict within the group.[12] Robyn Bunds, one of Koresh's earliest spiritual wives, defected as a result of sexual jealousies ignited when he began selecting other women for the House of David, including her mother.[13] Jeannine Bunds, in turn, defected when she did not conceive the child Koresh had promised, which would have legitimated their sexual relationship. Marc Breault started contemplating defection in 1989 when he began to fear that Koresh was going to claim as a spiritual wife his young Australian bride, Elizabeth Baranyai, who had decided that she could not comply. Breault quotes from a letter Baranyai wrote him (Breault and King 1993, 200–201) in which she concludes: "I don't believe I will be able to go through what is being asked. If I thought that it was possible, then I would have become part of the House of David rather than marry you in the first place. And believe me, I did think long and hard about it. . . . I don't know what to say or do any more. Marc I'm really scared. I don't want to disobey the Lord but I can't do what is being asked. I feel very lost at the moment." Both apparently finally concluded that their resistance would make it impossible for them to remain in the group on acceptable terms.[14]

The House of David also created incidents that left the group vulnerable to legal intervention. Koresh had inducted young women who were legally minors into the House of David. He avoided recording paternity on some birth registration forms, apparently to deflect official inquiries about the group's sexual practices. In one incident, Koresh responded to Robyn Bunds's defection by hiding their son, Wisdom, from her. After Robyn complained to the police, Koresh returned the child to Robyn's custody. Finally, in 1991, now apostate Mark Breault approached David Jewell, whose former wife, Sherri, and their nine-year-old daughter, Kiri, lived at Mt. Carmel, with the allegation that Kiri had been chosen as a member of the House of David. David Jewell immediately filed for custody of the child. In a prehearing settlement, the court stipulated that Kiri would live with David Jewell and his second wife; Sherri Jewell would retain visitation rights provided that Kiri was kept away from Koresh. These individuals continued to seek allies in the media, anticult organizations, and law enforcement agencies, ultimately making contact with the Bureau of Alcohol, Tobacco, and Firearms. There is little doubt that Koresh felt increasingly vulnerable and embattled and that his opponents recognized that they had found a means of gaining leverage against him. Given the sensitivity of the Branch Davidians to child custody issues and the larger society to child abuse issues, the mixture was a volatile one indeed.

Conclusions

Through most of their history the Davidian groups at Mt. Carmel were closely linked to their SDA heritage through a range of theological beliefs, organizational practices, and a preponderance of former SDA members even though they were rejected and ostracized by the SDA. The Adventist tradition always has been plagued by a contradiction between its transformative impulse and a tendency to adopt a more settled, preservative lifestyle. The various Davidian groups played on this contradiction by offering SDA members a promise of imminent transformation and a higher level of spiritual commitment. However, the Davidians themselves were a rather settled group at most points in time. We have argued that for the most part the various groups representing the Davidian tradition can be described in terms of patronal clan organization. There were brief transformative moments during the Houteff and Roden eras, but these seem to have represented an attempt to keep alive salvationist hopes and legitimate the sacrifices required for life at Mt. Carmel. In the Koresh era there was a pronounced shift toward prophetic movement organization, which both energized the Branch Davidians and increased the level of tension with larger society.

During the first two eras Davidians legitimated themselves primarily as preservers and restorers of the authentic Adventist tradition, and indeed the Davidians professed the fundamental truth of SDA theology. Their spiritual errand was to recall to its original and true purpose a tradition that had been corrupted, and to preserve that tradition until the occasion of the second coming. During the Houteff era the Davidians in fact attempted to maintain SDA membership and regularly attended SDA churches, and throughout Davidian history evangelizing has been directed almost exclusively at current and former SDA members. Thus the Davidians expended a substantial amount of their symbolic and organizational effort in the direction of creating and maintaining continuity between present and past. There were transformative moments, most notably the 1959 millennial hope that became another "Great Disappointment," but such moments only interrupted much longer settled periods for the Davidians. Koresh created much more of a transformative orientation. In his preaching he emphasized the imminence of world transformation, and Bible study sessions were devoted to scripting the opening of the seven seals, as a prelude to the apocalypse. This process of continuous theological revelation spiritually energized the Branch Davidians and created in the group a sense of potent spiritual agency. Koresh also began moving the attack on the Branch Davidians closer in time and space and began the implementation of survivalism.

Leaders from the Houteff and Roden families provided primarily patronal leadership even though the effectiveness and durability of their leadership varied considerably. The Houteffs and Rodens legitimated themselves primarily by linking their own biographies to a biblically chronicled lineage to which they were the contemporary successors. There were, of course, revelatory moments during which present and future were more closely connected. These prophetic moments were not inconsequential to the community, as they energized Davidian spiritual life and reaffirmed prophetic authority so as to secure the community more firmly during the extended periods when it rested principally on patronal leadership. For the most part during the Houteff and Roden eras, leaders assumed highly centralized control, providing the residents at Mt. Carmel with leadership, an orderly and devotional community life, and a variety of services in return for tithing and loyalty.

While Koresh began by staking claim to leadership of the true Adventist tradition, he moved steadily toward a more prophetic orientation. By rebuilding the Mt. Carmel community through conversion of individuals who regarded him as their personal spiritual leader, Koresh created a nucleus of enthusiastic recent converts, demonstrated his charisma, and began the building of the faithful remnant. Through his New Light doctrine, which was implemented in the House of David, Koresh actually began moving the Branch Davidians into the divinely ordained future by creating the first generation of residents in this new order. To the extent that Branch Davidians accepted the New Light doctrine, they granted Koresh the highest spiritual status as the only person who could set in motion the forces that would ultimately lead to salvation for all humankind.

For most of Davidian history the group was organized as a religious clan, a network of spiritually interrelated families headed by the family of a patronal leader. Most families affiliated with the Davidians did not reside at Mt. Carmel; rather, Mt. Carmel served as the nucleus for this internationally dispersed network. Even at Mt. Carmel, independent families were the basic building blocks of the community. Families were recruited as units, financed the community, positioned themselves around the patronal family, and mediated between patronal leaders and individual adherents. The clan was founded on spiritual rather than biological consanguinity, and beginning in the Houteff era there was considerable pressure for religious homogamy. The spiritual lineage of each family was traced most immediately to the Davidian leader of the period who claimed to be heir to the biblically chronicled lineage. In this way the entire community conceived of itself as an embodiment of a purified tradition which it preserved until the time of the second advent.

During the Koresh era there was a decisive shift toward individuals becoming the basic unit of Branch Davidian organization. Family units initially created stability for the group by donating or lending money and property, and Koresh did continue to convert entire families. However, in the course of his proselytizing campaigns Koresh began converting teenage and young adult members of families who were attracted to him independently of their family membership. He urged new converts to take up residence at Mt. Carmel, and residents increasingly invested all their time, energy, and financial resources in the community. The New Light doctrine also undermined the autonomy of family units by privileging spiritual lineage, centered on his person, over biological or legal family lineage. Personal alliance with Koresh through membership in the House of David and Mighty Men became more significant than family membership. Family viability was further reduced through gender-segregated housing.

Finally, tension with the larger society rose dramatically during the Koresh era. Through the previous eras the Davidians were in conflict only with the SDA, from which they recruited members. Koresh's aggressive recruitment campaigns perpetuated this conflict. However, it was the House of David that left the Branch Davidians most vulnerable to external intervention. On the one hand, the practice symbolized the group's building of a divinely mandated order and legitimated Koresh's prophetic leadership. On the other hand, Koresh's practice of taking spiritual wives created internal dissension and a pool of disaffected members in search of allies. Ultimately these practices energized the coalition that mobilized against Koresh and began the tragic course of events that ended in the apocalypse at Waco.

Notes

1. We shall refer to the succession of groups that culminated in the Branch Davidians as the Davidians and to Vernon Howell as David Koresh throughout, although he did not legally adopt this name until 1990.

2. The most detailed compilations of early Davidian history are found in Pitts (this volume) and Bailey and Darden (1993).

3. Koresh later disclaimed the relationship, commenting that Roden was "as ugly as Medusa" (Kantrowitz et al. 1993, 56).

4. The sex ratio of adults was relatively evenly balanced between men and women. More than one-third of the population was composed of children, which is not surprising, given that most of the adults were twenty to forty years old. It was a multiracial and multinational community, reflecting the diversity in the SDA church. African Americans, Mexicans, and Asians constituted about half of the Branch Davidian community. Although Americans were the largest nationality, there was a sizable contingent from the United Kingdom (most of Jamaican heritage) and smaller groups from Australia/New Zealand, Canada, Jamaica, and the Philippines.

5. According to James Tabor (1993) Koresh believed that he had opened four of the seven seals, and so the Davidians were in the fifth seal. The extensive theological dialogue in which Koresh engaged with James Tabor and Phillip Arnold, with the blessing of federal authorities, prior to the assault on the Davidian community was intended to reach a mutual interpretation of the fifth seal that did not require a showdown with the forces surrounding the community.

6. According to Marc Breault, Koresh's wife, Rachel, accepted Koresh's adoption of spiritual wives; she "even wrote a short document describing how women should prepare themselves for love making with Vernon [Koresh]. The document described how they should bathe and perfume themselves" (Breault and King 1993, 80).

7. In another case, Koresh had a sexual liaison with Karen Doyle, daughter of Australian Davidian member Clive Doyle. Koresh reported to Doyle that he had a troubling vision ordering him to give his seed to Karen. After hearing Koresh's explanation, "Clive was convinced and gave his blessing for the union to continue" (Breault and King 1993, 63).

8. Even when Koresh did generally gain the approval of family members, agreement likely followed a period of considerable ambivalence and soul-searching. According to one former Davidian, "When I was there . . . . I mean guys were in tears about it, that God wanted them to give up their wives. . . . They were heartbroken" (England and McCormick, 1993, 8A).

9. Of course, Koresh's revelations also compelled him to demonstrate charisma commensurate with this elevated status. Breault quotes Koresh as complaining about the demands for sexual performance created by the House of David. "It ain't easy having all these wives. I know what all of you men are like. Everyone of you sits back and wishes you was the

Prophet so you could have all these women. But none of you men knows the pain that I endure to do God's work. These women are always jealous and they always complain about how they don't get enough. They're always wanting to be the one to come to my bedroom for the night. They don't understand. I get tired. I suffer. Sometimes I don't want them. And then they cry and say I don't love 'em. They just don't understand my work. They haven't caught the vision. They're not in the spirit" (Breault and King 1993, 85).

10. It is not clear whether Koresh believed that the apocalypse would begin in Israel or in the United States. Tabor (this volume) argues that Koresh expected the end-time events to take place in Israel in 1995. It is possible that Koresh was not sure of the particular location and held that either place was a possibility. Certainly, many of the events described in Revelation had to take place in Israel. In any case, Tabor's contention that Koresh's understanding of the standoff was still open to interpretation seems valid.

11. It seems clear that some of the young women who became Koresh's spiritual wives were infatuated with him. Mark Breault (Breault and King 1993, 90) reports that thirteen-year-old Aisha Gyarfas, whose family Koresh had converted on his 1988 trip to Australia, sometimes used to sleep on the floor outside the door of Koresh's bedroom when he was spending the night with another of his spiritual wives.

12. In some cases individuals who might have joined the group were apparently pressured by Koresh on sexual issues. In one instance, Shannon Bright, a musician whom Koresh invited along with his girlfriend to Mt. Carmel to participate in a late-night jam session, clearly was impressed with Koresh's knowledge of the Bible. He avers that "what Dave showed me made more sense than anything that anyone has ever shown me in my life." However, when Koresh approached Bright at the end of the evening and contended that his girlfriend really belonged to Koresh, Bright resisted. Bright recalls ending up in an argument when Koresh "said in God's eyes it wasn't right. She belonged to him." Bright simply left and never returned to Mt. Carmel (England 1993a, 1A, 4A).

13. Clearly there were romantic jealousies associated with the House of David (Davis 1936). In some of her comments Robyn Bunds intimated that she felt romantically betrayed: "Well, he always promises me things. Like, 'I'll take you to dinner.' Or something like this or something like—just little promises. And to me, a promise is a promise. He never kept a promise" (Oprah 1993, 16). Nonetheless, even members who did defect clearly continued to experience deep ambivalence about Koresh and their relationship to him. For example, Jeannine Bunds commented, "Even now I don't hate him. . . . Even after all he's done to my family. It's hard for me. I've seen both sides of him. He can be nice. He cares about people, or at least he seems to. I do have feelings for Vernon [Koresh]. Sometimes they overwhelm me" (England and McCormick, March 1, 1993, 9A).

14. According to Marc Breault, in the case of Steve and Judy Schnei-

der, Koresh apparently put pressure on the couple to give Judy to the House of David: "He would condemn her in the studies for still wanting to be with Steve. . . . She knew what was right, [Koresh] said. She should do it, otherwise she was a whore because she belonged to Vernon. She and Steve had gotten married just because they wanted to get married, Vernon said. They didn't have the Lord's permission. They were committing adultery" (England, March 8, 1993, 10A).

References

Bailey, Brad, and Bob Darden. 1993. *Mad Man in Waco: The Complete Story of the Davidian Cult, David Koresh, and the Waco Massacre.* Waco: WRS Publishing.

Bonfante, Jordan, and Sally B. Donnelly et al. 1993. "Cult of Death." *Time*, March 15, p. 38.

Breault, Marc, and Martin King. 1993. *Inside the Cult.* New York: Signet.

Bromley, David, and Bruce Busching. 1988. "Understanding the Structure of Contractual and Covenantal Social Relations: Implications for the Sociology of Religion." *Sociological Analysis* 49: 15–32.

Bromley, David, and Anson Shupe. 1993. "New Religions and Countermovements." In *Handbook on Cults and Sects in America*, part B, edited by David G. Bromley and Jeffrey K. Hadden, pp. 177–98. Greenwich, CT: JAI Press.

Butler, Jonathan. 1986. "From Millerism to Seventh-day Adventism: Boundlessness to Consolidation." *Church History* 3: 50–64.

Carey, James, ed. 1988. *Media, Myths, and Narratives: Television and the Press.* Newbury Park: Sage Publications.

Cheal, David. 1988. *The Gift Economy.* London: Routledge.

Cockerham, Jenny. 1993. "From Shepherd's Rod to Branch Davidians, Group Awaited Second Coming since 1929." *Mineral Wells Index*, April 20, pp. 1, 6.

Coser, Lewis. 1964. "The Political Functions of Eunuchism." *American Sociological Review* 29: 880–85.

Davis, Kingsley. 1936. "Jealousy and Sexual Property." *Social Forces* 14: 395–405.

Eisenstadt, S. N. 1984. *Patrons, Clients, and Friends: Interpersonal Relations and the Structure of Trust in Society.* Cambridge: Cambridge University Press.

———. 1968. *Max Weber: On Charisma and Institution Building.* Chicago: University of Chicago Press.

England, Mark. 1993a. "Still Having Doubts: Drummer Who Hung around Cult Continues to Wonder if Howell Isn't Christ." *Waco Tribune-Herald*, April 17, pp. 1A, 4A.

———. 1993b. "Follower 'Integral' in Negotiation." *Waco Tribune-Herald*, March 8, pp. 1A, 4A, 10A.

England, Mark, and Darlene McCormick. 1993. "The Sinful Messiah: Parts 3–7." *Waco Tribune-Herald*, March 1, pp. 1A-5A, 7A-9A.

Fair, Kathy. 1993. "Standoff at Cult Compound: Separated from Man with Answers, Follower Keeps Vigil." *Houston Chronicle*, March 13, p. 22A.

Fiske, Alan. 1991. *Structures of Social Life: The Four Elementary Forms of Human Relationships*. New York: Free Press.

Hinds, Michael de Courcy. 1993a. "A Believer, Stranded in Battle, Says Sect Has Peaceful Goals." *New York Times*, March 6, p. 8.

———. 1993b. "Cult Member Gives Details of Life inside Waco Compound." *Fort Worth Star-Telegram*, March 12, p. A-6.

Jordan, Mary, and Sue Anne Pressley. 1993. "Believers in Isolation." *Washington Post*, March 3, p. A-12.

Kantrowitz, Barbara, Andrew Murr, Peter Annin, Ginny Carrol, and Tony Clifton. 1993. "The Messiah of Waco." *Newsweek*, March 15, p. 56.

Linedecker, Clifford L. 1993. *Massacre at Waco, Texas: The Shocking Story of Cult Leader David Koresh and the Branch Davidians*. New York: St. Martin's.

Madigan, Tim. 1993. *See No Evil: Blind Devotion and Bloodshed in David Koresh's Holy War*. Fort Worth, TX: Summit Group.

Mahlburg, Bob. 1993. "Cult Member Sold Items at Gun Shows, Dealers Say." *Fort Worth Star-Telegram*, March 14, p. A-17.

Mantrowitz, Barbara, with Andres Murr et al. 1993. "The Messiah of Waco." *Newsweek*, March 15, p. 58.

McCormick, Darlene. 1993. "A Prophet for Profit?" *Waco Tribune-Herald*, March 6, pp. 1A, 5A.

McGee, Jim, and William Clairborne. 1993. "The Transformation of the Waco 'Messiah.'" *Washington Post*. May 9, p. A19.

The Oprah Winfrey Show. 1993. "Inside Waco and Other Cults." March 25. Transcript.

Ouichi, William. 1980. "Markets, Bureaucracies, and Clans." *Administrative Science Quarterly* 25: 129–41.

Pinkerton, James. 1993. "Sect's Money Was Welcome, Source Unclear." *Fort Worth Star-Telegram*, March 7, p. A-23.

Shils, Edward. 1965. "Charisma, Order, and Status." *American Sociological Review* 30: 199–213.

Sullivan, Tim. 1993. "Australian Follower of Koresh Praises 'Modern-day Prophet.'" *Fort Worth Star-Telegram*, March 12, p. A-4.

Tabor, James. 1993. "Apocalypse at Waco: Could the Tragedy Have Been Averted?" *Bible Review* (October): 25–32.

Tate, Bret. 1993. "Officials Dig Up Cultist's Body." *Waco Tribune-Herald*, May 5, pp. 1A, 4A.

Verhovek, Sam Howe. 1993. "In the Shadow of the Texas Siege, Uncertainty for Innocents." *New York Times*, March 8, p. A-14.

Wolff, Eric. 1963. "Kinship, Friendship, and Patron-Client Relations in Complex Societies." In *The Social Anthropology of Complex Societies*, edited by Michael Banton, pp. 1–21. London: Tavistock Publications.

Wright, Stuart. 1993a. Interview with Catherine Matteson. Waco, TX. September 10. Transcript.

———. 1993b. Interview with Rita Riddle. Waco, TX. December 17. Transcript.

———. 1993c. Interview with Wally Kennett. Waco, TX. December 23. Transcript.

Part Two

SOURCES AND DEVELOPMENT OF CONFLICT

4

STUART A. WRIGHT

Construction

and Escalation

of a Cult Threat

*Dissecting Moral Panic
and Official Reaction to
the Branch Davidians*

An enormous and alarming concentration of resources—taxpayers' money, government personnel and time, not to mention many lives—were expended on the social problem allegedly taking place in Waco. According to news sources, the planned raid of the Mt. Carmel Davidians' property by the Bureau of Alcohol, Tobacco, and Firearms was one of the largest civilian law enforcement actions in U.S. history. The initial operation involved approximately eighty federal agents, armed with semiautomatic and automatic weapons, orchestrated to execute a single search and arrest warrant. After the failed siege, in which at least six sect members and four agents died in a gun battle, and the ensuing fifty-one-day standoff, in which an estimated seventy-four Davidians died in the fire, twenty-one of whom were children, the final toll included the tragic deaths of eighty-four people, and cost the taxpayers over 100 million dollars. By the end of the whole affair, an army in excess of 700 federal and state officials were involved in one capacity or another (U.S. Department of Justice 1993, 2).

The cruelest irony of all is that it need never have happened in the first place. The U.S. Treasury Department report (1993), which reviewed the actions of BATF in Waco, later revealed gross errors of judgment by federal officials. Among other things, the agency failed to investigate sufficiently the possibility of serving the warrants to David Koresh while he was away from the church's property, thus avoiding the bloodshed altogether. BATF agents denied that Koresh had left the grounds in the preceding months before the raid, but the Treasury Department's report exposed this claim as a cover-up. In fact, the report details a number of false and misleading statements by senior BATF officials who engaged in a disinformation campaign after the failed siege in order to disguise their actions. There is now incontrovertible evidence that Koresh was aware of the BATF investigation. The Treasury Department report clearly documents the failure of BATF's undercover operation. Agents posing as students "did not fit the profile of . . . students," according to the report, and Koresh questioned neighbors about the agents and "expressed doubt that the men were students" (1993, 187). Another BATF agent posing as a UPS trainee elicited a harsher criticism by the report: "This undercover effort was so transparent that Koresh complained to the local sheriff's department" (1993, 188). Indeed, there is strong evidence that Koresh was made aware of the investigation by a gun dealer, Henry McMahon, seven months prior to the February 28 raid. Using McMahon as an intermediary, Koresh invited the special agent in charge of the case to visit the church's property and make an inspection of the weapons, which the agent declined (Smith 1993, 21A; McVicker 1993).

A careful analysis of the so-called problem posed by the Branch Davidians suggests one that is hardly proportional to the official reaction it prompted. Indeed, one of the most confounding questions that lingers from this lamentable episode in American history is why a relatively small, benign, unconventional religious sect in the rural farmlands of central Texas would evoke such a herculean response from authorities. Curiously, it appears that no attempts were made by the federal agents to secure less violent or more peaceable means of enforcing the law. The deployment of excessive force appears to be the only option ever considered by BATF, or what the Treasury Department report describes as "steps taken along what seemed at the time to be a preordained road" (1993, 174). The report's characterization seems quite accurate. But the reasons for the agency's actions are left unexplained.

It is clear now that many of the allegations and fears expressed by federal agents or reported by the media have little support and fail to provide a justification for the actions taken. Many of these allegations will be examined systematically in the course of the chapter. But even allowing that some of the accusations were true, such as the illegal weapons charges, conducting an elaborate, paramilitary assault without concerted efforts to consult with local law enforcement or consider less drastic options for executing the warrants, and without even attempting to communicate with the Davidians, requires explanation. In reviewing the documentation available through government reports and newspaper accounts, it now appears that BATF agents had already become convinced that the Davidians were a dangerous menace to society necessitating a swift and emphatic response. What the official reports or media accounts fail to explain are the sources, the dynamics, or the influences that contributed to the formulation of the problem in such an egregious manner.

In an effort to explain the marked discrepancy between the inconsiderable problem actually posed by the Branch Davidians and the exaggerated perception of an insidious threat leading to massive official reaction, this paper offers a "constructionist" approach (Spector and Kitsuse 1987) or perspective regarding the recognition and identification of the Davidian sect as a social problem. Here I want to advance the thesis that the Mt. Carmel Davidians became caricatures of evil constructed through specific, but highly subjective, social processes of recognition, interpretation, and claims-making by pressure groups and detractors. In effect, how the sect came to be *defined* as dangerous or threatening to society is a product of social activities, less reflective of an objective condition than the symbolic meanings imposed upon the religious sect by others. In gaining the attention of authorities, a particular definition of the problem was legitimated and given official sanction.

Constructing Social Problems: Selection, Definition, Claims-making

It cannot be assumed that any social problem is self-evident. Many problems in society never get serious attention by authorities, while others may get more than their share. This paradox is easily explained by constructionist theory as a process of selection, or selective recognition. In the initial stages of the AIDS epidemic, for example, the problem was generally ignored by government authorities under the Reagan administration because it was believed that the victims were largely homosexuals and IV drug users—disvalued social groups. On the other hand, the amount of attention given missing children who have been allegedly abducted by strangers appears to be greatly disproportionate to the actual figures, taking into account that most of these children are runaways or victims of custody battles between divorced or separated parents (Best 1990). Thus, the likelihood or degree of recognition of a problem may have no clear relation to the actual danger or threat posed to a society by a particular individual or group. Increasingly in recent decades, sociologists have come to appreciate the extent to which some social problems are selectively identified and symbolically defined.

By symbolic, I refer to the collective beliefs and meanings imputed to the actions or intentions of social groups or individuals. When the alleged problem represents a condition signifying a threat to the cherished norms or values of certain segments of society (Fuller and Myers 1941), when the particularistic moral order is challenged, a subjective definition may crystallize, finding shared indignation and consensual validation among select groups.

In this context, we find that collective action inevitably involves mobilizing ideas and meanings. Social actors engage in "meaning-work" (Snow and Benford 1992, 136), or what Hall (1982) call the "politics of signification," the struggle over the production of ideas and meanings. These productive efforts comprise an essential part of the core activities of social movements and moral crusades. According to Snow and Benford (1992, 136), such movements are not merely carriers of extant meanings but are "actively engaged in the production and maintenance of meaning for constituents, antagonists, and bystanders or observers."

A constructionist approach does not assume that a social problem can be taken at face value. It seeks to examine the social processes that lead to its definition by a social audience. There may be some debate among scholars as to whether an action can be inherently deviant or possess a known objective reality behind it (Lemert 1951; Spector and Kitsuse 1987; Rains 1975). It is not the purpose of this work to entertain that debate. What constructionism does make clear to our understanding of social problems, and particularly to the problem at hand, is that the official definition may not accurately reflect the situation or event.

Another key component in the analysis of social problems is the issue of *claims-making*. Some problems in society receive attention largely because of organized efforts by pressure groups to spotlight or herald the perceived dangers of a group or phenomenon. According to Kitsuse and Schneider (1989, xii-xiii), "The theoretical task is to study how members define, lodge and press claims; how they publicize their concerns, redefine the issue in question in the face of political obstacles, indifference or opposition; how they enter into alliances with other claims-makers." Successful efforts may take on the features and characteristics of a symbolic crusade. Gusfield's (1963) analysis of the temperance movement in the nineteenth century suggests that elite groups, faced with declining power and status, supported temperance as a symbolic issue that would enable them to recover their dominant status and reassert their power. Similar arguments have been made with regard to the new religious right, and the antipornography and prolife movements (Wald et al. 1989; Zurcher and Kilpatrick 1976).

Claims-makers often engage in what Becker (1963) calls "moral enterprise." Such activities are designed to influence, create, or reconstitute a new fragment of the moral order and are carried out by "moral entrepreneurs," an increasingly significant source of influence in shaping value conflicts in a pluralistic society. Cultural heterogeneity in modern society precludes value consensus, giving rise to divergent and competing ideas, moral codes, and worldviews. Individuals or groups seeking to promote a particular set of values or moral beliefs work toward building a moral hegemony whereby dominant social institutions and public policy reflect their own ideals.

Claims-making is more effective if the particular issues target problems that reflect pre-existing or widespread social fears and apprehensions. Various studies of witch hunts or witch trials suggest that they occurred in the context of social turmoil, disorganization, or acute anomie (Erikson 1966; Karlsen 1987). Consequently, the claims find resonance with a larger social audience, receptive to and willing to support the definitions promoted by certain interest groups, such as those made by the Puritan clergy in colonial America during the Salem witch trials (Chambliss and Mankoff 1976; Moore 1987). History is replete with claims of fanaticism lodged against new sects by institutional religionists engendering conflict and giving birth to far-fetched plans for moral rectification. Though frequently representatives of "official" religion are articulating the conventional moral codes of the status quo, the claims-makers need not be religious, in any strict sense. In the last century, for example, critics cite a shift in moral entrepreneurship from religion to the therapeutic and mental health communities (Gross 1978; London 1964; Reiff 1966; Szasz 1970a, 1970b, 1984).

According to Szasz (1970b), the purge of witches during the Inquisition served to heighten the scope of power held by the Medieval Church in much the same manner that clinical diagnoses of mental illness have been used by some to further the interests and power of mental health professionals. The "manufacture of madness" was an effective tool used by institutional psychiatrists during the McCarthy era to suppress socialist ideas (Szasz 1970b: 29), and even more insidious as a technique employed by the now dismantled Soviet state to punish political dissidents (Bloch and Reddaway 1977). Others have suggested that the widespread apprehension about youthful moorings and the growth of new or unconventional religions in recent years has given rise to a "cult scare," not unlike the witch hunts or Red scares of previous times (Bromley and Shupe 1981). The proliferation of psychiatrists, psychologists, and social workers who now specialize in cult deprogrammings, exit therapy, or counseling alleged survivors of satanic ritual abuse indicates the importance of interest groups in this phenomenon (Richardson, Bromley, and Best 1991).

The Role of Interest Groups

There are three critical areas of research in which an analysis of claims-making should focus (Best 1990; Gusfield 1963; Jenkins 1992). The first is the *interests* that particular groups or movement organizations and actors have in promoting a social problem. How or in what ways do these groups benefit or profit from promulgating a definition of an issue, lodging claims, and pressuring for an amelioration to the alleged crisis? These interests may be symbolic, material, or both. Interest groups may comprise individuals who perceive themselves as victims of some unjust system, group, or process. In this instance, the wronged victims invest themselves emotionally and psychologically in the cause so that it becomes analogous to a conversion experience. Often, the "convert" will embrace the cause with deep conviction and vigor, exhibiting the zeal of one involved in a religious crusade. Social movements are filled with activists or figures who attempt to turn their own misfortunes or bad experiences into moral or altruistic campaigns. For example, Candy Lightner, the founder of MADD whose daughter was killed by a drunk driver, used her personal tragedy to launch a career as an activist in the anti–drunk driving crusade (Nock and Kingston 1990). Similarly, Steven Hassan, an ex-Moonie, has been an outspoken activist in the anticult movement, speaking at rallies and conferences, participating in deprogrammings, and eventually settling into a career as an exit counselor (Hassan 1988). Other members of these interest groups or movements may have similar personal experiences, or have family members who have been "victims," or simply be sympathetic to or aligned with the values and beliefs represented.

A second area of focus is the *resources* available to an interest group. A successful campaign or movement is often predicated on its ability to mobilize sufficient resources, particularly those external to the movement. Financial support from sympathetic publics, voluntary help to conduct routine activities, outside experts or consultants who lend advice or give direction, political contacts or networks, and alliances with other groups with common goals all may be considered important resources. The development of resource mobilization theory in social movements has contributed significantly to our understanding of how movements and interest groups succeed (McCarthy and Zald 1977; Zald and McCarthy 1979, 1987).

The third area of concern in analyzing interest groups is the *ownership* that they eventually secure over the issue or problem. In effect, ownership refers to the extent that society accepts their definition and evaluation of a problem as authoritative. Here the rhetoric or language invoked to "frame" the issue by interest groups or movement sectors serves as the dominant explanation or perspective (Snow et al. 1986). Conflicting interest groups will compete for ownership of a problem, attempting to gain larger shares of public support and eventually recognition by authorities. The conflicts over abortion between prolife and prochoice movement organizations reflect just such a struggle for ownership of the problem.

Symbolic Politics, Deviance Amplification, and Moral Panic

Claims-makers may succeed in drawing attention to a special problem but fail to mobilize resources or force the actions of officials, particularly if the purported deviance is within a reasonable range of social tolerance. For example, moral crusades assailing pornography or homosexuality struggle to generate widespread public support because such deviations fall within the limits of tolerance in a democratic society. Issues of privacy or censorship prevent impulsive official reaction and defuse public outcry. Similarly, attacks on religious deviance are not likely to find a sympathetic audience because of the offsetting ethical concerns of free speech and freedom of religion.

Studies of moral or symbolic crusades, however, reveal that interest groups often circumvent this problem by engaging in what Jenkins (1992, 10) calls the "politics of substitution." Since they are unable to attack a particular issue directly, they shift the focus to a more serious offense, essentially substituting a more deviant claim for a less deviant one. Thus Jenkins found that in Great Britain, interest groups that had been organized to fight pornography introduced children into their claims, alleging links between pornography and child sexual abuse. He observed that previously impotent moral campaigns against pornography gained widespread public support when coupled with child sexual abuse. While allegations of links between the two phenomena lacked any solid empirical evidence, the campaigns were nonetheless successful in creating moral panic and generating public demands for increased law enforcement efforts, new legislation, education programs in schools, counseling and treatment centers for victims, and a host of other activities. The moral panic surrounding child sexual abuse led many to believe that the problem was near epidemic proportions even though reliable statistics could not substantiate any significant increase in prevalence rates.

This process of deviance amplification or escalation is discussed in the work of Hall et al. (1978, 223), who describe it as a "self-amplifying sequence within the area of signification: the activity or event with which the signification deals is escalated—made to seem more threatening" than it actually is. By amplifying or escalating the general threat to society, the deviant activity or event crosses over the threshold of tolerance, incurring official sanctions. Deviance amplification is accomplished through "convergence," a rhetorical tactic linking two or more activities so as to implicitly or explicitly draw parallels between them (p. 223). "One kind of threat or challenge to society seems larger, more menacing," they state, "if it can be mapped together with other apparently similar phenomena—especially if by connecting one relatively harmless activity with a more threatening one, the danger implicit is made to appear more widespread and diffused" (1978, 226).

This theoretical framework is helpful in understanding how David Koresh and the Branch Davidians came to be defined as a serious threat to society, requiring elaborate government response. Reports of child abuse, sexual abuse, and preparations to attack the city of Waco with illegal weapons can be analyzed as claims-making activities of certain interest groups who, though frustrated in initial efforts to persuade authorities to act, effectively mapped together relatively harmless activities with more serious acts of deviance and illegality, thus pushing the putative actions over the threshold of tolerance.

Interest Groups and Deviance Amplification in Waco

In the development of the alleged problem posed by the Branch Davidians in Waco, there appear to be at least three interest groups that helped shape the exaggerated and nefarious perception of Koresh and his followers: disgruntled apostates, the media, and anticult organizations. While there are certainly other players in this drama, the activities of these particular groups seem to be significant and can be readily documented and analyzed. Over time, and in varying degrees, these groups formed alliances to create, mutually reinforce, and help perpetuate a definition of Koresh and the Davidians as evil; they worked to gain the attention of government officials, and later served as advisors and sources of authority on the sect to federal agencies involved in the siege and the subsequent standoff.

Disgruntled Apostates

Atrocity tales about religious movements or organizations are commonly traced back to disgruntled apostates. Some famous historical examples include *Six Months in a Convent* by Rebecca Theresa Reed (1835), the *Awful Disclosures of the Hotel Dieu Nunnery of Montreal* by Maria Monk (1836), *The History of the Saints, or, An Expose of Joe Smith and Mormonism* by John C. Bennett (1842), and the anti-Shaker work, *Portraiture of Shakerism,* by Mary Dyer (1822). All these works were inflated, scurrilous accounts giving alleged details and facts about events from former members (Lewis 1989; Miller 1983). Such "facts," however, tend to be less than objective when placed in the context of motives and circumstances of leaving. Apostates may leave under unfavorable conditions and voice their grievances as a form of retaliation.

Studies of defectors from new religious movements generally indicate favorable or sympathetic responses toward their former groups (Wright 1984, 1987, 1988; Wright and Ebaugh 1993), despite popular opinion to the contrary. Exceptions are most likely to include individuals who have been deprogrammed or participated in exit counseling (Lewis 1986; Solomon 1981; Wright 1987). Defectors who leave over doctrinal quarrels to form their own schismatic sects and those who have been expelled are also more likely to voice recriminations. Thus, while acrimonious accounts by former members are not typical, they are certainly not unprecedented either.

Several former Branch Davidians played a key role in the claims-making activities that provoked official reaction. But none was more significant than Marc Breault, a self-described "right-hand" man of Koresh, who defected in 1989. In a sensationalized account, published shortly after the fatal fire, entitled *Inside the Cult*, he chronicles in great detail his efforts to gain the attention of authorities (Breault and King 1993). Breault's coauthor, Martin King, was the reporter for the Australian television show *A Current Affair* who attempted to expose Koresh tabloid-style in 1992. By his own account, Breault actively engaged in persuading Australian Davidians, particularly the Gent family, to defect. Curiously, Breault accomplished this task by claiming to be a rival prophet, challenging Koresh's leadership in the sect.

Not unlike other activists in interest groups or movements, Breault exhibited features of both victim and crusader. According to King, "Breault became a cultbuster. He committed his life to righting the wrongs of the past and, more importantly, to putting a stop to Vernon Howell before he could destroy many more lives" (Breault and King 1993, 208).

Breault boasts of a number of claims-making activities in order to provoke official reaction, including (1) flying to Waco to alert the police, (2) hiring a private investigator to gather damaging information on the sect, (3) approaching authorities in LaVerne, California, alleging statutory rape of young female adherents, (4) working with reporter King on the exposé, (5) contacting a sect member's estranged husband (David Jewell) and alleging sexual abuse of his daughter by Koresh, (6) serving as a witness in a custody battle over the sect member's daughter, and (7) contacting congressman Fred Upton of Michigan for assistance in gaining help from the FBI.

Largely as a result of this flurry of activity and lobbying, Breault was contacted by BATF special investigator Davy Aguilera in December 1992, approximately ten weeks before the raid, to obtain information about the Davidians (Breault and King 1993, 294). Breault became a primary source for the BATF and several other federal agencies. After the initial contact with the special investigator, Breault reports that he received "almost daily phone calls . . . (from) senior officials of the United States Government, which included the BATF, the FBI, Congress, the State Department, and the Texas Rangers" (1993, 295).

Other important apostates included the Bunds family, especially David and Debbie Bunds. David and Debbie Bunds were expelled from Mt. Carmel in June 1990 for violating dietary rules in the community. Soon after the expulsion, Breault contacted David Bunds and successfully "converted" him to "cultbusting" (1993, 218). Bunds subsequently persuaded his sister, Robyn, to defect and encouraged her to contact Breault. Robyn Bunds was reportedly one of Koresh's wives, and bore a child with him. Allegations lodged against Koresh by Robyn in LaVerne, California, centered around a custody battle for the child. The claims of child abuse made against the Davidian leader appear to begin at this juncture. Eventually, a group of former members solidified under the leadership of Breault and continued to level complaints against Koresh to authorities both in California and Australia. Debbie Bunds was interviewed by special agent Aguilera and her testimony appears in the BATF affidavit accompanying the search warrant regarding the possession of illegal weapons. According to the affidavit, Ms. Bunds "observed Howell shooting a machinegun behind the main structure of the compound" in 1989 (U.S. District Court 1993, 10). Some comments from Ms. Bunds regarding Koresh's "exclusive sexual access to the women" (p. 10) also appear in the affidavit. Robyn and Marc Bunds (Robyn's half brother) are quoted extensively in the initial days following the failed BATF raid in news stories, and the Bunds family is generally credited by Breault as being instrumental in the federal investigation (1993, 297). Finally, at the trial of eleven Davidian survivors, four members of the Bunds family were called as witnesses for the prosecution.

One of the most bewildering questions regarding the BATF's decision to mount an assault ("dynamic entry") rather than pursue a more modest course of executing the warrants is answered in the Treasury Department investigation. According to the report, the BATF concluded that a request for Koresh to surrender would be futile. These conclusions were based solely on "intelligence obtained . . . from former cult members" (U.S. Treasury Department 1993, 141). This is further corroborated in a transcript of an interview with Breault conducted by a federal agent and reproduced in Breault and King (1993, 306–7).

BATF: If Vernon received a summons to answer questions regarding firearms, would he show up?
Breault: No way.
BATF: If the good guys came with a search warrant, would Vernon allow it?
Breault: If Vernon were not expecting it, no. If Vernon had prior warning, yes. He'd have time to shift all the firearms.

Breault goes on to assert that Koresh might kill others, order a mass suicide, or start his own holy war if approached by government officials. However, accounts by local law enforcement and authorities in Waco directly contradict claims by Breault and other defectors. McLennan County's sheriff's department reportedly had good relations with the Davidians, having had several opportunities to visit

Mt. Carmel without incident over the years. The former district attorney in Waco, Vic Feazell, reported no difficulty in obtaining the cooperation of the Davidians in a 1987 trial that ended in an acquittal of Koresh. Indeed, Feazell criticized the siege as "a vulgar display of power on the part of the feds" and stated that "if they'd [the BATF] called and talked to them, the Davidians would've given them what they wanted" (Bragg 1993, 7A).[1]

An equally perplexing question about the raid concerns the BATF's failure to consult or work more closely with local law enforcement, thus likely avoiding a standoff or bloodshed. This question also appears to be answered by apostate claims. The Australian defectors were exasperated at unsuccessful efforts to get Texas authorities to act against Koresh (Breault and King 1993, 231). King echoes the sentiments of the ex-Davidians: "The Sheriff's Department told us over the phone, and none too politely, that they knew all about the allegations but refused to discuss what action, if any, they planned to take. In a nut-shell, we got the cold shoulder" (1993, 288).

When the former sect members finally gained the attention of the BATF, they expressed acute frustrations about the perceived inaction of Waco law enforcement. In his role as cult-buster and BATF advisor, Breault apparently convinced federal agents that the local authorities in Waco could not be trusted. In an account of a conversation with another apostate, Breault implies that there is a leak in the sheriff's department, and claims that the BATF was "bypassing local authorities" three days before the raid (1993, 318). David Jewell, who worked with Breault to gain custody of his daughter in a court battle, reports in an AP news story that he was transported to and from Waco by the BATF "because there was a concern of [sic] the integrity of local law enforcement" (*Houston Chronicle,* October 11, 1993, 15A). The link between apostates' claims and the decision by the BATF to avoid collaboration with local law enforcement helps explain the steadfast resolve of federal agents to conduct a military-style raid in the manner of the "pre-ordained road" cited in the Treasury Department report.

Media

Two media sources played a critical role in the claims-making activities generating official reaction, an Australian television station and the *Waco Tribune-Herald.* By his own account, Breault's initial claims and pleas made to American authorities "fell on deaf ears" (1993, 13). Subsequently, he found a sympathetic listener in the Australian media, namely reporter King. The following account is given in the cobiographical narrative.

In the meantime, Marc Breault had given up on the authorities, so he went to the American media. . . . But, amazingly, Marc couldn't get the American media interested in this devil in their midst. Then he turned to Australian television . . . . The network knew a good story when it saw one. As a reporter for 'A Current Affair,' (Australia) I took up the challenge that was to dominate my life for the next two years. But how would we convince Vernon to be a willing participant in a television report, *the secret agenda of which was to expose him as a sex-crazed despot?* (1993, 256; emphasis mine)

Since the Davidians had churches in Australia and New Zealand, the media interest was fueled by local concern. As the allegations and claims-making grew, the journalist's investigation grew and extended to the United States and Waco. Breault and King give a detailed account of this development. Relying on Breault as a confidant and advisor, King conducted and filmed interviews with the Australian apostates in December 1991, and later with Koresh at Mt. Carmel in January 1992. An interview with Robyn Bunds was also conducted and filmed during the same visit. The filmed interviews were shown on the Australian television program *A Current Affair,* and stereotypically cast the Davidians as a "dangerous cult," lodging a litany of claims against Koresh, including child abuse, sexual promiscuity, and brainwashing.

It is difficult to know what kind of impact the media attention had on Koresh and the Davidians, in terms of their own perceptions. But there would appear to be a linkage between the sensational Australian media coverage and a chain of events leading to the increased signification of previous claims by apostates and responses by media and government in the United States. The Australian television station divided the program into a series that ran for four nights, April 15–18, 1992. Simultaneously, the *Herald Sun,* an Australian newspaper, covered the story in print. Not coincidentally, the *Waco Tribune-Herald* began its investigation of the Branch Davidians the following month, in May. The connection between Breault and *Waco Tribune-Herald* reporter Mark England is recounted in Breault's book. The seven-part series, "The Sinful Messiah," published by the Waco paper, relied heavily on Breault's own framing of events, exhibiting a striking similarity to the lurid paperback.

Government documents suggest that the BATF investigation of the Davidians began in late May or early June. In the affidavit accompanying the search warrant, agent Aguilera reports meeting with an officer in the McLennan County sheriff's department on June 4 (U.S. District Court 1993, 1). The text of the account implies that the agent had earlier telephone conversations with the sheriff's department regarding a torn UPS package containing pineapple-type hand-grenade casings. The UPS incident was cited by BATF officials as the cause of the initial investigation. The affidavit states that the UPS information was received by the sheriff's department in May. However, against the backdrop of previously lodged claims by apostates, and further amplified by the Australian media coverage that filtered back to the States through video tapes, it is likely that the UPS incident was given much more serious attention by BATF than might otherwise have occurred. Both the BATF investigation and the *Waco Tribune-Herald* investigation began approximately one month after the Australian media coverage.

The Waco paper's investigative series, although largely just a recapitulation of apostate claims-making reproduced for American audiences, apparently had the effect of hurrying and perhaps competing with the BATF investigation. According to the editor, Bob Lott, the paper was prepared to publish the series a full month before the siege (Trounsen 1993). Accounts by the *Tribune-Herald* and spokespersons for the BATF concur that federal agents requested a delay of the series publication. Though the paper agreed to postpone the series while the government proceeded with its operation, the editor eventually grew impatient and released the first part in the series the day before the raid. In the aftermath of the failed siege, a flurry of allegations by federal agents blamed the publicity generated by the *Tribune-Herald* for the adverse outcome (Fair and Bragg 1993: 1A). In Breault's book (1993, 301), he notes that the "BATF is becoming increasingly paranoid about the media" and specifically refers to the *Tribune-Herald*.

Anticult Organizations

The actions and goals of the anticult movement are well documented in the research literature (Bromley and Shupe 1979, 1987, 1993; Shupe and Bromley 1980, 1985). By definition, the anticult movement is a countermovement engaged in a symbolic campaign to defeat, or at least curtail, the growth and spread of unconventional religious groups or "cults." In recent years, a national coalition of discrete movement organizations has been forged under the umbrella organization Cult Awareness Network (CAN), formerly the Citizens Freedom Foundation. The involvement of CAN officials, anticult organizations, and deprogrammers in the Branch Davidian conflict is probably the least surprising and the most predictable element of the claims-making and social construction of the so-called cult problem in Waco.

The involvement of anticult movement actors can be traced to the deprogramming of a former Branch Davidian, David Block, in the summer of 1992. According to a sworn affidavit, Block was deprogrammed by Rick Ross in the home of CAN national spokesperson, Priscilla Coates, in California (Ross and Green 1993). Deprogrammer Ross apparently obtained information from Block about stored weapons on the Davidian property. According to the Treasury report, much of the information about the weapons "was based almost exclusively on the statement of one former cult member, David Block" (1993, 143). In a review of the BATF's actions, the report criticizes the agency's "failure to consider how Block's relations with Koresh . . . might have affected the reliability of his statements" (p. 143), suggesting that the deprogrammed apostate may have been less than objective. The report also acknowledges Block's relationship with Rick Ross. The link between Ross and the BATF was confirmed by the deprogrammer himself on several occasions by news media shortly after the failed raid. Ross described himself as a "cult expert" and consultant to the BATF investigation (Robertson 1993). This is corroborated in Breault's account of the events leading up to the BATF raid (1993, 314). Breault initially learned of deprogrammer Ross from *Tribune-Herald* reporter Mark England. Cult-buster Breault subsequently recounted his efforts to contact Ross and referred to an intermediary who "has detailed information on cult awareness groups and cultbusters" (1993, 315). Breault also stated that Ross knew that "something was about to happen real soon" on February 16, and that Ross urged family members to "get Steve (Schneider) out as soon as possible" (1993, 317). Ross's apparent knowledge of the BATF raid twelve days before the event suggests more than a peripheral role as a government advisor.

In the first segment of "The Sinful Messiah" series published by the *Waco Tribune-Herald* on February 27, the day before the raid, reporters Mark England and Darlene McCormick acknowledged that they had information from interviews with more than twenty "former members" and quoted a man "deprogrammed" by Ross. Herein, the transmission of constructed meanings as "news" was accomplished. The language and rhetoric of apostate claims clearly regurgitated anticult framing and signification: "Former cult members also said Howell uses traditional mind-control techniques to entrap listeners" (England and McCormick 1993, 12A). Mind control and brainwashing attributions were pervasive throughout the series, reflecting the core concepts and ideology of the anticult movement.

An addendum to Nancy Ammerman's report to the Justice Department made evident the significance of deprogrammer Ross as an FBI advisor, describing him as "closely involved with both the

BATF and the FBI" and as having "the most extensive access to both agencies of any person on the 'cult expert' list" (Ammerman 1993). Ammerman's direct access (as a behavioral science expert) to government officials and nonpublic documents critical to the Waco catastrophe lends particular credence to the claim of the deprogrammer's influence (see also Ammerman, this volume).

In the House Judiciary Committee hearings following the Waco debacle, evidence surfaced that CAN had established regular contact with at least one congressman—apparently William Hughes of New Jersey—who subsequently supplied information about the Branch Davidians to the attorney general (Milne 1994, 141). Janet Reno confirmed that she had obtained this information involving the identification and use of "cult" advisors in the future, and indicated that she had a copy of an anticult article ("How Many Jonestowns Will It Take?"). Also, FBI special agent in charge at Waco, Jeffrey Jamar, stated in response to questioning that the bureau had been in possession of a "white paper" on cults prior to the Waco standoff and that they had found it "very useful" (Milne 1994, 142). The so-called white paper refers to a twelve-page document parroting anticult constructions of "harmful cult" characteristics, largely clinical in description and conspicuously void of contravening evidence or substantive empirical studies or references ("Cults" n.d.). Religious leaders are painted as manipulative, duplicitous, and even psychotic, while members are cast as victims of devious mind control techniques. To assert that the document is an objective treatment of marginal religious sects is akin to suggesting that Ku Klux Klan materials are dispassionate assessments of racial minorities. However, the white paper provides a helpful clue to the actions, or rather the *rationale* of such actions, taken by FBI agents. As a primer on "cults," the white paper may be seen as giving some explanation to the moral panic that federal law enforcement demonstrated so inexplicably on the grounds of Mt. Carmel.

Conclusion

The argument has been advanced in this chapter that alliances and networks among key interest groups—apostates, media, and anticult organizations and actors—had a marked influence on the recognition, selection, and definition of the problem eventually adopted by federal authorities. The groups in question successfully achieved ownership of the problem, convincing government officials that they possessed the knowledge and expertise to define and explain the putative crisis at Mt. Carmel. Claims-making activities conducted in concert by the key interest groups helped shape a unified and cohesive, albeit exaggerated, framing of the Branch Davidians as a cult threat, posing alleged dangers to sect members, children, and even citizens of Waco. By linking or mapping together less harmful activities (communal organization, charismatic authority, polygamy or sexual pluralism, millennial expectations) with more threatening ones (child abuse, sexual abuse, mental enslavement of members, or brainwashing, and preparations for launching an armed assault on the government[2]), antagonists were able to make benign activities appear to be more perilous and menacing. The extreme actions of excessive force by federal agents can best be understood in light of the processes of claims-making and deviance amplification, giving credence to official decisions that now, in retrospect, can only be described as tragically narrow and shortsighted.

Notes

1. In an alarming and somewhat prophetic statement to the news media on March 2, 1993—six weeks before the FBI assault and tragic fire—former District Attorney Feazell said, "The Feds are preparing to kill them [noting the mobilization of military equipment into nearby staging areas]. That way they can bury their mistakes and they won't have attorneys looking over what they did later. . . . I'd represent these boys for free if they'd surrender without bloodshed, but I'm afraid I'm going to wake up and see the headlines that say they all died" (Bragg 1993, 7A).

2. This is precisely the claim made by the government in the trial of eleven Branch Davidians in San Antonio in early 1994. However, the jury was not convinced by government arguments, acquitting all of the sect members of charges of murder and conspiracy to murder. In effect, the jury rejected the claim that the Davidians conspired to provoke federal authorities into a gun battle and then ambushed the agents serving the warrants.

References

Becker, Howard. 1963. *Outsiders.* New York: Free Press.

Best, Joel. 1990. *Threatened Children.* Chicago: University of Chicago.

Bloch, Sidney, and Peter Reddaway. 1977. *Psychiatric Terror: How Soviet Psychiatry Is Used to Suppress Dissent.* New York: Basic Books.

Ammerman, Nancy T. 1993. "Report to the Justice and Treasury Department Regarding Law Enforcement Interaction with the Branch Davidians in Waco, Texas." In *Recommendations of Experts for Improvements in Federal Law Enforcement after Waco.* Washington, DC: U.S. Department of Justice.

Bragg, Roy. 1993. "Ex-Prosecutor Laments Agent's 'Storm Trooper' Tactics." *Houston Chronicle*, March 2, p. 7A.

Breault, Marc, and Martin King. 1993. *Inside the Cult*. New York: Signet.

Bromley, David G., and Anson D. Shupe. 1979. *Moonies in America*. Beverly Hills: Sage.

———. 1981. *Strange Gods: The Great American Cult Hoax*. Boston: Beacon.

———. 1987. "The Future of the Anticult Movement." In *The Future of New Religious Movements*, edited by David G. Bromley and Phillip E. Hammond, pp. 221–34. Macon: Mercer University.

———. 1993. "Organized Opposition to New Religious Movements." In *The Handbook on Cults and Sects in America*, edited by David G. Bromley and Jeffrey K. Hadden, pp. 177–98. Greenwich, CT: JAI Press.

Chambliss, William, and M. Mankoff. 1976. *Whose Law? What Order?* New York: Wiley & Sons.

"Cults." N.a., n.d. (Document referred to as the "white paper"). On file with author.

England, Mark, and Darlene McCormick. 1993. "The Sinful Messiah." *Waco Tribune-Herald*, February 27, p. 11A.

Erikson, Kai. 1966. *Wayward Puritans*. New York: Wiley & Sons.

Fair, Kathy, and Roy Bragg. 1993. "ATF Agent's Suit Claims Newspaper Warned Cult." *Houston Chronicle*, March 18, p. 10A.

Gross, M. L. 1978. *The Psychological Society*. New York: Random House.

Gusfield, Joseph R. 1963. *Symbolic Crusade: Status Politics and the American Temperance Movement*. Urbana: University of Illinois.

Hall, Stuart. 1982. "The Rediscovery of Ideology: Return of the Repressed in Media Studies." In *Culture, Society, and the Media*, edited by Michael Gurevitch et al., pp. 56–90. New York: Methuen.

Hall, Stuart, Chris Critcher, Tony Jefferson, John Clarke, and Brian Roberts. 1978. *Policing the Crisis: Mugging, the State, and Law and Order*. London: Macmillan.

Hassan, Steven. 1988. *Combatting Mind Control*. Rochester, VT: Park Street.

Jenkins, Phillip. 1992. *Intimate Enemies: Moral Panics in Contemporary Great Britain*. New York: Aldine de Gruyter.

Karlsen, Carol. 1987. *The Devil in the Shape of a Woman*. New York: Norton.

Kitsuse, John I., and Joseph Schneider. 1989. Preface to *Images of Issues*, edited by Joel Best, pp. i-iv. New York: Aldine de Gruyter.

Lemert, Edwin. 1951. *Social Pathology*. New York: McGraw-Hill.

Lewis, James R. 1986. "Reconstructing the Cult Experience: Post-Involvement Attitudes as a Function of Mode of Exit and Post-Involvement Socialization." *Sociological Analysis* 47: 151–59.

———. 1989. "Apostates and the Legitimation of Repression: Some Historical and Empirical Perspectives on the Cult Controversy." *Sociological Analysis* 49 (4): 386–96.

London, Perry. 1964. *The Modes and Morals of Psychotherapy*. New York: Holt, Rinehart & Winston.

McVicker, Steve. 1993. "Assault on Mt. Carmel." *Houston Press*, July 22–28, pp. 17–22.

McCarthy, John, and Mayer N. Zald. 1977. *The Dynamics of Social Movements*. Boston: Winthrop.

Miller, Donald E. 1983. "Deprogramming in Historical Perspective." In *The Brainwashing/Deprogramming Controversy*, edited by David G. Bromley and James T. Richardson, pp. 15–28. New York: Edwin Mellen.

Milne, Andrew. 1994. "The Cult Awareness Network: Its Role in the Waco Tragedy." In *From the Ashes: Making Sense of Waco*, edited by James R. Lewis, pp. 137–42. Lanham, MD: Rowman and Littlefield.

Moore, R. I. 1987. *The Formation of a Persecuting Society*. Oxford: Blackwell.

Nock, Steven L., and Paul W. Kingston. 1990. *The Sociology of Public Issues*. Belmont, CA: Wadsworth.

Rains, Prudence. 1975. "Imputations of Deviance: A Retrospective Essay on the Labeling Perspective." *Social Problems* 23: 1–11.

Reiff, Philip. 1966. *The Triumph of the Therapeutic*. New York: Harper & Row.

Richardson, James T., David G. Bromley, and Joel Best. 1991. *The Satanism Scare*. New York: Aldine de Gruyter.

Robertson, George. 1993. "Cult Awareness Network Charged with Responsibility for Waco Texas Religious Sect Shoot-out." Media briefing, March 8. Typescript.

Ross, Nancy, and Linda Green. 1993. "What Is the Cult Awareness Network and What Role Did It Play in Waco?" Washington, DC: Ross and Green Legal Firm. Typescript.

Shupe, Anson D., and David G. Bromley. 1980. *The New Vigilantes: Deprogrammers, Anti-Cultists, and the New Religions*. Beverly Hills: Sage.

———. 1985. *A Documentary History of the Anticult Movement*. New York: Edwin Mellen.

Smith, Mark. 1993. "Agent Allegedly Refused Koresh's Offer." *Houston Chronicle*, September 11, p. 21A.

Snow, David A., and Robert D. Benford. 1992. "Master Frames and Cycles of Protest." In *Frontiers in Social Movement Theory*, edited by Aldon D. Morris and Carol McClurg Mueller, pp. 133–55. New Haven: Yale University.

Snow, David A., E. Burke Rochford, Jr., Steven K. Worden, and Robert D. Benford. 1978. "Frame Alignment Process, Micromobilization, and Movement Participation." *American Sociological Review* 51: 464–81.

Solomon, Trudy. 1981. "Integrating the 'Moonie' Experience: A Survey of Ex-Members of the Unification Church." In *In Gods We Trust*, edited by Thomas Robbins and Dick Anthony, pp. 275–96. New Brunswick: Transaction.

Spector, Malcolm, and John I. Kitsuse. 1987. *Constructing Social Problems.* New York: Aldine de Gruyter.

Szasz, Thomas. 1970a. *Ideology and Insanity.* Garden City, NY: Doubleday.

———. 1970b. *The Manufacture of Madness.* New York: Harper & Row.

———. 1984. *The Therapeutic State: Psychiatry in the Mirror of Current Events.* Buffalo, NY: Prometheus.

Trounsen, Rebecca. 1993. "Questions Persist about Coverage by Press, TV." *Houston Chronicle,* March 7, p. 15A.

U.S. Department of Justice. 1993. *Report to the Deputy Attorney General on the Events at Waco, Texas: February 28 to April 19, 1993.* Redacted version, October 8. Washington, DC: U.S. Government Printing Office.

U.S. Department of Treasury. 1993. *Report of the Department of Treasury on the Bureau of Alcohol, Tobacco, and Firearms Investigation of Vernon Wayne Howell, Also Known as David Koresh.* Washington, DC: U.S. Government Printing Office.

U.S. District Court. 1993. Application and Affidavit for Search Warrant. W93–15M. Western District of Texas. Filed February 26, 1993.

Wald, Kenneth, Dennis E. Owen, and Samuel S. Hill. 1989. "Evangelical Politics and Status Issues." *Journal for the Scientific Study of Religion* 28 (1): 1–16.

Wright, Stuart A. 1984. "Post-Involvement Attitudes of Voluntary Defectors from Controversial New Religious Movements." *Journal for the Scientific Study of Religion* 23 (2): 172–82.

———. 1987. *Leaving Cults: The Dynamics of Defection.* Washington, DC: Society for the Scientific Study of Religion.

———. 1988. "Leaving New Religious Movements: Issues, Theory, and Research." In *Falling from the Faith,* edited by David G. Bromley. Newbury Park, CA: Sage.

Wright, Stuart A., and Helen R. Ebaugh. 1993. "Leaving New Religions." In *Handbook of Cults and Sects in America,* edited by David G. Bromley and Jeffrey K. Hadden, pp. 143–65. Greenwich, CT: JAI Press.

Zald, Mayer N., and John McCarthy. 1977. *The Dynamics of Social Movements.* Cambridge, MA: Winthrop.

———. 1979. *The Dynamics of Social Movements: Resource Mobilization, Social Control, and Tactics.* Cambridge, MA: Winthrop.

———. 1987. *Social Movements in an Organizational Society.* New Brunswick: Transaction.

Zurcher, Louis, and Roger J. Kilpatrick. 1976. *Citizens for Decency: Anti-Pornography Campaigns as Status Defense.* Austin: University of Texas.

5

JAMES R. LEWIS

Rodney King's beating captured the nation's attention for more than a year. The extermination of more than 80 Americans during an armed attack by federal agents outside Waco [quickly slipped off] the front pages. But then, King is a black man whose maltreatment came to symbolize police violence against the poor. The Davidians were "a cult," and thus exempted from justice and compassion.

Alexander Cockburn,
LA Times

Self-Fulfilling Stereotypes, the Anticult Movement, and the Waco Confrontation

While certain anticult organizations expressed satisfaction with the attention their interpretations of events received in the mass media during the Branch Davidian drama, the direct influence of organized anticultism upon federal and other agencies involved in the siege was probably less significant than some have claimed.[1] Of course, this is not to deny the direct but limited involvement of anticult organizations in the BATF investigation or its continued influence and lobbying after the failed assault at Mt. Carmel, as other contributors to this volume attest. But upon close examination, it may be argued that the anticult movement has been most influential in its successful campaign to construct and rein- force—indirectly—negative stereotypes about nontraditional reli- gions in the media and in the general public. Moreover, it reflects the pervasive receptivity of society to such disparaging labels, historical- ly imputed to ethnic, racial, or religious minorities. Thus the wide- spread popularity of the cult stereotype that was invoked in Waco is suggestive of a disposition to accept rigid and denigrating images that is deeply ingrained in American culture long before the first shot was fired at Mt. Carmel.

By attending to certain themes in anticult discourse, it should be possible to identify some of the forces that effectively enhance the receptivity of contemporary society to negative, stereotyped images of cults. Specifically, relevant social-psychological research indicates that, once a stereotype has been accepted, it structures and molds our perceptions so that we tend to notice and process information that conforms to our image of the stereotyped group, and to neglect or dis- regard other kinds of information. What this meant for the Waco con- frontation was that once the label "cult" was successfully applied to the Branch Davidians, the information that the mass media gathered about Koresh and his followers was selectively appropriated so that almost everything the public heard or saw about the Davidians con- formed to our stereotype about cults, and thus helped to fuel the final, fiery holocaust of the Mt. Carmel community.

The Anticult Movement

In the early seventies opposition to religious innovation was cen- tered around deprogrammers—individuals who forcibly abducted members of nontraditional religions, locked them up in motel rooms, and assaulted their beliefs until they gave up their religious faith (Kelley 1977; Shupe and Bromley 1980). Despite claims that deprogramming was and is a therapeutic intervention that breaks through the cult members' "hypnotic trance" and forces them to think more clearly (see Hassan 1988; Langone 1993; Ross and Lan- gone 1988), it is evident that many deprogrammers are little more than vigilantes or moral entrepreneurs acting at the behest of parents upset by the religious choices of their adult children (Bromley and Richardson 1983; Bromley and Shupe 1987, 1993). This critical eval- uation of deprogramming is reinforced by the observation that, as a group, deprogrammers often have little or no training in counseling, though there is an increasing professionalization among some psychologists and social workers specializing in "exit counseling" (Bromley and Shupe 1987; Robbins 1988; Wright and Ebaugh 1993).

Deprogramming, controlled entirely by independent entrepreneurs, however, could never have developed into a viable profession without the simultaneous development of secular "cult watchdog groups." These organizations, despite vigorous public denials to the contrary, regularly refer concerned parents to deprogrammers. The evidence for this connection is overwhelming. For example, the former national director of a large anticult group once sent me an "information" sheet that can best be described as a consumer's guide to deprogramming—a set of questions one should ask prospective deprogrammers. Also, at the national gatherings of the Cult Awareness Network (CAN; formerly the Citizens Freedom Foundation, or CFF), one always finds a host of deprogrammers actively marketing their services to the concerned parents in attendance. Deprogrammers, in turn, allegedly kick back a certain percentage of their fees to CAN. John Myles Sweeney, former national director of CAN/CFF, described this arrangement recently in a sworn affidavit: "Because of the large amount of money they make due to referrals received from CFF members, deprogrammers usually kick back money to the CFF member who gave the referral. . . . The kick backs would either be in cash or would be hidden in the form of a tax-deductible 'donation' to the CFF" (Sweeney 1992, 1).

One of the results of the financial linkages between anticult groups and deprogrammers is that anticult groups acquire a vested interest in promoting the worst possible stereotypes of nontraditional religions. In other words, if one is profiting from referring worried and distraught parents to deprogrammers, it makes no sense to inform parents that the religion their child has joined is comparatively benign. Instead, one tends to paint such religions in the exaggerated colors of fear and fanaticism, creating the anxiety that unless their child is "rescued" immediately, he or she could end up as a lobotomized robot, suffering from permanent emotional and psychological damage.

Similarly, it makes little sense to propagate a balanced view of alternative religions to the press. If one profits from the fear associated with such groups, then one takes every opportunity to repeat frightening rumors. It is, in fact, the two-decade-long interaction between the anticult movement and the media that has been largely responsible for the widespread view that all new or unconventional religions, that is, "cults," are dangerous organizations—this in spite of the fact that comparatively few such groups constitute a genuine threat, either to themselves or to society.

Direct Influence of the Anticult Movement in the Waco Tragedy

The general atmosphere of distrust toward minority religions contributed significantly to public support for the BATF assault on Mt. Carmel, and probably even explains why the BATF selected a group like the Davidians for their dramatic, public raid. It may be argued, from a law enforcement perspective, that the BATF knew that the press would readily accept their portrayal of the Branch Davidians as violent, fanatical cultists, and thus that the deeper kinds of questions about the sortie would be short-circuited (Oliver 1994). Unlike other minority groups, nontraditional religions are not protected by a consensus of favorable public opinion (see Bromley and Breschel 1992; Richardson 1992), nor do they enjoy the usual patronage of those with liberal political leanings. Compare, for example, the public response to the assault on Rodney King with the response to the Waco attack. What if, instead of King, police had chased a speeding David Koresh around the streets of Los Angeles, and then beat the Davidian prophet senseless? Would there have been the same public outcry against the brutality of the LAPD? In any case, certainly the city would not have erupted into riots if police had been absolved from excessive-force violations against Koresh.

While there were comparatively few direct connections between the BATF and the anticult movement that contributed to the Waco fiasco, they were significant. In particular, the testimony of a deprogrammed former Davidian, David Block, was adduced to support the contention that Koresh possessed massive firepower and illegal weapons, which appears to have been instrumental in the BATF's ability to obtain a search warrant (U.S. Department of Treasury 1993, 143). Indeed, evidence for the warrants appears to rest largely on the accounts of apostates. The Treasury Department record shows that the investigative agent for the BATF sought to secure a warrant on November 2, 1992, which was denied by the magistrate for insufficient evidence (p. D-5). However, on November 20, less than three weeks later, the agent returned and was able to secure warrants. The only additional evidence apparently acquired during this time, according to the Treasury Department record, was "soft" data—information obtained from interviews with apostates and family members of Davidians (pp. 46–47, D-5).

Equally important was the advisory role that Rick Ross played with the BATF prior to the attack. Before the blood had even dried in the fields surrounding Mt. Carmel, Ross was busy promoting himself to the media on the basis of his role as advisor to the BATF. What were the qualifications that allowed this person to have the ear of the BATF? Ross, it turns out, had deprogrammed several Branch Davidians. What was his background and training? It was certainly not counseling. Ross is an ex-convict with a psychiatric record. After completing an apprenticeship in petty crime, he graduated to the more lucrative career of deprogrammer, and as someone who makes his living deprogramming "cult" members for money, Ross clearly has a vested interest in portraying nontraditional religions in the worst possible light. For example, in his forward to Tim Madigan's *See No Evil: Blind Devotion and Bloodshed in David Koresh's Holy War*, Ross paints a picture of the evils of all nontraditional religions in the boldest possible colors:

> America must take a long, hard look at Vernon Howell, later known to the world as David Koresh, because among cult leaders, he is not atypical. It seems they are all the same. As I travel the country and delve into different destructive cults, I meet the same cult leader over and over again. Only the names are different. They are self-obsessed, egomaniacal, sociopathic and heartless individuals with no regard whatsoever for their followers. They seek only their personal aggrandizement, financial well-being and physical pleasure. Such leaders exercise total control over their followers. The personalities of those adherents have been dismantled by systematic brainwashing to the point where the leader's desires become their own. Cult victims and fanatical followers of radical sects are deceived, lied to, manipulated and ultimately exploited. (Ross 1993, x)

From these characteristically facile and indiscriminant statements, it is possible to see how the BATF's distorted impressions of the Branch Davidians could easily have been created by misinformation received from Ross and others.

Even after the senseless BATF raid, Ross continued to be consulted by the relevant law-enforcement agencies. He spoke with the FBI in early and late March. In the latter meeting, he recommended that the FBI employ tactics that would humiliate Koresh, in an attempt to alienate the Davidians from their leader. While Ross may or may not have been directly responsible, such tactics were, in fact, deployed. This strategy, while often effective in a deprogramming situation (with which Ross was intimately familiar), was clearly inappropriate for a siege (with which Ross had no experience whatsoever). The FBI's utilization of this tactic merely increased Koresh's distrust of the agency.

The great bulk of the information that Rick Ross communicated to the BATF and the FBI, however, would have done little other than reinforce the widely prevalent stereotype of cults as criminal organizations ready to commit the worst atrocities at the mere bidding of a maniacal leader. The anticultists' main contribution to the Branch Davidian holocaust was in the preceding two decades of their influence over the mass media, and, in turn, over public opinion, which has resulted in the adoption of an essentially "demonic" (Pfohl 1994) view of nontraditional religions.

The long-term effectiveness of anticult propaganda was evident from the very beginning of the crisis, when the media immediately, unreflectively, and irresponsibly began referring to the Branch Davidians as a "cult." This labeling activity began with the original affidavit in which Special Agent Davy Aguilera consistently used the term—never once affording the respect implied in a less stigmatic term like "church" or "religion"—and continued unabated until the Davidians went up in flames. Anticultists candidly acknowledged the impact of their ongoing propaganda efforts in shaping the public response to Waco. For example, the following remarks from the *Cult Observer* appeared not long after the Waco tragedy ended: "Our efforts at educating and informing the news disseminators as well as the general populace, while we may at times have felt overwhelmed by the challenge, have very clearly paid off" (*Cult Observer,* 1993 [10]: 2).

Anticultists, particularly the self-appointed "cult experts" associated with the secular anticult movement, were quick to exploit the incident for purposes of self-promotion. CAN Executive Director Cynthia Kisser gave numerous interviews during and after the raid, as did CAN spokesperson Patricia Ryan. Just a few days after the tragic conflagration, Kisser, in characteristic disdain for constitutional protections, opined that "tighter controls on such cult trademarks as home schooling and faith healing could give officials reasons to inspect cult communities and gather evidence of wrongdoing" (Warren 1993, 15A). The *Cult Observer,* in a column entitled "AFF Was Ready," noted that "the AFF office, and professionals from many fields associated with AFF committees and programs, were able at every stage to provide studied commentary and analysis to major national and international media" (1993 [10]: 2).

Yet, while the media eagerly gathered sound bites from anticult spokespersons, the social institutions with the real power to decide the fate of the Branch Davidians—namely, the federal government and the law enforcement agencies in Waco—neglected to consult organizations like CAN or AFF, either before, during, or after the Mt.

Carmel siege.[2] Even Ross found himself out in the cold when questions began to be raised about the appropriateness of the BATF and FBI consulting a deprogrammer. Thus the anticult movement was in an awkward position with respect to Waco. On the one hand, it seemed that the anticult perspective on nontraditional religions completely dominated public perceptions of the incident. On the other hand, anticult organizations had little direct input into the agencies that ultimately decided the fate of the Branch Davidians.

Though some direct involvement of anticult organizations occurred, I want to advance the argument that the influence exercised by the anticult movement was more indirect, providing a subtle but pervasive stereotype of intolerance. Anticultism feeds upon— and in turn feeds—a public predisposition to perceive nontraditional religions in a disparaging light.[3] We might best understand this predisposition in terms of the social psychology of stereotyping.

Stereotyping Cults

Over a decade ago, sociologist Tom Robbins observed that if someone at a previously unknown vegetarian community died from being squashed by a giant cabbage, tomorrow's headline news story— spread sensationally across the front page—would be a report on an act of "cult violence."[4] The incident would also immediately become fodder for the propaganda mill of anticult organizations, and be offered as an example of "what these awful groups are capable of." This hypothetical community, which prior to the member's unfortunate death, had never been considered "cultic," would then be mentioned in all future discussions of *destructive cults.*

Robbins's observation provides a fitting analog for the Mt. Carmel fiasco. Prior to the BATF attack, the Branch Davidians were a little-known religious group on the outskirts of Waco. Although some people familiar with the community had found it to be somewhat eccentric, the Davidians enjoyed reasonably good relations with their neighbors and the citizens of Waco (Pitts, this volume). There is no evidence that the group was considered to be a "cult," and it was certainly not cast in the same mold as such groups as the Manson Family or People's Temple, as it was contended later.[5] In the wake of the tragedy, however, the Branch Davidians were transformed overnight into the paradigmatic *evil cult.* Instantaneously, the actions of Koresh and his followers became the penultimate examples of abuse, manipulation, violence—actions that, in the view of anticultists, should force the government to now "do something" about these sinister cults. Public (and law enforcement) acceptance of this revisionist history of the Branch Davidians requires some systematic explanation.

The post hoc reasoning demonstrated here is the same illogic of stereotyping from which many minorities have suffered:

- •If a black man rapes a woman, then all black men must be rapists.
- •If a Jew cheats a neighbor, then all Jews must be cheaters.
- •If a homosexual molests a young boy, then all homosexuals must be pedophiles.
- •If a nontraditional religious group in the boondocks of Texas shoots four lawmen, then all nontraditional religions must be violent cults.

We immediately recognize these prejudiced stereotypes for what they are when applied to racial, ethnic, and sexual lifestyle minorities, but often fail to recognize such flagrantly demeaning stereotypes when applied to nontraditional religions.

What is a stereotype? Stereotypes are generalizations about *other* groups of people, but they are a peculiar type of generalization. "Stereotypes are used to ascribe incorrectly certain characteristics to whole groups of people and then explain or excuse social problems in light of these characteristics" (Rothenberg 1988, 253). Stereotypes are usually held rigidly, in that we tend to ignore or to dismiss evidence that flies in the face of our generalization. Such rigidity indicates that the stereotype "may be relatively fundamental to our conceptual scheme, it may protect our self-esteem, it may help bring about some desirable situation, or it may shield us from facing [some] unpleasant fact" (Andre 1988, 257). Thus the stereotype depicting certain races as lazy (NORC 1989, 27), for example, would simultaneously boost the self-esteem of society's dominant racial group as well as blind one to the inequalities of existing social arrangements. It is relatively easy to recognize that most generalizations about new religions are little more than negative stereotypes; but what are the social forces that make such stereotypes peculiarly attractive to contemporary society?

One of the more widely accepted dictums of sociology is that societies need enemies, particularly societies that are going through a disturbing period of change. External threats provide motivation for people to overcome internal divisiveness in order to work together as a unit. Conversely, "the unity of the group is often lost when it has no longer any opponent" (Simmel 1955, 97). Having an enemy one can portray as evil and perverse may provide social solidarity and support for the normative values and institutions of one's society

(Durkheim 1960; Erikson 1966). According to Durkheim, it creates a sense of mutuality among people in the community by supplying a focus for group feeling and a fusing together of private sentiments. Like a war, a flood, or some other emergency, an enemy can bring individuals together in a common posture of dependency, anger, or indignation. For example, such dynamics were evident in cold-war rhetoric: "They" are Communists; "we" are capitalists. "They" are totalitarian; "we" are democratic. Typically, the highest expressions of patriotism were attacks on communism.

One of the corollaries of this theory is that in situations where external enemies no longer threaten, a society will find groups or individuals within its own perimeters that it can construe as threatening and evil. Such enemies become particularly important to communities passing through a crisis in which fundamental values are being called into question. In the words of Albert Bergesen, "A community will commence to ritually persecute imaginary enemies— conduct a witchhunt—to manufacture moral deviants as a means of ritually reaffirming the group's problematical values and collective purposes" (1984, vii). Deviants come to symbolize or personify changes, threats to the status quo, where "the community is confronted by a significant relocation of (moral) boundaries" (Erikson 1966, 68). Thus there appear to be two independent variables that can account for this phenomenon; one is the crisis of cultural change and the other is existence of external threat. The latter has been effectively supported by various historical studies. For example, in a seminal work on New England witchcraft, John Demos (1982) found that the persecution and execution of "witches"—usually unsocial, churlish old women—abated during periods of war, and reappeared after peace had returned.

As a potent international threat, communism has largely disappeared. The only significant remaining Communist power is Red China, and the Chinese are more interested in cooperating with the West than in challenging it. Other threats, such as Iraq, flare up and pass rather quickly. The lack of pressing external enemies in combination with our current, ongoing social crisis would lead the sociologically informed observer to anticipate that our culture might have a tendency to seek out groups within its own boundaries to take the place of Communists (see Richardson, this volume).

Unless there are groups that are consciously antisocial or criminal—such as gangs—the deviations from the norm that a community chooses to perceive as threatening are somewhat arbitrary. The people traditionally construed as deviants by our culture have been racial, ethnic, and sexual minorities (e.g., African Americans, Jews, and homosexuals). In recent years, however, it has become socially unacceptable to castigate or malign these groups, at least in the overt manner in which they have been attacked in the past. This leaves few groups of any significant size to persecute. Unfortunately, one of the few minorities that liberals have been slow to defend are nontraditional religions. This is due to a number of different factors, including the resistance of traditionally conservative religions to liberal politics and policies advocating progressive change. The failure of normally open-minded people to protect religious pluralism has allowed contemporary witch-hunters to declare open season on marginal religions or "cults."

Groups of people seen as threatening frequently become screens onto which a society projects its fears and anxieties. If, for example, a culture is troubled by sexual issues (as is often the case), then its enemies are perceived as perverse, sexually deviant. Racial minorities, who have often been viewed as promiscuous and sexually aggressive, have suffered from this stigma. This was also a dominant theme in nineteenth-century anti-Catholic and anti-Mormon literature (Lewis 1989; Miller 1983). Contemporary unconventional groups, of course, suffer the same fate.

In the classical formulation of psychological projection, Freud (1938), who was especially concerned with sex and violence, viewed it as a defense mechanism against unacceptable inner urges. Thus in a society with strict sexual mores, an individual who perpetually repressed such urges might perceive rather ordinary dancing, let us say, as sexually suggestive. Becoming enraged at such "loose" behavior, one might then attempt to lead a movement to impose prohibitions against dancing, restrict the activities of musicians and promoters (purveyors of "dirty" dancing), and have all of the dance halls closed down. According to Freud, this hypothetical individual's inner struggle was "projected" externally to provide a script for an outer struggle (i.e., internally he or she is repressing libidinal urges while symbolically battling the same desires in the external world). The same process may be at work in the collective interaction of society, perceiving marginal groups as sexually deviant. For instance, the stereotype of the sexually abusive cult leader, routinely forcing devotees to satisfy his or her sexual whims, perfectly captures the fantasy of many members of society who desire to sexually control any person they wish.

The same analogy holds true for aggressive urges. We live in a society with relatively strict sanctions against overt violence; simultaneously, violence is glorified in the entertainment media. This introduces a cultural contradiction that is projected onto enemies and deviant groups, with the result that minorities are often perceived as violent and belligerent. This accusation is also regularly aimed at nontraditional religions. In particular, the radical actions of a tiny handful of alternative religions is mistakenly taken to indicate a widespread tendency among all such groups.

We can generalize beyond Freudian psychology's emphasis on sex and aggression to see that many other cultural anxieties and contradictions are selectively assigned to minority groups. For instance, our society gives us contradictory messages about the relative importance of wealth, property, and material success. On the one hand, we are taught that economic pursuits are supposed to be secondary to higher moral, social, and religious concerns. On the other hand, we receive many messages from the surrounding society that the single-minded pursuit of wealth is the principal activity of economic life. This inherent contradiction is typically ignored or overlooked with regard to mainstream religions where gross socioeconomic inequities exist within the same community, or where religious elites and hierarchies enjoy favored status and privilege. However, that such tensions are seen with any clarity only in alternative religions, as represented in the infamous stereotype of the money-hungry cult leader who demands that her or his followers lead lives of squalor or poverty while the leader wallows in riches, begs the question.

Similarly, the child abuse accusation and contemporary society's seeming obsession with child abuse flows out of another cultural contradiction. Our cultural heritage (at least post-Victorian), supported by modern psychology, holds out the ideal of a child who is constantly under the wing of a loving parent, usually the mother. Current economic conditions, however, often require both parents to work full-time, which usually entails leaving young children in the care of strangers. This results in a good deal of guilt, generating a widespread anxiety about the precariousness of children, which is easily displaced and projected in the form of stereotypes of deviance in such groups as nontraditional religions (see Ellison and Bartkowski, this volume). Is there any reason to assume that the incidence rates among marginal sects exceeds that of more mainstream religious organizations, such as in the Catholic church? Like the isolated instances of violence, the radical actions of a tiny handful of adherents to alternative religions who have abused children is mistakenly taken to indicate a pervasive tendency among all such groups. Despite the outcry against the Branch Davidians, for example, our best current information is that, while strict, the Davidians did not abuse their children. The readiness of the media and the public, however, to embrace the stereotype of child abusing cultists convicted David Koresh before he was able to receive a fair hearing.

One of the more important cultural contradictions indexed in alternative religions is tied to the brainwashing/mind control notion that is the core accusation leveled against such groups. Discourse that glorifies American society usually does so in terms of a rhetoric of liberty and freedom. However, while holding liberty as an ideal, many Americans experience an occupational environment that is often quite controlled and restrictive. Only about one in six persons works in a professional occupation where greater autonomy and independent decision making are commonly exercised. Most citizens work as employees in highly disciplined or regimented jobs where the only real freedom is the freedom to quit. Also, we are bombarded by advertising designed to influence our decisions and even to create new needs. Our frustration with these forms of influence and control is easily displaced and projected onto the separated societies of alternative religions, where the seemingly restricted flow of information offers a distorted reflection of the situation we experience as members of the dominant society.

The accusation of control is both curious and puzzling because of its role in the Waco debacle. Readers who followed the siege on Mt. Carmel may recall the FBI spokesman who made the peculiar complaint that David Koresh was in "total control" of the situation. Here was a community pinned down by a small army of federal agents. The FBI had cut off Mt. Carmel's water, electricity, and telephones. Tanks had crushed and demolished the community's vehicles (cars, buses, motorcycles), vegetable garden, and the children's toys. A disorienting, agitating, sound-and-light assault dominated the night. Finally, the FBI controlled the flow of information to reporters by keeping them isolated and feeding the media only the information the FBI saw fit to share. Indeed, it was the federal authorities who had total control over the situation. But the agents were frustrated by their inability to control David Koresh enough to force him to surrender, and, in the heat of their frustration, leveled the accusation of "being in total control" at him—not realizing how ridiculous they sounded.

The components of the cult stereotype that have been enumerated thus far help to explain certain themes in anticult discourse as well as why this stereotype tends to resonate with public opinion. Without this disposition to construe nontraditional religions negatively, the anticult movement would have little or no social influence. However, while the anticult movement has relatively little direct social power, the stereotype it has helped to shape has taken on a life of its own, independent of organized anticultism.

Self-Fulfilling Stereotypes

Once a stereotype is in place, a variety of studies have shown that it becomes self-fulfilling and self-reinforcing. In a study by Snyder and Uranowitz (Snyder 1988), for example, students were asked to read a short biography about Betty K., a fictitious woman. Her life story was constructed so that it would fulfill certain stereotypes of both het-erosexuals and lesbians. In Snyder's words, "Betty, we wrote, never had a steady boyfriend in high school, but did go out on dates. And although we gave her a steady boyfriend in college, we specified that he was more of a close friend than anything else" (1988, 266). A week later, they told some of the students that Betty was currently living with her husband, and another group of students that she was living with another woman in a lesbian relationship. When subsequently requested to answer a series of questions about Betty, they found a marked tendency on the part of students to reconstruct her biography so as to conform to stereotypes about either heterosexuality or homosexuality, depending on the information they had received.

> Those who believed that Betty was a lesbian remembered that Betty had never had a steady boyfriend in high school, but tended to neglect the fact that she had gone out on many dates in college. Those who believed that Betty was now a heterosexual, tended to remember that she had formed a steady relationship with a man in college, but tended to ignore the fact that this relationship was more of a friendship than a romance. (1988:266–67)

More directly relevant to the case at hand is a study by Pfeifer (1992). Pfeifer reported the results of an experiment that compared responses to the biography of a fictitious student, Bill, who dropped out of college to: (1) enter a Catholic seminary, (2) join the Marines, or (3) join the Moonies. The short biography incorporated elements of indoctrination or thought control often attributed to cults. The fol-lowing excerpt is an example:

> While at the facility, Bill is not allowed very much contact with his friends or family and he notices that he is seldom left alone. He also notices that he never seems to be able to talk to the other four people who signed up for the program and that he is continually surrounded by [Moonies, Marines, Priests] who make him feel guilty if he questions any of their actions or beliefs. (1992, 535)

When given a choice in how to describe Bill's indoctrination experience, subjects who thought Bill had joined the Catholic priesthood most often labeled his indoctrination "resocialization"; those who were told that he had joined the Marines most frequently labeled the process "conversion"; and those who were under the impression that he had become a Moonie applied the label "brainwashing." On various other questions regarding the desirability and fairness of the indoctrination process, subjects who were told that Bill had joined the Moonies consistently evaluated his experience more negatively than subjects who were under the impression that Bill had joined either the Marines or a priestly order.

Summary

The implications of these studies and supporting arguments for the Waco situation should be clear. The Branch Davidians' chances for a fair hearing were severely damaged as soon as the label "cult" was applied. After that, the mass media selectively sought out and presented information about Koresh and his community that conveniently fit the stereotype. It was only a matter of time before law enforcement and the media had completely demonized Koresh and his followers. Anticult organizations provided ample fodder for the ritual and symbolic castigation of this little-known religious sect, simplistically reducing the beliefs and practices of the community to vapid, inane categories of brainwashing rhetoric. After this demonization had been successfully accomplished, the entire community—men, women, and children—could be consigned to their tragic fate with little more than a peep of protest from the American public, a public which overwhelmingly approved of the FBI's tragic final assault on Mt. Carmel.

Notes

1. I refer here to some of the allegations that amount to conspiratorial theories about the role of the Cult Awareness Network (CAN) by right-wing groups and patriot organizations. While CAN undoubtedly exercised some influence on the entire Waco debacle, it would be misleading to accord them more power and influence than they actually had throughout the incident. In this way, I think it more appropriate to concentrate the analysis on the pervasive but indirect influence on public opinion that the anticult movement has had over the long term, especially since Jonestown.

2. While the evidence certainly points to individuals such as Ross, whose affiliation with CAN is well known, it is less clear that any organizations were directly consulted. It is also likely that BATF and FBI investigators were unaware of Ross's ties to CAN.

3. Paradoxically, one could turn the notion of "destructive cults" on

its head to refer to "destructive anticults"—organizations of religious hate groups formed for the purpose of ridding society of marginal religions. If the proposition is true that anticults contributed to the destruction of the Branch Davidians, then one can entertain the logical conclusion that some anticult organizations are also "destructive."

4. The statement was made offhandedly during a session at the annual meetings of the Society for the Scientific Study of Religion in 1982.

5. Of course, apostates and anticultists made such claims in their narratives or accounts when attempting to gain the attention of authorities. But the fact that they were largely dismissed by local and state officials in Texas (see Breault and King 1993, chap. 23) indicates the extent to which the cult label was publicly adopted only after the raid.

References

Andre, Judith. 1988. "Stereotypes: Conceptual and Normative Considerations." In *Racism and Sexism,* edited by Paula Rothenberg, pp. 257–62. New York: St. Martins.

Bergesen, Albert. 1984. *The Sacred and the Subversive: Political Witch-Hunts as National Rituals.* Storrs, CT: SSSR Monograph Series.

Bromley, David G., and Edward Breschel. 1992. "General Population and Institutional Support for Social Control of New Religious Movements: Evidence from National Survey Data." *Behavioral Sciences and the Law* 10: 39–52.

Bromley, David G., and James T. Richardson. 1983. *The Brainwashing/Deprogramming Controversy.* New York: Edwin Mellen.

Bromley, David G., and Anson Shupe. 1987. "The Future of the Anticult Movement." In *The Future of New Religious Movements,* edited by David G. Bromley and Phillip E. Hammond, pp. 221–34.

———. 1993. "Organized Opposition to New Religious Movements." In *The Handbook on Cults and Sects in America,* edited by David G. Bromley and Jeffrey K. Hadden, pp. 177–98. Greenwich, CT: JAI Press.

Cockburn, Alexander. "From Salem to Waco, by Way of the Nazis." *Los Angeles Times,* April 27, 1993, p. B7.

Demos, John Putnam. 1982. *Entertaining Satan: Witchcraft and the Culture of Early New England.* New York: Oxford University Press.

Durkheim, Emile. 1960. *The Division of Labor in Society.* Translated by George Simpson. New York: Free Press.

Erikson, Kai. 1966. *Wayward Puritans.* New York: Wiley.

Freud, Sigmund. 1938. *The Basic Writings of Sigmund Freud.* Translated by A. A. Brill. New York: Modern Library.

Hassan, Steven. 1988. *Combatting Mind Control.* Rochester, VT: Park Street Press.

Kelley, Dean. 1977. "Deprogramming and Religious Liberty." *Civil Liberties Review* (July/August): 22–33.

Langone, Michael D. 1993. *Recovery from Cults.* New York: Norton.

Lewis, James R. 1989. "Apostates and the Legitimation of Repression:

Some Empirical and Historical Perspectives." *Sociological Analysis* 49 (4): 386–96.

Miller, Donald E. 1983. "Deprogramming in Historical Perspective." In *The Deprogramming/Brainwashing Controversy*, edited by David G. Bromley and James T. Richardson, pp. 15–28. New York: Edwin Mellen.

NORC. 1989. *General Social Surveys, 1972–1989: Cumulative Code-book*. Chicago: National Opinion Research Center.

Oliver, Moorman, Jr. 1994. "Killed by Semantics." In *From the Ashes: Making Sense of Waco*, edited by James R. Lewis, pp. 71–86. Lanham, MD: Rowman and Littlefield.

Pfeifer, Jeffrey E. 1992. "The Psychological Framing of Cults: Schematic Representations and Cult Evaluations." *Journal of Applied Social Psychology* 22: 531–44.

Pfohl, Stephen. 1994. *Images of Deviance and Social Control*. New York: McGraw-Hill.

Richardson, James T. 1992. "Public Opinion and the Tax Evasion Trial of Reverend Moon." *Behavioral Sciences and the Law* 10: 53–64.

Robbins, Thomas. 1988. *Cults, Converts, and Charisma*. Newbury Park, CA: Sage.

Ross, Catherine, and Michael D. Langone. 1988. *Cults: What Parents Should Know*. Weston, MA: American Family Foundation.

Ross, Rick. 1993. Forward to *See No Evil: Blind Devotion and Bloodshed in David Koresh's Holy War*, by Tim Madigan, pp. ix–xii. Fort Worth, TX: Summit Group.

Rothenberg, Paula. 1988. "The Prison of Race and Gender: Stereotypes, Ideology, Language, and Social Control." In *Racism and Sexism*, edited by Paula Rothenberg, pp. 252–56. NY: St. Martins.

Shupe, Anson D., and David G. Bromley. 1980. *The New Vigilantes: Deprogrammers, Anti-Cultists, and the New Religions*. Beverly Hills: Sage.

Simmel, George. 1955. *Conflict and the Web of Group Affiliations*. Translated by Kurt Wolff and Reinhard Bendix. New York: Free Press.

Snyder, Mark. 1988. "Self-Fulfilling Stereotypes." In *Racism and Sexism*, edited by Paula Rothenberg, pp. 263–69. NY: St. Martins.

Sweeney, John Myles, Jr. 1992. "Declaration of John Myles Sweeney, Jr." Maricopa County, Arizona. Affidavit, March 17.

U.S. Department of Treasury. 1993. *Report of the Department of the Treasury on the Bureau of Alcohol, Tobacco, and Firearms Investigation of Vernon Wayne Howell, Also Known as David Koresh*. Washington, DC: U.S. Government Printing Office.

Warren, Susan. 1993. "Cult Guidelines Become Urgent Need." *Houston Chronicle*, April 25, p. 15A.

Wright, Stuart A., and Helen Rose Ebaugh. 1993. "Leaving New Religions." In *The Handbook on Cults and Sects in America*, edited by David G. Bromley and Jeffrey K. Hadden, pp. 117–38. Greenwich, CT: JAI Press.

6

CHRISTOPHER G. ELLISON AND

JOHN P. BARTKOWSKI

"Babies Were

Being Beaten"

Exploring Child Abuse
Allegations at Ranch
Apocalypse

Soon after the fire at Mount Carmel on April 19, 1993, federal authorities offered a series of child-centered legitimations for the assault. They renewed allegations of extensive child abuse by David Koresh and the Branch Davidians, and they charged that sanitary conditions and the quality of life inside the facility were deteriorating (Kantrowitz et al. 1993b; Reuters 1993). In establishing the urgent need to end the standoff

An earlier version of this chapter was presented at the 1993 meeting of the Society for the Scientific Study of Religion, Raleigh, NC, October 28-31. The authors wish to thank Philip Arnold, David Bromley, Sharon Sandomirsky, and especially Stuart Wright for helpful feedback and suggestions. However, the views and conclusions presented here are those of the authors alone.

between the Branch Davidians and federal agents, Attorney General Janet Reno specifically raised the specter of gruesome forms of child abuse: "We had information that babies were being beaten," she said, "I specifically asked, 'You really mean babies?' 'Yes, he's slapping babies around.' These are concerns that we had" (Verhovek 1993b). Officials close to Reno maintained that her primary concern was the welfare of the children remaining inside the structure at Mt. Carmel (Kantrowitz et al. 1993b). Justice Department spokesman Carl Stern commented: "There were probably half a dozen different factors, but the one that drove [Reno] the most was her concern about the children" (Labaton 1993b).

The day after the fire, President Clinton held a press conference to explain the various rationales behind the fatal assault. After outlining a number of interrelated concerns (e.g., limited federal resources and increasing frustration among law enforcement agents), he reiterated that federal officials "had reason to believe that the children who were still inside the compound were being abused significantly as well as being forced to live in unsanitary and unsafe conditions" (Reuters 1993). Clinton had concluded—largely on Reno's recommendation—that the precarious welfare of the children translated into a need to promptly resolve the standoff (Niebuhr and Thomas 1993). The emphasis on the children's welfare continued. By midweek, White House spokesperson George Stephanopoulos claimed that there were "mountains of evidence" of long-term child abuse by Koresh and his followers, and on Friday Clinton charged: "We know that David Koresh had sex with children . . . Where I come from, that qualifies as child abuse" (Niebuhr and Thomas 1993).

Yet, even as the administration emphasized concerns about the threat of ongoing child abuse, key FBI officials—including Director William Sessions—disclosed that there was, in fact, "no contemporaneous information" of baby beatings or child abuse which justified immediate action (Labaton 1993b). Soon after this information was divulged, public statements by federal officials began to downplay concerns about child abuse, emphasizing instead that increasing pressure on Koresh was necessary because agents had concluded that Koresh would never surrender voluntarily (Labaton 1993b; see also Labaton 1993c).

This apparent confusion among key federal officials invites a careful analysis of the role of child abuse allegations in the Branch Davidian conflict. We believe that these allegations and the institutional and public responses to them are best understood within the context of the current moral panic regarding welfare of the children. Our analysis proceeds as follows. First, we outline historically changing constructions of childhood, which by the late twentieth century have culminated in (1) the hypervaluation of the modern child, (2) the rise of "permissivist" parenting and the democratic family, (3) the proliferation of child-saving movements, and (4) a pervasive anxiety about various threats to the well-being of children (i.e., a contemporary moral panic). These factors enabled former Branch Davidians and other detractors of Koresh to mobilize institutional resources and the media, and attract widespread public attention, with their allegations.

Then, we attempt to assess the child abuse claims themselves and the evidence bearing upon them. We address three types of child abuse allegations faced by Koresh: (1) severe corporal punishment, (2) sexual abuse, and (3) psychological abuse and material deprivation. To be sure, we have no wish to downplay the seriousness of these allegations, or to vindicate Koresh and his followers unduly. Nevertheless, we conclude that the empirical evidence in most of these areas is more limited and more ambiguous than media accounts and government portrayals typically indicated, and we believe that a review of the evidence regarding child abuse at Mt. Carmel reveals a number of inconsistencies that amply suggested the need for more cautious interpretation and adjudication.

The Family and the Child in Historical Perspective

It is now widely recognized that the modern nuclear family—defined by domesticity (i.e., relative social isolation), affective familial relationships, and a quasi-egalitarian family structure—is a relatively recent family form, animated partly by the rise of market capitalism and the demise of traditional local economies (Aries 1965; Shorter 1977; Stone 1977). Many historians also agree that beliefs regarding the nature of children and proper parenting are culturally and historically specific (Aries 1965; Degler 1980; deMause 1974; Hernandez 1993; Shorter 1977; Strathman 1984; Zelizer 1985). Indeed, much of the contemporary wisdom about the appropriateness of democratic and egalitarian modes of family organization and practice, and about the intrinsic moral goodness of children, is of quite recent origin, as is the ubiquitous concern—sometimes bordering on hysteria—about the vulnerability and (allegedly) widespread victimization of children by adults (Best 1990; Jenkins 1992; Nelson 1984). We argue that the emergence, content, and reception of the child abuse allegations leveled against David Koresh and the Branch Davidians are best understood in light of the contemporary "moral panic" about child welfare issues. This context afforded a cultural environment in which such allegations were treated rather uncritically by media, public officials, and the general public, as well as a fertile legal environment in which detractors of the group and various moral entrepreneurs could press their attacks on the group for its alleged maltreatment of children.

The Nature and Social Value of Children

In contrast to the traditional view of children as miniature adults, the modern perspective holds that *children are inherently different from adults* (Aries 1965; Degler 1980). The assignment of roles within the modern family, for example, often hinges on a distinction between parental obligations (e.g., paid labor outside the home) and tasks assigned to children (e.g., school attendance, menial duties within the home). In addition, the modern view of children rejects the traditional notion that youngsters are innately evil (Degler 1980; deMause 1974), and instead holds that *children are innocent, vulnerable, and in need of parental love and protection* (Aries 1965; Degler 1980; Demos 1973; Shorter 1977; Stone 1977). Prior to the seventeenth century, traditional religious perceptions about the depravity of children led many parents to treat youngsters with indifference or to promote feelings of inadequacy in their "willful" children (Demos 1973; Illick 1974; Osborne 1989). Beliefs about the inherent sinfulness of children led evangelical Protestant parents in early America to seek to "break the will" of their youngsters (Greven 1977, 1990). To exact conformity from their "rebellious" children, parents frequently bound their children with cloth (swaddling), imposed food restrictions upon them, threatened youngsters with frightening images, or physically punished children (Greven 1977; see also deMause 1974). Leading evangelicals of the day argued that a failure to curb childish license would result first in the overt rejection of parental authority, and would lead ultimately to the eternal damnation of the child.

In sharp contrast to these earlier practices, modern perspectives on children have been strongly influenced by the ideas of Locke, who saw children as morally neutral and, more recently, by the humanistic insights of Rousseau, who emphasized the innate goodness of children (see Osborne 1989; Nelson 1984; Strathman 1984; Walzer 1974). Thus, historians suggest that, beginning in the late eighteenth and early nineteenth centuries, child-rearing methods tended to rely less on frequent and severe corporal punishment (deMause 1974; Degler 1980; Walzer 1974), and increasingly involved maternal affection and greater parental involvement (Shorter 1977; Aries 1965; Strathman 1984).

During the twentieth century, modernist conceptions of morally pure children and nonpunitive parenting became the received wisdom, promulgated by various child-rearing experts (Strathman 1984).[1] Indeed, analyses of public opinion and other types of data indicate that since the early decades of the twentieth century, American parents have downplayed the importance of children's obedience, instead emphasizing their intellectual autonomy and personality development (Miller and Swanson 1958; Alwin 1984, 1988).

While the views of contemporary secular child-rearing experts vary widely, several themes surface consistently in popular advice manuals produced since the 1960s (Bartkowski and Ellison, 1995). First, secular specialists often focus on the need for parents to develop "healthy" self-concepts (i.e., self-esteem, personal mastery, confidence) and interpersonal competence in their youngsters. Second, these secular child-rearing experts tend to endorse relatively egalitarian and democratic models of family practice, centering on the "rights" and "interests" of children, and on processes of negotiation between parents and children. Third, perhaps the most common image of the ideal parent in secular child-rearing literature is that of the proactive tactician or household manager, who manipulates the child's environment to minimize the potential for family conflict and to facilitate the child's safe exploration of the physical and social world. Finally, secular specialists are virtually unanimous in vigorously rejecting the use of corporal punishment; indeed, a growing number of academics and policymakers label as "child abuse" any use of physical force by parents (see the recent exchange between Straus [1994] and Larzelere [1994]). Instead of corporal punishment, child-rearing experts promote the use of positive reinforcement, time-out, empathetic communication and reasoning, natural consequences, and a plethora of nonconfrontational disciplinary tactics.[2]

Hypervaluation and Moral Panic

In addition to these dramatic shifts in prevailing conceptions of childhood and parenting, public concern about the welfare of the Branch Davidian children may be traced to two interrelated twentieth-century developments: (1) the hypervaluation of children; and (2) the proliferation of "child-saving movements" (Best 1990; Jenkins 1992; Nelson 1984; Parton 1985). According to Zelizer (1985), the redefinition of youngsters as innocent and vulnerable within the early nineteenth-century family had, by the late 1800s and early 1900s, led to the hypervaluation of children throughout the public sphere as well. For instance, accidental deaths of children, once treated with relative indifference, now had become a cause for public mourning. And bereaved parents, who formerly were reimbursed solely for the estimated wages of their deceased youngster, could now seek compensation based on the tragic loss of their dearly loved child. In effect, the sacralized child became an economically "worthless," yet emotionally "priceless," member of family and society (Zelizer 1985). The late nineteenth and early twentieth centuries also witnessed a dramatic escalation of fears about various types of "child-victims" in society at large (Best 1990). In addition to concern over accidental child death, anxieties increased about child kidnaping, missing children, child labor, child pornography, the sexual abuse of children, and black-market babies (Best 1990, Jenkins 1992; Parton 1985; Zelizer 1985).

This historic explosion of concern about threats to children might best be described as a *moral panic*, that is, a periodic state of heightened moral anxiety in which a society identifies an issue or group as a threat to social values. Jenkins (1992) has examined various moral panics over the welfare of British children (e.g., child murder, pedophilia, child abuse) and has suggested some similarities between recent definitions of "social menaces" in Britain and the United States. Jenkins maintains that the rapid acceptance of child sexual abuse as a British social problem was due, in part, to the successful lobbying activities of various groups (e.g., child advocates, social service agencies, and feminists concerned with sexual violence) interested in identifying this problem and proposing solutions to it. An examination of American public debate about child abuse reveals a remarkably similar pattern. Best (1990) has traced current concerns about missing children to a series of previous anxieties about the safety and well-being of American youngsters: the battered child syndrome in the early 1960s; runaways and Halloween sadism later in that same decade; sexual abuse, child pornography, and child snatching in the 1970s; and ritual abuse and missing children in the 1980s. Taken together, these concerns suggest that anxieties about the welfare of American children have intensified considerably over the last several decades.

Child Abuse Legislation

Among the earliest promoters of child advocacy, private child protective societies were organized in the late 1800s to rescue children from threats to their morals, safety, health, and welfare (Nelson 1984; Parton 1985; Pfohl 1977). By the early twentieth century, the efforts of these societies were complemented by those of federal agencies, such as the Children's Bureau. Following the decline of the private protective societies, the 1950s witnessed a resurgence in concern about child abuse, due in part to broader public debates about social equity (e.g., the civil rights movement and, later, the War on Poverty). The Children's Bureau, with an increased postwar budget at its disposal, began sponsoring research on child abuse and disseminating relevant findings to American families (Nelson 1984).

During the 1950s and early 1960s, the subject of child abuse also began attracting increased attention from physicians (specifically, pediatricians and radiologists) and from the media (Nelson 1984; Johnson 1985, 1989). Like child welfare workers, these interest groups sought to make the American public aware of the recently discovered "battered child syndrome." During the early 1960s, the Children's Bureau, the American Academy of Pediatrics, and the Council of State Legislatures proposed model statutes to encourage reporting of physical abuse. Between 1963 and 1967, every state and the District of Columbia passed some form of a child abuse reporting law (Nelson 1984).

Such a rapid adoption of reporting laws at the state level was facilitated by a narrow definition of child abuse, namely as "physical injuries or injury which appear to have been inflicted upon the child by other than accidental means" (quoted in Nelson 1984, 14). This narrow definition reflected the leadership role of medical personnel in the mobilization against child abuse; pediatricians and technicians characterized abuse primarily in terms of physical conditions they could identify and measure. However, by the time federal legislation was passed in 1974, child abuse was defined much more comprehensively to include "physical or mental injury, sexual abuse, negligent treatment, or maltreatment [and harm or threats to] . . . the child's health or welfare" (quoted in Nelson 1984, 14).[3] This broadening of the definition of child abuse reflected not only the finesse of liberal politicians, but also the engagement of social workers, clinicians, and other child advocacy interests. Consistent with the broader federal definition of child abuse, the adoption of "protective custody" provisions permitted police, physicians, and in some cases child welfare workers to remove children immediately from families when harm seemed imminent (Nelson 1984).

Sexual Abuse Legislation

The identification of and legislative response to child sexual abuse followed a historical trajectory that is remarkably similar to that of physical abuse, and provides further evidence of the strength and pervasiveness of twentieth-century concerns about the victimization of children (Best 1990, 71–74; Johnson 1985; Weisberg 1984; see Berrick and Gilbert 1991, 1–6; Kocen and Bulkley 1981; Russell

1984; Viinikka 1989 for related historical overviews). Until the late 1800s, legal measures were designed to protect only very young children from sexual exploitation (Kocen and Bulkley 1981). Girls over the age of ten were protected solely from nonconsensual sex, and only by broader laws against forcible rape. However, twentieth-century concerns about the victimization of children caused increasing attention to be given to adult-child sexual contact and led to several significant definitional and legal changes related to child sexual abuse (Weisberg 1984). In the 1930s, psychiatrists diagnosed child molesters as suffering from "sexual psychopathy," a disorder which was believed to be remedied by extending appropriate medical treatment to the patient. Early child sex abuse laws, which stressed rehabilitating rather than punishing the perpetrator, were modeled on this medical interpretation of the problem. Since the 1950s, however, other interested professionals have successfully challenged the early medicalization of child sexual abuse. Over the past several decades, psychologists and social workers gradually have redefined child sex abuse as a family problem (rather than a psychological malady) caused by a criminal "sex offender." This dramatic change in "expert" opinion has had serious legal implications, as evidenced by the post-1950 evolution of statutory rape and child sexual abuse laws. In the 1950s, reformed provisions raised the statutory age to sixteen or eighteen (with variations between states), and became applicable to both consensual and nonconsensual sexual intercourse with young girls (whose chastity was viewed as needing legal protection)(Kocen and Bulkley 1981). In addition, most states enacted provisions which punished other forms of sexual contact with children (e.g., touching a young child's genitals), which had come to be known as "molestation."

By the 1960s and early 1970s, a flurry of legislation prompted new reforms of existing statutory rape and child sexual abuse laws. Heightened concerns about child abuse during this time (described above) led to an increased focus on protecting children from sexual exploitation (Best 1990, 71–74; Nelson 1984). Reformed statutes incorporated some components of earlier provisions (e.g., minors were still defined as sixteen or eighteen years of age and younger), but also: (1) distinguished between different *degrees of statutory rape* for an expanded range of prohibited sexual acts with graduated penalties based on the age of the minor; (2) defined criminal sexual intercourse based on an *age differential between the victim and the perpetrator,* so that sex between adolescents close in age was no longer a punishable offense; (3) called attention to *the relationship between the victim and the perpetrator,* whereby specific penalties could be direct-

ed against perpetrators who occupy a position of power over a youngster (including not only parents, legal guardians, or blood relatives,
but also household members, or individuals who use their authority
to exact submission from the victim)(Kocen and Bulkley 1981). Thus,
these reformed statutes gave legal expression to growing concerns
about the sexual abuse of all minors (i.e., both young children and
teenagers) perpetrated by an adult who may exercise supervisory care
over them. Soon after this new legislation was enacted, sexual impro-
prieties with children were relabeled and underwent a process of
"domain expansion" (see Best 1990). Incest and child molestation
were renamed "child sexual abuse" to highlight the inherently harmful nature of adult-child sexual contact (Best 1990: 71). And, some
claims-makers sought to expand the domain of child sexual abuse in
order to (1) include a wider range of potentially abusive behaviors
(e.g., routinely walking about the home unclothed), and (2) encompass sexual misconduct which occurred in a variety of other, nondo-
mestic settings (child pornography, adolescent prostitution, and ritual abuse)(Best 1990, 71–74).

In this context, we argue that the intensive focus of the media,
government officials, and the general public on allegations of child
abuse at Mt. Carmel must be located within a historical perspective
on the family and changing social constructions about the nature of
children. As outlined, traditional understandings of children and
child-rearing have been supplanted by modern commitments to individualism, affective familial relationships, and a relatively older
accepted marital age. In addition, premodern notions about the
depravity of children and traditional religious legitimations for corporal punishment have been replaced in many quarters by a belief in
the moral purity of children, and (at least rhetorical) opposition to
the regular and severe physical punishment of youngsters. Moreover,
recent years have witnessed a sacralization of the child, and a succession of moral panics about the vulnerability of innocent children
and the perceived increase in their victimization by adults (both
strangers and intimates). These cultural changes have both stimulat-
ed and reflected the mobilization of various interest groups, including doctors, therapists, and activist private and federal child welfare
organizations. Taken together, these trends have resulted in (1) a
heightened public and official sensitivity to issues of children's welfare, as well as (2) a burgeoning array of new legal tools with which
children's advocates and others can press claims of child abuse. Having provided the historical context in which child abuse accusations
were leveled against Koresh and his followers, we now attempt to
review and assess the specific charges faced by the Branch Davidians.

We begin with an analysis of physical abuse allegations, followed by an examination of child sexual abuse, material deprivation, and psychological abuse charges.

Severe Corporal Punishment and Physical Abuse

The claim that Koresh and the Branch Davidians engaged in severe corporal punishment of very young children stems primarily from a small number of alleged incidents. These disturbing incidents were reported by defectors to law enforcement officials in LaVerne, California, in 1991 (Niebuhr and Thomas 1993), and later to officials in Texas as well (Langford 1993). A group of defectors, led by Marc Breault, included these allegations of physical abuse in their testimony at a 1992 child custody hearing in St. Joseph, Michigan. These claims were first introduced to the general public by the *Waco Tribune-Herald* in a seven-part report on the group (England and McCormick 1993a, 1993b, 1993c), and subsequently recycled by national media in the weeks following the raid on the Mt. Carmel facility (Beck et al. 1993; Carroll et al. 1993; Gregory 1993; Kantrowitz et al. 1993a; Rimer 1993; Verhovek 1993a; Woodward and Hamilton 1993).

One incident of physical abuse is said to have occurred in 1986, when the group still resided in Palestine, Texas (England and McCormick 1993a, 1993c). At that time, Koresh's son Cyrus—then approximately one year old—had been left alone inside a school bus while the rest of the group held Bible study. According to former Branch Davidians, Koresh became irritated with the cries of Cyrus, and responded to this disruption by making several trips to the bus, allegedly whipping the child severely for several minutes on each occasion. Accounts indicated that no Branch Davidian adults went to comfort the youngster because they were reluctant to miss the Bible study sessions, and this was represented as yet another indicator of the sinister charisma and control exercised by David Koresh over the group.

On another occasion in late 1988, Koresh is said to have beaten the eight-month-old daughter of another member for some forty minutes, until the little girl's bottom was bruised and bleeding, because she refused to sit on his lap (England and McCormick 1993c). Koresh is also alleged to have hit his son Shaun Bunds, then ten months old, with a wooden paddle after the baby would not come to him when he asked. Again, this paddling was sufficient to bruise and draw blood (England and McCormick 1993c). Finally Larry Little, a Michigan man involved in a custody battle to extract his child from

Mt. Carmel, claims to have witnessed the beating of a young boy (age unspecified) with a stick during a 1990 visit to the facility. According to Little, the beating, which occurred at Koresh's direction, lasted for approximately fifteen minutes (Carroll et al. 1993).

Based on these disturbing anecdotes, official statements and news accounts widely depicted David Koresh as a chronic child abuser engaged in an extensive and ongoing campaign of harsh punishment against the youngest members of the Branch Davidian community. While it is conceivable that this portrait is accurate, the evidence is murkier, and the issues involved are more complex, than media accounts and official pronouncements indicated. Surveying the evidence at hand, two features are immediately striking: (1) only a small number of alleged incidents have surfaced; and (2) the best-known incidents of physical abuse—those described graphically by defectors and noted above—are alleged to have occurred during the 1986–90 period, rather than in more recent years.

Why might we lack detailed and corroborated accounts of more recent abusive conduct by Koresh or his followers? Several possible explanations deserve consideration. First, of course, child abuse is often difficult to document, owing to the inherently sensitive and intimate character of parent-child relations. Further, it has been suggested that sustained Branch Davidian contacts with the surrounding community were diminished in the months prior to the initial raid, thereby reducing outsiders' access to information about the group. In particular, the availability of incriminating information about childrearing at Mt. Carmel may have been attenuated by the 1989 departure of Marc Breault and his wife Elizabeth Baranyai, along with other prominent apostates, who were key sources of the disturbing anecdotal evidence presented above (England and McCormick 1993b, 1993c).

These explanations, however, are not entirely satisfying. For one thing, the beliefs and lifestyles of the Branch Davidians have been under intense scrutiny from media organizations, government agencies, academicians, and others. Acquaintances, neighbors, former members, and survivors of Mt. Carmel have been interviewed extensively, sometimes revealing highly intimate details of life within the community. Such persistent probing from many different quarters might have been expected to turn up contemporaneous evidence of physical abuse, if it existed. Instead, the direct questioning of a long-time resident of Mt. Carmel, Catherine Matteson, yielded only a flat denial that harsh physical punishment ever occurred (Wright 1993). Moreover, because Breault expressed particular concern about the welfare of the children (England and McCormick 1993a, 1993c), and even maintained computer files detailing incidents of various types of child abuse, the lack of information about more recent episodes of physical abuse is especially puzzling.

While the graphic anecdotes of harsh physical punishment furnished by former Branch Davidians may well be accurate, prudence commends skepticism for several reasons. It is unclear whether babies of this age would have survived a steady diet of such severe beatings. In addition, the theology articulated by Koresh accorded a central role to children—especially those fathered by Koresh with the women of the House of David—in establishing and sustaining the future Kingdom of God (Bromley and Silver, this volume). While love and abusive discipline are not always incompatible, there are signs that Koresh genuinely cared for these children, and that they loved him as well.

Media accounts and official statements regarding Koresh's child abuse generally took apostate claims at face value. However, a critical evaluation of these accounts introduces us to a tangled web of personal agendas and counteragendas. It is clear that some prominent former members had incentives to hurl child abuse accusations at Koresh, just as Branch Davidian sympathizers have every incentive to discredit the apostates. For instance, survivors of Mt. Carmel have suggested that Marc Breault was jealous of Koresh's charisma, scriptural knowledge, and appeal to women (Wright 1993). Indeed, some Koresh loyalists have claimed that Breault wished to supplant Koresh as prophet and leader of the group, although those who observed Breault in Australia following his departure from Mt. Carmel doubt this (England and McCormick 1993b). In any event, it is clear that Breault resented the evolving direction of Koresh's New Light doctrine, which eventually led him and wife Elizabeth Baranyai to depart the group on less than favorable terms.

The claims of Robyn Bunds, formerly a wife of Koresh, invite similar skepticism. Bunds graphically described how Koresh subjected son Wisdom (also known as Shaun Bunds) to corporal punishment, including a severe beating at approximately the age of ten months. Unsympathetic survivors paint Bunds as an attractive but spoiled member of the community who wanted and expected Koresh's undivided attention (Wright 1993), and turned vengeful when Koresh subsequently took other wives into the House of David, including her mother (England and McCormick 1993b, 1993c). Others note that Bunds was embroiled in an ongoing conflict with Koresh over custody of their son (Niebuhr and Thomas 1993), and that a large percentage of child abuse allegations first surface within the context of such custody battles.

Perhaps most important, although Robyn Bunds has attacked Koresh for using corporal punishment to discipline Wisdom (Shaun), she has admitted using physical punishment herself on numerous occasions, granting that she possibly spanked the child more often than David Koresh did. Moreover, she maintains that this corporal punishment is responsible for a host of problems subsequently experienced by Wisdom, including low self-esteem, short attention span, cognitive deficits, and emotional difficulties. When confronted with her potential culpability, however, Bunds blames Koresh, insisting that she was only following his teachings, and that she was under his charismatic influence during this period (England and McCormick 1993c).

To be sure, none of the foregoing should lead us to dismiss the testimony of Marc Breault, Robyn Bunds, or other former Branch Davidians out of hand. However, these issues do suggest that authorities should have weighed the possible emotional conflicts, complex motivations, and personal agendas of these and other prominent apostates, and that authorities should have treated the allegations and claims of these detractors as something other than accurate, unbiased, insider information.

One potential source of empirical information about the allegations of harsh physical punishment at Mt. Carmel is a 1992 investigation of the Branch Davidians by the Children's Protective Services (CPS, a division of the Texas Protective and Regulatory Services). However, the investigation and its results remain the focus of heated dispute. It would appear that the inquiry yielded little clear support for the allegations. Acting on an anonymous tip, CPS caseworkers made three separate trips to the community, eventually interviewing David and Rachel Koresh, along with several adults and children (England and McCormick 1993a; National Public Radio 1993; Niebuhr and Thomas 1993). They also talked with Koresh at the CPS offices in Waco. In the interviews, children denied experiencing abuse, and denied knowing of other cases of abuse at Mt. Carmel. Adults denied engaging in abusive disciplinary practices. No significant injuries were found in physical examinations of twelve of the children. Given the lack of evidence supporting allegations of physical and other forms of child abuse by the Branch Davidians, CPS supervisors decided to terminate the investigation after two months (Smith 1993; *Houston Chronicle,* October 11, 1993).

However, within the CPS some felt that the decision to terminate the investigation was premature, and that the child abuse allegations against the Branch Davidians merited further monitoring (Tedford 1993b, 1993d). After the fire, this disagreement erupted in a series of

public recriminations. Joyce Sparks, the lead CPS caseworker, insisted that the results of her investigations seemed to support the allegations against the Branch Davidians, although she did not produce
further evidence to this effect (National Public Radio 1993). Sparks
denounced her superiors at CPS for failing to support the investigation. She also claimed that McLennan County Sheriff Jack Harwell
had discouraged her inquiries, insisting that Branch Davidian child-
rearing practices were "none of her business," although her CPS
supervisor denied any impropriety by sheriff's department personnel
(*Houston Chronicle,* October 11, 1993).[4]

Although information about dramatic violence against young
children remains elusive, there is ample evidence that Koresh and
other Branch Davidians did employ corporal punishment to discipline the children of Mt. Carmel. While examinations of some twenty-one children of various ages released during the standoff turned up
no evidence of past or current physical injuries, these examinations
did reveal small circular bruises on the buttocks of some youngsters
(Carroll et al. 1993). When questioned, the children indicated that
they were spanked for misbehavior or disobedience with a wooden
spoon or paddle, called "the helper." These spankings generally took
place in a room designated for this purpose at the Mt. Carmel facility (Gregory 1993; Rimer 1993; Verhovek 1993a). Psychiatrists and
social workers caring for the children who were released during the
standoff reported that the youngsters inquired about the presence of
a "helper" and a "whipping room" in their new environment, and
that they apparently feared that they would be spanked for behavioral infractions. Nevertheless, the children generally spoke of Koresh with fondness and admiration. When asked about the physical
punishment experienced at Mt. Carmel, fourteen-year-old Kalani
Fatta seemed unfazed: "If you were punished, [Koresh] said it was
because you had done something wrong, and maybe it hurt him to
have to do it" (quoted in Verhovek 1993a). However, Baylor psychiatrist Bruce Perry, who monitored the released children, cautioned
that abused children (especially those subjected to long-term abuse)
often love their abusers, and often adopt adult rationalizations which
define the violence as something other than abuse (Carroll et al.
1993; *Beaumont Enterprise,* May 5, 1993).

Whether David Koresh engaged in physical abuse hinges partly on
a key definitional issue: Does the use of corporal punishment constitute physical abuse? A significant—and perhaps growing—number
of social workers, therapists, and academic researchers are inclined
to take this position (e.g., Maurer 1974; Straus 1994), and this view
was also implicit in some media discussions of the Branch Davidi-

ans. However, other experts reject this blanket assessment, as does a large segment of the American public—particularly contemporary religious conservatives. Corporal punishment is widely endorsed by American adults, and widely used by American parents. For instance, in the 1990 General Social Survey, a large national probability sample of adults, approximately 80 percent of the respondents agreed with the following statement: "It is sometimes necessary to discipline a child with a good, hard spanking" (Davis and Smith 1990). In the 1987–88 National Survey of Families and Households, approximately 50 percent of the parents of toddlers (ages 1–4) and nearly 25 percent of the parents of preadolescent children (ages 5–11) reported "spanking or slapping" their youngster during the week preceding the interview (Ellison, Bartkowski, and Segal 1994).

Further, data from these sources, and from several other recent surveys, consistently show that Conservative Protestants (i.e., fundamentalists, evangelicals, and charismatics) support and use corporal punishment significantly more than other Americans (Ellison and Sherkat 1993; Ellison, Bartkowski, and Segal 1994). As we noted earlier (see note 2), Conservative Protestant parenting writers have expressed strong support for carefully delineated forms of physical punishment, particularly in response to disciplinary infractions that are perceived as "willful disobedience" (Dobson 1970, 1976; LaHaye 1977; Lessin 1979; Fugate 1980).[5] Thus, while the alleged incidents in which babies were subjected to harsh punishment clearly depart from the methods endorsed by some experts, many of Koresh's well-documented disciplinary practices appear similar to those employed widely by many Texans and other Americans.

Did David Koresh and his followers engage in extensive, ongoing physical abuse of children, as apostates and other detractors have alleged? It is certainly possible that they did. However, several alternative interpretations of the data are also plausible. In reporting anecdotal violence against babies, some former Branch Davidians may have exaggerated their descriptions of episodes of corporal punishment. Given the public concern and institutional power devoted to issues of children's welfare, and the legal resources available for the detection and prosecution of child abuse, some apostates might have embellished these reports deliberately, adding physical child abuse to a long litany of grievances and complaints designed to discredit Koresh. Finally, it is possible that, as an inexperienced and frustrated parent during the 1986–90 period, Koresh did use excessively harsh punishment, but also that he moderated his child-rearing practices in later years. Despite the prominence of the child abuse allegations in the rationales for the final assault on Mt.

Carmel, numerous questions persist regarding the evidence, its sources, and its interpretation. In the aftermath of the fire at Mt. Carmel, much of the information needed to clarify this issue may be lost forever.

Child Sexual Abuse

Perhaps the most celebrated allegations against David Koresh involved claims of child sexual abuse. Apostates, authorities, and others alleged that Koresh (1) had multiple underage sexual partners (which he termed "wives"); (2) fathered numerous children through these liaisons; (3) used charisma and manipulation to fashion a harem of girls and young women at Mt. Carmel; (4) molested (or raped) at least one underage female Branch Davidian; and (5) provided an unwholesome environment for minors and adults alike through constant references to, and graphic descriptions of, sexual acts in his Bible studies and other public statements. As in the case of the physical abuse allegations, the issues involved here are more complex, and the evidence supporting the allegations is less clearcut, than official statements and media accounts usually acknowledged. Nevertheless, the evidence of sexual abuse—or at least illegal sexual activity—appears somewhat stronger than the evidence buttressing the other allegations against Koresh.

There is evidence that Koresh engaged in sexual relations with female minors, although it is not clear exactly how many liaisons were involved. Koresh married Rachel Jones, the daughter of longtime Branch Davidians and Koresh loyalists, in 1984, when she was fourteen years old. This relationship was monogamous for a period of two or three years, and Rachel bore two children with Koresh, Cyrus and Star. Koresh also became interested in Rachel's younger sister, Michelle Jones, and allegedly began to have sexual relations with her in 1987, when the girl was twelve. Michelle gave birth to a daughter in February 1989, at age fourteen.

In 1987, Koresh also initiated a sexual relationship with Robyn Bunds, a Californian who was then seventeen. Like Rachel, Robyn Bunds was part of a Branch Davidian family with close ties to Koresh, and she bore a son with Koresh, named Wisdom (Shaun), in November 1988. Robyn Bunds subsequently became alienated by Koresh's sexual pluralism, and dropped out of the community in 1990, after she became aware that he had had sex with her mother, Jeannine Bunds. Jeannine Bunds also left the group in 1991, and she and her daughter later became key figures in the coordinated effort to discredit and displace Koresh in the community.

While the cases of the Jones sisters and Robyn Bunds are the best-known instances of Koresh's sexual involvement with underage female Branch Davidians, there are rumblings and piecemeal accounts of others. In a sworn affidavit, BATF agent Davy Aguilera recounted a December 1992 interview with Jeannine Bunds in which she indicated (1) that Koresh had fathered at least fifteen children with "various women and young girls" at Mt. Carmel, (2) that some of the mothers were "as young as twelve," and (3) that she personally delivered seven of the babies (U.S. District Court 1993). It is not clear from this document, or from subsequent public statements and commentaries by the principals, exactly how many female minors are alleged to have given birth to Koresh's progeny.

In addition, Aguilera cites information supplied by Joyce Sparks of CPS. According to Sparks, an unidentified underage female Branch Davidian claimed during an interview (date unknown) that Koresh molested her in a Waco motel room. At the time of the incident, the girl was twelve years old, and in the interview she reported feeling "scared but privileged" (U.S. District Court 1993; Johnson 1993).[6] In addition, Aguilera also named a New Zealand woman (Mrs. Poia Vaega), who claimed that Koresh and another unnamed Branch Davidian physically and sexually abused her sister at Mt. Carmel (Johnson 1993). The dates of these alleged incidents of abuse are unclear.

Along with the allegations contained in Aguilera's affidavit, there are other scattered claims of sexual abuse and impropriety. In 1992, after the Texas CPS investigation of the Branch Davidians was terminated, LaVerne, California, police decided to reopen their probe of Koresh and his followers at the urging of apostates. Although an earlier LaVerne inquiry turned up no evidence of abuse, this time one of the unnamed girls alleged as a victim was out of the group, in her father's custody. After extensive interviewing, the girl confirmed that she had engaged in sexual relations with Koresh (Niebuhr and Thomas 1993).

According to apostates, Koresh himself had revealed information about several additional cases of sexual abuse. For instance, Marc Breault claimed that in 1986 Koresh told Branch Davidians at a Passover service held in Palestine, Texas, that God commanded him to have sex with a shy, unidentified fourteen-year-old girl in the group. In Breault's account of this occasion, Koresh and the girl were to unite and have a child called Shoshonna, who would marry Cyrus, Koresh's son by legal wife Rachel. The two children of Koresh would rule in God's kingdom. In addition, Breault provided information about a widely cited incident involving a thirteen-year-old Australian girl, probably Aisha Gyarfas, which allegedly occurred in 1989. After hearing Koresh speak suggestively of this girl, Breault claims that he sought to investigate Koresh's behavior. Breault pretended to be working on a computer in an office below Koresh's quarters for the entire night, and observed the underage girl leaving the room of the Branch Davidian leader at dawn the following morning. Breault has identified this event as a turning point in his evaluation of Koresh as leader of the group. This account, however, has been seriously questioned by surviving Davidians who point out that Marc Breault is legally blind, and would have had great difficulty seeing the girl from across a dimly lit room in the early hours of the morning.[7]

Finally, the case of Kiri Jewell is widely represented as an aborted instance of child sexual abuse by Koresh. After leaving the Branch Davidians, Breault claims that he became aware that Koresh might want to include Jewell (who was then either nine or ten years of age) in a group of female minors with whom he allegedly engaged in sexual relations. According to Breault, Koresh had approached Kiri Jewell and had made suggestive remarks to this effect, even giving her a Star of David pendant as a symbol of his intentions. In 1991, Breault contacted the girl's father, a Michigan disc jockey who was not a Branch Davidian, and in response the father initiated a custody suit and other actions against Koresh. Many of the allegations of sexual abuse and other forms of abuse by Koresh were first aired in affidavits sworn by defectors in connection with that custody case, which was resolved in favor of the father in 1992 (England and McCormick 1993a, 1993c). Further, in the wake of the initial raid and subsequent standoff at Mt. Carmel, Kiri Jewell—apparently encouraged by her father—emerged as a key source of various types of unfavorable information about Koresh and the Branch Davidians.[8]

While the claims regarding sexual relations between Koresh and female minors grabbed headlines and attention during and after the standoff at Mt. Carmel, apostates also leveled other allegations at Koresh and his followers. According to Robyn Bunds, Koresh recounted the details of at least one sexual encounter with twelve-year-old Michelle Jones to members of the community, and his description clearly indicated to Bunds that the sexual contact was not consensual (England and McCormick 1993c).[9] Several other apostates—including Michelle Jones's brother Joel—have endorsed Bunds's recollection of the events.

In addition to this allegation of sexual coercion, apostates portray Koresh as obsessed with sex and willing to use his power and charisma to manipulate female Branch Davidians to provide sexual favors for him. Marc Breault claimed that Koresh confided frequently about these matters, discussing his favorite sexual partners in detail, as well as the problems he encountered in trying to please all of his partners. Several apostates indicated that Koresh frequently peppered his Bible study sessions with frank (even crude) sexual language. According to these accounts, Koresh emphasized the importance of constraining sexual impulses and behavior, including masturbation, and imposed strict regulations limiting the role of men in changing the diapers of female babies, apparently out of fear that the men of Mt. Carmel would become sexually aroused by this experience. In other widely reported allegations, Breault and his confederates recounted Koresh's graphic public instructions concerning how young, relatively undeveloped girls should use tampons to prepare themselves for sexual relations with him.

A careful review of the evidence supporting these allegations raises several troubling issues. First, the strength of the detractors' case rests primarily on the testimony of apostates and some of their sympathetic family members. At one level, this is understandable; few others would have inside information about Koresh's statements and about the intimate details of Branch Davidian life. However, historical analyses of societal responses to marginal religious groups in America (e.g., Mormonism, Catholicism) refer frequently to allegations of debauchery and atrocity—most of which appear to have been wild exaggerations or outright falsehoods (see Bromley and Shupe 1981; Fogarty, this volume; Lewis 1989). And, apostates—whose material and ideological interests frequently shift with their defection—may offer pejorative accounts or highly inaccurate information about the internal workings of marginal groups (Wright 1991; Wright and Ebaugh 1993).

Nonetheless, Koresh's public statements—prior to the siege—about his "wives," his "children," and his "family" were cryptic, probably deliberately so. He denied these relationships in other places, acknowledging only two children, Cyrus and Star.[10] On some occasions, however, Koresh also showed awareness of the external hostility that he might face because of his unorthodox and polygynous practices, which would account for the vague and contradictory nature of his statements. In a videotape released to federal agents during the standoff, Koresh posed with his "family," which included a large number of children. Comments from this tape clearly indicate that he had fathered children by several of the women who appeared with him (e.g., Katherine Andrade, Nicole Gent). Smiling, he told viewers, "Our ways are not your ways. . . . What we do, people would not understand." Thus while some form of plural marriage (see Kilbride 1994) is openly acknowledged on the videotape, what is not clear is at what age these women became "wives."

Considerable attention has been devoted to the fact that a number of births at Mt. Carmel after the late 1980s were unregistered with McLennan County authorities. In some instances where birth certificates were filed (in Texas and in California), the identity of the baby's father is not listed. Apostates, in some cases relatives of the mothers, have contended that Koresh restricted the filing of birth certificates in order to disguise the number of babies born without a known father at Mt. Carmel. Jeannine Bunds, a trained nurse who was once a registered midwife in McLennan County, recounted a specific instance in which Koresh directly ordered her not to file birth certificates for twin girls delivered at Mt. Carmel in 1991, shortly before Bunds's departure from the group. This information, which appears to be accurate, strongly suggests that Koresh intended to conceal from authorities the number and circumstances of births (England and McCormick 1993a, 1993c).

Several aspects of the Branch Davidian case make these various allegations of child sexual abuse especially unusual. First, in at least some cases, Koresh sought and obtained the consent of Branch Davidian parents prior to (or shortly after) engaging in sexual liaisons with their daughters (see Bromley and Silver, this volume). This appears to have been true for the Bunds family in the case of Robyn (then age seventeen), and for the Gent family in the case of Nicole (then nineteen). There are some indications that Koresh may also have enjoyed the support of the Jones family in his relationships with Rachel and Michelle. For other cases, however, this issue is, and may remain, unclear. Detractors point out that Koresh had a history (dating at least to 1980) of (1) feeling that God called him to marry, or at least to have sexual relations with, various girls and women; and (2) attempting (not always successfully) to persuade the parents that the impending relationship was divinely inspired (see England and McCormick 1993b).

Koresh apparently overcame the initial reluctance of the Bunds, Gent, and Jones families by persuading them that his liaisons were not purely physical, but rather that they entailed a distinctive spiritual bond. In an increasingly elaborate theological rationale, Koresh maintained that the purpose of these liaisons was to produce children who would rule in God's kingdom. Indeed, some accounts suggest that Koresh believed that these children existed in heaven prior to their birth in this world, and that his goal was to fulfill the prophecy in Revelation 2:4–5 by bringing twenty-four children into the world (i.e., "twenty-four elders to rule on earth") for the future leadership of a geopolitical kingdom to be based in Israel. Some even speculate that Koresh and some of his followers believed that these children were genetically different from ordinary youngsters, that they were earthly manifestations of supernatural children (Arnold 1994).

In sum, an array of sexual impropriety charges were leveled against Koresh. Given the quantity and breadth of the charges that we have overviewed above, it seems likely that Koresh did violate some Texas statutory laws. Investigations, however, proved inconclusive. Why could investigators find no evidence of sexual abuse? It is possible that the unusual nature of the sexual abuse claims, and the complex circumstances surrounding them (especially the isolated communal lifestyle and parental consent within the patronal clan), made the task of documenting these allegations extraordinarily difficult for investigative personnel. It is also possible that the psychological or emotional trauma normally associated with premature sexual activity was mitigated somewhat by their parents' approval or by the group's culturally specific expectations about sexual activity for young girls.

Material Deprivation and Psychological Abuse

Along with the allegations of harsh physical punishment and sexual abuse, apostates and other detractors argued that David Koresh and his followers also endangered their children in less dramatic ways. Of particular interest are widespread criticisms of (1) the material deprivation and spartan lifestyle and (2) the putatively damaging psychological effects of the apocalyptic theology and militaristic environment at Mt. Carmel. Defending the FBI action that resulted in the fatal fire on CNN's *Larry King Live,* Attorney General Janet Reno indicated that her "horrible fear" was that "if I delayed, without sanitation or toilets there . . . I could go in there in two months and find children dead from any number of things" (quoted in Kantrowitz et al. 1993b). Nevertheless, a review of these various claims and the supporting evidence raises a number of complex issues.

Material Deprivation and Spartan Lifestyles

Published reports and survivor testimony indicated that the Mt. Carmel facility lacked indoor plumbing, and that Branch Davidians were required to haul buckets of human waste out of the residential area and to dump them elsewhere on the premises. Therapists and social workers treating the children who were released prior to the fire often emphasized the youngsters' fascination with flush toilets and other modern conveniences (*Beaumont Enterprise*, May 5, 1993; Tedford 1993c). While the absence of indoor plumbing was a fact of daily life at Mt. Carmel, the impact of this condition was exacerbated by the BATF/FBI siege. Fearing that they would be shot by FBI snipers, the Branch Davidians discontinued their practice of transporting buckets of waste outside the main buildings. Instead, it appeared that they simply tossed the waste out the doors of the facility (Kantrowitz et al. 1993b). While official spokespersons and media accounts contended that sanitary conditions were deteriorating during the weeks preceding the final assault, they rarely elaborated on the contribution of federal policies to these problems.[11]

In addition to the sanitation issue, apostates and others alleged that Koresh imposed a spartan, even harsh, lifestyle on his followers, including Branch Davidian youngsters (Gregory 1993). Children released from Mt. Carmel during the standoff indicated that they performed regular chores around the facility. Boys participated in "gym," which involved vigorous exercise and possibly paramilitary activities such as simulated combat. Gym was held each day beginning "as early as 5:30 AM," according to some reports (*Beaumont Enterprise*, May 5, 1993). Although girls were permitted to sleep much later, they handled food preparation and other household responsibilities.

Another aspect of this spartan lifestyle concerned the strict regulation of children's food consumption (*Beaumont Enterprise*, May 5, 1993). Survivors, including children, noted that the Branch Davidians focused considerable energy on stockpiling provisions. Overall food intake was limited for most members of the community, with the partial exception of Koresh himself. The children ate primarily fruits and vegetables, and especially grain products; the consumption of fast foods, ice cream and other sweets, and meat was sharply constrained (Gregory 1993; Tedford 1993c). According to Joyce Sparks of CPS, her 1992 investigation of Koresh yielded "indications" that food was being withheld as punishment, although no specific anecdotal or systematic evidence to this effect was released to the public (National Public Radio 1993). Statements by Bruce Perry, the Baylor psychiatrist who examined the children released before the fire, also claimed that Branch Davidian children occasionally were kept without food for "up to a day" (*Beaumont Enterprise*, May 5, 1993). Similar allegations against Koresh date from the late 1980s, when the Branch Davidians lived in California (England and McCormick 1993c), and it is unclear whether the "indications" mentioned by Sparks and Perry were references to these earlier incidents, or whether these were fresh allegations.

The diverse claims regarding material deprivation at Mt. Carmel raise a number of thorny issues. First, the use of child protection legislation as a means by which to remove children from poor households and to enforce middle-class values and lifestyles has been a persistent source of controversy since the initial drafting of the 1974 Mondale Act (Kocen and Bulkley 1981; Nelson 1984). The Branch Davidian case raises the question of whether parents who choose to raise their children in a spartan environment are guilty of abuse. As Dick DeGuerin, an attorney who represented Koresh, put the matter shortly after the fire: "At what point does society have a right to step in and say you have to raise your family our way? It's applying yuppie values to people who choose to live differently" (quoted in Carroll et al. 1993).

The claims of apostates and other opponents of the Branch Davidians notwithstanding, it remains unclear whether, and to what extent, the lifestyle embraced at Mt. Carmel was actually harmful to the children. For instance, it is interesting that media accounts routinely portrayed Koresh as a tyrant for regulating children's nutrition and for requiring that children engage in vigorous exercise. Recent medical reports indicate that obesity is on the rise among American children, owing largely to indulgent dietary practices and sedentary lifestyles. While there is little question that Branch Davidian children experienced an exceptionally regimented daily routine, and a relatively homogeneous diet (Tedford 1993c), physicians who examined the children released during the standoff pronounced them healthy and fit.

In a similar vein, much was made of the fact that the Branch Davidian children were educated at home. However, social workers assigned to survivors indicated that these children were generally bright, competent readers (although they used mainly the Bible as their text), adept at arithmetic, and skilled at describing the world around them (*Beaumont Enterprise,*May 5, 1993; Verhovek 1993a). Although being taught at Mt. Carmel meant that these children had reduced social contacts outside the community, social workers and therapists often commented on the close, familial bonds among surviving children, and on the ease with which these children related to others, including adults (Verhovek 1993a).

Was Branch Davidian child-rearing "abusive?" In weighing the evidence, it is important to consider whether the parents and adults of Mt. Carmel cared for the children. There is ample evidence that these children were treated with love and affection (Hoversten and Hall 1993). Medical examinations of surviving children revealed that they were "in good health," although there were allegations by one examining doctor that they had been "emotionally neglected" (Rimer 1993). When the children were released prior to the fire, parents provided detailed notes about favorite toys, foods, and stories (Verhovek 1993a). Surviving youngsters (and attorneys who visited the community) reported that the children's living quarters were modest, but clean and attractively decorated (Carroll et al. 1993), and that the children were the focus of frequent expressions of affection from Koresh and the other adults. Before the fire killed their families and friends, most of the released children expressed a desire to return to Mt. Carmel to see their parents, and they discussed a number of pleasing aspects of community life (Verhovek 1993a).

Stress and Psychological Abuse

In addition to criticisms about the material conditions and lifestyles within which the Branch Davidian children were being raised, apostates and detractors also expressed concern about the putatively detrimental psychological impact of Branch Davidian theology and culture on these children. For instance, some worried that a steady diet of Koresh's lengthy Bible study sessions, apocalyptic imagery, and pronouncements about a fiery cataclysm were fostering anxiety and psychological distress among the children. Further, Koresh's preachings often centered on themes of sin and punishment; he was known to reproach children at length about their sins and transgressions, and even to discuss these sins with other youngsters.

Moreover, psychiatrist Bruce Perry and others were particularly concerned about the exposure of the children—especially the boys—to violence. There is ample evidence that they were permitted—even encouraged—to watch war videos, and that they were surrounded by weaponry and by the preparations for violent conflict. It was suggested that these children might be desensitized to the horrors of violence and more likely to perpetrate violence as adults. Finally, according to at least one report, Koresh and other Branch Davidians instructed children on how to commit suicide (with cyanide, a gun, etc.). Kiri Jewell, who was removed from Mount Carmel via a 1992 custody battle, has reiterated these claims on several occasions, thus far with little corroboration from sources other than her father (Hoversten and Hall 1993).

Although Koresh's evolving theological views clearly differ somewhat from those of the American religious mainstream in their apocalyptic nature, there are dangers in certain of these arguments about stress and "psychological abuse." On the one hand, critics have marshalled little evidence to buttress their claims that Koresh's teachings promoted aggressiveness and violence among the Branch Davidian children. And although some psychological critics have long argued that the religious preoccupation (especially in conservative traditions) with themes of human sinfulness holds grave consequences for self-esteem and psychological functioning (Ellis 1962; Branden 1994), the empirical evidence bearing on this contention is actually mixed (Bergin 1983; Watson, Morris, and Hood 1988). Nevertheless, in media accounts and in the anticult pronouncements of government officials and psychological "experts," the scientific language of child abuse was deployed in an attack, not on the structure or processes of the group, but on the Branch Davidian theology and belief system. In essence, critics suggested that exposure to conservative, apocalyptic theology itself was harmful to children.

Further, while the emphasis on martial themes is a bit unusual, it is not clear how dramatically the experiences of Branch Davidian children diverge from those of other youngsters in Texas, or elsewhere in the South. After all, many middle-class, suburban men and boys exhibit a fascination with war games, military history, and related topics, and every year war movies with violent characters and gruesome special effects are national box office favorites. In support of the initial search warrant, an affidavit filed by BATF agent Davy Aguilera repeated the claim of CPS investigator Joyce Sparks that "a boy 7 or 8 years old . . . [said that he] could not wait to grow up and be a man" so he could get "a long gun just like all the other men there" (U.S. District Court 1993; quoted in Smith 1993). While some media accounts made much of the children's fascination with guns, this is hardly a sign of abuse throughout much of the South. Numerous studies demonstrate that southerners are much more likely than other Americans to own firearms for sport and defense, and are more supportive of defensive or retaliatory violence than other Americans (e.g., Ellison 1991a, 1991b). Given that firearms ownership is a rite of passage for many young southern men, it is not surprising to find similar patterns within the Branch Davidian community.

Definitive answers to many questions about the impact of Branch Davidian teachings and lifestyles on the well-being of the children remain elusive. According to Baylor psychiatrist Bruce Perry and others close to this case, the answers to many of these questions will become more apparent as the children gradually open up and become comfortable discussing their experiences at Mt. Carmel.[13] This may be true. However, another scenario is also possible: as the children become more removed—temporally and cognitively—from the Branch Davidian community, and more acclimated to the values and practices of the outside world, they may become more inclined to accept prevailing negative definitions of the Branch Davidians and to restructure their own thinking in this direction, especially if these views are reinforced by therapists and others in the broader society.

Such a development might limit the availability of accurate information from the children about the group, its values, and its practices. In addition, knowledgeable observers suggest that this might also have undesirable implications for the children themselves, especially in the aftermath of the fire. Charles Hart Enzer, chairman of the peer-review committee of the American Academy of Child and Adolescent Psychiatry, has asserted that it is important for the orphaned children to retain positive images of their time at Mt. Carmel: "The challenge is to give them reason to be proud of each parent. The worst-case situation is where children are taught to hate the parents, hate their heritage, hate their history, hate themselves, and feel guilty and bad for being angry" (quoted in Verhovek 1993a).

Discussion

In this chapter, we have explored the role of child abuse allegations in the conflict at Mt. Carmel. Clearly the charges of physical, sexual, and psychological abuse and material neglect helped to shape public perceptions of Koresh and the Branch Davidians, and provided a justification for the series of government actions that culminated in the final assault and fatal fire. To summarize briefly, we began by situating these claims, and the public and official responses to them, within the context of major shifts in child-rearing values in the U.S. and other industrialized societies. Three recent developments are especially important: (1) the growing popularity of what some have termed "the protected childhood" (which stresses the moral goodness and "emotional pricelessness" of children); (2) the pervasiveness of affective parenting (which downplays the need for harsh discipline or physical punishment); and (3) the current moral panic over the welfare of children (which stresses the myriad real and perceived threats to the physical, emotional, and sexual welfare of youngsters in contemporary industrialized societies). Owing to these emerging value commitments, apostates and other detractors gained access to unprecedented political, institutional, and legal resources with which to press their claims, and made use of heightened public attention to the allegations, including widespread sympathy for official intervention at Mt. Carmel in the name of child-saving.

We then turned to an examination of the child abuse allegations themselves, including a critical assessment of the evidence bearing upon them. This is a difficult task for obvious reasons: Child abuse is a sensitive issue, and we have no wish to trivialize the importance of child abuse in its various forms, or to absolve Koresh and his followers unduly. Nevertheless, our analysis demonstrates that the issues raised by the various abuse allegations are often quite complex, and the evidence supporting them is more ambiguous than authorities or the media acknowledged. For instance, while apostates and other detractors have claimed that David Koresh engaged in the physical abuse of children, a review of the evidence raises troubling questions concerning the dearth of contemporaneous evidence, the elastic definitions of "abuse," the possibly complex motivations of anti-Koresh claims-makers, and other issues. There is stronger evidence that the sexual liaisons between Koresh and several female minors may have violated Texas laws. Even here, however, the apparent theological underpinnings of these relationships and the consent given freely by the parents underscore the complexity of these situations, dictating some degree of interpretive caution. Further, when examined carefully, the evidence supporting various allegations of material deprivation and psychological abuse appears underwhelming, especially in the absence of compelling indications that the children were harmed by their stay at Mt. Carmel. Interestingly, some aspects of the Branch Davidian lifestyle that were presented as deviant or menacing by federal authorities and national media (e.g., home schooling, emphasis on guns, corporal punishment) actually seem to parallel practices that are common in Texas and throughout much of the South.

While the vigorous pursuit of child abuse allegations failed to protect the presumed child victims from harm, in retrospect these claims did serve a variety of other interests. Apostates were able to use largely unsubstantiated allegations in their unrelenting campaign to demonize David Koresh. Although their initial efforts to alert state and federal law enforcement agencies via an Australian private investigator failed, they ultimately succeeded by inserting these claims into a child custody case (involving Kiri Jewell), and by arousing the interest of CPS personnel in Texas, and subsequently federal authorities as well. These accusations were so sensational and compelling that Breault's earlier fantastic allegations that Koresh planned the ritual sacrifice of children were seldom mentioned and did not detract from his credibility (Melton 1993).

The extensive attention to the child abuse allegations by government officials and media accounts placed CPS in the spotlight (and occasionally in the hot seat). The issues of child abuse received considerable coverage, as children's advocates underscored the seriousness of child abuse, and raised questions about the adequacy of (1) existing protective statutes in Texas and elsewhere, (2) the ability and commitment of law enforcement and other government agencies to intervene on behalf of children. Crusading CPS investigator Joyce Sparks was often depicted as a heroine, who alerted authorities and the public about the menace posed by Koresh, and who ministered tirelessly to children released prior to the fire (Prather 1993).

While Sparks's judgment appears vindicated to many in the aftermath of the disaster at Mt. Carmel, her activities raise several disturbing questions for authorities and children's advocates. First, Sparks pressed her superiors at CPS to continue their investigation of the Branch Davidians, despite the lack of supporting evidence after a two-month inquiry. (Although some argue that this seems wise in retrospect, Sparks went public with her complaints about CPS supervisory policies, and for whatever reason is no longer employed by CPS.) Will open-ended investigations—based largely on hunches and suspicions—become the norm for children's advocates in the future? In addition, Sparks apparently went beyond her official capacity, alerting various state and federal agencies, including the BATF and FBI, freely circulating anecdotal evidence about sexual abuse and unsubstantiated rumors about physical abuse (National Public Radio 1993). Given such revelations, it may be important to establish clearly the limits (if any) of legitimate professional activities by social workers engaged in child-saving endeavors.

Moreover, Sparks's own discussions of her involvement indicate clearly that she established a personal relationship with Koresh, including several individualized Bible study lessons, largely out of antipathy toward his theology. In one interview, she freely admitted: "This had nothing to do with my professional responsibilities . . . I was fascinated by how he used the Old Testament to write his own script, and I was very concerned about his apocalyptic views" (quoted in Prather 1993). She also unsuccessfully sought the approval of her superiors at CPS to assist the BATF during the initial raid and subsequent standoff (National Public Radio 1993). Sparks's comments raise legitimate concerns about whether, and to what extent, individual social workers should be permitted to use their professional positions to pursue personal or theological campaigns against marginal religious groups.

The child abuse allegations also proved quite valuable to government agencies and officials. Although the BATF lacks statutory authority to investigate or adjudicate allegations of child abuse, they took a keen interest in the information about Koresh that was disseminated by Joyce Sparks of the CPS. In a sworn affidavit filed to obtain the initial search warrant, BATF agent Davy Aguilera included detailed allegations of child sexual abuse provided by Sparks (U.S.

District Court 1993). There was no accompanying documentation for these claims, save for attribution to Sparks, and no indication that they were corroborated independently. Thus, child abuse allegations were helpful to agents of the BATF in promoting their institutional agenda.

Further, the FBI, the Justice Department, and the attorney general were able to establish public credibility and to forestall criticism by emphasizing child-saving themes. Indeed, in a variety of ways children were rhetorically and symbolically front and center throughout the weeks of the standoff. Although such child-saving rhetoric ultimately resulted in the deaths of these youngsters, it appears to have been a smashing public relations success. Public opinion polls conducted in the days after the fire showed widespread support for the government.[13]

Finally, the child abuse allegations were a boon to anticult organizations, who saw renewed public, political, and media receptivity to their perennial campaigns against marginal religious groups. During and after the standoff at Mt. Carmel, spokespersons for groups like the Cult Awareness Network (CAN) and others enjoyed extensive access to the print, radio, and television media, through which to articulate their central message that many of these small groups are dangerous and destructive. Child abuse allegations were prominent in these public statements. When media representatives asked Priscilla Coates, a longtime CAN leader in California, about the Branch Davidian experience in her state, she provided few specifics. Instead, Coates asserted simply: "I know how these types of groups work and children are always abused" (quoted in Niebuhr and Thomas 1993).

Indeed, the Branch Davidians are not the first marginal religious group in recent years to be accused of child abuse; other groups—particularly communal fundamentalist groups—have also been the focus of such claims. One previous case involved a 1982 raid against the Northeast Kingdom Community at Island Pond, in northern Vermont. That raid, later termed an "illegal fishing expedition" by a state judge, was designed ostensibly to rescue nearly a hundred mostly African-American children from a small Christian commune whose adult members were allegedly committing child abuse. No evidence of abuse was found, and the children were subsequently returned to the community (Melton 1993; Ross and Green 1993). More recently another fundamentalist Christian communal organization, the Family (formerly the Children of God), has been attacked in several countries (e.g., Argentina, Australia, France, Spain) and in the United States has been accused of promoting various forms of child sexual abuse. There are indications that these attacks on the Family have been instigated by various international anticult organizations (Richardson 1994). To date, no charges of child abuse against the group have been sustained, although government sources have vowed to continue their prosecution in Argentina.

Emphasizing claims of child abuse may be an attractive strategy of the anticult movement because of the potentially broad appeal of such allegations. In contrast to coercion-persuasion ("brainwashing") claims, which are debated primarily by social and behavioral scientists with highly specialized technical knowledge, child abuse claims are more accessible and intrinsically interesting to members of the public, many of whom are parents. Interest is particularly strong given the contemporary moral panic about child-rearing and child welfare issues. In addition, child abuse allegations have the potential to cement an odd anticult alliance from forces of the sociopolitical left and right: law enforcement agents, therapists, social workers and other children's advocates, as well as diverse segments of the religious establishment (ranging from Southern Baptists to Reform Jews), and others.

As the essays in this volume emphasize, stocktaking is crucial if we are to avoid future disasters like the conflict at Mt. Carmel. Toward that end, our analysis suggests several policy recommendations. First, authorities and media representatives should investigate carefully the complex process of claims-making surrounding marginal religious groups and their child-rearing practices. When assessing competing claims, it is important to link conflicting accounts about the group to the divergent ideological, psychological, and material interests and agendas of the adversarial parties. Second, "child abuse" should be defined very carefully, so as to avoid loose and ideologically laden uses of this stigmatizing label. Children who are physically punished, taught a distinctive (e.g., apocalyptic) theology, or raised in an unusual set of circumstances (e.g., communally) are not necessarily being abused by their caregivers. However, individuals who are committed to nonphysical forms of discipline, to liberal theological views, or to the notion that marginal religions typically prey upon innocent children may well perceive and portray such practices as abusive.

Third, authorities who must adjudicate the various claims and counterclaims about marginal religious groups should solicit and take seriously the input of social scientists who are familiar with the theology, history, and collective dynamics of such groups (see Ammerman, this volume). Moreover, when child abuse claims are at issue, these investigators should be attentive to the growing body of scholarly research that treats such accusations critically. Among other key findings, studies in this tradition suggest that child abuse allegations often turn out to be inaccurate for various reasons, and that a substantial proportion of such allegations emerge from child custody battles, or from other intrafamily or intragroup conflicts (Besharov 1986, 1990). Academic investigators are also interested in a host of thorny methodological issues pertaining to child abuse research, including the implications of divergent strategies of child examinations (Lloyd 1992; Wakefield and Underwager 1994), child suggestibility (Ceci and Bruck, 1993), and "repressed memories" that are subsequently released through therapeutic intervention (Coleman 1992; Coleman and Clancy 1990), among other contested topics.

At each step in the investigative process, it must be the responsibility of authorities to weigh carefully the tradeoffs between the preservation of religious liberty for minority religious groups and the welfare of the children. They must avoid taking steps which might jeopardize the physical or emotional well-being of the youngsters. As we learned at Mt. Carmel, without vigilant attention to these concerns, good intentions and child-saving rhetoric are not enough.

Notes

1. In the 1920s, modern "scientific" child-rearing emphasized parental awareness of the needs and developmental capacities of children; behaviorists suggested that parents avoid situations necessitating punishment and, instead, stressed the importance of positive reinforcements to instill self-discipline in the child. In the 1930s, specialists began urging parents to recognize the unique qualities of each child, and to appreciate the world from their child's point of view. The 1940s and 1950s witnessed the rise of "permissivist" parenting, in which the child was construed as the natural and most competent "architect of his or her own upbringing" (Strathman 1984, 9).

2. It is testimony to the scope and impact of these dramatic changes in popular parenting ideologies that a backlash has emerged among evangelical Protestants (Dobson 1970, 1976; LaHaye 1977; Fugate 1980; see Bartkowski and Ellison, in press). Embracing traditional notions of scriptural inerrancy and original sin, today's conservative religious writers echo many of the core themes from early American evangelical child-rearing. For instance, they reject democratic family models in favor of a vision of hierarchical and patriarchal family relations, in which the primary responsibility of parents is to exercise loving but decisive leadership. Perhaps most important, many contemporary evangelicals argue strongly in favor of the judicious use of the "rod," on both theological and pragmatic grounds (Ellison and Sherkat 1993). Empirical evidence indicates that Conservative Protestants (1) favor corporal punishment

more strongly than other Americans, and (2) use corporal punishment more frequently than other parents, to discipline both toddlers and preadolescent children (Ellison, Bartkowski, and Segal 1994).

3. The law was enacted as the Child Abuse Prevention and Treatment Act, sometimes referred to simply as the Mondale Act. The broadening of the original definition of child abuse apparently occurred in conference committee prior to the final approval of the legislation (see Nelson 1984).

4. Further, Sparks's various public statements raise questions about the specific circumstances under which the CPS investigation was conducted. For instance, she and her staff expressed concern that access to the Davidian children was restricted by adults at the facility (England and McCormick 1993a, 1993c; National Public Radio 1993). Detractors also suspect that Koresh was tipped off by phone prior to each CPS visit, permitting him to hide certain children and to suppress evidence. Sparks has accused deputies from the McLennan County Sheriff's Department, who accompanied the CPS team on each visit, of interfering with the CPS investigation by (1) instigating these leaks, and (2) demanding that the caseworkers abandon at least one visit to Mt. Carmel soon after their arrival. Some sources within the sheriff's department defend such phone calls as appropriate, given the reclusiveness of the group and the presence of weapons at Mt. Carmel, while others recall CPS personnel indicating that they, not sheriff's deputies, alerted Koresh about impending visits (England and McCormick 1993a).

5. It is interesting to note that while the news that Koresh used a wooden spoon or paddle to punish children proved controversial in some media outlets, Beverly LaHaye (1977, 128–32), founder of Concerned Women for America, reports that she and husband Tim (a minister) maintained a large wooden spoon to be used specifically for spanking their children.

6. This story surfaced in several other places as well; according to the Justice Department report, the girl was ten rather than twelve years old (Roth 1993).

7. Breault appeared on the Maury Povich show in October 1993 to recount this episode, and was challenged by Davidian survivor Wally Kennett. Kennett stated: "He (Breault) told me in 1988 that he was legally blind. If you all noticed, he had to be helped up on the stage, and when he reads he has to hold the paper right in front of his eyes. . . . He could not have seen the things he claimed he saw. These things he claimed he saw were at night in the dark. How could a man that is legally blind have seen these things?" Breault's reply was hardly convincing: "Well. . . , legally blind people do have brains and I can hear pretty well."

8. If these various allegations are accurate, then Koresh may have violated several Texas statutes. Perhaps the most serious possible offense, *aggravated sexual assault of a child*, occurs when an adult has sexual intercourse with a child under age fourteen. This is a first-degree felony punishable by a prison sentence of from five to ninety-nine years. In addi-

tion, Texas law prohibits *indecency with a child*, which occurs when an adult has sexual contact with a child under age seventeen. This offense is a second-degree felony, punishable by up to twenty years in prison. It is considered a mitigating circumstance if the child is fourteen or older and has engaged in promiscuous sexual behavior. Further, *sexual assault of a child* (sexual intercourse with a child fourteen or older) is a second-degree felony punishable by up to twenty years in prison. It is also conceivable that Koresh could have been charged with *endangering a child*, an offense that occurs when a person who has custody of a child under fifteen places that child in danger of physical or mental injury. This Class A misdemeanor is punishable by up to one year in the county jail.

9. Bunds concluded: "Now that I'm out here, living a normal life, I realize it was rape. . . . She resisted, but he kept on going because he said God told him to. Psychologically, it's weird. But you got used to it. It was normal" (quoted in England and McCormick 1993c).

10. Some survivors suggest another intriguing, albeit exotic, possibility: while Koresh did lie with young girls, it is conceivable that no sexual consummation took place (Arnold 1994). Instead, some note the biblical account of King David who, as he became elderly, began the practice of lying with young virgins of Israel in sleep only to "get heat in old age" (most probably to stimulate the blood flow and promote longevity). This Rite of Abashak, a secret and private ritual, offers one possible explanation for Koresh's behavior. However, other sympathizers have suggested that the young girls were simply betrothed to Koresh—i.e., promised to him for later liaisons.

11. Although the CPS inquiry led by Joyce Sparks turned up no evidence of sexual abuse at Mt. Carmel, save for her interview with the unnamed twelve-year-old (or ten-year-old) girl mentioned earlier, the limited scope and duration of that investigation are noteworthy. No gynecological examinations were conducted. Indeed, a CPS spokeswoman conceded that children and adults were not actually asked about sexual abuse, because CPS staff feared that such queries would compromise the investigation: "If we had asked pointed questions like that, we would have gotten only a yes or no answer" (quoted in Beck et al. 1993). It appears that gynecological exams were not performed on the children released from Mt. Carmel prior to the fire, either. Further, experts in this area caution that clear physical evidence of child sexual abuse is often elusive, unless the gynecological exam is conducted immediately following the occurrence of abuse (Wakefield and Underwager 1994).

12. If material deprivation and stress undermine the welfare of children, then federal agents are guilty of augmenting these forms of abuse (Lewis 1994; Lilliston 1994; Robertson 1994). The initial exchanges of gunfire between BATF agents and members of the community posed grave hazards for the children of Mt. Carmel, yet the agents continued to attack the facility with automatic weapons and hollow-point ammunition for more than an hour (Tedford 1993a). During the siege, agents of the FBI cut off electricity and phones and prevented traffic and supplies

from entering the community, thus maximizing hardship. To make sleep and reflection more difficult, federal agents also shone searchlights through the uncovered windows and bombarded the complex with high-volume, tape-recorded squeals of dying rabbits (see Labaton 1993a). Further, despite conflicting opinions and evidence about the physical and psychological risks posed by the tear gas, Attorney General Janet Reno approved the final assault. Although an investigation team of "independent" arson investigators (the wife of the lead investigator was employed in the Houston office of the BATF) concluded otherwise, some critics of the government allege that federal agents initiated the fatal fire.

13. Baylor psychiatrist Bruce Perry has subsequently presented a starkly negative assessment of Branch Davidian child-rearing practices. In testimony submitted in connection with the prosecution of another marginal religious group, The Family (formerly the Children of God), in Australia, Perry summarized his experience with the Branch Davidian children this way:

> it was only over time and after establishing ongoing contact with these children (essentially living with them as their caretakers) that they began to reveal the true nature of their inner world— which reflected the world that they were raised in. It was only then that we saw the coercion, the destructive educational practices, the destructive practices regarding the development of "individual ego" functions—e.g., decision making. It was only after doing a thorough, longitudinal assessment [of] the Branch Davidian children was it [sic] clear that the majority of these children were emotionally and socially immature and maldeveloped. These children had a variety of deficits in their ability to exhibit independent cognition. (Perry 1994, p. 11)

14. An ABC News/*Washington Post* poll showed that 72 percent of those surveyed approved of the FBI's final assault, while in another poll 95 percent of the respondents blamed Koresh rather than the feds for the disastrous outcome (Labaton 1993d). In a *Newsweek* poll of April 22–23, 71 percent of those surveyed agreed that "the FBI [had] good reasons to launch their operation" (Press et al. 1993).

References

Alwin, Duane F. 1984. "Trends in Parental Socialization Values: Detroit, 1958–1983." *American Journal of Sociology* 90: 359–82.
———. 1988. "From Obedience to Autonomy: Changes in Traits Desired in Children, 1924–1978." *Public Opinion Quarterly* 52: 33–52.
Aries, Philippe. 1965. *Centuries of Childhood: The Social History of Family Life.* New York: Vintage Books.
Arnold, Philip. 1994. Personal communication with author [CE].
Bartkowski, John P., and Christopher G. Ellison. 1995. "Divergent Mod-

els of Childrearing in Popular Manuals: Conservative Protestants vs. the Secular Experts." *Sociology of Religion* 56: 21–34.

Beck, Melinda, et al. 1993. "'Someone Dropped the Ball'—Authorities Missed Child Abuse." *Newsweek*, May 17: 51.

Bergin, Allen E. 1983. "Religiosity and Mental Health: A Critical Reevaluation and Meta-Analysis." *Professional Psychology: Research and Practice* 14: 170–84.

Berrick, Jill Duerr, and Neil Gilbert. 1991. *With the Best of Intentions: The Child Sexual Abuse Prevention Movement.* New York: Guilford Press.

Besharov, Douglas J. 1986. "Unfounded Allegations—A New Child Abuse Problem." *Public Interest* 83: 18–33.

———. 1990. "Gaining Control over Child Abuse Reports." *Public Welfare* (Spring): 34–41.

Best, Joel. 1990. *Threatened Children: Rhetoric and Concern about Child-Victims.* Chicago: University of Chicago Press.

Branden, Nathaniel. 1994. *The Six Pillars of Self-Esteem.* New York: Bantam.

Bromley, David G., and Anson Shupe, Jr. 1981. *Strange Gods: The Great American Cult Scare.* Boston: Beacon Press.

Carroll, Ginny, et al. 1993. "Children of the Cult." *Newsweek*, May 17: 48–50.

Ceci, S. J., and M. Bruck. 1993. "The Suggestibility of the Child Witness: A Historical Review and Synthesis." *Psychological Bulletin* 113: 403–40.

Coleman, Lee. 1992. "Creating 'Memories' of Sexual Abuse." *Issues in Child Abuse Accusations* 4: 169–76.

Coleman, Lee, and Patrick E. Clancy. 1990. "False Allegations of Child Sexual Abuse: Why Is It Happening? What Can We Do?" *Criminal Justice* (Fall): 14–20, 43–47.

Davis, James A., and Tom W. Smith. 1990. *The General Social Surveys: Cumulative Codebook, 1972–1990.* Chicago: National Opinion Research Center.

Degler, Carl N. 1980. *At Odds: Women and the Family in America from the Revolution to the Present.* New York: Oxford University Press.

deMause, Lloyd. 1974. "The Evolution of Childhood." In *The History of Childhood,* edited by Lloyd deMause, pp. 1–73. New York: Psychohistory Press.

Demos, John. 1973. "Infancy and Childhood in the Plymouth Colony." In *The American Family in Social-Historical Perspective,* edited by Michael Gordon, pp. 180–91. New York: St. Martin's Press.

Dobson, James. 1970. *Dare to Discipline.* Wheaton, IL: Living Books/Tyndale House.

———. 1976. *The Strong-Willed Child.* Wheaton, IL: Living Books/Tyndale House.

Ellis, Albert. 1962. *Reason and Emotion in Psychotherapy.* Secaucus, NJ: Lyle Stuart.

Ellison, Christopher G. 1991a. "An Eye for an Eye? A Note on the Southern Subculture of Violence Thesis." *Social Forces* 69: 1223–39.

———. 1991b. "Southern Culture and Firearms Ownership." *Social Science Quarterly* 72: 267–83.

Ellison, Christopher G., John P. Bartkowski, and Michelle L. Segal. 1994. "Conservative Protestantism and Corporal Punishment of Toddlers and Preadolescents." Paper presented at the annual meeting of the Society for the Scientific Study of Religion, Albuquerque.

Ellison, Christopher G., and Darren E. Sherkat. 1993. "Conservative Protestantism and Support for Corporal Punishment." *American Sociological Review* 58: 131–44.

England, Mark, and Darlene McCormick. 1993a. "The Sinful Messiah, Part 1." *Waco Tribune-Herald*, February 27.

———. 1993b. "The Sinful Messiah, Part 2." *Waco Tribune-Herald*, February 28.

———. 1993c. "The Sinful Messiah, Parts 3–7." *Waco Tribune-Herald*, March 1.

Fugate, Richard. 1980. *What the Bible Says about . . . Child Training.* Tempe, AZ: Alpha/Omega Press.

Gregory, Sophfronia Scott. 1993. "Children of a Lesser God." *Time*, May 17: 54.

Greven, Philip. 1977. *The Protestant Temperament: Patterns of Child-Rearing, Religious Experience, and the Self in Early America.* New York: Alfred A. Knopf.

———. 1990. *Spare the Child: The Religious Roots of Punishment and the Psychological Impact of Physical Abuse.* New York: Alfred A. Knopf.

Hernandez, Donald J. 1993. *America's Children: Resources from Family, Government, and the Economy.* New York: Russell Sage Foundation.

Hoversten, Paul, and Mimi Hall. 1993. "Fears for Kids Led to Attack." *USA Today*, April 21.

Illick, Joseph E. 1974. "Child-Rearing in Seventeenth-Century England and America." In *The History of Childhood*, edited by Lloyd deMause, pp. 303–50. New York: Psychohistory Press.

Jenkins, Philip. 1992. *Intimate Enemies: Moral Panics in Contemporary Great Britain.* New York: Aldine de Gruyter.

Johnson, John M. 1985. "Symbolic Salvation: The Changing Meanings of the Child Maltreatment Movement." *Studies in Symbolic Interaction* 6: 289–305.

———. 1989. "Horror Stories and the Construction of Child Abuse." In *Images of Issues: Typifying Contemporary Social Problems*, edited by Joel Best, pp. 5-19. New York: Aldine de Gruyter.

Johnson, Dirk. 1993. "Forty Bodies of Cult Members Are Found in Charred Ruins." *New York Times*, April 22.

Kantrowitz, Barbara, et al. 1993a. "The Messiah of Waco." *Newsweek*, March 15: 56–58.

————. 1993b. "Day of Judgement." *Newsweek*, May 3: 22–27.

Kilbride, Philip L. 1994. *Plural Marriage for Our Times: A Reinvented Option.* Westport, CT: Bergin and Garvey.

Kocen, Lynne, and Josephine Bulkley. 1981. "Analysis of Criminal Child Sex Offense Statutes." In *Child Sexual Abuse and the Law*, edited by Josephine Bulkley, pp. 1–51. Washington, DC: American Bar Association.

Labaton, Stephen. 1993a. "Reno Sees Error in Move on Cult." *New York Times*, April 20.

————. 1993b. "Confusion Abounds in the Capital on Rationale for Assault on Cult." *New York Times*, April 21.

————. 1993c. "A Strategy of Openness Aims to Avert Backlash." *New York Times*, April 22.

————. 1993d. "Reno Wins Praise at Senate Hearing." *New York Times*, April 23.

LaHaye, Beverly. 1977. *How to Develop Your Child's Temperament.* Eugene, OR: Harvest House.

Langford, Terri. 1993. "Officials Say They Had No New Complaints of Child Abuse Charges against Cultists." Associated Press, April 24.

Larzelere, Robert. 1994. "Should the Use of Corporal Punishment by Parents Be Considered Child Abuse? No." In *Debating Children's Lives: Current Controversies on Children and Adolescents*, edited by Mary Ann Mason and Eileen Gambrill, pp. 204–9. Thousand Oaks, CA: Sage.

Lessin, Roy. 1979. *Spanking: Why When How?* Minneapolis: Bethany House.

Lewis, James R. 1989. "Apostates and the Legitimation of Repression: Some Historical and Empirical Perspectives on the Cult Controversy." *Sociological Analysis* 50: 386–96.

————. 1994. "Child Abuse at Waco." In *Sex, Slander, and Salvation*, edited by James R. Lewis, pp. 133–38. Stanford, CA: Center for Academic Publication.

Lilliston, Larry. 1994. "Who Committed Child Abuse at Waco?" In *From the Ashes: Making Sense of Waco*, edited by James R. Lewis, pp. 169–74. Lanham, MD: Rowman and Littlefield.

Lloyd, Robin M. 1992. "Negotiating Child Sexual Abuse: The Interactional Character of Investigative Practices." *Social Problems* 39: 109–24.

Maurer, Adah. 1974. "Corporal Punishment." *American Psychologist* 29: 614–26.

Melton, J. Gordon. 1993. "Child Abuse, Suicide and the Branch Davidians." Paper presented at the annual meetings of the American Academy of Religion. Washington, DC.

Miller, Daniel R., and Guy E. Swanson. 1958. *The Changing American Parent.* New York: John Wiley.

National Public Radio. 1993. "Morning Edition: Social Worker Sheds Light on Branch Davidian Cult," May 20 (broadcast).

Nelson, Barbara J. 1984. *Making an Issue of Child Abuse: Political Agenda Setting for Social Problems.* Chicago: University of Chicago Press.

Niebuhr, Gustav, and Pierre Thomas. 1993. "Abuse Allegations Unproven." *Washington Post,* April 25.

Osborne, Philip. 1989. *Parenting for the '90s.* Intercourse, PA: Good Books.

Parton, Nigel. 1985. *The Politics of Child Abuse.* London: Macmillan.

Perry, Bruce D. 1994. Destructive Childrearing Practices by the Children of God. Report to Health and Community Services, Melbourne, Australia, March 28.

Pfohl, Stephen J. 1977. "The Discovery of Child Abuse." *Social Problems* 24: 310–23.

Prather, Judy Henderson. 1993. "Baylor Community Responds to the Mount Carmel Tragedy." *Baylor Line* (Summer): 27–29.

Press, Arie, et al. 1993. "General Reno Captures the Capital." *Newsweek,* May 3, 27.

Reuters 1993. "Excerpts from Clinton News Conference: 'The Right Thing.'" *New York Times,* April 21.

Richardson, James T. 1994. "Social Control of New Religions: From 'Brainwashing' Claims to Child Sex Abuse Accusations." Paper presented at the annual meetings of the Australian Sociological Association, Sydney, Australia.

Rimer, Sara. 1993. "Cult's Surviving Children: New Lives, New Ordeals." *New York Times,* April 27.

Robertson, George. 1994. "Suffer the Little Children." In *From the Ashes: Making Sense of Waco,* edited by James R. Lewis, pp. 175–80. Lanham, MD: Rowman and Littlefield.

Ross and Green. 1993. "What Is the Cult Awareness Network and What Role Did It Play in Waco?" Washington, DC. Typescript.

Roth, Bennett. 1993. "Reno Inaccurate on Cult Child Abuse, Review Says." *Houston Chronicle,* October 9.

Russell, Diana E. H. 1984. *Sexual Exploitation: Rape, Child Sexual Abuse, and Workplace Harassment.* Beverly Hills: Sage.

Shorter, Edward. 1977. *The Making of the Modern Family.* New York: Basic Books.

Smith, Mark. 1993. "Officials Frustrated Trying to Prove Abuse." *Houston Chronicle,* April 22.

Stone, Lawrence. 1977. *The Family, Sex, and Marriage in England, 1500–1800.* New York: Harper and Row.

Strathman, Terry. 1984. "From the Quotidian to the Utopian: Child Rearing Literature in America, 1926–1946." *Berkeley Journal of Sociology* 29: 1–34.

Straus, Murray A. 1994. "Should the Use of Corporal Punishment by Parents Be Considered Child Abuse? Yes." In *Debating Children's Lives: Current Controversies on Children and Adolescents,* edited by Mary Ann Mason and Eileen Gambrill, pp. 197–203. Thousand Oaks, CA: Sage.

Tedford, Deborah. 1993a. "Cult Children Hid under Beds during Battle." *Houston Chronicle*, March 2.

———. 1993b. "Closing of Abuse Probe Assailed." *Houston Chronicle*, May 6.

———. 1993c. "Couple Recalls Two Months with Cult Kids." *Houston Chronicle*, June 19.

———. 1993d. "Caseworker Says CPS Ignored Koresh Sex Abuse Allegations." *Houston Chronicle*, August 29.

U.S. District Court. 1993. Application and Affidavit for Search Warrant. W93–15M. Western District of Texas. Filed February 26, 1993.

Verhovek, Sam Howe. 1993a. "In Shadow of Texas Siege, Uncertainty for Innocents." *New York Times*, March 8.

———. 1993b. "Scores Die as Cult Compound Is Set Afire after F.B.I. Sends in Tanks with Tear Gas." *New York Times*, April 20.

Viinikka, Simmy. 1989. "Child Sexual Abuse and the Law." In *Child Sexual Abuse: A Feminist Reader*, edited by Emily Driver and Audrey Droisen, pp. 132–57. Washington Square: New York University Press.

Wakefield, Hollida, and Ralph Underwager. 1994. "The Alleged Child Victim and Real Victims of Sexual Misuse." In *Handbook of Forensic Sexology*, edited by James Krivacska and John Money. Buffalo: Prometheus Books.

Walzer, John F. 1974. "A Period of Ambivalence: Eighteenth-Century American Childhood." In *The History of Childhood*, edited by Lloyd deMause, pp. 351–82. New York: Psychohistory Press.

Watson, Paul J., Ronald J. Morris, and Ralph W. Hood. 1988. "Sin and Self-Functioning, Part 1: Grace, Guilt, and Self-Consciousness." *Journal of Psychology and Theology* 16: 254–69.

Weisberg, D. Kelly. 1984. "The 'Discovery' of Sexual Abuse." *U.C. Davis Law Review* 18: 1–57.

Woodward, Kenneth, and Kendall Hamilton. 1993. "Children of the Apocalypse." *Newsweek*, May 3: 30.

Wright, Stuart A. 1991. "Reconceptualizing Cult Coercion and Withdrawal: A Comparative Analysis of Divorce and Apostasy." *Social Forces* 70: 125–45.

———. 1993. Interview with Catherine Matteson: Branch Davidian Survivor. September 10. Transcript.

Wright, Stuart A., and Helen Rose Ebaugh. 1993. "Leaving New Religions." In *Handbook of Cults and Sects in America*, edited by David G. Bromley and Jeffrey K. Hadden, pp. 143–65. Greenwich, CT: JAI Press.

Zelizer, Viviana A. 1985. *Pricing the Priceless Child: The Changing Social Value of Children*. New York: Basic Books.

Part Three

**MEDIA COVERAGE AND
PUBLIC OPINION**

7

JAMES T. RICHARDSON

Manufacturing Consent about Koresh

A Structural Analysis of the Role of Media in the Waco Tragedy

How could the Waco tragedy have happened, an event still bewildering to those who value social order, freedom of religion, and the safety of children in our society? The episode, which cost many lives and millions of dollars, riveted the attention of the nation and the world for months, before ending in a fiery holocaust that claimed the lives of those the authorities in charge said they were seeking to help the most—the children.

The official answer, one that apparently most Americans are willing to accept, is that David Koresh was to blame (see U.S. Department of Treasury 1993). If he had not been a crazy religious fanatic who was willing to die and take his followers with him, then the standoff would have ended peacefully. This psychologizing of the "Waco problem" is as wanting now as it was when such explanations were offered for the tragedy of Jonestown (Richardson 1980). A slightly different version of this simplistic notion is that Koresh was so irrational and unpredictable that he probably would have ordered a mass suicide no matter when authorities acted, so that actions taken on that fateful fifty-first day were irrelevant. This view was developed in the trial of Davidians in San Antonio, where prosecutors expounded on the "theology of death" integral to Koresh's beliefs (Pressley 1994).

The official versions of the tragedy have been roundly criticized by a number of people, not the least of whom were the four behavioral science experts invited by the Justice Department to evaluate the FBI's role in Waco. The reports to the Justice Department by Ammerman (1993), Stone (1993), Cancro (1993), and Sullivan (1993), which are to varying degrees critical of what happened, all suggest that the holocaust probably could have been avoided (see especially Labaton 1993b; Wood 1993; McVicker 1993[1]). Some of their comments are scathing, with accusations that the Bureau of Alcohol, Tobacco, and Firearms and the Federal Bureau of Investigation did not understand or take seriously Koresh's beliefs and statements. Instead, religious aspects of the situation were trivialized and the working model used by law enforcement officials was that Koresh was a con man using religion as a cover, and that his followers were dupes or fanatics so enthralled with him that they could not resist. Law enforcement authorities ignored in-house expertise and used questionable sources when they did seek opinions from outsiders. Disagreements over tactics were glossed over and a "them-against-us", "action-imperative" (Stone 1993) mentality won the day, leading inexorably to a tragic ending.

Justice Department experts Sullivan and Stone were quite critical of decisions to "tighten the noose" around the Davidians and to use psychological warfare tactics, an approach that all four experts suggest backfired because it fulfilled Koresh's apocalyptic prophecies. The failure to allow others, including family members, to communicate with Koresh and his followers during the siege, and the refusal to use a third-party negotiator also drew strong criticism. Acceptance of a basic definition of the episode as a "hostage/rescue" situation by authorities was especially problematic (see Ammerman, this volume). Koresh's followers had joined the group of their own free will, and then most apparently opted to stay with him even during the siege.[2]

Given available alternative modes of action, some of which were even recommended by FBI behavioral science experts, why did law enforcement command officials persist in the approach being taken toward the Davidians? How could authorities proceed with the raid even after it was clear that the element of surprise had been lost? After the abortive initial assault, why did the FBI proceed with its "tighten the noose" policy in the face of considerable evidence that the tactics were not working? How was an official mind-set formed which allowed actions that encouraged the unthinkable to happen— deaths of all the children still inside the building? What was the public thinking as the situation at Mt. Carmel unfolded, and what role did such views play in Waco?

These questions guide the present effort, which will make use of the provocative work of Herman and Chomsky (1988), as well as material from the "politics of representation" literature. My thesis is simple: *Authorities were able to take actions against the Davidians with such impunity because they and members of the general public shared a view of Koresh and his followers and the situation that allowed, even required, such actions.* How this view of Koresh and his followers was developed and maintained is of great interest. Knowing how specific ideas about Koresh and his followers were so quickly tied to the anticultist ideology that has achieved hegemony in the United States (Dillon and Richardson 1991) is crucial to understanding events such as the Waco tragedy.

Manufacturing Consent

Herman and Chomsky (1988) offer a detailed "propaganda model" to explain the performance and organization of mass media in the United States. They claim that the mass media is both directly and indirectly an instrument of dominant corporate and governmental elites, even in an open society such as the United States. They state that (1988, 298): "a propaganda model suggests that the 'societal purpose' of the media is to inculcate and defend the economic, social, and political agenda of privileged groups that dominate the domestic society and the state. The media serve this purpose in many ways: through the selection of topics, distribution of concerns, framing of issues, filtering of information, emphasis and tone, and by keeping debate within the bounds of acceptable premises."

Herman and Chomsky marshall considerable evidence for this thesis, focusing on political events of the past few decades to support their arguments. They do not discuss religion in any direct way, but it seems reasonable to extend their model to encompass religious phenomena, particularly since some religious movements have garnered significant attention in recent years in the media. Such phenomena have become quite politicized, often requiring positions to be taken by politicians and others, including members of the media, from corporate executives and editors to the beat reporter. "Cults" have become big news and are thought of by many as a major new social problem in the United States and elsewhere (Beckford 1985; Robbins 1988; Bromley and Richardson 1983; Barker 1984; Kilbourne and Richardson 1984).

There are strong antipathies expressed toward these religious groups (Bromley and Breschel 1992; Richardson 1992b), and those in positions of authority in the media have contributed directly to these sentiments through choices made about how to cover such stories (van Driel and Richardson 1988a, 1988b; Beckford and Cole 1988; Selway 1989, 1992). The media are the most significant mediating structure between the mass public and marginal religions. Moreover, the media, in confluence of interests with some other institutional structures, have promoted a narrow and particularistic approach consistent with certain American values (Richardson, Kilbourne, and van Driel 1988).

Most people have never met a "Moonie," but large majorities know of them and do not like them (Bromley and Breschel 1992; Richardson 1992b; Pfeifer 1992), an unfounded but negative view generalizable to other new religions that have attracted attention in recent years. Indeed, even groups such as Koresh's that do not fit the usual definition of a new religious movement can be quickly typed as one simply by assigning it to the category of "cult" or by alleging so-called brainwashing and mind control. Such labeling has been a powerful weapon to use against groups thought to be deviant by some.[3] Herman and Chomsky's work, applied to so-called cults, can aid understanding of this circumstance, which contributed in no small measure to what happened at Waco. Only against a backdrop of pervasive anticult sentiment could those in positions of authority concerning Waco adopt the disastrous tactics they chose.

The development of such thoroughgoing contempt for new religions can fruitfully be examined using specific ideas from Herman and Chomsky, who posit a series of five "filters" that determine the quantity and character of coverage in the mass media. First, Herman and Chomsky (1988, 3–14) explain the developmental history of the acute *concentration of ownership in the mass media*, which is an industry dominated by large corporations seeking profits. They discuss the way major media are integrated, wherein major print and electronic media outlets are often controlled by the same companies and even specific families; and they point out that major media corporations have strong ties with other business institutions such as banks, through overlapping directorates and the use of credit and financial arrangements. Thus, the big business of media is highly interconnected with other institutional structures in our society, raising serious questions about its independence, and about idealized notions of freedom of the press.

The concentration of ownership and control of which Herman and Chomsky write has the potential to affect coverage of religious as well as political topics, especially since cults have become so politicized (Bromley and Robbins 1992). Once major media organizations decide how (or whether) to cover a topic or event, then the decision results in consistent reporting within fairly narrow bounds. There is usually little contrasting coverage, simply because of the much weaker position of the alternative press that might choose to treat a topic differently.

While explanations may vary about why the media have treated new religions in such a negative fashion,[4] it is clear that this has been done. Van Driel and Richardson's (1988a, 1988b) study of major print media over a ten-year period demonstrates the general antagonism toward these organizations, particularly groups such as the Unification Church ("Moonies"), Peoples Temple, Scientology, and Hare Krishna (also see Beckford and Cole's [1988] follow-up of this study in the United Kingdom, as well as Selway's [1989] study of Australian media). Many examples can also be found to illustrate this point with electronic media, as well, even though no systematic content analysis of electronic media exists on this issue. All the major networks have shown made-for-television movies with the theme of "rescuing brainwashed cult members," some a number of times.

Some observers have suggested that this orientation reflects similar values between media representatives and members of the general public—values that fail to acknowledge religion as a serious alternative to secular occupational and material pursuits typifying the individualistic and competitive cultural milieu of the United States (Richardson, Kilbourne, and van Driel, 1988). It may also be that this type of coverage has developed because of increased public interest in titillating stories framed in terms of "cults stealing children" or "breaking up families." Such emotion-laden, demonizing stories sell newspapers and gain viewers; thus those operating the commercial newspapers, and television and radio networks and outlets have been more apt to take that approach.[5]

This latter reason coincides with the second filter of Herman and Chomsky's model—namely *the role played by advertising in the competitive media market.* Herman and Chomsky point out that newspapers and television networks are in the business of selling advertising so they can survive and generate profit, a context that severely limits the approach taken by media outlets toward controversial topics. Herman and Chomsky suggest that media leaders learn quickly what topics will attract advertising, and they are likely to exploit those topics. Moreover, those media choosing to offer particular orientations or "frames" (Goffman 1974) not popular with advertisers are penalized by receipt of less revenue. Framing stories, television movies, and specials on the theme of "cults stealing innocent children," for example, has been a popular seller to advertisers. This perennial anticult myth has achieved the status of urban legend and has been adopted by virtually all mass media outlets.

Herman and Chomsky's third filter focuses on *sources of information.* News organizations have to allocate resources efficiently; they cannot be everywhere at once. Thus, they come to depend on sources—people or places where key information can be found. This leads them inexorably to institutional or governmental sources of information that furnish the official version of an event. Certainly there have been some major statements and presentations about the "cult problem" by governmental entities (Bromley and Robbins 1992; Richardson 1995c, Forthcoming). Federal agencies such as the Immigration and Naturalization Service, the Internal Revenue Service, and the Justice Department have adopted aggressive positions toward new religions that have sometimes become quite public matters. There have been several congressional hearings and reports, some very widely publicized. The federal court system has also rendered decisions in cases involving new religions that have caused great consternation among supporters of freedom of religion (Laycock 1991). A number of state governments have become entangled as well, issuing special studies, reports, and even questionable legislative actions (Richardson 1986, 1990). Local governments and legal systems have also become possible sources of such news, as battles have been fought over zoning laws and solicitation regulations. Some civil and criminal actions involving marginal religions have become newsworthy at the local, regional, and even national levels, leading to well-publicized decisions, many of which imply that these religious groups are a social problem requiring intrusive regulation and control.

While a focus on official sources seems well-placed with reference to the new religions, Herman and Chomsky also posit crucial importance on *private sources* of information. Their analysis focuses on the role large corporations and their surrogate organizations have in presenting a benevolent view of their activities, and the substantial expenditures devoted to accomplish that end. Thus corporations such as General Electric (which owns the NBC television network), perhaps the largest producer of nuclear weaponry, funds enormous advertising budgets on the theme of "making a better tomorrow" for ordinary citizens. And organizations such as the U.S. Chamber of Commerce spend millions in lobbying and information campaigns to cultivate and protect the dominant position of corporations in the United States.

On a smaller scale, private sources of information have also played a key role in developing the image of new religions shared by most Americans. Anticult organizations such as the American Family Foundation (AFF) and Cult Awareness Network (CAN) have had impressive success in shaping public attitudes in the United States and overseas (Bromley and Shupe 1994; Shupe and Bromley 1994; Richardson 1995a, Forthcoming; Richardson and van Driel 1994). These particular organizations operate on budgets mostly garnered from private foundations and individual contributions, spending their resources on public relations and lobbying campaigns aimed at attacking the "cult menace."[6] The organizations, especially CAN, issue regular press releases on major events in the cult wars. AFF publishes a popularly oriented newsletter, the *Cult Observer*, and also an attempt at a refereed professional journal, *Cultic Studies Journal*.[7] Quite often press releases from such anticult groups are treated seriously by media outlets. There are examples of even major papers printing such releases virtually verbatim.

Why organizations like CAN and AFF have had such success is, of course, a significant question. Plainly they have become experienced at what they do, institutionalizing efforts to instill public fears about so-called cults. But they have an impact that far exceeds the relatively meager budgets on which they operate, and they have overcome some major public relations disasters to become a primary source of information.[8] The answer seems to be twofold: (1) CAN and AFF have developed important political alliances, and (2) they are sending a message for which the American public has a certain receptivity.

Friends and allies, which vary in terms of "social distance," include powerful political figures and representatives of some important professions and interest groups in our society. CAN (and its precursor organizations and other groups like it) has furnished information to and worked with state governors, attorney generals, and legislators; U.S. Senators and Congressmen; the federal Justice Department, and other agencies such as the Immigration and Naturalization Service. Moreover, CAN and AFF work closely with, and even include in their leadership, representatives of the therapeutic and helping professions and certain religious organizations. Consequently, there is a significant confluence of interest among CAN and similar groups: (1) therapists who think current and former members of new religions need psychological help, (2) politicians who want to legislate against cults, (3) social workers and counselors who think cults destroy families, and (4) religious leaders who, through gate-keeping functions, attempt to protect their respective domains, alleging that cults steal children, or that they are the work of the devil. In some cases, parents of converts are involved, some of whom are quite well-enough placed socially and politically to cause trouble for such groups and to assist those who oppose them (Shupe and Bromley 1980; Richardson 1992a, 1995a).

The receptivity of the American public to the message of the anticult movement—what Shupe and Hadden (this volume) call the "anticult narrative"—is not difficult to understand. The new religions have attracted some young, upwardly mobile, high-status individuals. The investment in children of status-conscious Americans is often considerable. Thus conversion to a new religion may disrupt plans for law school or a career in medicine, eliciting outrage from parents (Richardson, Kilbourne, and van Driel 1988). Explanations about conversion are demanded, and anticult groups have an appealing answer that scapegoats these religious groups and absolves parents and their offspring. This account posits that the convert was tricked by a mysterious and inscrutable (if they were from the East) religious charlatan who was adept at the use of powerful psychotechnology developed first by Communists and subsequently imported for the insidious use in America against "our children" (Richardson, Van der Lans, and Derks 1986).

The account ignores, however, the most common pattern—that persons join volitionally, and that participation is usually brief and often ameliorative, all well-substantiated findings from research by scholars in this field of study (see work of Wright 1983, 1987; Barker 1984; Bird and Reimer 1984; Levine 1984; Galanter 1989; and reviews by Richardson 1985a, 1985b, 1993c, 1994a). The neglect or omission of these findings and the perspective they support occurs quickly and easily, however, because such findings do not fit the brainwashing model that is more conducive to the self-interest of the parties involved.

The Waco tragedy furnishes a case study of how such influence can work. CAN and AFF leaders were highly visible immediately after the initial attack, and CAN's press release capabilities mobilized to the task. CAN and AFF seized this opportunity to interpret the standoff and offer their "expertise" to the media. Literally hundreds of interviews were given by CAN/AFF spokespersons volunteering as self-appointed experts, furnishing narratives of the deadly initial assault, and suggesting tactics. Deprogrammer Rick Ross appeared on major network programs a number of times, talking about his role in advising authorities about the Davidians and what actions should be taken to terminate the siege.

When the fateful fifty-first day arrived and the siege was ended, CAN-affiliated spokespersons were prominent media personalities, condemning Koresh and drawing parallels with Jonestown. One of the most blatant examples of hegemonic, anticult framing occurred when the well-respected *McNeil-Lehrer News Hour* featured psychiatrist Louis Jolyon West, a prominent personage in the movement and a member of the board of directors of CAN. West has a history of long involvement in questionable causes and projects, including research for the CIA on mind-control issues. West's former academic position at UCLA affords him some credibility, and apparently *McNeil-Lehrer* staff thought him the proper spokesman for the evening news on that day. Thus the anticult frame enjoyed a lengthy and influential airing on this premier news show, on an evening when virtually all of America was focused on this tragic event.[9] The involvement of CAN continued with disturbing reports that CAN personnel had been involved in deprogramming surviving Branch Davidians so they would "become productive witnesses for the prosecution" (Wood 1993, 239).

Organizations such as CAN and similarly minded groups also serve an important function referred to in Herman and Chomsky's fourth filter, the *production of "flak" and enforcement of proper perspectives.* Herman and Chomsky discuss the wide range of organizations that have developed to criticize the media when they stray from the politically correct position on some issues. These organizations maintain pressure on media outlets and target media programming that is unacceptable.

This filter is not as important to the issue of the spread of ideas about the new religions, if only because there is so little favorable coverage about these groups, as has been noted. Thus, there is little to criticize, after the fact. However, one could argue that CAN and similar groups serve something of a pre-emptive role, with their readiness to furnish a strict anticult explanation for any possibly ambiguous event involving a minority religious group (see Lewis, this volume) and some unpopular political groups, as well.

The fifth filter through which any news must pass concerns *anticommunism as a control device*, a filter that now seems a bit antiquated. Herman and Chomsky refer to an overarching ideology that guides the interpretation of all news, but, more important, furnishes a way to harangue or intimidate dissenters into submission. If media personnel or others who were worthy of media attention strayed from the status quo position, they could, during the Cold War, be accused of being soft on communism, a very effective social weapon.

It should be noted, however, that there are clear ties between anticommunism and anticultism, in that development of the mysterious psychotechnology allegedly used by so-called cults was attributed to Communists in Korea, China, and the former Soviet Union (Anthony 1990; Richardson and Kilbourne 1983). In one important sense then, anticultism fits neatly with the overarching anticommunism theme pervasive in American ideology until recently, and it should be remembered that anticultism began twenty years ago, when fear of communism was still strong.

Anticultism also contains other discrete elements that resonate with the anticommunism theme (Richardson and Kilbourne 1983). Many new religions are communal, or at least most of the controversial ones have been, which can inspire reactions reminiscent of the anticollectivism of anticommunist ideology. Furthermore, there were often elements of racism and antiethnic sentiments associated with anticommunism, themes that also can be found in anticultism.[10]

It would be impolitic to argue that anticultism has assumed the prominence of anticommunism. However, anticultism has become diffused in American society. The Gallup Poll (1989) discussed in Richardson (1992b) and the work of Bromley and Breschel (1992), and that of Pfeifer (1992) have shown that there is a pervasive fear of "cults," and that they have become perhaps the most hated groups in America. In a nationwide survey of 1,000 adults conducted by Gallup, 62 percent said that they would not like to have religious sects or cults as neighbors, a figure twice as high as the next most disliked category (fundamentalists) and four or five times as high as the figures for categories such as African Americans, Koreans, Hispanics, Russians, and Vietnamese. As Lewis suggests in an earlier chapter, anticult antipathies have spread widely throughout America, setting the stage for the kind of actions taken at Mt. Carmel.

Worthy and Unworthy Victims

Herman and Chomsky (1988, 31–35) claim that the impact of the five filters narrows the range of what becomes news, a process which leads to a "dichotomization" of subjects. This refers to a simplification whereby topics are defined in black or white terms. An overarching frame is developed within which to present stories about the topic. In short, a selected slant is developed that influences how journalists write about a topic that has become newsworthy.

One crucial choice is to determine whether those being written about are "worthy" or "unworthy" victims. Many newsworthy episodes involve people being harmed, even if the connection seems indirect.[11] Harm itself is not the issue: people being hurt is to be expected in news stories. What is the issue is whether those being harmed deserve it or not. Herman and Chomsky state (1988: 35): "Our hypothesis is that worthy victims will be featured prominently and dramatically, that they will be humanized, and that their victimization will receive the detail and context in story construction that will generate reader interest and sympathetic emotion. In contrast, unworthy victims will merit only slight detail, minimal humanization, and little context that will excite or outrage."

The slant taken with most stories about new religions clearly demonstrates this dichotomization, as research on media coverage shows (van Driel and Richardson 1988a, 1988b; Beckford and Cole 1988; Selway 1989). "Cults," of course, "brainwash" innocent victims, taking advantage of the naivete and idealism of America's youth. Thus, participants are generally defined as worthy victims, as are their families. Media themes concerning the "rescue" of these worthy victims are prominent in television programming about new religions and in print media coverage.

The proposition offered here is that, for reasons discussed, those associated with David Koresh at Mt. Carmel never made it into the category of "worthy victims." Instead, there was an expressed ambiguity about their status. Those living at Mt. Carmel, including even the children, were never fully humanized in the eyes of the general public. We knew little about them as individuals, including details of their lives—their hopes and desires, their hobbies, their goals. We did not see many depictions of them as real human beings. The public was told repeatedly about the crude demographics—how many men, women, and children there were inside Mt. Carmel, and what countries they were from—in large part because media representatives had virtually no access to those inside the besieged site.

The dehumanization of those inside Mt. Carmel, coupled with the thoroughgoing demonization of Koresh, made it easier for those in authority to develop tactics that seemed organized for disaster (see McVicker 1993, 22). The American public seemed less concerned about those inside Mt. Carmel than they were enthralled with the "Waco miniseries" that unfolded on their television screen every night for seven weeks. The evening news had all the elements to guarantee high ratings—religion, sex, guns, child abuse, and other violence, in tandem with the intrigue and complex plotting by both sides. The drama seemed to imitate a Greek tragedy, moving inexorably toward its predictable climax, and we know that Greek tragedies always involve predetermined sacrifices. That tragic sense of the "meaning" of the Waco tragedy was borne out on April 19 when authorities did what Koresh had been predicting all along to his followers (Richardson 1994b).

Direct Control of the Media

It would be misleading to conduct the analysis without some comment on the direct control of media at Mt. Carmel. Herman and Chomsky's (1988) theoretical scheme focuses on the situation of a competitive media operating within an environment (the five filters) that is "managed," not controlled overtly, such as in an authoritarian state. However, even in a managed society such as the United States, overt control is sometimes sanctioned. This occurs when the society is at war or when law enforcement personnel are involved in an action against alleged criminals. In both situations usual rules of access for the media do not apply, as ample court rulings and laws demonstrate. Those in authority have immense control in such situations, and this allows them to manage the news directly. This certainly happened in Waco. Indeed, some media personnel have said that in the Waco situation there was more governmental control than they had ever experienced in long careers of covering the news (Freedom of Information Foundation Conference 1993).

Federal officials made an early decision that was enforced throughout the long episode that reporters would not be allowed access to Koresh and his followers.[12] There was little serious thought given by authorities even to organizing effective pool coverage that would allow the limited access for a few media representatives that is sometimes used in situations where danger exists, such as a prison riot with hostages or a war setting (Freedom of Information Foundation Conference 1993). Instead, a total ban on communication with sect members inside Mt. Carmel was established, and reporters, of whom there were hundreds, were moved progressively back from the front lines until they were some three miles from Mt. Carmel.

Although the BATF was initially in charge, the FBI assumed control shortly after the abortive raid and retained it until April 20, when the Texas Department of Public Safety assumed control. All these law enforcement agencies used the media for their own ends, inhibiting and restricting information and preventing any empathetic account from the residents of Mt. Carmel. The BATF used the Waco paper and a television station as a scapegoat early on, blaming them for notifying Koresh about the impending raid (U.S. Department of Treasury 1993, 82–88, 157–63). The FBI exploited the media throughout the episode by carefully editing information and issuing only reports that placed their actions in the most positive light. Early in the standoff, the FBI requested that some of Koresh's "ramblings" be played on a radio station, as Koresh had asked, in order to try to gain his surrender. FBI officials became upset when Koresh called CNN directly at one point, and stopped the activity immediately by cutting all phone lines except the one they wanted kept open.[13] Since the FBI was in charge of all press conferences, it was apparent that they were sending messages directly to Koresh, messages that were not necessarily true in a technical sense, but were the result of a concerted strategy by the agency to bring an end to the standoff (see U.S. Department of Treasury 1993, 193–210; Holley 1993, 52; Freedom of Information Foundation Conference 1993).

When enterprising reporters did seek to get closer than the three-mile limit, they were treated harshly. A number of photographers, tired of the "lens wars" that had developed as media outlets sent stronger and stronger lenses to Mt. Carmel, violated distance limitations imposed by the FBI (Wilson 1993; Freedom of Information Foundation Conference 1993, 20). They were summarily arrested, thrown to the ground, handcuffed, and taken away to jail. There were other examples of physical and verbal abuse of reporters trying to get the story (Department of Treasury 1993, 110). Such treatment was protested strongly by media representatives. Shelly Katz, *Time-Life* photographer, declared that "in over thirty years, twenty-seven of which have been with *Time-Life*, I have covered everything from wars to riots—you name it. I have never been restrained as I was in Waco, and I will say needlessly and senselessly" (Freedom of Information Foundation Conference 1993, 7). But such treatment continued and did send a message that violating the rules was serious business, and would be dealt with harshly.[14]

Koresh and his followers knew that they were losing the media war, for they continually requested access, sometimes even unfurling homemade banners made from bedsheets ("God Help Us, We Need Press") asking for contact with the media. Some of the reports by the behavioral scientists cited earlier criticized this ban on such interaction and communication, as did attorney Dick DeGuerin (Freedom of Information Foundation Conference 1993, 14–17). It now seems quite plausible that had the media been allowed better access, it might have resulted in a different outcome. Better access, however, would have perhaps had the effect of humanizing Koresh and his followers, which would have undercut the seemingly official policy of demonization. This might have made it more difficult to contemplate the kinds of actions that were taken against the men, women, and children at Mt. Carmel. Better interaction might also have put more people in contact with Koresh, who could have discussed his theological ideas in a serious way that would have led to some modification of those ideas. And most important, allowing media personnel some access might have served to defuse the intense situation that was obviously developing within Mt. Carmel, as the noose was tightened day after day. Media personnel could even have served as third-party negotiators with Koresh, not an unprecedented occurrence in such situations.

But none of this happened, of course. Instead, FBI tactics, and Koresh's response to those tactics, moved the situation tragically toward the conflagration that occurred, unimpeded by the scrutiny or assistance of the media. The effort at managing and controlling the media was virtually a total success, but the "operation" itself was a complete failure: most "patients," including the children, died.

Concluding Comment

This structural analysis has been critical of both the media and the authorities handling the situation in Waco. The media have contributed directly to development and promotion of the anticult paradigm, to the extent that it can reasonably be referred to as a dominant hegemony of thought about new religions among the general public (Dillon and Richardson 1991). There is a politically correct ideological position on so-called cults. Any group that drifts far from the bounds of ordinary acceptable values and behaviors stands to be accused of being a "cult," and anyone who defends such groups stands to be called a "cult-sympathizer," with all that is implied by those terms (see Richardson 1993a).[15] Such pervasive anticult sentiment makes it easier to justify and defend the kinds of strategies that were implemented at Mt. Carmel. Indeed, such a hegemonic view was essential to what happened, and grasping that fact makes the fiery holocaust itself more understandable.

Having made that general point, however, it must be said that the media cannot be blamed for the specific way the tragedy developed. The several authorities in charge, from beginning to end, must be held responsible for the many bad judgments and misguided plans that were developed before, during, and even after the fire. A key element of the strategy taken, particularly by the FBI, was to exercise total control over the media. Authorities treated the media simply as a resource to be allocated and used as they desired, and as a nuisance to be dealt with severely if they refused to comply. In the end, of course, official reports about the tragedy blame the "irresponsible media" for much of what happened, an account that ironically is suggestive of further controls over the media in future situations of this kind.[16]

This authoritarian and even disdainful way of dealing with media by the authorities should concern all citizens of our society who value individual freedom and who think that a reasonably unfettered press is essential to democracy. Those studying what happened at Waco should add to the list of casualties the idea of a free press, even as we have seen it developed within the American context Herman and Chomsky describe. Also, those who want to avert future tragic episodes such as occurred at Waco should carefully re-examine the process whereby simplistic anticult views about the meaning of new religions have achieved such hegemony in American society.

Notes

1. James Wood, editor of the *Journal of Church and State*, observes (1993: 239), "If the state had intervened elsewhere in the world against a religious group as had occurred at the Branch Davidian compound, it would have been reported in the U.S. as an act of oppression." Dick DeGuerin, Koresh's attorney, claimed (in McVicker 1993) that (1) the BATF was attempting to grandstand to support their budget request, which was before Congress in March; (2) that the BATF had a "long history of . . . excessive force, abusing their authority" (p. 17); (3) the search warrants were deficient in crucial ways; and (4) the BATF refused an invitation from Koresh prior to the raid to come to Mt. Carmel to inspect the guns.

2. Obviously one cannot say that the small children had chosen to join and stay of their own free will. Therefore it makes some sense to think of the children as hostages, as did the FBI's own behavioral experts. However, it is virtually impossible to understand why, if that was the think-

ing, the FBI authorized the tactics it did at the end. The CS gas was extremely irritating, even lethal, to all, especially young children who did not have proper gas masks (see Stone's detailed discussion of this point). As Stone notes (1993, 35), autopsies revealed that most of the children died of suffocation.

3. This labeling was done post hoc to People's Temple, about which few were concerned until the mass suicide in Guyana. But once the event had occurred, it was politically expedient for antagonists of new religions to exploit that tragedy to promote anticult themes and interests (Richardson 1980). See Robbins, Anthony, and McCarthy (1983) for one of the first systematic analyses of the use of so-called brainwashing and mind-control accusations as a powerful social weapon to stigmatize unpopular groups.

4. It would be interesting to find out whether any offspring of members of major media families have been involved with some of the new religions. This would not be surprising, given the educational levels and class origins of many members of some of the groups, which were higher than those of the general public (Barker 1984; Wuthnow 1978). Certainly the sons and daughters of some quite prominent and wealthy Americans have had this type of experience, an involvement that might have served as a catalyst for a more negative orientation of major media corporations. The beginnings of "medicalization" of participation in new religions owes much to such a direct personal connection. The author of the first article about "destructive cultism" in a major professional journal Eli Shapiro (1977), was writing from his experience of attempting to extract, through deprogramming and the use of conservatorship laws, his son Edward from the Hare Krishnas (Richardson and Stewart, 1990; Richardson, 1992a). The term "destructive cultism" coined by Shapiro has become a byword of those concerned about new religions, used as if it refers to a new psychological syndrome.

5. I have encountered this deliberate selectivity in working with the media over years of research in the area of new religions. When my perspective or analysis did not fit with the view that the reporters had, then they were much less interested in what I had to say. I have also had several discussions with reporters who were interested in a perspective other than the anticult party line, but who said that upper management might not agree, and that the story might not run. Sometimes they were correct in that assessment.

6. Information on CAN, a tax-exempt charitable and educational organization, is available through its "990" forms, which are filed with the IRS and become public records. This data source reveals a number of foundations that give regular amounts to CAN. Also, there are allegations that CAN serves as a go-between for concerned parents and deprogrammers, and then receives kickbacks from deprogrammers. Such allegations are hotly denied by CAN officials, but are belied by such information as that contained in affidavits filed by some former CAN officials and deprogrammers, as well as the federal trial of deprogrammer

Galen Kelly, who was found guilty of federal kidnaping charges in 1993 and was sentenced to a seven-year prison term.

7. The effort to bootleg this journal into the arena of refereed professional journals has followed on the heels of severe criticism of some anticult legitimators for not presenting their brainwashing-based theories in legal, legislative, and professional forums. One prominent criticism was that such ideas had not been published in refereed professional journals, and thus were not subject to the rigors and scrutiny of the relevant disciplines. After this criticism gained momentum, some major figures in the anticult movement established a "professional organization" and assumed sponsorship of the *Cultic Studies Journal*, now promoted as a refereed professional journal.

8. One former CAN leader, Reverend Michael Rokos, was dropped when it became known that he had been arrested on morals charges. Rokos was arrested in Baltimore in 1982 for soliciting sex with a male police officer posing as a minor. The former president of CAN resigned in 1990. CAN's contacts with deprogrammers, some of whom seem quite disreputable, also have detracted.

9. It is noteworthy that Herman and Chomsky (1988, 25) chose participation on the *McNeil-Lehrer* program as a major indicator of what type of people are selected as experts in the areas of defense and terrorism. This program, which is seen overseas in a number of countries, as well, is a major validator of experts in American society.

10. The consequences of widespread acceptance of anticultism are somewhat similar to those of pervasive anticommunism. Herman and Chomsky (1988, 30) discuss the effects in an insightful passage that I shall quote, with anticultism substituted for anticommunism, to illustrate the point: "When [anticult] fervor is aroused, the demand for serious evidence in support of claims of [cult] abuses is suspended, and charlatans can thrive as evidential sources. Defectors, informers, and assorted other opportunists move to center stage as 'experts,' and they remain there even after exposure as highly unreliable, if not downright liars."

This passage seems to describe well what has happened, especially as demonstrated with the tragic Waco episode.

11. For instance, a story could simply be a report about the official U.S. position on a violent episode in a Latin American country. The position assumes, however, that one side is correct and the other is the aggressor. As Herman and Chomsky point out, the politically correct side can literally get away with murder, for its cause is deemed just, whereas those designated the aggressors can do only evil, receiving no credit for any good deeds they might do.

12. Wilson (1993) quotes a *Houston Post* reporter, Terry Kliewer, as saying: "The FBI . . . was kind of using us like tools. Most of us could sense it at the time, but we did not have a great deal of alternative. When the FBI said something as a matter of fact, we tried to be reasonably skeptical about it . . . but it wasn't easy to juxtapose it next to somebody else's version of the same thing. They [the FBI] had the only version . . .

because, of course, [Koresh] was incommunicado to the general public. We were all hamstrung that way."

13. Herman and Chomsky (1988: 307) close their book with a brief comment about the development of cable and satellite communications systems such as CNN, which they think is a major structural change in opposition to centralized control of the propaganda system based on traditional oligopolies in the print and electronic media. The kind of access allowed via satellites and cable directly attacks traditional controls, making the operation of the five filters discussed herein somewhat skewed if not yet obsolete. The best example of this lack of control was the presence of CNN personnel in Baghdad during the Gulf War, giving the world "the other side of the story." CNN was severely attacked for having people there because it upset the usual control of the news afforded authorities in a war situation. The attacks against CNN, of course, were made using the rationale that CNN was forced to become a propaganda arm for the Iraqis by virtue of the tenuous position CNN reporters occupied there. However, the spoon-feeding of reporters at the daily arranged briefings did not compare well with the kind of coverage coming from Baghdad directly via CNN. Hence the attacks on CNN. Perhaps the experience of authorities in the Gulf War with the new technology even contributed to new media control procedures such as those used at Mt. Carmel, which were extremely rigorous.

14. Attorney DeGuerin (McVicker 1993; Freedom of Information Foundation Conference 1993) was very critical of media representatives for agreeing to accept the kind of control exercised on them by the government, saying that this acquiescence helped governmental authorities protect themselves and their agencies from criticism. Also, at the FOIF conference, John Lumpkin, Texas AP bureau chief, complained mightily about how he was treated when trying to gather information about the situation at the courthouse in Waco. He was not allowed even to talk to a federal judge about an aspect of the situation. The Waco situation reminds one of the collusion between media and police authorities in the famous Hilton bombing case in Australia, also involving an unpopular religious group (Ananda Marga), which resulted in long prison sentences for three innocent people (see Anderson 1992, especially chapter 27, "Crime and the Mass Media")

15. There is currently a declaratory judgment motion pending in Federal District Court in New York's Southern District to stop the FBI and other federal authorities from referring to the New Alliance Party as a cult. This left-oriented political party, which was successful in getting its candidate for U.S. president, Dr. Lenora Fulani, an African American woman, on the ballot in all fifty states, has been very critical of established ways of doing things in American society, especially focusing on endemic racism in America. They claim a disinformation campaign against them by the FBI and other federal agencies, in conjunction with Cult Awareness Network and the Anti-Defamation League, who have issued reports on the NAP that have been circulated by the FBI through-

out the country, as part of an ongoing investigation of the NAP. The motion alleges that the FBI has chosen in their press releases and comments of late to use the term "organized political cult" to refer to the NAP, a tactic that the NAP claims undercuts its ability to function as a political party. The NAP seems well aware of the hegemonic implications of this subtle but effective way of designating the organization, and wants it stopped. The motion claims that the NAP fears that this labeling by officials is a prelude to another military-like action such as occurred in Waco. Another political group sometimes referred to as a cult by CAN and the media is that headed by Lyndon LaRouche.

Note that a motion was filed in the San Antonio Davidian trial, requesting that the prosecution be precluded from using the term "cult" to refer to the Davidians. The motion was rejected by the judge, however (Fair 1994). A similar motion was granted in a major Australian child custody case in 1994 (Richardson 1995d), establishing a first such legal precedent.

16. This is reminiscent of the recommendations from official studies of the Jonestown tragedy. The huge official report, which was mostly a compilation of newspaper coverage, ended with recommendations that the Freedom of Information and Privacy Acts be weakened to allow more thorough investigation of such groups and the people associated with them in order to avoid future events such as the mass murder/suicide of Jonestown (see Richardson 1980).

References

Ammerman, Nancy. 1993. "Report to the Justice and Treasury Departments Regarding Law Enforcement Interaction with the Branch Davidians in Waco, Texas." *Recommendations of Experts for Improvement in Federal Law Enforcement after Waco.* Washington, DC: U.S. Department of Justice.

Anderson, Tim. 1992. *Take Two: The Criminal System Revisited.* Sydney: Bantam Books.

Anthony, Dick. 1990. "Religious Movements and Brainwashing Testimony: Evaluating Key Testimony." In *In Gods We Trust,* edited by T. Robbins and D. Anthony. New Brunswick, NJ: Transaction Books.

Barker, Eileen. 1984. *The Making of a Moonie: Brainwashing or Choice?* Oxford: Blackwell.

———. 1989. *New Religious Movements.* London: Her Majesty's Stationary Office.

Beckford, James. 1985. *Cult Controversies.* London: Tavistock.

Beckford, James, and Melanie Cole. 1988. "British and American Responses to New Religious Movements." *Bulletin of the John Rylands University Library of Manchester* 70 (3): 209–24.

Bird, Frederick, and Bill Reimer. 1982. "Participation Rates in New Religious Movements." *Journal for the Scientific Study of Religion* 21: 1–14.

Bromley, David, and Edward Breschel. 1992. "General Population and Institutional Support for Social Control of New Religious Movements: Evidence from National Survey Data." *Behavioral Sciences and the Law* 10: 39–52.

Bromley, David, and James T. Richardson, eds. 1983. *The Brainwashing/Deprogramming Controversy.* New York: Edwin Mellen.

Bromley, David, and T. Robbins. 1992. "The Role of Government in Regulating New and Nonconventional Religions." In *The Role of Government in Monitoring and Regulating Religion in Public Life,* edited by James Wood and Derek Davis. Waco, TX: Dawson Institute of Church-State Studies, Baylor University.

Bromley, David, and A. Shupe. 1994. "Organized Opposition to New Religious Movements." In *The Handbook on Cults and Sects in America,* edited by David G. Bromley and Jeffrey K. Hadden, pp. 177–98. Greenwich, CT: JAI Press.

Bromley, David,, Anson D. Shupe, and Joseph Ventimiglia. 1979. "Atrocity Tales, the Unification Church and the Social Construction of Evil." *Journal of Communication* 29: 42–53.

Cancro, Robert. 1993. "Letter to Philip Heymann, Deputy Attorney General, Department of Justice." *Recommendations of Experts for Improvements in Federal Law Enforcement after Waco.* Washington, DC: U.S. Department of Justice.

Cockburn, Alexander. 1993. "From Salem to Waco, by Way of the Nazis." *Los Angeles Times,* Tuesday, April 27.

Dillon, Jane, and James T. Richardson. 1991. "Social Construction of the 'Cult' Concept: A Politics of Representation Analysis." Paper presented at the annual meeting of the Society of the Scientific Study of Religion, Pittsburgh, PA.

Fair, Kathy. 1993a. "Legal Expert: Treasury Plan Suspect." *Houston Chronicle,* September 15: 13A.

———. 1993b. "Two Media Groups Protest Secrecy on Cult Raid Report." *Houston Chronicle,* September 16: 28A.

———. 1994. "Eleven Davidians' Trial to Open Amid Secrecy." *Houston Chronicle,* January 9, p. 1A.

Freedom of Information Foundation Conference. 1993. "Mount Carmel: What Should the Public Know?" Austin, TX, September 10–11. Transcript.

Galanter, Marc. 1989. *Cults and New Religious Movements.* Washington, DC: American Psychiatric Association.

Gallup, George. 1989. "Members of Cults Head List of Least Desirable Neighbors." *Palm Beach Post,* March 16. West Palm Beach, FL.

Goffman, Irving. 1974. *Frame Analysis.* New York: Harper and Row.

Herman, Edward S., and Noam Chomsky. 1988. *Manufacturing Consent: The Political Economy of the Mass Media.* New York: Pantheon Books.

Holley, Joe. 1993. "The Waco Watch." *Columbia Journalism Review* (May/June): 50–53.

Isikoff, Michael. 1993a. "FBI Clashed over Waco, Report Says." *Washington Post*, October 9, p. A1.

Isikoff, Michael. 1993b. "FBI Faulted on Warnings of Waco Mass Suicide." *Washington Post*, October 3, p. A8.

Kilbourne, Brock, and James T. Richardson. 1982. "Cults versus Families: A Case of Misattribution of Cause?" *Marriage and Family Review* 4 (304): 81–101.

———. 1984. "Psychotherapy and the New Religions in a Pluralistic Society." *American Psychologist* 39: 237–51.

Labaton, Stephen. 1993a. "Outside Review Criticizes FBI on Raid on Cult." *New York Times*, November 16, p. A7.

———. 1993b. "Report on Initial Raid on Cult Finds Officials Erred and Lied." *New York Times*, October 1, p. A1.

———. 1993c. "Report on Assault on Waco Cult Contradicts Reno's Explanations." *New York Times*, October 9, p. A1.

Laycock, Douglas. 1991. "The Remnants of Free Exercise." *Supreme Court Review 1990*. Chicago: University of Chicago Press.

Levine, Saul. 1984. *Radical Departures: Desperate Detours to Growing Up*. San Diego, CA: Harcourt, Brace, Jovanovich.

McVicker, Steve. 1993. "Assault on Mount Carmel." *Houston Post*, July 22, pp. 17–22.

Perrin, Robin. 1991. "Religion as Deviant Behavior." Paper presented at annual meeting of the Pacific Sociological Association, Irvine, CA.

Pfeifer, Jeffrey. 1992. "The Psychology of Framing Cults: Schematic Presentations and Cult Evaluations." *Journal of Applied Social Psychology* 22: 531–44.

Pressley, Sue Anne. 1994. "Waco Cult Adept in 'Theology of Death,' Trial Told." *Washington Post*, January 13, p. A3.

Richardson, James T. 1980. "People's Temple and Jonestown: A Corrective Comparison and Critique." *Journal for the Scientific Study of Religion* 19: 239–55.

———. 1985a. "The Active vs. Passive Convert: Paradigm Conflict in Conversion/Recruitment Research." *Journal for the Scientific Study of Religion* 24: 163–79.

———. 1985b. "Psychological and Psychiatric Studies of New Religions." In *Advances in the Psychology of Religion*, edited by L. Brown. New York: Pergamon.

———. 1986. "Consumer Protection and Deviant Religion." *Review of Religious Research* 28: 168–79.

———. 1988. *Money and Power in the New Religions*. New York: Edwin Mellen Press.

———. 1990. "New Religions on Trial: The Case of Oregon." Paper presented at annual meeting of the Pacific Sociological Association, Spokane, WA.

———. 1991. "Cult/Brainwashing Cases and the Freedom of Religion" *Journal of Church and State* 33: 55–74.

———. 1992a. "Mental Health of Cult Consumers: A Legal and Scientific Controversy." In *Religion and Mental Health*, edited by J. Schumaker. New York: Oxford University Press

———. 1992b. "Public Opinion and the Tax Evasion Trial of Reverend Moon." *Behavioral Sciences and the Law* 10: 53–64.

———. 1993a. "Definitions of 'Cult': From Sociological-Technical to Popular-Negative." *Review of Religious Research* 34: 348–56.

———. 1993b. "Religiosity as Deviance: Negative Religious Bias in and Misuse of the DSM-III." *Deviant Behavior* 14: 1–21.

———. 1993c. "A Social Psychological Critique of 'Brainwashing' Claims about Recruitment to New Religions." In *The Handbook of Cults and Sects in America*, edited by David G. Bromley and Jeffrey K. Hadden, pp. 75–98. Greenwich, CT: JAI Press.

———. 1994a. "Clinical and Personality Assessment of Participants in New Religions." *International Journal for the Psychology of Religion.* Forthcoming.

———. 1994b. "Lessons from Waco: When Will We Ever Learn?" *From the Ashes: Making Sense of Waco*, edited by James Lewis. Rowman & Littlefield.

———. 1995a. "Evolution of Social Control Methods with New Religions." *Law and Society Review.* Forthcoming.

———. 1995b. "Journalist Attitudes toward New Religions in the U.S. and Australia." Paper presented at the annual meeting of the Pacific Sociological Association, San Francisco.

———. 1995c. "Legal Status of Minority Religions in the U.S." *Social Compass.* Forthcoming.

———. Forthcoming. "Minority Religions and the 'New Europe.'" *Journal of Church and State.*

Richardson, James T., and Brock Kilbourne. 1983. "Classical and Contemporary Applications of Brainwashing Models: A Comparison and Critique." In *The Deprogramming/Brainwashing Controversy*, edited by David G. Bromley and James T. Richardson, pp. 29–46. New York: Edwin Mellen.

Richardson, James T., and Mary Stewart. 1990. "Medicalizing Participation in New Religions." Paper presented at annual meeting of the Society for the Scientific Study of Religion, Washington, DC.

Richardson, James T., J. Van der Lans, and Frans Derks. 1986. "Leaving and Labelling: Voluntary and Coerced Disaffiliation from Religious Social Movements." In *Research in Social Movements, Conflicts and Change*, vol. 9, edited by K. Lang, pp. 97–126. Greenwich, CT: JAI Press.

Richardson, James T., and Barend van Driel. 1984. "Public Opinion on Legislative Control of New Religions: A Research Note." *Journal for the Scientific Study of Religion* 23: 412–18.

Richardson, James T., and Barend van Driel. 1994. "New Religions and Their Opposition in European Countries." In *Anti-Cult Movements in Comparative Perspective*, edited by A. Shupe and D. Bromley, pp. 129–170. Greenwich, CT: JAI Press.

Richardson, James T., Brock Kilbourne, and Barend van Driel. 1989. "Alternative Religions and Economic Individualism." In *Research in the Social Scientific Study of Religion,* 1: 3–56. JAI Press.

Robbins, Thomas. 1988. *Cults, Converts, and Charisma.* Newbury Park, CA: Sage.

Robbins, Thomas, Dick Anthony, and James McCarthy. 1983. "Legitimating Repression," In *The Brainwashing/ Deprogramming Controversy,* edited by David G. Bromley and James T. Richardson, pp. 319–28. New York: Edwin Mellen.

Robbins, Thomas, and David G. Bromley. 1992. "Social Experimentation and the Significance of American New Religions." *Research in the Social Scientific Study of Religion* 4: 1–28. JAI Press.

Robbins, Thomas, William Shepherd, and James McBride. 1985. *Cults, Culture, and the Law.* Chico, CA: Scholars Press.

Selway, Deborah. 1989. "Religion in Print Media: A Study of the Portrayal of Religion in the *Sydney Morning Herald* 1978–88." Honor's Thesis, University of Queensland.

———. 1992. "Religion in the Mainstream Press: The Challenge for the Future." *Australian Religious Studies Review* 5 (2): 18–24.

Shapiro, Eli. 1977. "Destructive Cultism." *American Family Physician* 15: 80–83.

Shupe, Anson D., and David G. Bromley. 1980. *The New Vigilantes.* Beverly Hills, CA: Sage.

———, ed. 1994. *The Anti-Cult Movement in Comparative Perspective.* Greenwich, CT: JAI Press.

Stone, Alan A. 1993. "Report and Recommendations Concerning the Handling of Incidents Such as the Branch Davidian Standoff in Waco, Texas." Washington, DC: U.S. Justice Department.

Sullivan, Lawrence E. 1993. "Recommendations Concerning Incidents Such as the Branch Davidian Standoff in Waco, Texas, between February 28, 1993, and April 19, 1993. *Recommendations of Experts for Improvements in Federal Law Enforcement after Waco.* Washington, DC: U.S. Justice Department.

U.S. Department of Treasury. 1993. *Report of the Department of Treasury on the Bureau of Alcohol, Tobacco, and Firearms Investigation of Vernon Wayne Howell, Also Known as David Koresh.* Washington, DC: U.S. Government Printing Office.

van Driel, Barend, and James T. Richardson. 1988a. "Cult vs. Sect: Research Note on the Characterization of New Religions in the American Print Media." *Sociological Analysis* 49 (2): 171–83.

———. 1988b. "Print Media Coverage of New Religions: A Longitudinal Study." *Journal of Communication* 38: 377–91.

Wood, James. 1993. "The Branch Davidian Standoff: An American Tragedy." *Journal of Church and State* 35 (2): 233–40.

Wilson, D. J. 1993. "Reporters, Guns, and Money." *Houston Post,* July 22, p. 18.

Wright, Stuart A. 1983. "Defection from New Religious Movements: A

Test of Some Theoretical Propositions." In *The Brainwashing/Deprogramming Controversy,* edited by David G. Bromley and James T. Richardson, pp. 106–21. New York: Edwin Mellen.

———. 1987. *Leaving the Cults: The Dynamics of Defection.* Washington, DC: Society for the Scientific Study of Religion.

———. 1993. "Construction and Escalation of a Cult Threat: Dissecting Official Reaction to the Branch Davidians." Paper presented at the annual meeting of the Society for the Scientific Study of Religion, Raleigh, NC.

Wuthnow, Robert. 1978. *The Consciousness Reformation.* Berkeley, CA: University of California Press.

8

ANSON SHUPE AND
JEFFREY K. HADDEN

Cops, News

Copy, and

Public Opinion

*Legitimacy and the Social
Construction of Evil in Waco*

Introduction

Few Americans had ever heard of a sectarian group called the Branch Davidians until the last day of February in 1993. The American public was not alone in being unaware of the Davidians. Fully 96 percent of the residents of the Waco area reported that they knew "little" or "nothing at all" about the Branch Davidians prior to publicity surrounding the shoot-out (Baylor 1993, 4). Fifty-one days later, when the Mt. Carmel compound went up in flames, the Davidians were known to hundreds of millions around the world. Public opinion polls in the United States showed little sympathy for the Davidians and, in sharp contrast, substantial support for the actions of federal agents in handling the siege.

The absence of public criticism of the federal agents' behavior is not very surprising. From the onset, the mass media substantially reported the story without much scrutiny of the details of the raid and siege as these were presented to them in government press briefings in Waco. In presenting the story largely without criticism, the mass media contributed significantly to legitimating the government's role and portraying the federal agents as: (1) properly assuming responsibility for abused and endangered children, (2) duly authorized agents charged with responsibility for bringing to justice a band of criminals who had assembled an enormous cache of illegal weapons and ammunition, and (3) guardians of a community at risk of an armed assault by the followers of the fanatical and dangerous cult leader and his brainwashed followers.

Independent investigations by the departments of Treasury and Justice came to very different conclusions about the incidents in Waco. The Department of Treasury report was candid and quite critical of the Bureau of Alcohol, Tobacco, and Firearms (BATF), while the Department of Justice report laid the blame for the tragic outcome on Koresh while praising the Federal Bureau of Investigation (FBI) for "patience and restraint." Attorney General Janet Reno and President William Clinton blamed the Davidian leader, who would never be able to stand trial for his alleged crimes, while publicly exonerating each other and the public agents involved. Our task for this paper is not to debunk or criticize the media for their coverage of the story of David Koresh, his followers, and their conflicts with federal agents. Nor is it our purpose to expose the mistakes or alleged wrongdoings of government officials. We leave it to others, and to history, to sort out a great deal of conflicting evidence and self-serving rhetoric on the part of all parties involved. Rather, our goal is to develop a conceptual model that is capable of objectively describing and analyzing both the accounts rendered by government agents and the story as it was reported by the mass media.

News and the Stock of Cultural Knowledge

Our point of departure may be characterized as a sociology-of-knowledge perspective. Our theoretical premise, widely accepted by scholars of the media as well as some journalists, is that news is not an objective reality that happens and needs merely to be transmitted to the public by those who report the news. Rather, news, like all social reality, is socially constructed.

Those who make the news, or who get caught up in news stories, usually have a perspective on what they are doing or what has happened. That is to say, people interpret what they do or what happens to them; they may accept responsibility, proffer blame, or attribute happenings to fate or supernatural forces. Likewise, those who report the news bring a wide array of predispositions to the task. They will search for the facts, but that inquiry is shaped by prior knowledge or presuppositions they bring to the investigation. When public authorities get involved, they too have a perspective and presuppositions. The "news" is a composite that incorporates, to varying degrees, the wide array of perspectives and presuppositions that these actors—newsmakers, public authorities, and news reporters—bring to the event.

Alternately, the general public does not just "hear" the news. Audiences filter the information and images through their own perspectives and experience. In many instances, a reader or viewer may not have prior knowledge about specific individuals or groups who make news, but they have attitudes, values, and presuppositions that both directly and indirectly come into play as they seek to make sense of any given news item. For example, an urban crime or drug story may automatically trigger the presupposition of a perpetrator or victim who is a member of a minority, lower socioeconomic class, and so forth.

When the Branch Davidian story broke, almost no one had foreknowledge of the group. However, a large proportion of the public was not without presuppositions, so the story did not break in an experiential vacuum. Once a little information about the group and what had happened was presented, many viewers or listeners were able to bring their presuppositions to bear in such a way that the story immediately "made sense."

Some of what people bring to bear in interpreting a news story is particularistic, that is, unique to that individual's experience. But we can also speak of a common stock of cultural knowledge, or information and perspectives that are broadly shared by the general public. To speak of something as being part of a common stock of cultural knowledge is not to imply that the knowledge is prima facie true. It is merely to assert that the knowledge is widely accepted.

When the Branch Davidian story broke, there was a substantial reservoir of cultural knowledge that was widely shared by the general public, the mass media, and the federal agents who pursued what they believed to be illegal and immoral activities at Mt. Carmel. First, and foremost, the episode in Waco was a "cult story." Cults are widely believed to be led by fanatical leaders who hold unusual sway over their followers. Both the leaders and their followers are capable of doing bizarre things and, furthermore, they are potentially danger-ous both to themselves and to others.

This image of cults is firmly anchored in American history, but has been recently reinforced by the plethora of new religions over the past two decades. Virtually everyone knows about the mass suicide of hundreds of followers of Jim Jones in Guyana. But many other groups, such as the Unification Church (Moonies), Hare Krishnas, the Children of God, and Scientology, have been the subjects of high-profile and highly negative publicity. Hence, the mere labeling of a group as a cult conjures up the most scandalous of images.

We have, on the other hand, a shared respect in this culture for law enforcement officers. We accept that their work can be dangerous, and we regularly exhibit public honor and sympathy when law enforcement officers fall while performing their duty. Thus, the fact that four agents of law enforcement lost their lives and an addition-al sixteen were wounded in the initial confrontation evoked great sympathy for the BATF agents and, concomitantly, repugnance toward the presumed perpetrators.

The initial contours of the story, thus, were heavily weighted against much sympathetic play for the Davidians. But there is much more to understanding the framing of the Branch Davidian story than a widely shared stock of cultural presuppositions regarding cults, which the death and wounding of federal law enforcement agents confirmed at the onset. What is required is a more complex analyti-cal framework that can explain the unwavering character of the story, especially in the face of alternative perspectives that possessed certain compelling qualities.

Such a model needs to explain why all the actors in this drama per-ceived the crisis as they did and behaved according to those presup-positions. It should be a model that provides general explanatory power, not just an accounting for the outcome at Waco. The concep-tualizations to follow are predicated on the assumption that actors in crisis situations are not so much oriented toward specific behaviors or outcomes but, rather, seek to sustain a narrative or account of what is happening so as to render their own behavior legitimate.

Action and the Problem of Managing Legitimacy

Our analysis of the behavior of the key actors in the Branch Davidian crisis begins with an examination of the sociological concept of *legit-imacy*. Contemporary sociological analysis of legitimacy is signifi-cantly informed by Weber's delineation of the relationship between power, authority, and legitimacy (Weber 1947, 124–32). Weber's tripartite distinction between rational, traditional, and charismatic authority is well known in several subdisciplines of sociology.

Social order and stable governance is possible because collective cognitions and affective sentiments render legitimacy to established patterns. It is not normally necessary to call in the militia to enforce the laws passed by a congress or parliament because these institutions are broadly perceived to have the authority to make laws. Further, it is widely understood that there are structures in place to sanction those who do not comply with the laws. While the threat of sanctions may contribute to legal compliance, most such compliance is anchored in the perception that laws are legitimate. The reasons that laws are perceived to be legitimate may be explained, in varying degrees, by the imputed reasons analyzed by Weber.

In modern democratic societies, power and authority are widely diffused in both public and private institutions. Thus, we can conceptualize all institutions, as well as the roles within them (particularly leadership roles), as having greater or lesser degrees of legitimacy. For example, public education in America—especially in the inner cities of large metropolitan areas—is widely perceived to have failed. This perceived failure significantly undermines public trust and feeds the flames of critics who declare public education to be illegitimate. The perception of illegitimacy countervails and thus contributes to a self-fulfilling prophecy. Widespread negative sentiment, in turn, leads to a growing reluctance by some to commit resources to public education.

In the same sense that it is possible to think of institutions as having greater or lesser degrees of legitimacy, so also may the idea of legitimacy be applied to specific individual actors, or incumbents of roles within an institution. Generally, the application of the concept would be restricted to agents of considerable organizational responsibility. For example, in American democracy there is virtual consensus regarding the legitimacy of the office of the president and there has been little variance on that consensus from the inception of the nation. Yet, there have been numerous occasions where there was widespread belief that the individual incumbent of the role was not legitimate. Presidents typically experience considerable fluctuation in popularity during their terms of office and, hence, popularity is, at best, an indirect and probably not very useful indicator of perceived legitimacy.

It needs to be stressed that legitimacy is not to be equated with popularity. Weber's penetrating analysis cautions against such a conclusion. On the other hand, modern democracies, with relatively unfettered free presses, can turn unpopular actions—including evidence of inadequate or improper job performance—into major crises for role incumbents. This is so not only for presidents, but for incumbents of any high-profile public role.

Clearly, legitimacy involves a great deal more than public perception. At the same time, it is clear that widespread public disapproval of an institution, or role incumbent, can constitute a potentially serious problem for the institution or individual in question.

Established institutions tend to have a taken-for-granted legitimacy. Still, there exists the ever present possibility of unfavorable events reflecting negatively on an institution and challenging its legitimacy. Thus, it is axiomatic that institutional leaders will strive to guard against the emergence of events that might undermine either their institutions or their leadership. Further, when threatening events do emerge, leaders will act in ways they believe to be consistent with eliminating or controlling threats to legitimacy.

Analysis of how this occurs requires the development of a simple nomenclature or set of concepts. We begin with the proposition that all organizations face an ongoing series of events that present either an opportunity or obligation to respond. We distinguish between routine or normal *events*, and *crisis events*.

Events are happenings or activities that normally require a response from appropriate public officials (public agents). Response to some events may be characterized as obligatory, as the case of the death of a prominent public figure. Other events may be seen as opportunities for public officials to identify with popular activities, for example, offering congratulations to the winner of the Super Bowl, or receiving Olympic medal winners at the White House. This broad array of routine events may have the impact of enhancing the esteem of an institution, an institutional agent, but the high public expectation of a response tends to place the worth of such responses in the category of institutional or role maintenance. Habitual neglect, or conspicuously inadequate response, could have negative consequences.

Crisis events also require appropriate public agents to respond, but how they respond has potential implications for their perceived legitimacy. Responses normally include both *accounts* and *actions*. Accounts are narratives or explanations about what has happened which may include assignment of responsibility. Actions may involve direct and highly visible activities, such as mobilizing the National Guard, or symbolic activities, such as a presidential visit to the site of a disaster, or the appointing of a commission to investigate the event.

The responses of public agents to crisis events may be viewed as *crisis management activities.* In the age of instant mass media, crisis prevention and crisis management have increasingly become important activities. Skillful management of crisis events affirms the legitimacy of an institution. Failure to manage a crisis calls forth the precariousness of legitimacy. The appearance that a situation is out of control constitutes a serious blow to agents and the institutions involved.

The perception that a crisis was handled skillfully may enhance the reputation of the public agents involved. On the other hand, the perception that it has been mishandled has the impact of drawing attention away from the event to the agents responsible for responding. When this happens, there is a risk that the responsible officials and the institutions they represent will face a challenge to their legitimacy. Agents who fail to manage a crisis event may suffer loss of popularity or esteem, reassignment and career derailment, dismissal, failure to win reelection, or—at the extreme—indictment or impeachment. Institutions may lose public support, suffer budget and staff cuts or—at the extreme—be abolished altogether.

Reporting Events

What we have here characterized as events, both routine and crisis, are essentially public happenings. The mass media, or media agents, gather, sort, analyze, and communicate news about events to the general public. What media agents elect to report, and the interpretation they give to an event, may well determine whether it is to be understood as a normal or crisis event.

Awareness of the role of the media in shaping public perceptions of events has been generally acknowledged since 1922 when Walter Lippmann published his classic work, *Public Opinion.* There is also a growing consciousness that journalists are like everyone else in the sense that they have attitudes and values about all sorts of subjects (Lichter, Rothman, and Lichter 1986). Further, these sentiments do not disappear when journalists go to work, although some would like to convince themselves and others that their work role is pursued with objectivity and total neutrality toward any and all subject matters. Gans (1980, 68) terms this unconscious, rarely reflected-upon bias as a "paraideology" that exerts a steady influence even if journalists are unaware or deny its existence. It helps determine what is covered, how it is covered, and how it is reported.

The mass media, of course, have been the subject of much criticism in recent years. Some critics regard the mass media as a conscious or, at best, inadvertently driven tool to apologize for and but-

tress the status quo (Parenti 1986, 10). Others see the media as clos-
et crusaders who mask their moral reform goals behind a shroud of
objectivity (Lichter, Rothman, and Lichter 1986, 299). Altheide
(1976, 24) describes the process of television news reporting as so
"decontextualized" that electronic journalists have virtual free rein
in shaping an event to the meaning that producers and writers consciously or unconsciously intend.

Most journalists readily acknowledge that the act of reporting
involves more than mirroring some objective events that are "out
there." David Broder, syndicated columnist and veteran reporter for
the *Washington Post*, candidly and insightfully discusses the need for
and difficulties in developing a cohesive story line (1987, 94): "Plot
creation is an inescapable part of journalism. We are offered, or we dig
up, fragments of information, often buried in a mass of irrelevancies,
and we have to render a comprehensive, plausible scenario from these
fragments . . . there are times when the journalistic product looks like
a mastodon that was assembled from a fossil toenail find. Some plots
described in the press don't bear much resemblance to reality."

From a sociology-of-knowledge perspective, news is a negotiated
product that reflects the interaction of a complex web of factors
including (1) the information available, (2) the values and interests of
reports and their editors, and (3) the commercial or market imperatives within which the newsmaking industry is embedded.

Further, crisis events trigger public response. *Public Opinion* con-
sists of the perceptions people have regarding the legitimacy of the
accounts and actions offered by public agents. The opinions that
publics form about crisis events are often superficial and subject to
rapid change. This is especially likely at the onset of a crisis event if
the public is ill-informed about the specific details or the context of
the event. Information disseminated by media agents gives shape to
the crisis event and helps to locate it within the broader value structures of the public. Yet mishandling of crisis events can turn public
opinion against an institution and thus threaten its legitimacy. As a
result, public opinion must be taken seriously.

Public agents may occasionally utilize the infrastructure of mass
media to access the public directly for the purpose of offering
accounts and announcing actions. For example, presidential address-
es to the nation normally are proceeded and followed by the appearance of media agents who contextualize and analyze (1) the crisis
event, (2) the president's account, and (3) the proposed actions. The
mass media, thus, are not merely a conduit in the transmission of
information about crisis events to the public. The selection of information for transmission, as well as how the information is present-

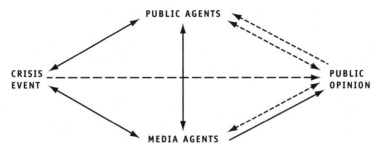

Figure 1

ed, can have a significant impact upon the definition and outcome of crisis events.

The nexus of relations between crisis events, public agents, media agents, and public opinion is diagramed in figure 1. A few comments need to be offered about the directions of influence in the model. First, note that the relation between the public and public agents is characterized by broken arrows. This is because direct access is at best a fleeting moment. Most of the information that public agents communicate to the public is mediated through media agents. And even brief moments of direct access are usually circumscribed by media agent commentary. Second, note the broken feedback arrows from public opinion to both public and media agents. While clearly there is a limited amount of direct public feedback to public agents, most of the feedback comes indirectly through opinion polls as well as secondary and even tertiary feedback from persons having access to public agents. Media agents also receive limited feedback in the form of letters and calls, but they too rely substantially on indirect information. Finally, note the one-way broken arrow from the crisis event to the public. In an age when millions of Americans have witnessed the unfolding of crisis events on Cable News Network (CNN) or C-Span, one might question whether the arrow should be direct rather than broken.

We offer several reasons for suggesting that the relationship between a crisis event and the public should be characterized as mediated. First, the number of persons watching an event actually unfold is usually quite small. Consider, for example, CNN's live coverage of the ramming of the walls of the Branch Davidian compound to insert CS gas, and later the engulfing of the structure in flames. The large majority of the public who watched these events saw only a highly edited version on the evening news. Second, the events were not merely broadcast. Reporters on the scene discussed and interpreted what was happening for audiences. Thus, even live coverage does not represent unadulterated transmission of a crisis event but one that is mediated by instant commentary from broadcasters. In addition, most crisis events do not just suddenly happen in a cultural vacuum but are contextualized by prior public sentiments. In the case of the Branch Davidian fire, this crisis event was part of a larger crisis that had been unfolding for fifty days. Further, the framing of the story was, from the beginning, understood in the broader context of "cult stories."

The tension between public agents and a free mass media is inherent in the structure of their relationship. Probably every president since Thomas Jefferson has frequently looked upon the press as a personal menace, and at least occasionally, has seen the press as a threat to governance of society. The press, in turn, has frequently pursued a modus operandi that assumes that anything less than full disclosure is automatically evidence that public agents have something scandalous to cover up.

The tension between the press and government intensifies whenever a crisis event unfolds. Crisis events evoke a special measure of caution on behalf of public agents, while the crisis often brings forth the "killer instinct" on the part of media agents (e.g., Sabato 1993).

In democratic societies, where the mass media are not monopolized, competition for audience share and advertising revenues figures importantly in the production of news. While most media organizations probably do not consciously or ordinarily calculate how to treat a specific crisis event in order to maximize audience share and profits, most have general strategies or formulas that shape their orientation.

The rules of engagement between public agents and media agents can, thus, be highly variable. A crisis event may emerge anywhere. The centripetal structure of news gathering usually results in national crisis events quickly reaching the White House press room. Here, usually with limited information, the task of formulating an account, that is, a story line about what has happened and who is responsible, commences. This is followed by a centrifugal flow of information gathering as news agencies fan out to fill in the details of the story.

While media agents seek to "tell the story," they also endeavor to "get behind the facts." This involves the pursuit of a whole range of issues. Is the account offered by the public agents creditable? Are there alternative accounts that may have credence? Is the action proposed appropriate and adequate to address the crisis event? Are there resources available to pursue the proposed action?

Public agents operating at many levels of responsibility and authority provide the media with information relevant to the story. This broad class of individuals we characterize as *players*. The media's pursuit of the story also involves gathering information and opinions from individuals and agencies who are neither directly involved nor responsible for dealing with the crisis event. They are actors because of the knowledge they possess, or profess to possess, about the crisis event. This broad class of individuals we characterize as *experts*.

Experts can generally be categorized as either *corroborators* or *doubters*. Corroborators provide information and voice that support the accounts proffered or actions advanced by public agents. Doubters come in many shades. The may range from skeptics regarding the accounts offered or actions proposed to aggressive contrarians. *Contrarians* seek to refute the accounts and actions advanced and to introduce alternative accounts or propose alternative actions.

The media may utilize experts in a variety of ways. Their most common usage in news stories is to provide information and perspective that help the media agent understand issues relevant to the crisis event. Second, quotations in print journalism and commentary or sound bites in broadcast journalism help lend credibility to the story as framed by the media agent. The media's use of experts may have the effect of corroborating information available through public agents or it may serve to challenge credibility. Some media formats are structured to maximize controversy, such as by providing a format for aggressive contrarians.

Space does not permit a more detailed elaboration of the interactive model we have sketched. We hope we have provided adequate detail to apply the model to interpret the dynamics that ensued as the result of the raid by the BATF on the Branch Davidian compound near Waco, Texas. One final caveat, however, is important. The mass media, and individual journalists, are also subject to assessment regarding their legitimacy. Like the office of the president, a free press is highly institutionalized and legitimated, but particular actions and policies are subject to assessment.

Narratives and the Social Construction of Legitimacy: An Interactive Account of the Branch Davidian Siege

The story of Waco as it emerged in public opinion is the product of sometimes conflicting, sometimes reinforcing narratives and subnarratives. Each narrative has been constructed by participants who seek not only to tell the story as they see it, but also to frame the story in a manner that renders their own roles legitimate. Specific behaviors, or even the final outcome, are less important, ultimately, than public perceptions of what happened and why. Thus, consciously or unconsciously, the issue of legitimacy is the starting point of the accounts or narratives that various participants construct.

Of all the narratives and subnarratives that were at play in the Waco story, five can be identified as major narratives that have significant impact in explaining the outcome: (1) the public agent narrative, (2) the Branch Davidian narrative, (3) the mass media narrative, (4) the anticult narrative, and (5) the contrarian narrative. Utilizing the conceptual model presented above, we shall seek to demonstrate how each narrative is an attempt to legitimize a perspective and how each contributes to the formation of public opinion.

The Public Agent Narrative

There were a number of public agents as the story unfolded, beginning with the McLennan County Sheriff's Department. They were quickly overshadowed by the BATF, which in turn was eclipsed by the FBI. In the course of the siege, the U.S. attorney general and the Department of Justice, the governor of Texas and the Texas Rangers, and the president of the United States became actors contributing to the legitimation of the initial raid and the final confrontation that ended in the tragic fire.

While there was some evidence of tension between the various public agents, they seemed to have quickly reached closure on the narrative that legitimated their actions and subsequent crisis management of events in Waco. The key components of this narrative included: (1) a statutory mandate to search for illegal weapons, (2) a humanitarian in loco parentis responsibility to rescue Brand Davidian children and dependents from abuse and neglect, and (3) an obligation to round up illegal aliens.

Though the latter two concerns are beyond the statutory mandate of the BATF, they were included as part of a prima facie justification for the initial application and affidavit for a search warrant presented by BATF Special Agent Davy Aguilera (U.S. District Court 1993). Despite the inability of a local child welfare investigator to confirm the practice of child abuse, and despite the total lack of attention to the case by Immigration and Naturalization Service authorities, such concerns played a role in the overall official acceptance of the February 28 BATF raid (U.S. Department of Treasury 1993, 28ff.).

The mass media did initially raise questions about the wisdom of such an elaborate plan to storm the Branch Davidian compound merely in order to serve a warrant (which, in fact, the BTAF assault team failed to bring). But the fact that a shoot-out occurred, and that federal agents were killed and wounded, overrode critical examination of other accounts. From the onset of the siege, the BATF story line of being "ambushed" and "outgunned" not only appeared to have credibility; it also overrode consideration of other possible narratives. More important, it confirmed the federal agents' contention that David Koresh and his followers were a "present danger" to the public and to the government.

When such events occur, it is the official duty of public agents to intervene. Those who resist them are ipso facto illegitimate regardless of other existing issues. Two alternating paradigms quickly surfaced: Koresh was criminalized as an inveterate "con artist" who had duped his followers. He was also medicalized as a psychopath against whom rational guardians of society could have little effect. The FBI's quick assumption of responsibility for the siege operations further legitimated the government's initial ground for intervention. In the long run, the FBI involvement laid the foundation for questioning the ability of the BATF to pursue its operations objectives, but it did not challenge the legitimacy of the raid.

From the federal agents' perspective, the early days of the siege confirmed their understanding of David Koresh as devious, manipulative, unreliable, and extremely dangerous. In the course of the fifty-one day siege, federal agents pursued an unusual number of psychological warfare measures. The FBI tactics included the use of loudspeakers to bombard the Davidians with propaganda and harassment. Presumably the agents held out some hope that they would overcome the grip that Koresh held over his followers. At all hours of the night and day, the loudspeakers belched forth such curious content as audiotapes of rabbits being killed, chanting Tibetan monks, and Nancy Sinatra singing "These Boots Were Made for Walking."

If these tactics at times seemed to match the bizarre theological pronouncements coming forth from Koresh, in the end they served to legitimate the federal agents' conclusion that they had done everything they could to get the Davidians out. That they held out against psychological warfare tactics "demonstrated" that the Davidians were dogmatic, determined, and unrelentingly devoted to their leader. For their own safety and well-being, they had to be rousted out by any means necessary. Thus, the tactics of tear gas and battering armored vehicles that might have seemed indefensible during the first few days of the siege seemed less so on the fifty-first day. This tactic was further legitimated by returning the narrative to concern for the welfare of the children.

The FBI cast the fifty-one-day siege in the context of a battle of wills between its agents and the forces of Koresh. Increasingly, the objective of the agents was to confront Koresh with the "fact" of his eroding power during the siege (despite protests about this strategy from the FBI's own behavioral science experts) and "to assert control and demonstrate to Koresh that they were in control" (Stone 1993, 14ff).

In reality, the federal agents were not in control of events. Repeatedly, their efforts to bring the standoff to a quick conclusion were foiled. There can be no question that the FBI agents were tired and frustrated. As one anonymous congressional aid commented: "I think you not only need to understand the psychology of cults but you need to understand the psychology of law enforcement as well. They [the BATF and FBI] had been challenged . . . there was the day-in-day-out appearance of impotence in a profession in which control is so important" (Riley et al. 1993, 43).

Federal agents had to know that there were risks associated with the plan to insert CS gas into the compound with armored vehicles. The possibility of a mass suicide had been entertained, even discussed with Koresh, but dismissed by those in decision-making roles.

We may never know whether the federal agents in charge seriously entertained the possibility of a calamitous ending. If they did, their behavior during the siege seems clearly to point to an explicit, or at least implicit, narrative that placed full responsibility for such an outcome on the shoulders of David Koresh. Koresh was taking the Branch Davidians with him down a Pyrrhic path of defiance. When the seemingly unthinkable tragedy occurred, Edward S. G. Dennis, Jr. (1993, 3) provided an internal Department of Justice report for Attorney General Janet Reno that concluded: "The events of April 19 were the result of David Koresh's determined efforts to choreograph his own death and the deaths of his followers in a confrontation with federal authorities to fulfill Koresh's apocalyptic prophecy." The government, in this account, was not at fault.

Independent reports by the Department of the Treasury and the Department of Justice served further to legitimate the public agents in the handling of the crisis event in Waco. The Treasury report in particular was unusually candid. Most important, the report acknowledged that the BATF agents undertook the raid, which was predicated on the element of surprise, despite the knowledge that Koresh had been tipped off that the assault was imminent, and that they then proceeded systematically to make "false or misleading public statements about the raid" that had the impact of "undermining the integrity of their agency" (U.S. Department of Treasury 1993, 194).

Having admitted that "mistakes were made," BATF Director Stephen Higgins and two assistants were permitted to resign (though the latter were reinstated). By assigning blame and getting rid of key officials, the Treasury report may be viewed as a form of damage control. Agents responsible for failed management of the crisis event had to go, in order to preserve the credibility and legitimacy not only of BATF, but also of the Department of Treasury.

The Department of Justice report, on the other hand, focused substantially on the wrongdoings of Koresh and the Davidians. Significant criticism or reflection about the handling of the entire crisis event was in short supply.

By the time the two investigations were released, almost six months after the siege ended, the story had passed from the front page. While the reports made the network television news and the front pages of most major newspapers, the revelations of misconduct by public agents did not register long in public memory. Long before the reports were released, even before the tragic conclusion of the siege, the public agents had succeeded in presenting a narrative of the crisis event that portrayed it as largely self-imposed by David Koresh and his Branch Davidian followers.

The Branch Davidian Narrative

The sequence of events precluded the media from obtaining authentic insider accounts of what the Davidians were experiencing and how the siege was interpreted. On the day of the initial confrontation, CNN aired a live interview with Koresh, and Dallas radio station KRLD aired messages and scripture readings from Koresh through an agreement worked out with the BATF.

All other contacts with Koresh and his followers were mediated in one way or another. Federal agents cut off telephone communications except their own. Thus, most of what was subsequently learned of the Davidian narrative was filtered through both government and media agents, and some of it through two attorneys for the Davidians, Dick DeGuerin and Jack Zimmerman, who were allowed into the compound.

There were also, of course, a few sensational personal narratives offered by disillusioned and hostile former members who had abandoned the group before the crisis events occurred (e.g., Breault and King 1993). However, these narratives display all the earmarks of being colored by apostate and commercial motivations (Shupe and Bromley 1981).

Few of the principle actors survived the final conflagration. While the trials of surviving Branch Davidians did offer some vindication,[1] their testimony is suspect as literal history, given the pressures to slant memories coming from both prosecutors and defense attorneys. In addition, survivors experienced a wide variety of counseling and interviews that likely contributed to their understanding of what they had experienced. All in all, the methodological problems of interpreting the testimonies of the survivors are considerable (Wright and Ebaugh 1993).

Some independent evidence of the Branch Davidian narrative survives.[2] There are films of Koresh's millennial preaching and knowledge of his claims and his remarks to both the media and the FBI negotiators. From Koresh's perspective, he was intensely engaged in interpreting critical parts of the book of Revelation which would conclude what he believed to be a divine theological mission. This mission is the heart of the Branch Davidian narrative. Koresh believed that he could decipher the allegorical meaning of the seven seals mentioned in Revelation and that he and his loyal followers would be part of the second coming of Christ. This claim was Koresh's source of authority over his followers (see Tabor, this volume).

Ironically, the raid and subsequent siege functioned to strengthen Koresh's vision of his prophetic role in history as well as his hold over his followers. These events confirmed Koresh's prophecies based on his interpretation of the book of Revelation. He had preached that in the last days there would initially be a killing spree aimed at the faithful. Koresh said that God had commanded him to wait under siege until others were killed. Phillip Arnold, a theologian whose advice to the FBI went unheeded, said in hindsight that "David felt that the prophecies of the Book of Revelation were being fulfilled this very week, this very day, in Waco, Texas" (Prime Time 1994).

This perspective was, of course, significantly at odds with FBI tacticians who considered Koresh's theology to be a hoax and the man himself a charlatan. Had federal agents taken this theological perspective seriously, they perhaps would have understood how their tactics inadvertently confirmed the legitimacy of Koresh's prophecies and, in turn, his hold over his followers. From the initial presence of so many BATF agents, to the prolonged siege, to the media hoopla, Koresh's world-transforming prophetic message must have been reinforced not only in the mind of Koresh, but in those of his followers as well.

This was a narrative that was incomprehensible to the federal agents who were responsible for the initial raid, and those later responsible for operations during the siege. Their dismissal of it as ravings unimportant to the "hostage/barricade" issue accounts for much of Koresh's alleged inconsistencies and erratic behaviors during negotiations. The narrative was also largely incomprehensible to the media agents assigned to cover the story.

Consultants to the investigations of the Justice and Treasury departments confirmed the presence of agents in the behavioral science division of the FBI who had at least rudimentary understanding of the Davidians' theological perspective, but the advice of these agents was ignored (Ammerman 1993; Stone 1993). Religion writers, including several working for Texas newspapers, had appropriate training and experience to understand the Davidians' theological perspective. Again, ironically, they were not assigned to cover the story.

The Branch Davidians' narrative, thus, remains substantially a private narrative. To the extent that it received any attention, it was shrouded by skepticism. At best, the theological narrative was viewed as evidence that the Davidians were either deranged or hopelessly brainwashed by their leader.

The Mass Media Narrative

Mass media coverage of crisis events performs two functions: (1) the dissemination of information in the form of accounts of events to news consumers, and (2) more subtly, the legitimation of media agencies as knowledgeable authorities. In a competitive news market the process of self-legitimation is critical for the retention of both an audience and advertisers. In presenting both information and an interpretation, it is critical that media agents present a narrative that appears accurate and appropriate. When either or both of these imperatives appear to be violated, the media are vulnerable to accusations of bias which, in turn, constitute threats to the legitimacy of mass media.

In tipping off selected media agents about a vague but imminent law enforcement event (U.S. Department of Treasury 1993, 79), the BATF clearly anticipated favorable publicity that would aid their own pursuit of legitimacy. There were approximately a dozen members of the press, including a television cameraperson, present to witness the raid and ensuing gun battle.

The failed raid rapidly progressed from an event of no particular significance into a crisis event of major proportions with a siege of indeterminate duration. The BATF was quickly replaced by FBI agents just as national news eclipsed local and regional reporters. Almost simultaneously, media agents were cut off from communications with those inside Mt. Carmel and physically cordoned from the compound to a location that was dubbed Satellite City. Their access to information about what had happened was restricted to the telephoto lens and press briefings conducted by FBI spokespersons back in Waco.

Whenever a big story breaks, the media first scramble for basic information about what has happened. In the Branch Davidian story, the first eyewitnesses were primarily the BATF agents and the Davidians inside the compound. The law enforcement agents' perspective was available primarily through agency spokespersons. After the first few hours the Davidians were available only through secondary information fed by the enforcement agents' spokespersons.

The most readily available background information was the series of articles that appeared in the *Waco Tribune-Herald*. While there was clearly much about Koresh and the Davidians that was not especially flattering, the *Tribune-Herald* series was particularly inflammatory. The articles drew heavily on information from disgruntled former members, and there is evidence that anticultists also contributed significantly to framing the story. The articles cited no academic scholars of religious movements. The availability of the *Tribune-Herald* articles provided the national press with initial background and a trail to former members as well as anticultists.

Four factors worked together to quickly shape the Branch Davidian story line: (1) the initial armed confrontation, (2) the common stock of conventional wisdom about "cults," (3) the availability of the *Tribune-Herald* investigative articles that served to corroborate the conventional wisdom, and (4) the tightly controlled access to information imposed by the FBI. These factors maximized the ability of the law enforcement agents to frame the narrative to suit their objectives, and they did not hesitate to do so. What ensued, then, was a codependent relationship of mutual legitimizing: the public agents needed to justify the government's prolonged siege tactics and the correctness of its presiege actions, while the media needed information to present a coherent story line.

It is possible to challenge the supposition of media dependency. Why did we not witness the dogged, aggressive investigation that often typifies the mass media, especially when there is the slightest hint of scandal? We can only speculate, of course, but it would appear that the "destructive cult" story line not only appeared to be compelling, it was also very popular with the public, as judged by opinion polls that consistently showed strong support for the law enforcement agencies and condemnation of David Koresh. Thus, we see the subtle feedback loop of public opinion. To have gone aggressively after the BATF or the FBI would have given the appearance of sympathy for a leader and his followers who were not viewed as deserving of sympathy.

The Anticult Narrative

The anticult movement (ACM) is a loose confederation of organizations opposed to virtually all new or innovative religious movements. The first organizations were founded in the early 1970s by parents who were distressed over their children's decisions to affiliate with a religious movement (Shupe and Bromley 1980). In recent years these groups have professionalized, becoming information clearinghouses and watchdogs over developments in American religion that their constituents perceive as troubling.

While the anticult groups pay lip service to the notion that not all religious movements are alike, they tend to be monolithic in their vigorous promotion of the concept of cults as organizations controlled by cynical and manipulative leaders, destructive to those who become involved and a danger to the broader social fabric.

Anticult movement leaders played an important corroborative role for the narrative created by the law enforcement agents. Indeed, they appear to have contributed significantly to the formation of the BATF's initial story line, as several other contributors to this volume suggest. Ammerman (1993), in a report to the Justice Department, was critical of the government's reliance on anticult sources and stereotypical claims.

Priscilla Coates, an official in the Cult Awareness Network (CAN), claimed that no one in either Justice or Treasury spoke with anyone affiliated with CAN (1994). Her claim, however, is contradicted by others. Rick Ross, whom CAN executive director Cynthia Kisser described as "among the half dozen best deprogrammers in the country," asserted on more than one television program that he had consulted with BATF agents before the February 28 raid. The affidavits submitted by BATF special agent Davy Aguilera to U.S. Magistrate Judge Dennis G. Green contained idiomatic language strongly reminiscent of ACM ideology (U.S. District Court 1993). And, at least one FBI spokesperson allegedly affirmed to a reporter that the organization had consulted with CAN (Nancy Ross and Linda Green 1993, 13).

The FBI repeatedly claimed that it consulted with "cult experts," yet no one, to our knowledge, in the relatively small world of academic social scientists who specialize in new religions was ever consulted before the February 28 raid or during the siege. Thus, if the actual role of CAN and anticultist individuals is unknown, the thought and planning of BATT is certainly suggestive of anticultist input.

Whatever direct role anticultists may have had with law enforcement agents, their role as corroborators of the federal agents' story line was abundantly present in the mass media. They provided corroborative sound bites for network television news, commentary for special programming on the Waco crisis, and scores of quotations for print journalism. In addition, anticult leaders were frequent guests on television talk shows.

The anticultists also played an important role in framing the *Waco Tribune-Herald* story, the first background resource many journalists saw as they poured into Waco after the raid. Quotations from anticultists that appear in the story, as well as the one-sided character of the "Sinful Messiah" series, suggest a very strong influence in the development and presentation of the *Tribune-Herald* story. Rick Ross and Priscilla Coates are the subject of a sidebar story on "experts" that appeared in the series (McCormick and England, 1993).

In addition, Tim Madigan, a journalist who covered the Branch Davidian story for the *Fort Worth Star Telegram*, published a rushed-to-print potboiler in which he cites and quotes extensively from ACM activists (1993). Deprogrammer Rick Ross wrote a foreword to the book.

While the mass media drew heavily upon the ACM activists for background and quotations, there was no parallel consultation with academic scholars of religious movements. If this appears curious, it is perhaps even more curious that editors did not assign religion writers to cover the Waco story. This suggests that "cult" stories are not perceived to be "religion" stories. Or, alternatively, it might suggest that the story line was well defined early on and that the expert input of a religion writer was neither required or desired.

The Contrarian Narrative

We have defined a contrarian narrative as one that is sharply at variance with the conventional wisdom about a crisis event. In a pluralistic media market it is virtually inevitable that contrarian voices will emerge. Leading the way in the Waco case were antigovernment libertarians and gun ownership groups that had pre-existing grievances with the BATF and the FBI. *Soldier of Fortune*, a gun magazine, ran several articles, including a carefully reasoned piece arguing that there was no probable cause for the raid on the Branch Davidians (Pate 1993). Another carefully reasoned article appeared in the *American Spectator*. Other articles, appearing in the alternative press, examined the past record of BATF and drew parallels between the collaboration between BATF and the FBI in a shoot-out with a separatist named Randy Weaver in Idaho who was currently on trial (e.g., Bock 1993).

Much of this literature appears to us to warrant critical examination. But there was yet another genre of literature emerging from the far right that espoused incredulous conspiracy theories. For example, Lyndon LaRouche (1993) wrote that the Waco tragedy was a deliberate setup conspired by CAN, the Anti-Defamation League, and their infiltrators in both the FBI and the BATF. Attorney Linda Thompson (1993) of the American Justice Foundation produced and disseminated a video entitled *Waco: The Big Lie*. This document presented a number of troubling accusations, with footage that appeared to support several of her allegations. But her claim that the BATF killed its own agents, several of whom had been Secret Service bodyguards for presidential candidate Bill Clinton, challenged the credibility of the document. Thompson's credibility was further undermined by an electronic bulletin essay in which she claimed that Waco was the tip of a one-world conspiratorial iceberg that included "reported citings [sic] of UN tanks going into Portland, Oregon" and various troop movements of unmarked military vehicles nationwide.

The contrarians variously accused the federal agencies involved of abuse of constitutional freedoms, of lying and covering up, and of essentially murdering an eccentric religious group that was minding its own business and not hurting anyone. In spite of the fact that some of the contrarian literature dealt seriously with anomalous and troubling issues—many of which turned out to be legitimate—these issues never surfaced as a serious problematic in the mainstream press. Only after the official narrative seemed firmly in place did the contrarian narrative gain limited credibility. For example, Fiddleman and Kopel, writing in the *Washington Post*, concluded in June that "[i]t is increasingly clear that the original federal raid on the compound never should have occurred, because the BATF's application to search the premises was far below legal standards." And William Safire, highly respected syndicated columnist for the *New York Times*, accused the Department of Justice and the U.S. attorney general's office of a "whitewash" in their internal reviews. But once the story is substantially off the front page, alternative truths or narratives don't matter much to either public agents or the public. Only under extraordinary circumstances can they be resurrected. For example, the conspiracy theory of the assassination of President John F. Kennedy is the most celebrated instance of a contrarian view that seemingly will not go away.

That the contrarian versions of what happened in Waco are largely unknown or unaccepted by most Americans is testimony to the legitimacy most citizens accord to public agents who maintain social order and to media agents who manage the news. From this perspective, contrarian views that cannot find a niche in the mainstream press face a far greater problem than merely seeking a forum to get the word out. They challenge the prestige and legitimacy of two powerful institutions which, when they are together, construct a social reality that most Americans accept without question. Whereas most contrarians have some basic sense of the social construction of reality when they see one account but believe others are possible, most consumers of public opinion do not.

The Dynamics of Narratives and Claims to Legitimacy in Waco

The argument advanced here is that the siege and ultimate conflagration in Waco had separate, though sometimes overlapping, meanings for different sets of actors in the drama. These meanings all clustered around the seminal issue of whose actions were legitimate and whose were not. Each set of actors sought to legitimate its own behavior. Actions aimed at accomplishing legitimacy by some sectors involved delegitimating other actors. In the most abstract sense, that is what the conflict was about.

The Branch Davidians, primed by the Armageddon theology of the charismatic David Koresh, seemed to have cast themselves in an antinomian role helping to usher in the apocalypse. Part of this role apparently entailed stockpiling large quantities of armaments, some of which they allegedly were in the process of altering to make fully automatic.

Like many postmillennialists who believe they must prepare in secular terms for the imminent time of social disorder and danger that precedes the second coming, this particular group wanted to prepare for Koresh's prophecy of attack and siege. The basis of social order in the fallen world was, in their sacred terms, illegitimate and in need of cleansing, and they were its faithful remnant. The BATF attack confirmed the prophecy of Koresh and, hence, his legitimacy.

The BATF, as part of the duly authorized structure responsible for monitoring illegal weapons, learned of arms-purchasing by the Davidians. Relying on a cultural stock of knowledge about unconventional religions, they planned a raid on the Mt. Carmel compound that would simultaneously uncover the true extent of the weapons stockpiling and, it was hoped, lend the agency favorable publicity.

Having miscalculated and mismanaged the raid, the BATF was

faced with restructuring their account of what they were doing, why, and what happened. This was facilitated by the FBI's assuming command of operations. But the FBI soon faced its own legitimacy problem. While the Branch Davidian violence against government agents unquestionably warranted a law enforcement response, the prolonged siege was complicated by several factors: (1) the government was in confrontation with a religious group; (2) many of the besieged occupants were clearly not combatants, but rather mothers, children, and some elderly, even infirm, citizens; and (3) the occupants believed that they followed a higher law than civil authority. Furthermore, the public agents were aware that any definitive strategy would become a major news item, and thus carried a potential challenge to their legitimacy. Hence, they were under pressure both to delegitimate those inside the compound while justifying their policy of media containment as necessary for carrying out safely their duties to restore social order.

The media, feeling that an appropriate story line was in place, chose to settle for this arrangement. They basically adopted the government's narrative of why its actions were justified. As the siege went on, and as the media reported a government-fed account of events at Waco, the media were increasingly faced with a loss of credibility if anomalies and hard questions about government strategy that they had failed to report and examine earlier were raised.

The media thus also accepted the cultural stock of knowledge about cults as a convenient lens through which to validate the government's (and their own) account. Meanwhile, it found the anticult movement a willing corroborator of all this.

Contrarians arose during and after the siege to challenge government and media accounts based on their own suspicions and presuppositions. But their different narratives were largely relegated to alternative media outlets and never seriously perforated the dominant public opinion about the meaning of Waco.[3]

The delegitimation of Koresh and the Branch Davidians, as a parallel of the government's own attempts to legitimate its handling of the siege, became a daily task. The FBI negotiators, insisting on treating Koresh as a hostage-taker or terrorist, repeatedly ran up against his prophetic, apocalyptic worldview. To them it was transparently alien. Field commanders therefore treated Koresh as mad, manipulative, and duplicitous. They dismissed his theological statements as gibberish rather than as a road map to his intentions.

The April 19 conflagration, regardless of who started the fire, was the end result of a breakdown of communication. Neither the public agents nor the media agents were able to grasp sufficiently the fact that Koresh and his followers took their religion seriously. The blatant strategy of power—the harassment while simultaneously trying to negotiate—was antithetical to a successful conclusion of the siege.

The federal agents viewed the Davidians' coming out as the rational conclusion to the standoff, and the insertion of CS gas was reported to have been designed for this result. One hardly needed insight into the Davidians' narrative to have understood that leaving under duress was not an option. Beleaguered and tormented for fifty-one days, they felt that a successful conclusion had to include an interpretation of coming out as part of a miraculous divine intervention. This was not an option the federal agents were capable of understanding or being a party to.

We view accounts not simply as retrospective explanations of actors' behaviors. They are also ongoing interpretations by actors and audiences of action in progress. Accounts, like all elements of culture, are sociologically emerging facts that have a habit of taking on lives of their own so as to influence persons' decisions and future behavior. Human beings use accounts to make symbolic sense of social order and disorder. Ironically, once created, these same human beings tend to have a vested interest in preserving the legitimacy of those accounts. The Waco story illustrates this axiomatic point as well as the fact that most persons cannot make the distinction between literal truth and the narratives of the truth-givers.

Notes

1. Government prosecutors failed to convince a San Antonio jury of the murder and murder conspiracy charges.

2. In addition to the films mentioned here, a videotape made by the Davidians during the standoff was only recently released, after the trial. It is approximately two hours in length and contains the comments of a number of members, as well as Koresh himself, all of whom later died in the fire. Several members offer their own accounts of what happened in the initial raid. Space did not permit an analysis of this tape to be included in the paper.

3. *Editor's note:* Of course, on the second anniversary of the April 19 assault by the FBI on Mt. Carmel, the Oklahoma City bombing, allegedly perpetrated by right-wing extremists, changed dramatically the meaning of Waco for many Americans by linking it to the contrarian narrative.

References

Altheide, David L. 1976. *Creating Reality: How TV News Distorts Events.* Beverly Hills, CA: Sage.

Ammerman, Nancy T. 1993. "Report to the Justice and Treasury Departments Regarding Law Enforcement Interaction with the Branch Davidians in Waco, Texas." In *Recommendations of Experts for Improvement in Federal Law Enforcement after Waco.* Washington, DC: U.S. Department of Justice.

Baylor. 1993. "Waco Area Opinions on the Mt. Carmel Raid and Siege." Baylor Center for Community Research and Development, Waco, TX. Poll #45, April.

Bock, Alan W. 1993. "Ambush at Ruby Ridge." *Reason* (October): 22–28.

Breault, Marc, with Martin King. 1993. *Inside the Cult.* New York: Penguin Books.

Broder, David S. 1987. *Behind the Front Page: A Candid Look at How the News Is Made.* New York: Simon & Schuster.

Coates, Priscilla. 1994. Correspondence to Anson Shupe. January 4.

Dennis, Edward S. G., Jr., 1993. *Evaluation of the Handling of the Branch Davidian Stand-off in Waco, Texas, February 28 to April 19, 1993.* Redacted public copy. October 8. Washington, DC: U.S. Department of Justice.

Fiddleman, Thomas, and David Kopel. 1993. "Unsettling Questions in Probe of Waco." *Washington Post.* June 1.

Gans, Herbert J. 1980. *Deciding What's News: A Study of CBS Evening News, NBC Nightly News, Newsweek, and Time.* New York: Vintage Books.

Heymann, Philip B. 1993. *Lessons of Waco: Proposed Changes in Federal Law Enforcement.* Report to the U.S. Attorney General, October 8. Washington, DC: U.S. Department of Justice.

LaRouche, Lyndon. 1993. "Cult Awareness Network Responsible for Waco Tragedy." Partial transcript of interview in *Executive Intelligence Review.* April 21.

Lichter, S. Robert, Stanley Rothman, and Linda S. Lichter. 1986. *The Media Elite: America's New Powerbrokers.* Bethesda, MD: Adler and Adler.

Lippmann, Walter. 1965. *Public Opinion.* New York: Free Press. Originally published 1922.

Madigan, Tim. 1993. *See No Evil: Blind Devotion and Bloodshed in Koresh's Holy War.* Fort Worth, TX: Summit Group.

McCormick, Darlene, and Mark England. 1993. "Experts: Branch Davidians Dangerous, Destructive Cult." *Waco Tribune-Herald.* March 1.

Pate, James L. 1993. "A Blundering Inferno." *Soldier of Fortune.* July, 38–41.

Parenti, Michael. 1986. *Inventing Reality: The Politics of the Mass Media.* New York: St. Martin's Press.

Prime Time. 1994. "Waco: The Untold Story." ABC's *Prime Time Live.* New York, January 13.

Riley, Michael, Richard Woodbury, et al. 1993. "Oh, My God, They're Killing Themselves!" *Time.* May 3, p. 43.

Ross, Nancy, and Linda Green. 1993. "What Is the Cult Awareness Net-

work and What Role Did It Play in Waco?" Report. Ross and Green
Legal Firm, Washington, DC. Typescript.

Sabato, Larry J. 1993. *Feeding Frenzy.* 2d ed. New York: Free Press.

Safire, William. 1993. "One Hand Whitewashes Other at Justice." *Houston Chronicle.* October 16.

Shupe, Anson D., Jr., and David G. Bromley. 1980. *The New Vigilantes: Deprogrammers, Anti-Cultists, and the New Religions.* Beverly Hills, CA: Sage Publications.

———. 1981. "Apostates and Atrocity Stories: Some Parameters in the Dynamics of Deprogramming." In *The Social Impact of New Religious Movements,* edited by Bryan Wilson, pp. 179–215. New York: Rose of Sharon Press.

———. 1982. "Shaping the Public Response to Jonestown: People's Temple and the Anticult Movement." In *Violence and Religious Commitment: Implications of Jim Jones's People's Temple Movement,* edited by Ken Levi, pp. 105–32. University Park: Pennsylvania State University Press.

Society of Professional Journalists. 1993. *Waco: What Went Right, What Went Wrong.* Greencastle, IN: Society of Professional Journalists.

Stone, Alan A. 1993. "To Deputy Attorney General Philip Heymann: Report and Recommendations Concerning the Handling of Incidents Such as the Branch Davidian Standoff in Waco, Texas." Report commissioned by the U.S. Justice Department.

Thompson, Linda. 1993. "Waco, Another Perspective." AEN News release. May 19.

U.S. Department of Treasury. 1993. *Report of the Department of the Treasury on the Bureau of Alcohol, Tobacco, and Firearms Investigation of Vernon Wayne Howell, Also Known as David Koresh.* Washington, DC: U.S. Government Printing Office.

U.S. District Court. 1993. Application and Affidavit for Search Warrant. W93–15M. Western District of Texas. Filed February 26.

Weber, Max. 1947. *The Theory of Social and Economic Organization.* Translated by A. M. Henderson and Talcott Parsons; edited by Talcott Parsons. Glencoe, IL: Free Press.

Wright, Stuart A., and Helen Rose Ebaugh. 1993. "Leaving New Religions." In *The Handbook of Cults and Sects in America,* edited by David G. Bromley and Jeffrey K. Hadden, vol. 3, pp. 117–38. Greenwich, CT: JAI Press.

Part Four

APOCALYPTICISM,
RELIGIOUS MARGINALITY,
AND VIOLENCE

9

JOHN R. HALL

Public Narratives and the Apocalyptic Sect

From Jonestown to Mt. Carmel

Long before the Bureau of Alcohol, Tobacco, and Firearms set out on their ill-fated raid against Mt. Carmel, David Koresh's apocalyptic sect was becoming another Jonestown. So said former Branch Davidians more than a year before the shoot-out with BATF (Breault and King 1993, 11–12). I believe that the apostates were prophetic: "Waco" has become a new Jonestown in the minds of the public. But was the prophecy in part self-fulfilling? To probe this question, I ask here how the central public meaning of Jonestown—mass suicide—came into play at Mt. Carmel.

There are two major approaches to cultural studies that could be used to address this question of public meaning. A neo-Durkheimian approach suggests that public meanings play out through alteration between two poles of one or another binary cultural code—sacred versus profane, good versus evil, democratic versus counterdemocratic (e.g., Alexander and Smith 1993). But the neo-Durkheimian approach runs the structuralist risk of forcing actual meanings into a preconceived framework. An alternative—more interpretive (or hermeneutic)—approach looks at the situated construction of local meanings instead of fitting them within some posited overarching cultural meaning system of binary oppositions.[1] Hermeneutic analysis can be carried out through the study of "intrinsic narratives"—the diverse stories that various social actors tell within emergent situations to which they are mutually oriented, but in different ways. Such analysis can help show how cultural meanings become nuanced, shaded, interpreted, challenged, and otherwise reworked by participants, and how such meaning shifts affect the course of unfolding events (Hall and Neitz 1993, 12–13; Hall forthcoming, chap. 4). Looking at narratives to trace emergent cultural meanings of mass suicide reveals how meanings about Jonestown became changed into meanings about the Branch Davidians. As I will show, the cultural opponents of David Koresh reinvoked and reworked narratives about mass suicide in ways that shaped the escalating trajectory of conflict at Mt. Carmel.

There is deep irony in the early prophetic warnings by former members that cast Mt. Carmel as another Jonestown, a "cult." The term "cult" has a variety of meanings. But whatever the possible dictionary definitions, in the late twentieth-century United States, the term has become almost universally recognized as a stigmatic label for countercultural religious groups. The term thus takes on its current cultural significance through meanings promulgated by the anticult movement. In this cultural sense, it is easy to understand Mt. Carmel as the second Jonestown—a prison-fortress that Jim Jones is said to have created in Jonestown, Guyana, a place where "brainwashed" and powerless individuals, broken of their will, were subjected to the whims of a megalomaniac who orchestrated their deaths in a "mass suicide" that was really an elaborate murder. But this comparison is superficial and misleading, because the people who put the most effort into labeling countercultural religious groups as cults are not passive bystanders or critics after the fact. They are active opponents. In the case of Jonestown, the movement against Peoples Temple contributed to the dynamic of accelerating conflict that ended in the murders and mass suicide (Hall 1987). The mass suicide thus could not be adequately analyzed solely through the "frame" (Snow et al. 1986) of the anticult movement. If, as I believe, Mt. Carmel now must be understood as another Jonestown, then it cannot be adequately understood as a "cult"; instead, we must ask whether anticult labeling played into the conflict. It is my thesis that because of our failure to learn from Jonestown, cultural opponents could take narratives about mass suicide from Jonestown and bring them to bear on the Branch Davidians in ways that proved central to how the tragedy at Mt. Carmel unfolded.

Peoples Temple and the Branch Davidians both approximated the "apocalyptic sect" as an ideal type. In such sects the end of the world is taken as a central tenet. But much depends on any given sect's response to their construction of the apocalypse. At one extreme, a group may retreat to an "other-worldly" heaven-on-earth, disconnected from the evil society in its last days. Alternatively, it may seek out the battle of Armageddon—that last and decisive struggle between the forces of good and manifest evil (Hall 1978). Moreover, these two contradictory tendencies sometimes remain in volatile play within the same group. Thus, no conclusions can be drawn in advance about the trajectory of an apocalyptic sect. For groups that have not stabilized a heaven-on-earth, the play of events is especially contingent upon the interaction of the group with the wider social world. Because neither Jim Jones nor David Koresh established a stable heaven-on-earth, we cannot understand either the Branch Davidians or Peoples Temple as a group with its own autonomous fate. Instead, we need to recognize that, like Jonestown, the conflagration at Mt. Carmel was the product of religious conflict between a militant sect and opponents who, wittingly or unwittingly, helped fulfill the sect's emergent apocalyptic vision.

The apocalyptic visions of Jim Jones and David Koresh were quite different, of course. Jones blended Pentecostal and liberal Christianity with political sympathies toward the world-historical Communist movement, and he consolidated a politically engaged movement built on the apocalyptic premise that Peoples Temple would offer an ark of refuge in the face of a prophesied U.S. drift toward race and class warfare. Koresh, by contrast, did not forge a new apocalyptic vision; he appropriated a long-standing one. The Seventh-Day Adventists, from whence the Branch Davidian sect had emerged, was founded in the nineteenth century on a prophecy of the end of the world. From this messianic beginning, Adventists have tried in the twentieth century to attain a legitimate denominational status within U.S. religion by suppressing their most florid apocalyptic visions, but in doing so they have opened themselves to the critique of Adventist splinter sects that reclaim the "true faith." The apocalyptic rhetoric of David Koresh differs little from the rhetoric of other such groups opposed to the Advent establishment, groups whose rhetoric is equally filled with references to the seven seals, plagues (AIDS), visions of glory, enemies of the faith, apostates, and the day of testing that is "just before us." Koresh could well have borrowed the warning of an Oregon group: "The members of the church will individually be tested and proved. They will be placed in circumstances where they will be forced to bear witness for the truth" (*Advent Review*, n.d.).

Jones's apocalyptic vision was a Marxist-Christian amalgamation tied to the social issues of the day, whereas Koresh continued the long-standing Adventist tradition of mapping highly detailed interpretations of the book of Revelation in relation to specific signs of the final days. Yet Jones's Temple and Koresh's Branch Davidians had much in common. Both Jones and Koresh took up the project of founding expansionary religious movements. Like early Mormon polygamists, both Jones and Koresh fathered children with multiple sexual partners, in Koresh's case, some of them under the legal age of sexual consent. Koresh also seems to have established a military "men's house" separated from the women (see Weber 1978, 357). Such communally organized sexual and gender patterns are culturally taboo within modern Western societies, even if (and perhaps because) they are tested, durable forms of social organization. Polygamy and the men's house can be used to create a militant, protoethnic religious movement bound together by the patrimonialist cadre of a prophet's followers and hereditary succession of prophecy. Following such a protoethnic formula, Jones and Koresh each established what amounted to a state within a state—Jonestown, close to Guyana's disputed border with Venezuela; and Mt. Carmel, a tiny principality on a back Texas road. Through interaction with real (and in Jones's case, sometimes imagined) opponents, both Jones and Koresh prepared for militant armed struggle. For Jones, the precipitating threats came from journalists and defectors in the early 1970s; for his part, Koresh consolidated his sectarian leadership through a violent confrontation in 1987 with the competing claimant to the Mt. Carmel legacy, George Roden. In the face of increasing external opposition, Koresh, like Jones, steeled his followers to "metanoia" (revolutionary rebirth) in which the meanings of life—and death—became bound up with unfolding events. In different ways, the dominant groups at both Jonestown and Mt. Carmel came to affirm their refusal to submit to an external authority they believed to be intent on destroying them.

Such parallels show that Peoples Temple and the Branch Davidians shared a propensity toward conflict with outside opponents and authorities, but they do not account for the tragedies at Jonestown and Mt. Carmel. Given that other standoffs between authorities and religious sects have been resolved peacefully, the outcome at Mt. Carmel, as at Jonestown, could have been different. How the standoff at Mt. Carmel was precipitated by the BATF raid already has been the subject of minute analysis. The U.S. Treasury Department report defended as legal and legitimate the BATF pursuit of Koresh for weapons violations (1993, 120). It strongly denied that the BATF acted against Koresh because of his deviant religious beliefs (p. 121). However, this claim is open to question, since Mt. Carmel was cast as a "cult" in the affidavit in support of application for the warrants (U.S. District Court 1993). Indeed, the Treasury review is self-refuting on the supposed irrelevance of Koresh's religion, since it evidences the threat that Koresh posed by reference to his apocalyptic theology. These incongruities suggest the need to understand how cultural rather than official lenses shaped the vision of BATF in the conflict.

Because cultural narratives about "cults" are distinctive in comparison to, say, the rhetoric of law enforcement, it is possible to trace the interplay between cultural constructions and legal ones. Anticult usage identifies "cults" as subversive both of families and individuals and of the core values of society as a whole. One cultural signification—mass suicide—is central in some ultimate sense to understanding both Jonestown and Mt. Carmel. After Jonestown, mass suicide has become a term of general cultural currency, a touchstone for describing the stark danger posed by "cults." This ambiguous but compelling motif was invoked frequently by opponents of the Branch Davidians, beginning more than a year before the BATF raid. The existence of diverse documents makes it possible to trace in detail the emergence of mass suicide as a cultural meaning about Mt. Carmel before the FBI standoff. In short, it is possible to examine a relatively circumscribed set of events to track the emergent play of cultural meanings that mediated an increasingly public religious conflict.

The shifts in the significance of mass suicide can be traced by examining the "intrinsic" narratives that were offered as events unfolded. By focusing on these accounts, it is possible to show connections that were established between previously existing cultural structures and the situated agency of individual and organized social actions (Sewell 1992; Hall and Neitz 1993, 11; Hall forthcoming, chap. 3). People use narratives ("stories," we can call them, if we refrain from judgments about truth status) in a variety of ways. They can "construct" reality by offering other people's accounts and reports of events beyond their own personal knowledge. People also individually and jointly compose narratives ("scripts" and "scenarios") in order to make sense of projects that they are undertaking. In a different way, accounts can be used to "reconstruct" events after the fact, and they can "deconstruct" competing stories in advance, as events unfold, and after the fact. Narratives in each of these forms may draw in "cultural meanings" that help render them coherent and accessible. Thus, analyzing narratives—in relation to the social identities, locations, and power of the narrators—can bring to light the specific connections between cultural constructs and situational public discourses about religious conflicts. As I will show, narratives are particularly important when the meaningful content shifts, when the narrative moves from one source to another, when affinities develop between the narratives of two individuals or groups, and when the incorporation of a received narrative rearranges other meanings for an individual or group. When such narratives are freighted with cultural meanings, they may exercise influence on a course of events in ways that exceed or do not depend upon merely factual, legal, or professional considerations.

How, then, did cultural meanings about mass suicide figure in the interwoven narratives of Waco? What accounts did Koresh and his followers at Mt. Carmel, the former sect members, authorities, and the media offer—to themselves and to others? How did various individuals assess other people's stories? To what extent were stories "cultural scripts"—that is, formulaic or liturgical narratives that bear significance independently of the actual circumstances? Tracing the narratives about mass suicide for the Waco affair up through the BATF raid on February 28, 1993, will show not only parallels with, but a genetic connection to, Jonestown; establishing these connections may offer some insight into how public discourse of citizens, media, and governmental authorities is built up through the reformulation of cultural meanings in successive historical events (Gamson et al. 1992).

The Narrative of Apocalyptic Militancy

The central narratives of Waco are, of course, those of David Koresh and his committed followers. Unfortunately, not only are they the ones about which we know the least, but most of what we know is filtered through their antagonists, both former cult members and governmental authorities. Yet available information suggests a pattern that parallels the emergence of the mass suicide motif at Jonestown. Jim Jones specifically appropriated Huey Newton's Black Panther party analysis. For Newton, the poor, the oppressed, and blacks in particular faced a choice between two kinds of suicide—the "reactionary" suicide of submitting to their oppression within the existing social order, or "revolutionary" suicide, that is, the rebirth of the individual to a revolutionary struggle that would become the central orienting meaning and ultimate commitment of their lives. Living for the cause could also mean dying for the cause. Mediated by Peoples Temple's struggles with its opponents, revolutionary suicide ultimately became mass suicide. But this outcome was not foreordained (Hall 1987, 135–36).

The Branch Davidians did not invoke the Black Panthers. If Koresh's political sentiments ran in any direction, it was to the antistate populism of right-wing Christian survivalist movements. But Koresh's and his followers' attachments to apocalyptic theology were, if anything, stronger than those of the Black Panthers and Peoples Temple. From its origins in the 1920s, the Branch Davidian movement was centered on the classic Seventh-Day Adventist questions about how exactly to interpret the book of Revelation's clues about the last days. Koresh did not have to create an apocalyptic theology from the ground up; he did not even have to shift it from a pacifistic to a militant dispensation, for Adventist discourse already had well-developed themes of militancy, sacrifices made by the faithful, their subjection to trials from the outside—in short, the strongest motifs drawn from a long tradition of Christian martyrdom that centuries earlier led Christians to fight for their faith, even to seek to die for their faith, in ways that likely had precipitated Augustine's injunction against suicide (Hall 1987, 296–98).

Yet there is considerable evidence that Koresh was an existentialist, not a predestinationist: he anticipated the apocalypse, but its form was open-ended. During the long standoff with the FBI, Koresh kept waiting for signs that would reveal the godly course of action. Before the BATF raid, he dealt with governmental officials, including a sheriff and deputy who served an arrest warrant over the Roden shoot-out in 1987. After the BATF raid, the prosecuting district attorney involved in the 1987 arrest, Vic Feazell, recounted, "We treated them like human beings, rather than storm-trooping the place. They were extremely polite people" (Bragg 1993, 7A). In this situation, when treated with relative civility, Koresh did not leap to a siege posture. He acted with courtesy and a degree of compliance. Koresh struck a similar chord during the BATF raid, in a recorded telephone conversation with the BATF: "It would have been better if you just called me up or talked to me. Then you all could have come in and done your work" (in Wood 1993, 2). This claim might be dismissed as self-serving but for the fact that it describes how Koresh had dealt with authorities in previous situations.

Still, it is fruitless to speculate about how Koresh might have responded if the BATF had approached him in a different way, for tensions heightened considerably early in 1992. Moreover, to note the existential civility of the Branch Davidians is not to deny that Koresh was willing to resort to violence. However, neither is it evident that Koresh was preparing to attack, and it is at least plausible, as even the Treasury Department review acknowledges, that he "might simply have been preparing to defend himself against an apocalyptic onslaught" (p. 127). In the final analysis, these considerations about what directions the apocalyptic struggle might have taken are moot, because Koresh came upon direct signs that he could interpret by way of ancient biblical prophecies about the last days.

The Narrative of Mass Suicide in the Opponents' Cries for Help

Given the long standoff before the final FBI assault and the subsequent fire, it is clear that David Koresh had no single apocalyptic scenario in mind before the BATF raid. Although there was a generalized apocalyptic vision within Mt. Carmel before the raid, the first specific invocation of mass suicide came from outside the Branch Davidians, from former sect members who had become opponents. What was this narrative, and how and where did it become more widely diffused? There were complex pathways, but as with Jonestown (Hall 1987, chaps. 9, 10), relatively small and converging clusters of opponents, informed by the discourse of the anticult movement, raised the alarm with the media and various government agencies. Like Temple opponents, the cultural opponents of Koresh invoked the threat that Koresh posed to his followers and the wider society by citing key incidents and "proof texts" taken from Koresh's preachings. In turn, as I will show, government agency scenarios for dealing with Koresh gradually became infused with the opponents' warnings about mass suicide, and in ways that shaped the logic of the BATF raid.

Certain details about how the discourse of mass suicide spread into the public and governmental domains have not yet (and may never) become public knowledge. But the major channels are clear. Mostly they trace from Marc Breault, who joined the Branch Davidians in 1986. Breault left after becoming increasingly dismayed about

Koresh's practice of engaging in sexual relationships and siring children with young teenage girls whom the leader initiated into the "House of David." As Breault recounted, he became disgusted by witnessing thirteen-year-old Aisha Gyarfas pass by his desk after spending the night with David Koresh sometime in July 1989. On August 5, 1989, Breault heard what he called Koresh's "New Light" doctrine justifying the sexual economy of the Branch Davidians, a doctrine connected to the role Koresh assumed as the "sinful messiah" (Tabor and Arnold, in Koresh 1993, 1–2). In September, Breault flew to Australia and took up the role of "cult-buster," working tirelessly to bring Koresh down. In early 1990, he used theological arguments to pry loose Australian followers of Koresh. Gradually, Breault consolidated a band of Australian apostates, and they began to engage in a clandestine struggle, even meeting in the middle of the night to avoid what they feared were stakeouts by Koresh loyalists (Breault and King 1993, 213).

By small steps, a story about possible violent retribution for their opposition emerged among the gathering apostates, as they worked to help other people break away from the Branch Davidians and raised the alarm to government agencies. Two families were central to their efforts—the Bunds and the Jewells. Koresh had banished David and Debbie Bunds. They later claimed that they received a threatening phone call after Breault got in touch with them, and they decided to move from Waco to California. There, they linked up with David Bunds's sister, Robyn, a Koresh "wife" who broke with Koresh over a period of months beginning in the summer of 1990. In Breault's description of Robyn's defection, he suggests a theme that went beyond vengeance against enemies—child sacrifice. Robyn Bunds had given birth to a child that remained with the Branch Davidians, and she became distraught: "I've heard that he's talking about sacrificing children! My God, what if he tries to kill Wisdom?" Robyn retrieved her son Shaun ("Wisdom"), apparently through the intervention of Sgt. John Hackworth, of the LaVerne, California, police (*Washington Post*, April 25, 1993; Linedecker 1993, 145–46). As Breault explains, "We were worried that Koresh might be thinking about human sacrifices. We didn't know for sure, but Koresh was unstable enough to make even our darkest nightmares seem possible" (Breault and King 1993, 220). This sort of atrocity tale became repeated, elaborated, and amplified over time. Breault later recounted that while he was a member, Koresh warned about outsiders coming in and killing the children. After Breault left, "we started hearing rumors that he was planning it himself" (*Washington Post*, April 25, 1993). Similarly, Breault became concerned about his own life:

"Koresh wanted to lure me back to Mount Carmel and kill me" (Breault and King 1993, 226, 233). To date, we have no way of tracing these stories back from Breault's accounts. Taken together, they weave a vision of sadistic violence and unrestrained retribution. But for the most part the narratives do not claim to be about actual events: they are about rumors, nightmares, and anticipated agendas. In an odd and disturbing way, Breault's accounts take a rhetorical form similar to some of the prophecies of Jim Jones (Hall 1987, 22, 33–36).

Nightmares are not cause for government intervention, but other matters were. Robyn Bunds reported to the U.S. Immigration and Naturalization Service that she had been a party to one of several sham marriages arranged between foreigners and U.S. citizens (Breault and King 1993, 245–46). Bunds's complaint was one of a barrage that Breault's group launched toward government officials in September 1990. The previous March, the defectors had hired an Australian private investigator, Geoffrey Hossack, to help in their struggle against Koresh, and they had begun collecting affidavits. In August, Breault called his band of defectors to a meeting in Australia and offered a "Bible study on human sacrifices." He told the assembled a story that he said he had been told by Koresh's close associate, Steve Schneider: "God was going to demand that Koresh do with his son Cyrus what Abraham of old was commanded to do with Isaac." (According to the book of Genesis, God instructed Abraham to sacrifice his son, and stopped him only at the last moment.) Breault's wording here is intriguing: he does not say that God actually made any such demand of Koresh, and although he asserts that he is in possession of damaging tape recordings of Koresh's preaching, he does not quote Koresh directly on the matter. Yet the story of child sacrifice, in various versions, became a key element in Breault's account of the dangers at Mt. Carmel. Borrowing a page from the tactics of so-called cults themselves (Hall 1987), Breault used the story at the Australia meeting to "shock" his audience, and "weeded out those [he] couldn't trust." Those whom Breault could trust drew up affidavits about statutory rape, immigration violations, food and water deprivation, and concerns about child sacrifices. Hossack flew to the United States with the affidavits, and in September 1990 he met with officers from the LaVerne, California, police department, and, in Waco, with an investigator from the Texas Department of Public Safety, Lt. Gene Barber of the McClennan County sheriff's department, the McClennan County district attorney, and the assistant U.S. attorney. Hossack also talked with the U.S. Internal Revenue Service and Immigration and Naturalization Service. Soon after these meetings, the FBI and the assistant U.S. district attorney, Bill Johnston, determined that no federal violations had occurred, and closed their case (U.S. Treasury Department 1993, D-3).

Like the opponents of Peoples Temple (Hall 1987, 228–35), Breault and his allies were frustrated at the lack of official response, and they pursued other avenues, namely the media, and their own court actions. In late 1991 and early 1992, they worked through two connected efforts—a television expose and a custody battle. Like certain Temple opponents, Breault hoped media attention would protect him: "If Vernon [Koresh] knew that Breault had gone public, he'd think twice about trying to kill him" (Breault and King 1993, 256; cf. Hall 1987, 268). Breault tried to interest the American media, but he got nowhere. In October 1991, however, he attracted the interest of the Australian television program, *A Current Affair*. Like one reporter who accompanied Congressman Leo Ryan on his ill-fated trip to Jonestown (Hall 1987, 257–58), the Australian television reporters projected an objective and impartial facade for most of their visit, and then confronted Koresh at the end with opponents' accusations. The crew of *A Current Affair* undertook what they believed to be a dangerous mission—exposing Koresh "as a cruel, maniacal, child-molesting, pistol-packing religious zealot who brainwashed his devotees." When the television crew visited Mt. Carmel in January 1992, they recalled Jonestown, where the reporters had been killed first. Already, they had been warned by "former cult members" that Mt. Carmel might become "another Jonestown" (Breault and King 1993, 256–57).

The Australian television program did not yield much in the way of direct results other than the footage of Koresh preaching that became so familiar to viewers after the BATF raid. But the other initiative, the custody battle, was critical to consolidating the movement against Koresh in the United States. The effort began in June 1991, well before the television program planning. Marc Breault had returned to the States from Australia, having decided to target Kiri Jewell, the daughter of Branch Davidian member Sherri Jewel and her former husband David, a disk jockey who was never a Davidian. Breault was concerned that the preteenager was "destined for" the "House of David," but he did not know how to reach David Jewell, and instead approached Sherri Jewell's mother, Ruth Mosher, with what he said was Robyn Bunds's firsthand account of Koresh's statements about his plan to take Kiri as a sexual partner. In front of Sherri Jewell's mother, he confronted Sherri with accusations about Koresh having sex with teenagers, and he got her to admit that a fourteen-year-old girl named Michelle had become pregnant at Mt.

Carmel. He transcribed the conversation and provided it to the LaV-
erne, California, police. (Police sergeant John Hackworth later
recounted that the charges were "unsubstantiated, and some of what
was alleged occurred in Texas.") Breault also telephoned Gene Barber, of the McClennan County, Texas, sheriff's department, and
found that an investigation of Koresh in Texas (probably the September 1990 investigation of sham marriages) had been closed for lack of
probable cause. On July 4, 1991, Breault wrote Barber a letter detailing his allegations of tax evasion and Koresh's sexual relations with
children, and claiming that a woman had been "raped by Vernon, . .
. and had a loaded gun pointed at her head." Enclosed with the letter
was a "tape of Vernon's [Koresh's] 'Bible study' in which he blatantly and clearly threatens to kill." These efforts did not result in any
specific law enforcement actions (Breault and King 1993, 233–45;
U.S. Treasury Department 1993, D5).

Marc Breault does not seem to have been very sophisticated about
the legal process in the United States, and he clearly became frustrated when his careful efforts to compile information did not seem
to go anywhere with the authorities. The custody struggle over Kiri
Jewell, however, involved a specific grievance on the part of someone
with legal standing. On October 31, 1991, in a telephone call from
Australia to Michigan, Breault was able to warn Kiri's father, David
Jewell, about the fate that awaited Kiri in the "House of David."
David Jewell promptly engaged an attorney, coordinated with Breault
by e-mail on CompuServe, and worked to obtain a Michigan court
order for temporary custody of Kiri when her mother sent the child to
Michigan for the Christmas holidays of 1991. Breault and the staff of
A Current Affair had planned the January 1992 visit by the Australian television crew partly to distract Koresh's attention from Kiri
Jewell. As these events unfolded, the opponents received information that reinforced their vision of cultic destruction, and they in
turn, used the information to further spread alarm. In a January 1,
1992, letter to Breault, David Bunds reported that his sister had told
him what his mother, Jeannine Bunds, had said sometime the previous summer. In this thirdhand account, Koresh was said to be telling
people that his goals would be accomplished in half a year. "My
mother also got the impression of mass suicide or homicide, she was
not really sure." Breault also claimed to have learned from former
members (the likely source is Jeannine Bunds) that he was at the top
of a "hit list" prepared by Koresh.

The custody battle was the focal point. Koresh sent Steve Schneider to help Sherri Jewell in the February court case, and Breault and
his allies decided to contact the Schneider family. On February 22,

1992, during preparations for the Jewell custody case, Sue Schneider, Steve's older sister, gave Breault chilling news:

> She said that Steve had called them to say goodbye. He said that he would probably have to do something which would cause him to die, but that he would be resurrected shortly thereafter and fulfill Isaiah 13 and Joel 2. . . . He sounded suicidal. The something which would cause him to die was termed "the end." This was not something limited entirely to Steve himself, but concerned the whole group. (Breault and King 1993, 268)

Breault could not sleep one night, "thinking of my best friend blowing his brains out, or taking cyanide [part of the Jonestown mass suicide potion], or getting shot in a gun-fight with the authorities" (Breault and King 1993, 276; U.S. Treasury Department 1993, 28; cf. Hall 1987, xii).

The struggle between Jim Jones and Grace and Tim Stoen over the custody of John Victor Stoen—the "child-god" whom Jim Jones claimed as his son—had been a cause celebre of the movement against Peoples Temple. The parallels between the custody battles of the Peoples Temple and the Davidians are striking. On February 28, 1992, before the court case was concluded, David Jewell and Sherri Jewell reached an agreement for joint custody of Kiri. The custody case was over, but like the apostates and relatives who opposed Jim Jones, the vision of David Jewell, Marc Breault, and others transcended their own individual interests in the custody of their own children. They collectively worked to stop someone they regarded as morally abhorrent. When David Jewell learned of "two thirteen-year-old friends [of Kiri] also targeted to become brides in the House of David, he telephoned the Texas Department of Human Services" (Breault and King 1993, 279; Linedecker 1993, 144 [quotation]; *Washington Post*, April 25, 1993; *Waco Tribune-Herald*, March 1, 1993, 9A). On the basis of a complaint on February 26, 1992, from "outside the state of Texas," as the affidavit supporting a search warrant put it, Joyce Sparks, of Texas Child Protective Services (CPS), visited Mt. Carmel with two sheriff's deputies the next day. In early March, Koresh came to see Joyce Sparks at the Waco CPS office, and Sparks visited the compound two more times, on April 6 and 30, 1992. Davidian children and adults denied any abuse, and examinations of children produced no evidence of current or previous injuries. Over the objections of Sparks, the nine-week investigation was closed. Sparks then became a key informant for other government agencies, talking with the FBI in May 1992, maintaining contact by telephone with Koresh through June 1992, and providing the BATF with floor plans of the Mt. Carmel compound in early December 1992 (U.S. Treasury Department 1993, D3 4; ABC Primetime, January 13, 1994).

Whether or not Koresh's opponents were directly in contact with the anticult movement's Cult Awareness Network (CAN), they increasingly followed the playbook of that organization, operating on multiple fronts to inform authorities and the media, and trying to turn individual Branch Davidian members to their cause, using their own affidavits, media clips, and evidence gathered from defecting members to build documentation that could in turn be used with subsequent initiatives. In at least one case, a former Davidian, David Block, was "deprogrammed" by someone associated with CAN— Rick Ross. It seems odd that Block could have developed such strong Davidian beliefs as to require deprogramming after living at Mt. Carmel for only around two months, from March or soon thereafter until he left in June 1992 (Cable News Network, transcript #260–61, March 2, 1993; U.S. Treasury Department 1993, D9). There is thus room to wonder whether Block was a bona fide convert in the first place or a plant sent in from the outside, either by opponents or by an investigating law enforcement agency (both Texas CPS and FBI investigations were active at the time of Block's presence at Mt. Carmel).

Soon after the custody court case, in March 1992, Breault, David Jewell, and their allies began to spread the word that the Branch Davidians might commit mass suicide. All the substantive evidence that Breault and King offer on this key question comes from the second- and thirdhand statements of Jeannine Bunds and Sue Schneider. Apparently, the statement from Steve to Sue Schneider and the account of an unnamed young female apostate carried particular weight (Linedecker 1993, 152–53). The cited evidence is ambiguous at best, but like Peoples Temple dissidents (Hall 1987, 234), Koresh's opponents embellished their accounts in order to magnify the dangers of the organization that they sought to expose. In March 1992, both Jewell and Breault wrote quite specific letters to David Jewell's congressman in Michigan, Fred Upton, about the possibility that the Branch Davidians would end their lives during Passover. In Breault's words, "the cult leader, one Vernon Wayne Howell, is planning a mass suicide somewhere around April 18th of this year. . . . Time is fast running out and I need to talk to the FBI or someone who can do something. If this does not happen, I believe that over 200 persons will be massacred next month. . . . Every day brings us closer to another Jonestown" (Breault and King 1993, 290–91). Upton forwarded the letter to Chet Edwards, the congressman from Waco, and

Edwards passed it to the FBI. In April 1992, the FBI opened an investigation of Koresh for "involuntary servitude." In May they interviewed Joyce Sparks of Texas CPS. But in June, the FBI closed the investigation, apparently for lack of evidence (U.S. Treasury Department 1993, D4).

The account of mass suicide began to percolate through other channels. An April 1992 statement by Australian Bruce Gent argued that government authorities would take notice only "when there's a pile of bodies . . . and then they're going to go in and find them and then it's all over. It'll be another Jonestown" (Breault and King 1993, 249). Also in April, the U.S. consulate in Australia sent a cable to Washington, citing "local informants" to the effect that the Branch Davidians were gathering at Mt. Carmel, "where they expected to die as part of a mass suicide." The cable went on, "The informants also told us that they believe that [Koresh] has armed himself with guns and ammunition in order to effect a shoot-out with authorities if they attempt to enter the cult's Waco property to take away any of the children now living there, or investigate living conditions." The same month, a reporter from the *Waco Tribune-Herald* began his investigation of the Branch Davidians, after hearing reports from the Australian press about a possible mass suicide over the Davidian Passover (Bailey and Darden 1993, 152; U.S. Treasury Department 1993, D4; *Washington Post*, April 25, 1993).

Whether there was ever any plan for mass suicide in April 1992, we have no direct evidence. Koresh's opponents spread the report, and although the event failed to materialize, the only public account of why is a cryptic statement, "The suicide plan was called off," made in the *Washington Post* a year later (April 25, p. 1). Breault's book with Martin King is silent on why the suicide prediction was not fulfilled. The first record of David Koresh making any statement on the subject was his response to *Waco Tribune-Herald* reporter Mark England at the time. Koresh questioned why, if the stories were true, the Branch Davidians would be improving the facilities at Mt. Carmel: "I've got the water-well man coming in. I mean, two weeks in a row we're supposed to be committing suicide. I wish they'd get their story straight" (quoted in Bailey and Darden 1993, 152).

My own view is that the opponents of David Koresh engaged in a long-standing fundamentalist practice—citing "proof texts"—to build a particular theological interpretation out of the deeply apocalyptic discourse that Koresh shared with other renegade Adventist sects. However, it is also evident that Koresh would have perceived increasing external signs of opposition during the first half of 1992. In January, he was the target of the Australian television story informed by his opponents' claims against him. Over January and February there was the custody struggle over Kiri Jewell. At the end of February Mt. Carmel was visited by Joyce Sparks of the Texas CPS. During the same days in early March that Koresh met in Waco with caseworker Sparks, a SWAT (Strategic Weapons and Tactics) law enforcement team undertook practice exercises near the "Mag Bag," a building some miles from Mt. Carmel owned by the Branch Davidians. It was in these circumstances, beginning on February 1, 1992, and accelerating on and after March 9, 1992, that Koresh made his great leap forward toward a siege mentality. He began arming his followers at Mt. Carmel with assault rifles and other paramilitary equipment, and he called upon some forty Branch Davidians to come to Mt. Carmel from California and England (U.S. Treasury Department 1993, B168–95, D3–4). The timing in relation to the custody dispute and subsequent Texas CPS investigation suggests a not unreasonable inference: Koresh likely believed that authorities might try to forcibly remove Branch Davidian children from the compound (as has happened at other religious communities both before and since[2]), and he may have decided to resist by force any such possible move. No CPS raid ever occurred. However, the efforts of Koresh's opponents precipitated a distinctively heightened siege posture at Mt. Carmel. In addition, the reports of plans for mass suicide and Koresh's decision to further arm his followers played directly into the events that led to the ill-fated BATF raid and the subsequent standoff with the FBI. As with Peoples Temple, the stories about the group told by their cultural opponents shaped the dynamic of religious conflict between the sect and the wider world. In form, content, and audience, the accounts by Koresh's opponents invoke the generalized collective memory embodied in the formulaic narratives told within the anticult movement about "cults" (e.g., Zilliox and Kahaner n.d.; cf. Fentress and Wickham 1992, 55).

Mass Suicide as a Narrative of Strategic Law Enforcement

To this point, I have shown how the cultural opponents of David Koresh gleaned a narrative about mass suicide from Koresh's preachings and the hearsay accounts of defectors, and concretized and spread that narrative to government agencies and politicians at the state, federal, and local levels, and to the media in Australia and the United States. The question to be addressed in turn is how narratives about mass suicide became infused into the scenarios that authorities constructed in relation to the Branch Davidians. To be sure, much other information came into the hands of officials, but by sticking to the question of mass suicide, it is possible to trace the influence of a central cultural motif.

The BATF investigation was initiated in May 1992, after a United Parcel Service driver discovered inert grenade casings in a package to the Branch Davidians and reported his discovery to the McClennan County Sheriff's Department, which passed the information to the BATF office in Austin. BATF agent Davy Aguilera was assigned to investigate, and he met on June 4, 1992, with Waco Assistant U.S. Attorney Bill Johnston and with Gene Barber of the sheriff's office—both of whom had been at the 1990 meeting with the Breault faction's private investigator, Geoffrey Hossack. Gene Barber briefed Aguilera on the Branch Davidians. The BATF may be technically correct to deny finding evidence of any motivation that "targeted Koresh because of his religious beliefs and life-style." And, to be sure, the BATF had its own interests in demonstrating its effectiveness as a law enforcement agency in relation to an armed "cult." But from the outset, the BATF investigation was immersed in webs of discourse that had been spun by Koresh's opponents (U.S. Treasury Department 1993, D4, 121, 125).

The BATF investigation was slow getting started. On July 23, 1992, Aguilera sent a report to BATF headquarters listing shipments to the Mag Bag and requesting analysis of whether the Davidians were "possibly converting or manufacturing Title II weapons." In October 1992, around the time a *Waco Tribune-Herald* reporter asked Bill Johnston about whether the Davidians' firearms were legal, Aguilera was told to begin preparing an affidavit for search and arrest warrants (he also was authorized to set up an undercover house near the Mt. Carmel compound). On November 2, 1992, BATF headquarters reported that there was not sufficient evidence based on the firearms listed in the July 23 report to justify a search warrant (U.S. Treasury Department 1993, B190, 193–94, D5). It was only—and immediately—after the disappointing news about lack of probable cause for a search warrant that the BATF began to contact former members and relatives of Branch Davidians directly.

The contacts were extremely sensitive, because the BATF did not want to compromise their secret investigation; for this reason, it would seem, they limited themselves to interviewing committed opponents of Koresh. The contacts were substantial. On November 3, Davy Aguilera flew to California, and met both with LaVerne police and with Isabel and Guillermo Andrade, who had two daughters living at Mt. Carmel, one of whom, they said, had given birth to a child fathered by Koresh. Aguilera arranged for the Andrades to fly to Waco to visit their daughters on November 5 through 7, and then he "debriefed" them (what information he obtained is not clear). In addition, on the basis of sexual allegations raised by the defectors, the BATF contacted Joyce Sparks, the Texas CPS caseworker, who reported that she had never been able to confirm any abuse because of staged tours, but that she had seen a target range and heard a child talk about (and saw herself) "long guns." She also quoted Koresh as having told her, "My time is coming. When I reveal myself as the messenger and my time comes, what happens will make the riots in L.A. pale in comparison." Defectors and relatives related similarly apocalyptic visions. From LaVerne police sergeant Hackworth, Aguilera learned about Marc Breault and the Bunds family on December 12. Jeannine Bunds told Aguilera about a "hit list" that she said Koresh once mentioned to her, and David Bunds recounted a conversation in which his father, Donald, had said that he was armed and prepared to die for Koresh. When Aguilera telephoned Breault on December 15, Breault reinforced these accounts by providing the BATF with the affidavit he had prepared in Australia and offering new information—about the posting of armed guards around the compound with instructions to "shoot to kill," and a story of how, in the Treasury Department's words, "a cult member had taken a shot at a newspaper delivery person" (pp. 27–30, 211, B-24, D5–7; Breault and King 1993, 294–301).

The BATF operatives drew no clear and hard line between the gathering of evidence to establish probable cause for the search warrant and obtaining intelligence for tactical planning, which began even while agents continued to gather information for probable cause. Moreover, the BATF tended to treat opponents' accounts as facts without considering whether the former members had "individual biases, or if they had an ax to grind," as two outside reviewers later pointed out (U.S. Treasury Department 1993, B19, 129–30). Thus, both the warrant and the BATF's tactical plan for responding to Koresh used information supplied by Koresh's opponents. Tactical planners adopted the view that the BATF had to take action to deal with the Mt. Carmel case. They did so partly because Koresh's documented 1987 attack on George Roden established his propensity toward violence, and partly because of reports to the BATF about "alleged threats against former cult members." The BATF "simply did not want to risk the added possibility that cult members would turn their weapons against members of the community," although they did not specify what evidence led them to this concern. With the decision to take action made, at various points the BATF envisioned three alternative scenarios: (1) attempting to serve warrants peaceably and, if they met resistance, laying a siege against Mt.

Carmel with negotiations for surrender, (2) staging a "dynamic entry," in which agents would storm the compound and secure it for the search and any arrests, and (3) luring Koresh away from the compound in order to facilitate an execution of the search warrant. Planners tended to discount the third option, partly because Joyce Sparks (incorrectly) told BATF that Koresh rarely, if ever, left Mt. Carmel. The BATF's initial plan, laid out at a meeting in Houston on December 18, 1992, was to pursue the serve-and-siege option. But a December 24 briefing at BATF headquarters in Washington led to demands for slowing down tactical operations planning and requests for further documentation of probable cause. At the request of tactical planners, Davy Aguilera subsequently made arrangements to interview Breault and others jointly with William Buford, a BATF agent who had participated in the 1985 FBI and BATF siege against the Arkansas communal settlement of armed white supremacists who called themselves the Covenant, the Sword, and the Arm of the Lord (CSA). Buford was a member of the Special Response Team (SRT) that would be conducting any tactical operation at Mt. Carmel (U.S. Treasury Department 1993, B-47, 44, D7–8, 43).

Aguilera and Buford went to California, where the two agents interviewed Marc Breault, the Bunds, and the Andrades from January 7 to 9, 1993. After Breault was interviewed, he also helped the BATF locate David Block—the man who had spent several months at Mt. Carmel. Breault knew that Block had submitted to deprogramming, and he contacted both *Waco Tribune-Herald* reporter Mark England and Steve Schneider's sister, Sue Schneider, who kept "detailed information on cult awareness groups and cultbusters." From the reporter, Breault managed to get the name of David Block's deprogrammer, Rick Ross, who, it turned out, was trying to convince Sue Schneider to hire him to deprogram her brother. Breault passed on Ross's name to Aguilera. Apparently Aguilera reached David Block through Ross, and on January 25, 1993, Aguilera and Buford interviewed Block (U.S. Treasury Department 1993, 38, 53, 151, D7–8; Breault and King 1993, 303–9).

The BATF agents' interviews with former Davidians and other opponents of Koresh contributed to the tactical thinking of the BATF concerning how to approach enforcement of weapons laws at Mt. Carmel. Aguilera and Buford asked Breault what Koresh would do if he were issued a summons. Breault told them that Koresh would not answer a firearms summons, but that he thought Koresh would respond to a Texas CPS summons because he "feels he has beaten that rap." What would Koresh do if authorities surrounded the compound: would he let the women and children go free? "No way,"

Breault replied, "He would use them as hostages" (U.S. Treasury Department 1993, 46, 53; Breault and King 1993, 305–6).

> Several former cult members, most forcefully Breault, noted the distinct possibility that Koresh might respond to a siege by leading his followers in a mass suicide; Breault expressed a particular fear for the children at the Compound. One child who had lived at the Compound told a California police officer, who in turn informed Aguilera, that she had been trained by Koresh and his "Mighty Men"—Koresh's closest and most trusted advisers—to commit suicide in several different ways, including placing the barrel of a handgun in her mouth and pulling the trigger. (U.S. Treasury Department 1993, 46)

The BATF agents knew that Block had been deprogrammed by Rick Ross. Professional intelligence procedures would have suggested that the validity of both his and other opponents' accounts should remain an open question. Instead, the BATF inserted tropes from the reports of opponents into the scenario that they began to work up about the situation they faced at Mt. Carmel. David Block claimed that Koresh controlled the distribution of weapons. It may be that this account was out of date, but it aligned closely with Breault's anticult portrayal of Koresh as a despot who possessed "absolute control" over his followers. Overinterpreting information of questionable accuracy, the BATF made serious strategic errors in developing its final tactical plan. More generally, the opponents' accounts concerning Koresh's stance of forcible resistance to authority and the threat of mass suicide shaped the development of a tactical plan for BATF action. The BATF largely discounted the possibility that Koresh would willingly submit to a peacefully served warrant, so serving a warrant became strongly linked to the siege option. In late December 1992, the tactical planners saw logistical difficulties in a siege because of the open terrain around the compound and the possibility of injuries, but as late as January 21, they were still developing the siege option. However, a January 25 interview with David Block, combined with information provided by other opponents and other analysis, led planners to shift their strategy toward the dynamic-entry option (U.S. Treasury Department 1993, 143–44, 45, D-9). Agent Buford's experience with the CSA standoff led him to fear that a siege would give the Davidians an opportunity to destroy evidence. Tacticians also were concerned that a siege might end in mass suicide. For these reasons, "the concept of surrounding the compound and announcing their intention to enforce a warrant was discarded by BATF agents" at tactical meetings in Houston from January 27 to 29. Having come to regard the luring-away option as unlikely to materialize, and having rejected the siege option, the tactical planners overinterpreted the (probably inaccurate) information provided by David Block, that Koresh controlled the weapons. Given the timing of the BATF shift in strategy relative to the times of interviews with opponents, it is likely that bad analysis of intelligence from David Block tipped the balance toward "increasing optimism" about the strategy of dynamic entry. If the assault could be carried out quickly under conditions in which Koresh's followers could not get to the weapons, the element of surprise would minimize the threat of mass suicide—a point that the tactical planners emphasized when they briefed BATF leadership in Washington about their plan on February 11 and 12. Subsequently, on February 26, two days before the raid, BATF director Stephen Higgins explained to Treasury Department officials—who wanted to call off the raid—that the use of scores of heavily armed agents to execute the warrant by force was necessary "because BATF feared that Koresh and his followers might destroy evidence or commit mass suicide if given the opportunity" (U.S. Treasury Department 1993, 53, B126 [quotation], 142, B49, 65, 179 [quotation]; also Breault and King 1993, 303–9).

No doubt sensing that a dynamic-entry raid was a risky undertaking, BATF strategists continued during February 1993 to think about luring Koresh away from the compound. They decided to try to request that Koresh come to Waco, apparently following the scenario envisioned by Marc Breault, when he had told investigators that Koresh might respond to a summons concerning child abuse. However, Texas Child Protective Services caseworker Joyce Sparks already had closed her investigation without taking any action, and her supervisor refused to allow the scheduling of such a meeting, so the BATF tried another avenue to the same end. On February 12, 1993, an BATF agent met with the Waco district attorney, Elizabeth Tobin, to discuss the possibilities. Kiri Jewell, the child at the center of the custody battle a year earlier, came to Austin, Texas, with her father on February 18. She is probably the "female minor" who was taken by BATF agent Aguilera to District Attorney Tobin's office three days later. Whoever the child was, she "decline[d] to testify against Koresh," and the effort to lure Koresh away from Mt. Carmel came to an end five days before the BATF raid on the compound (U.S. Treasury Department 1993, 64, D-11–12 [quotation]; see also Bailey and Darden 1993, 157–58; Breault and King 1993, 306).

The final scenario for the BATF raid was dynamic. "Ideally, if all went according to the script, all SRT teams would be able to 'exit the transportation vehicles in eight seconds, get into position and make entry at the front door in approximately 33 seconds.'" This rapid execution of the raid was deemed essential to the BATF's ability to keep men [sic] separated from the weapons supposed to be under Koresh's control (U.S. Treasury Department 1993, B-128).

Paradoxically, the accounts about mass suicide that shaped this scenario of dynamic entry may also have contributed to the failure of the BATF coordinators and commanders to call the raid off, once the element of surprise was known to have been lost. The strategy of dynamic entry invested a great deal in the narrative of surprise. According to BATF reviewers, any dynamic raid gathers "momentum" from participants' bravado and will to succeed, and from the specters of failure, loss of tactical advantage, judgment by higher officials, and bad public relations. At Mt. Carmel these pressures were exacerbated by the lack of any tactical alternative—a fallback or contingency strategy (U.S. Treasury Department 1993, 73–75).

Why was there no fallback strategy? It must be recognized that a latent narrative of mass suicide would resurface if the scenario of dynamic entry were abandoned. There is no way to pinpoint the exact magnitude of this influence on command decisions during execution of the attempted raid. But certain evidence is suggestive. The BATF had come to the scenario of dynamic entry by a contorted process that eliminated an alternative scenario—serving a warrant and falling back to a siege position if resistance were encountered. Both in the discussions of tactical planners and in briefings up to the highest levels in the chain of command, the execution of a surprise raid was justified because the alternative scenario of siege might lead to mass suicide. Perhaps because any scenario of failed surprise would be a scenario of siege, there was an "absence of any meaningful contingency planning for the raid" (p. 175). On the day of the raid, to lose the element of surprise thus was to reopen the scenario of siege, and by extension, mass suicide. The lack of contingency planning, articulated in latent ways with the narrative of mass suicide, amplified the momentum of the raid. Ironically, taking mass suicide seriously had the effect of avoiding it within tactical planning, by designing a scenario in which it would not be an issue.

In turn, the repressed narrative of mass suicide may have also more directly influenced the actions of BATF commanders on the day of the raid—Sunday, February 28, 1993. On Sunday morning, Robert Rodriguez, the BATF undercover agent who was visiting the compound, heard Koresh announce, "Neither the BATF nor the National Guard will ever get me. They got me once and they'll never get me again. They are coming for me but they can't kill me." Rodriguez knew that he had been "burned" (i.e., that his cover had been lost), and he knew that Koresh was making specific reference to the raid that had been planned for an hour later. Rodriguez left the compound, returned to the undercover house across the road, and reported on his conversation with Koresh. On hearing the news, one BATF "forward observer" at the undercover house was so convinced that the raid would be called off that he started to pack up his gear. But the response of the raid commanders at the command post some miles away was exactly the opposite. BATF agent Chuck Sarabyn, who took the call from Rodriguez, learned that the element of surprise had been lost. In turn, he asked Rodriguez whether he had seen any weapons, a call to arms, or preparations. Rodriguez replied that when he had left the compound, people had been praying. After confirming with another agent, who was watching the compound, that there was no sign of activity there, Sarabyn offered the opinion that the raid could still go forward if the agents moved quickly. He briefly conferred with other raid commanders. They broke from their huddle and moved to various tasks, using language like "Let's go," "Get ready to go, they know we're coming," "We better do this ASAP," and "They know BATF and the National Guard are coming. We're going to hit them now." Despite the effort to hurry up, the agents conducting the raid did not arrive at the compound until forty minutes after the first report from Rodriguez (U.S. Treasury Department 1993, 89 [quotation], 91 [quotation], 195 [quotations], 166–67 [quotation], 197, B-43).

The Treasury Department review argues that the decision to hurry up "made no sense": either Koresh was not going to prepare for the raid, in which case accelerating the schedule was unnecessary, or he was going to prepare, in which case—given the time required to get the raid under way—acceleration was useless (U.S. Treasury Department 1993, 171–72). In short, hurrying up does not salvage lost surprise. Was there then some other available meaningful definition of the situation? One alternative motive that offers at least some rationale for hurrying up is the "prevention of an imminent event." If something is about to happen, quick action may prevent it. But what was about to happen? The imminent event cannot be "lost surprise" because at the time of the decision to "hurry up," the lost surprise was an event of the past, not the future. However, a clear concern that shaped the development of tactical strategies in the months before the raid was that Koresh and his followers might commit mass suicide. With the loss of surprise, might the raid commanders ask whether such an action was imminent? The three BATF raid commanders had all been present at the meetings in Houston from January 27 to 29 where concerns about mass suicide were discussed.

With this concern already established in all their minds, once the element of surprise was lost, it would have been reasonable for the raid commanders to consider the possibility of mass suicide. At the compound were deeply apocalyptic religious people, reading the Bible after having been informed that the authorities were coming after them. In his conversation with Robert Rodriguez, Koresh referred to "the Kingdom of God," and stated that "the time has come" (U.S. Treasury Department 1993, 89). Whether the raid commanders received this information from Rodriguez and explicitly interpreted it within the framework of mass suicide, I have no way of knowing. But the motive structure for accelerating the raid makes a good deal more sense within such a framework than it does within the context of lost surprise.

Moreover, even if preventing the imminent event of mass suicide was not a conscious motive for "hurrying up," the narrative of mass suicide was embedded in the de facto fallback position. On the day of the raid, with the media looking on, if the scenario of dynamic entry failed, then a siege—with its latent element of mass suicide—would be the consequence. Presciently, one tactical planner already had understood that with a siege, as the Treasury Department review put it, "BATF probably would have to assault the Compound anyway, once public pressure on BATF to resolve the situation grew and the government's patience wore thin" (p. 53). The only way to avoid a siege was to "hurry up." On the day of the raid, BATF raid commanders discounted the importance of lost surprise because accepting it would have required canceling the raid, and canceling the raid would precipitate a siege. Because of the specter of mass suicide, a siege was not a fallback option; it was an imminent event to be avoided.

The Blurred Meanings of Narratives

Government authorities in the United States have a long tradition of using the state's monopoly on the legitimate deployment of violence to control utopian social movements. During the last quarter century, the most violent example that comes to mind is the 1985 Philadelphia police use of fire to destroy the rowhouse of the radical sect MOVE (a fire that killed people and destroyed many other homes in the process). This was not police enforcement action, but annihilation. Such cases suggest an implicit state policy to fulfill purposes of state that go beyond any narrowly conceived issues of law enforcement. In the Treasury Department review of the BATF raid, Frederick S. Calhoun, a historian at the Federal Law Enforcement Training Center, explains that "the raid fit within an historic, well-established and well-defended government interest in prohibiting and breaking up all organized groups that sought to arm or fortify themselves. . . . From its earliest formation, the federal government has actively suppressed any effort by disgruntled or rebellious citizens to coalesce into an armed group, however small the group, petty its complaint, or grandiose its ambition" (p. G-7).

I think that this is a true account. It evidences a concern about armed groups independently of whether the arms are legal or not. Both historically and currently, the BATF and its antecedents have been particularly concerned when groups obtain weapons in a way that monopolizes territory, and especially on the basis of some ideology that justifies their cause. The BATF thus may have been predisposed, more than other agencies, to read the narratives about an apocalyptic group in ways that went to the core of their historic mission.

What the statement fails to mention is government antipathy toward groups which, although not armed, advance social visions that are alien to established social mores. It would be a mistake to think that antipathy toward utopian sectarian groups is universally shared by government officials. But it would be equally mistaken to ignore an ideology of state social control of radical sects that binds together officials from a variety of agencies at the federal, state, and local levels of government. Governmental agencies other than the BATF investigated the Branch Davidians, but they lacked the hard evidence necessary to intervene in the affairs of the sect. Yet broader concerns of the state about the Branch Davidians—especially concerning sexual and physical abuse of children—were strongly raised in BATF Aguilera's application for a search warrant for Mt. Carmel. In effect, the BATF became the lead agency because it was the agency of the state with the strongest claim of jurisdiction (even though the evidence of weapons violations was circumstantial and inferential, and the basis for the arrest warrant for Koresh—who was to be detained without bond—is unclear). As a BATF spokesperson later noted, a successful BATF operation would have opened up Mt. Carmel to the intervention of other government agencies (*Washington Post*, April 25, 1993).

The BATF raid was a monumental failure. Subsequently, the April 19, 1993, FBI CS gas assault on the compound and the ensuing fire (whatever its cause) fulfilled only one state objective—that of suppressing an armed group. The children who were to be saved from abuse died instead. Was this the mass suicide that Marc Breault and the other opponents had predicted? The government disclaims any responsibility for the fire and hence, for the deaths (Scruggs et al. 1993). But theirs is a narrow analysis. It seems to me incontrovertible that the fire that did occur would not have happened in the absence of the FBI assault. Even if the FBI assault was not the sole cause of the fire, the assault was an antecedent condition causally necessary to any explanation of the subsequent fire, the deaths that ensued, and the obliteration of Mt. Carmel. If the Branch Davidians actually started the fire on purpose, their act certainly could be understood as an act of mass suicide. Because such an act would snatch victory away from their opponents at the cost of their own lives, it would directly parallel the deaths of over nine hundred people in the 1978 mass suicide and murder at Jonestown. In both cases, the actions emerged in the process of extended and pitched conflict with opponents. At Jonestown, the threat to the destruction of the community was more emblematic than immediate, but at Mt. Carmel on April 19, the FBI was engaged in the rapid and systematic physical destruction of the Branch Davidians' home. The mass suicide at Mt. Carmel—if that was what occurred—lacked the ritualistic and collective character of the mass suicide at Jonestown. In the face of the continuing assaults, people at Mt. Carmel died in different parts of the building, some from the fire, others from gunshot wounds, either self-inflicted or "mercy killings" at the hands of others.

The play of narratives about mass suicide in the FBI standoff with the Branch Davidians up to April 19 is a subject in its own right. However, even a cursory examination of the FBI construct of mass suicide suggests that they viewed it as an inherent and static predisposition, rather than a sect's possible response to a dynamic and shifting situation. After the conflagration, the FBI justified the tactical view they had taken in planning the assault—that mass suicide would not be a likely outcome—by citing David Koresh's future-oriented statements *in the absence of the assault,* such as his interest in auctioning his book rights (*New York Times,* April 22, 1993, A1). This static view of predisposition is based on a tendency that governmental authorities share with the anticult movement, a tendency to see the dynamics of "cults" as internal to such groups, rather than examine external social interaction in conflict between a sectarian group and opponents and authorities themselves.

Unfortunately, both authorities and opponents (and sometimes the media) have compelling vested interests in depicting the dynamics of religious social movements as internal rather than external, and they are thus systematically biased toward misunderstanding the very social processes in which they assert the legitimacy of their interests. Despite the clear significance of their actions, cultural opponents have never seriously weighed their own roles in negative outcomes of pitched conflicts with alternative religious movements.

This avoidance of critical review does not align well with the legitimacy routinely extended by some government authorities and the media to operatives of the anticult movement. The modus operandi of anticult groups is to target "cults" with increasing pressure on a number of fronts (Zilliox and Kahaner n.d.). At both Jonestown and Mt. Carmel, the cultural opponents succeeded in bringing authorities and the media to their side. In turn, the opponents could point to the tragic outcomes to validate their initial alarm. I believe that Koresh's opponents must have pursued their mission according to the dictates of their consciences, and I cannot think that any opponent of alternative religions would want to precipitate violence in order to prove a point. Nevertheless, in effect, the anticult movement benefits from "cult" tragedy. It is worth noting that in cases where the anticult movement did not play an active role in precipitating conflict, governmental authorities have sometimes—as with the CSA—been able to bring a standoff to a peaceful resolution. On the other hand, there have been truly devastating and disastrous results in two cases where the anticult movement played a strong role—Jonestown and Mt. Carmel. My own assessment based on these facts is this: insofar as participants in the anticult movement fail to acknowledge that their strategies can lead to the escalation of apocalyptic conflict, both the media and government authorities should treat the movement as lacking in portfolio in matters concerning deviant religious sects. More generally, governmental authorities would do well to bring certain anticult movement practices—especially kidnaping and forced deprogramming—under strict law enforcement.

The media bring a cultural perspective to their reportage on events (Gans 1979; Gamson and Modigliani 1989). As the cases of Jonestown and Mt. Carmel both demonstrate, they are particularly vulnerable to subordination by cultural opponents of unusual religious groups. With freedom of the press, limitations on the media are largely ethical. Unfortunately, the ethical response of journalism as a profession to media coverage of the Waco affair (Society of Professional Journalists 1993) sometimes seems shallow and self-justifying. Until journalists take more seriously the social dynamics of religious conflict between opponents and groups that they label as cults, stories of "cult-busting" will continue to follow the genre of the heroic expose.

The first amendment to the U.S. Constitution legally prescribes the state, in contrast to the media, from taking sides in matters of religion. Defenders of state action will no doubt emphasize the obligation of the state to enforce its laws. They already claim (for example in the Treasury Department review) that this was the objective at

Mt. Carmel. But such a defense of state action is flawed. It would be one thing if cultural opponents and governmental authorities acted independently of one another, even if they shared an affinity of goals due to different interests. But the emergence of narratives about mass suicide shows something quite different. The degree to which certain governmental authorities consciously took up the cause of the cultural opponents remains an open question. Whatever the answer to that question, the connection of governmental action to cultural opposition runs much deeper. Mt. Carmel does not simply bear comparison to Jonestown as a parallel but independent event. Instead, there was a *genetic* bridge between Jonestown and Mt. Carmel. Specifically, the opponents of Koresh took tropes about mass suicide derived from the apocalypse at Jonestown, reworked them, and inserted them into accounts that they offered about the Branch Davidians. In turn, the opponents' reports about mass suicide directly structured the development of tactical scenarios for the BATF raid, and they may well have figured in the motive structures of BATF commanders on the day of the raid. In these direct yet presumably unselfconscious ways, BATF operations became subordinated to the narratives of cultural opposition.

Meanings in the realm of public life are formed in part by the stories that people tell, and the ways that other people hear these stories. On the basis of the stories that they hear, along with their own personal and cultural structures of meaning, and in relation to their own readings of their resources and situations, people make new meanings in both their accounts of past events and their scenarios of projected actions (cf. Sewell 1992, 16–17). Understanding public meanings, then, depends upon the hermeneutic excavation of narratives embedded in lifeworldly activities that feed into the domain of public life. Sociologists Jeffrey Alexander and Philip Smith (1993) have suggested that such processes of public meaning formation depend on the operation of binary codes, and they have analyzed a number of situations where people have invoked "Democratic" and "Counter-Democratic" codes in public controversies in the United States. The present analysis of narratives about mass suicide shows that such binary analysis is at best incomplete, and potentially misleading. No doubt the anticult movement's stereotype of "cults" portrays cultists and their cultural structures of social organization as counterdemocratic. The anticult narrative of mass suicide is a virtual Triptik along the route of the counterdemocratic code's description of "passive," "hysterical," "unrealistic," and fundamentally "mad" people engaged in "secret" and "suspicious" activities that depend on "arbitrary" exercise of "power" at the whim of a "personality" (Alexander and Smith 1993, 162–63). But the transmission of stories in the lifeworld, even ones that fit a code—does not necessarily, or even typically, work in binary ways. Instead, public meanings about the Branch Davidians suggest something else for cases of intrinsic narratives. In these emergent situations, where different social actors tell their own stories about issues and events to which they are mutually oriented, there is a historicity of emergent meanings. People do not frame their own meanings simply by invoking two sides of a binary set of codes. Instead, cultural meanings become reworked and revised through the shading that occurs in the shift of narrative from one meaningful circumstance to another (Geertz 1973, 7). Koresh's opponents certainly invoked a counterdemocratic code, but they did so in narratives drawing on cultural meanings about mass suicide that were both historically formed and specific. For Koresh's opponents and the BATF, those accounts became revised through improvisational play, resulting in novel, nonbinary shifts in nuance and contexts of significance that altered meanings. The study of intrinsic narratives helps get at such shifts of meaning, because such narratives are not contained within any single frame of social reality, such as the public sphere. Instead, public meanings may be shaped by the most private experiences. Personal narratives of salvation from the evil of a "cult" can shape cultural cries for help, and in turn become elements of official state discourse.

Notes

I am grateful to Elaine Hoye, Gene Burns, Sonya Rose, and Guenther Roth for comments on an earlier version of this essay.

1. I say a "more interpretive" approach because the neo-Durkheimians have themselves embraced hermeneutics, at least programmatically (Alexander, Smith, and Sherwood 1993). For my part, I do not doubt the power of Durkheim's model of ritual in relation to public "sacred" and "profane" meanings (Hall 1987, chap. 12), but neither do I believe that the model captures all processes of public meaning formation. Thus, as a point of departure for cultural studies, it poses exactly the danger of reductionism which Alexander and Smith (1993) rightly criticize. To avoid this reductionism, it is necessary to begin at the hermeneutic end of interpretive analysis, invoking the Durkheimian model of binary ritual distinction only where the play of meanings takes that, rather than some other, form.

2. Armed state troopers took 112 children from communal houses of the Northeast Kingdom Community Church in Island Pond, Vermont, in June 1984. Later they were ordered released by a judge who ruled the raid "grossly unlawful." One of the early opponents of the sect was a woman who also had contact with defectors from the Branch Davidians—Priscil-

la Coates, in 1982, a director of the Citizens Freedom Foundation (*New York Times*, April 12, 1987). More recently, the sect called the Family has been the subject of similar raids in France, Spain, Australia, and Argentina (*New York Times*, September 26, 1993).

References

Alexander, Jeffrey C., and Philip Smith. 1993. "The Discourse of Civil Society: A New Proposal for Cultural Studies." *Theory and Society* 22: 151–207.

Alexander, Jeffrey C., Philip Smith, and Steven Sherwood. 1993. "Risking Enchantment: Theory and Method in Cultural Studies." *Culture* 8 (1): 10–14.

Bailey, Brad, and Bob Darden. 1993. *Mad Man in Waco: The Complete Story of the Davidian Cult, David Koresh, and the Waco Massacre.* Waco, TX: WRS Publishing.

Bragg, Roy. 1993. "Ex-Prosecutor Laments Agent's 'Storm Trooper' Tactics." *Houston Chronicle.* March 2, 7A.

Breault, Marc, and Martin King. 1993. *Inside the Cult: A Member's Chilling, Exclusive Account of Madness and Depravity in David Koresh's Compound.* New York: Penguin Signet.

Fentress, James, and Chris Wickham. 1992. *Social Memory.* Cambridge, MA: Blackwell.

Foster, Lawrence. 1991. *Women, Family, and Utopia: Communal Experiments of the Shakers, the Oneida Community, and the Mormons.* Syracuse, NY: Syracuse University Press.

Gans, Herbert. 1979. *Deciding What's News.* New York: Random House.

Gamson, William A., and Andre Modigliani. 1989. "Media Discourse and Public Opinion on Nuclear Power: A Constructionist Approach." *American Journal of Sociology* 95: 1–37.

Gamson, William A., David Croteau, William Hoynes, and Theodore Sasson. 1992. "Media Images and the Social Construction of Reality." *Annual Review of Sociology* 18: 373–93.

Geertz, Clifford. 1973. "Thick Description." In *The Interpretation of Cultures,* by Clifford Geertz, pp. 3–30. New York: Basic.

Hall, John R. 1978. *The Ways Out: Utopian Communal Groups in an Age of Babylon.* Boston: Routledge & Kegan Paul.

———. 1987. *Gone from the Promised Land: Jonestown in American Cultural History.* New Brunswick, NJ: Transaction.

———. Forthcoming. *Cultures of Inquiry: Discourses and Practices in Historical, Social, and Cultural Studies.* Chicago: University of Chicago Press.

Hall, John R., and Mary Jo Neitz. 1993. *Culture: Sociological Perspectives.* Englewood Cliffs, NJ: Prentice-Hall.

Koresh, David. 1993. "The Decoded Message of the Seven Seals of the *Book of Revelation.*" With an editorial preface and comments and clarifications by James D. Tabor and J. Phillip Arnold. Photocopied manuscript.

Linedecker, Clifford L. 1993. *Massacre at Waco, Texas: The Shocking True Story of Cult Leader David Koresh and the Branch Davidians.* New York: St. Martin's Paperbacks.

Scruggs, Richard, Steven Zipperstein, Robert Lyon, Victor Gonzalez, Herbert Cousins, and Roderick Beverly. 1993. *Report to the Deputy Attorney General on the Events at Waco, Texas, February 28 to April 19, 1993.* Redacted version. Washington, DC: U.S. Department of Justice.

Sewell, William H., Jr. 1992. "A Theory of Structure: Duality, Agency, and Transformation." *American Journal of Sociology* 98: 1–29.

Snow, David A., E. Burke Rochford, Jr., Steven K. Worden, and Robert D. Benford. 1986. "Frame Alignment Processes, Micromobilization, and Movement Participation." *American Sociological Review* 51: 464–81.

Society of Professional Journalists. 1993. "Waco: What Went Right, What Went Wrong." Greencastle, IN: Society of Professional Journalists.

U.S. Department of the Treasury. 1993. *Report of the Department of the Treasury on the Bureau of Alcohol, Tobacco, and Firearms Investigation of Vernon Wayne Howell, Also Known as David Koresh.* Washington, DC: U.S. Government Printing Office.

U.S. District Court. 1993. Application and Affidavit for Search Warrant. W93–15M. Western District of Texas. Filed February 26, 1993.

Weber, Max. 1978. *Economy and Society.* Edited by Guenther Roth and Claus Wittich. Berkeley: University of California Press.

Wood, James E., Jr. 1993. "The Branch Davidian Standoff: An American Tragedy." *Journal of Church and State* 35 (Spring): 1–9.

Zilliox, Larry, Jr., and Larry Kahaner. N.d. "How to Investigate Destructive Cults and Underground Groups." Photocopy.

10

THOMAS ROBBINS
AND DICK ANTHONY

Sects and

Violence

*Factors Enhancing
the Volatility of
Marginal Religious
Movements*

I n the aftermath of the fiery deaths of the
Branch Davidians in Texas, the issue of violence in marginal religions ("cults") has been
highlighted in popular consciousness.[1] While
spectacular mass violence such as exploded
in Jonestown, Guyana, and more recently in Waco,
Texas, is very rare, smaller-scale instances of deadly
violence have been associated with a variety of groups
in recent decades. The Manson Family, Synanon, Hare
Krishna, the Lundgren group, the House of Judah, several polygamous "fringe Mormon" groups, the Bha-
gawan movement of Sri Rajneesh, the Order of the
Solar Temple, and the followers of Lindberg "Black

Jesus" Sanders are just some of the other religiousgroups which have experienced violent episodes and whose leaders have been accused of wrongdoing in this connection. This chapter explores the factors that operate to enhance the volatility of relatively new or marginal religious groups.

Why are marginal or noninstitutionalized religious movements more volatile or potentially violent than institutionalized churches (assuming the validity of the premise)? What factors determine how much physical danger a group may pose to its members or others? There are indeed so many factors that may be identified as bearing upon these issues that the initial aim of this paper is simply to group, list, and briefly explore these factors.

We may initially list the factors pertinent to our inquiry under two headings: *exogenous* and *endogenous* factors. The former include factors related to the hostility, stigmatization, and persecution that "religious outsiders" often receive at the hands of forces in the social environment in which they operate. The latter category denotes properties of a movement: its leadership, beliefs, rituals, and organization. Exogenous and endogenous variables are interrelated (Richardson 1985); indeed, the separation and mutual autonomy of these factors may ultimately seem illusory.[2] Nevertheless, in this paper we will focus primarily on the endogenous conditions and processes within religious movements which appear to enhance volatility and the potential for violence. We note, however, the importance of exogenous factors, which Melton (1985) emphasizes: "Given the high level of tension with society under which some nonconventional groups have been forced to operate, it is not surprising that the violent tendencies of some cult leaders have emerged" (p. 57). Violence generally erupts "only after a period of heightened conflict" in which "both sides" have contributed to escalation (p. 58).

It is worth noting, however, that the relative weight or significance of the contribution of exogenous and endogenous factors may vary from one situated event to another. Thus to elicit a fatal violent response from Jim Jones's Peoples Temple required only that a congressman and a press entourage visit Jonestown and attempt to return to the United States with a handful of defectors. In contrast, to set off the immolations in Waco (assuming that the Davidians were responsible for setting the fire), what had to transpire was not only the initial military-style raid on the "cult compound" by the Bureau of Alcohol, Tobacco, and Firearms (BATF) but also the subsequent breaking down of the walls of the compound by armored vehicles and the insertion of CS gas. It may therefore be a viable thesis that the role or weight of exogenous factors was smaller at Jonestown compared to Waco. Or to put it another way, the Branch Davidian community at Waco was less internally volatile or violence-prone than the Peoples Temple settlement in Guyana.

Unfortunately, evaluations of the relative salience of exogenous and endogenous contributions to particular explosive events are highly controversial and sometimes elicit accusations of "blaming the victim." Resolving these issues is beyond the scope of the present survey, which will try to identify and group the most salient characteristics of movements which often operate to enhance volatility and the likelihood of violence. It should be noted that no factor discussed below produces violence automatically or autonomously. The eruption of violence generally reflects the interaction of several endogenous conditions with exogenous variables.

Pertinent endogenous factors may be tentatively grouped under three headings: (1) factors related to the consequences of *apocalyptic* beliefs and fervent millennial expectations; (2) factors related to the nature and characteristic volatility of *charismatic* leadership, and (3) residual factors that are more loosely interrelated but that might be viewed as relating to the significance of some social movements as communal-ideological *systems* with "boundaries" and systemic problems that may be given different priorities by different groups and leaders, who may attempt to resolve them in different ways. These headings do not denote single variables, but ensembles of variables. As with the distinction between endogenous and exogenous factors, the autonomy or separate identity of these groups of variables is ultimately illusory. "Charismatic," "apocalyptic," and "communal-systemic" factors are often closely interrelated; moreover, the same condition or pattern may sometimes be classified under more than one heading.

This survey is written from a sociological perspective. Factors related to the alleged phenomenon of "mind control," to the degree to which they have any validity, may entail some of the conditions and patterns that will be discussed under the headings delineated above. On the other hand, a partly autonomous and pertinent realm of factors may entail the predispositions and personality patterns of persons who are attracted to movements or ideologies of a certain kind, that is, militant, authoritarian, apocalyptic, or charismatically led (Anthony and Robbins 1994; Jones 1989), although we cannot devote much space here to a discussion of individual psychodynamics. We will deal first with the impact of apocalyptic beliefs.

Apocalypticism

Apocalyptic belief systems and millennial visions of the imminent "last days" or "end times" appear to characterize almost all violent religious sects. Such notions certainly characterized the Branch Davidians at Waco led by David Koresh. Originally a Seventh Day Adventist, Vernon Howell (David Koresh) was initially captivated by the grim apocalyptic message of the church-sponsored revivalist "Revelation Seminars" featuring "dramatic, even frightening images in a multimedia portrayal of Armageddon" (McGee and Clairborne 1993, 10) conducted by evangelist Jim Gilley. In the Branch Davidians, Howell found a special attention and emphasis given to the culmination of the end time, mystically represented in the seven seals, which could be opened only by a new prophet (see Tabor, this volume).

Jim Jones, prophet-leader of the ill-fated Peoples Temple, also developed a complex apocalyptic vision that was drawn from several sources. "With elements of socialism, messianism, and biblical prophecy, Jones crafted a worldview that made an impending apocalypse plausible." Jones "used biblical imagery to persuade his followers that they were on a divine pilgrimage through a wasteland to paradise" (Jones 1989, 212).

Distinctly apocalyptic and millennial worldviews have characterized a number of religious groups that have experienced violent altercations with outsiders, including the early Mormons (Boyer 1992, 1993), early Anabaptists and radical Reformation Protestants (Boyer 1992, 1993; Cohn 1961; Palmer 1994), and groups involved in pre-Jonestown episodes of mass/collective suicide such as the Old Believers in early modern Russia who immolated themselves (Cherniavsky 1970; Crummey 1970; Robbins 1986) or the violent Circumcellion fringe of the Donatist "Church of Martyrs" in late antiquity in North Africa (Frend 1950; Knox 1950; Robbins 1989).[3]

What is it about apocalyptic beliefs that may encourage volatility and enhance the likelihood of violence? The perceived imminence of the last days may be expected to relativize conventional norms and rules. Received arrangements are seen to be doomed! Apocalyptic visions thus have inherent antinomian implications. More specifically, apocalyptic movements often anticipate that an environing climate of violence will pervade the last days and that, in particular, persecutory violence will be directed against "The Saints" or "The Elect," that is, against the spiritual vanguard that the movement represents. The latter must therefore prepare themselves to defend their enclave, to survive to inherit the world. A defensive survivalist orientation may crystallize.

This was certainly the view of David Koresh, who frequently quoted the second Psalm, "The Kings of the Earth set themselves, and the rulers take counsel against the Lord and against His Anointed" (quoted in Boyer 1993, 30). Koresh clearly anticipated a government assault, and the actual military-style raid that the BATF perpetrated against the Waco Davidian settlement in late February 1993 "seemed to those inside to validate at least part of Koresh's prophecy. The Branch Davidians and their leader began preparing for the end" (McGee and Clairborne 1993, 11). After the shoot-out began, Koresh may well have wished to find a peaceful resolution to the confrontation. He was probably inhibited from surrendering to the BATF not only because his power would then be destroyed but also because his apocalyptic vision would be compromised if the confrontation ended "not with a bang but with a whimper."

Anticipation of ruthless persecution tends to be encouraged by beliefs that assign to the apocalyptic group a special sanctity and a special key role in the unfolding of end times or in the birth of a new order. Such beliefs, however, do not necessarily follow from a commitment to an apocalyptic scenario (Sharot 1982).

Perhaps what renders apocalyptic spirituality potentially explosive is that it is often linked to something broader and deeper to which we may apply Ronald Knox's terms "enthusiasm" or "ultrasupernaturalism" (Knox 1950). The enthusiast "expects more evident results from the grace of God than we others." Faith must fully transform devotees, who are therefore set apart from ordinary folks and live on a higher plane. The enthusiast prophet "insists that members of his society [movement], saved members of a perishing world, should live a life of angelic purity, of apostolic simplicity" (Knox 1950, 2); although in practice what has historically resulted from this orientation is "strange oscillations of rigorism and antinomianism," as emancipation from conventional rules validates the speciality of the Elect.

Enthusiasm, according to Knox, implies "a different Theology of Grace" whereby the "traditional doctrine" that "grace perfects nature" is supplanted by the idea that "grace has destroyed nature and replaced it. The saved man has come out into a new order of being, with a new set of faculties appropriate to his state; David must not wear the panoply of Saul" (Knox 1950, 2). Enthusiasts need not be violent—indeed religious enthusiasm can motivate pacifism, as in early Quakerism; however, an antinomian volatility can sometimes proceed from the phenomenological condition of God's Elect, who, "although they must perforce live cheek by jowl with the sons of perdition, *claim another citizenship and own another allegiance*" (Knox 1950, 2, our emphasis). When true religious enthusiasts submit themselves to public law and authority, which they may often readily do, it is "always under protest."

> Worldly governments, being of purely human institution, have no real mandate to exercise authority, and sinful folk have no real rights, although out of courtesy their fancied rights must be respected. Always the enthusiast hankers after a theocracy in which the anomalies of the present situation will be done away, and the righteous bear rule openly. Disappointed of this hope, a group of sectaries will sometimes go out into the wilderness and set up a little theocracy of their own, like Cato's senate at Utica. The American continent has more than once been the scene of such an adventure; in these days, it is the last refuge of the enthusiast (Knox 1950, 3).[4]

Clearly, apocalypticism or apocalyptic enthusiasm is not inexorably violent. Indeed, apocalypticism is somewhat like religion writ large: it reflects and hypostatizes the moral duality of religion, which can bind persons together and uplift them but can also provoke paranoid anxieties and fierce antipathy toward and dehumanization of the ungodly. Apocalyptic images of the future may often impart a particular volatile quality to a group. However, throughout history such volatile apocalypticism has often been elicited or intensified by the exogenous factor of *persecution*. Consider, for example, the violent Anabaptist chiliasm of the early sixteenth century which culminated in the seizure of Munster (or "New Jerusalem") by apocalyptic visionaries who eventually came to be led by Jon Bockelson, "a monomaniacal young tailor who, like David Koresh, anointed himself Messiah, imposed his absolute rule with the aid of loyal lieutenants and demanded free access to his female followers" (Boyer 1993, 30). Bockelson's followers "saw Munster as the birthplace of Christ's new world order as foretold in the final chapter of the Book of Revelation" (Boyer 1993, 30). Yet, as Norman Cohn (1961, 274) notes, "most Anabaptists were peaceful folk who in practice were quite willing, except in matters of conscience and belief, to respect the authority of the state." Yet, "even the most peaceful Anabaptists were ferociously persecuted and many thousands were killed." Anabaptist hostility to the state was thereby reinforced. Anabaptists "interpreted their sufferings in apocalyptic terms as the great onslaught of Satan and Antichrist against the Saints, as those 'messianic woes' that were to usher in the Millennium" (Cohn 1961, 275). In this context Anabaptists became obsessed by an expected "Day of

Reckoning" when the mighty would be overthrown by the faithful and Christ would return to establish the millennium and place the sword of retribution in the hands of the rebaptized and purified saints. Thus, alongside the persisting "tradition of peaceful and austere dissent" there emerged a new expression of "an equally ancient tradition of militant chiliasm" (Cohn 1961, 275).[5]

The exogenous factor of persecution is only one limiting condition on any explanation of religious violence and sectarian volatility in terms of apocalyptic worldviews. Consideration must also be given to the fact that apocalyptic beliefs are increasingly common, and only a tiny minority of groups and movements expressing such ideologies appear to have violent proclivities or to pose a threat to civil peace. David Koresh may have engaged in deviant practices, "But his alienation and core doctrines are shared by millions of Americans, perhaps even a majority. . . . the general contours of Koresh's beliefs were neither unique nor particularly unusual" (Boyer 1993, 30). Churches that embrace prophetic, millennial doctrines are presently experiencing rapid growth in the United States, where such currents have always run powerfully (Boyer 1992, 1993).

Are some varieties of apocalypticism more associated with violence and volatility than other varieties? We have already discussed "enthusiasm," as delineated by Ronald Knox (1950), however, it is clear that most apocalyptic religious enthusiasts are fairly peaceful. Some writers have identified "exemplary dualism" as an apocalyptic mystique that is particularly volatile (Anthony and Robbins 1978; Jones 1989). "Exemplary dualism" denotes an apocalyptic orientation in which contemporary sociopolitical or socioreligious forces are viewed as exemplifying absolute contrast categories in terms not only of moral virtue but also of eschatology and the millennial destiny of humankind. An example of such a worldview is the old Protestant millennial indentification of the papacy with Antichrist and the "Whore of Babylon." Exemplary dualism detranscendentalizes apocalypticism. It confers ultimacy on contemporary religiopolitical conflicts that are seen to have cosmic significance. The present authors originally developed this concept in an analysis of the ideology of the Unification Church (Anthony and Robbins 1978) and it has been subsequently applied to Jim Jones and the Peoples Temple by Jones (1989), a seminar student of Anthony. In Jim Jones's worldview:

> Themes of destruction, redemption, flight and salvation taken from the book of Isaiah were used to justify a prophecy of the destruction of the fattened nations and escape of the righteous into a new nation . . . the United States, its institutions and even its

standards of beauty were portrayed as the "beast"—totally irre-deemable—to be overcome by the "redeeming remnant." Well-versed in both doctrinal and operational aspects of the conflict of opposing forces of absolute good and evil, members of the Peoples Temple were prepared for sacrifice, struggle and an apocalyptic "final showdown" (Jones 1989, 212).

Exemplary dualism is volatile because it confers deep eschatological significance on the social and political conflicts of the day, thereby raising the stakes of victory or defeat in immediate worldly struggles. Thus communism, radical feminism, the papacy, and exotic cults have all been identified by some Protestant millenarians with the biblical Beast or the "Whore of Babylon." Yet there are surely many more groups with an exemplary-dualist worldview than there are violent or highly volatile movements. Indeed, the arguably exem-plary-dualist Unification Church, though labeled a "destructive cult" by anticult crusaders, has not been shown to be violent or volatile.

As John Hall (1989, 1990) observes, the Peoples Temple commu-nity at Jonestown represented the type of the "other-worldly apoca-lyptic sect." Such groups, "typically founded by charismatic leaders, establish a radical separation between themselves and the estab-lished social world, which they regard as hopelessly evil" (Hall 1989, 78). Yet as Hall (1990) notes in an analysis of the Jonestown tragedy, there have been many more world-rejecting apocalyptic sects than there have been violent (and particularly suicidal) movements. According to Hall, most apocalyptic sects conceptually situate them-selves "on the other side of the apocalypse" in the sense that they define themselves as inexorably "saved"—the corrupt world will be destroyed but they will survive by God's grace—and thus they are safe and cannot be hurt by the hostility of outsiders; they need not anticipate or prepare for violent conflict. A different kind of apoca-lyptic sect, however, a "warring sect," prosecutes a holy war "to van-quish the infidels from dominion over a world where they exercise their evil ways" (Hall 1989, 78). Jim Jones's problem was that under his leadership the Peoples Temple was unable to opt clearly for either pattern. The relocation to Guyana (from California) was a retreatist tactic and an attempt to insulate the group from outside pressure. But this strategy was undercut by Jones's emphasis (somewhat simi-lar to that of David Koresh) on the inescapability of conflict with an overpowering and relentless enemy. Although probably functional in terms of sustaining internal solidarity and control, Jones's paranoid themes undercut the insulated sanctuary conception that many world-rejecting sects construct and which enable them to condemn the surrounding society as hopelessly corrupt while making a partial de facto accommodation with the society. "Jones vacillated between an ethic of confrontation and an ethic of sanctuary" (Hall 1987, 298). Mass suicide, conceived as a vehicle for what Robert Lifton has called "revolutionary immortality," finally united "the divergent public threads of meaningful existence at Jonestown—those of political revolution and religious salvation" (Hall 1987, 300).

In an analysis of the Bishop Hill community, whose volatile charismatic leader, Eric Jansen, was murdered in 1850, Hall notes that his ideal typical conceptions of two different kinds of apocalyptic movements are often conflated in practice, "especially when believers who want to 'flee' this world find themselves embroiled in conflict with their own detractors" (Hall 1989, 78). Thus, as Hall emphasizes, the key to apocalyptic violence and suicide ultimately lies in the dynamics of tension between an apocalyptic community and an external political order. An apocalyptic sect may demonize the external order. The escalation of external pressure "thus forces a choice between the sacred and evil," which becomes "a question of honor, and it is the seedbed of martyrdom" (Hall 1987, 296).

It is possible to speculate as to what variety of apocalyptic or millenarian orientation is most conducive to volatility and violence.[6] It would appear, however, that millenarian-apocalyptic worldviews are most likely to be associated with volatility and violence when they are embodied in charismatic "messianic" leaders who identify the millennial destiny of humankind with their own personal vicissitudes and demonize any opposition to their aspirations and personal aggrandizement. "Koresh, of course, identified *himself* as the Lord's anointed and saw the standoff at Waco as the literal fulfillment of an intensifying campaign by demonic earthly rulers to destroy the righteous remnant" (Boyer 1993, 30, emphasis in original). To the volatility and destructive potential associated with fervent apocalyptic-millenarian expectations is added the volatility and instability associated with charismatic, messianic leadership. It is to the latter issue that we now turn.

Charismatic Leadership

Charismatic authority is a factor (or embodies a number of conditions) that may affect the volatility and violent potential of religious movements. The importance of this factor probably exceeds that of apocalypticism. Charismatic authority is really a hallmark, almost by definition, of noninstitutionalized movements that therefore partake of whatever instability or volatility is associated with charismatic leadership. Apocalyptic beliefs, on the other hand, characterize many relatively institutionalized churches with stable bureaucratic structures with little destructive potential. Apocalyptic, even millenarian, beliefs are not unique to marginal or noninstitutionalized churches or movements; the Seventh-Day Adventist Church and various fundamentalist churches are examples of stable organizations that adhere to apocalyptic (e.g., premillennial) expectations.

Nevertheless, despite the existence of institutionalized churches with doctrinal commitments to apocalyptic visions, there may be a sense in which charismatic leaders and apocalyptic scenarios fit together. Prophecies presuppose prophets, and apocalyptic beliefs are often associated with "world-rejecting" sects whose stance of total rejection of, or opposition to, the broader environing society requires the legitimation of a revered charismatic prophet with a compelling vision (Wallis 1984: Wallis and Bruce 1986a). Institutionalized or institutionalizing apocalyptic movements that are becoming more accommodating to conventional society appear to be prone to defections by volatile followers who become attracted to new and frequently schismatic prophets proclaiming new messages entailing new and nonaccommodative extrapolations of the original millenarian vision. Nonaccommodative apocalyptic sects often experience continual schisms entailing conflicts between competing leaders with differing extrapolations of an original vision. "Offbeat sects are composed of people who are fearful about the future, who hope that by placing their faith in some charismatic leader they will eradicate the past and protect their lives against unknown and unseen dangers" (Fogarty 1993, 486).

Ultimately the volatility of movements with charismatic leadership is related to the intrinsic volatility or *precariousness* of charismatic authority (Wallis 1984; Wallis and Bruce 1986a), which lacks institutional supports. As Wallis (1993, 176) notes, "Charismatic leadership is a fundamentally precarious status." This is largely because the charismatic leaders' claim to authority "rests purely on subjective factors. The 'gift of grace' may evaporate in the eyes of the claimant or his followers in the face of failure." In this connection Johnson (1979) has published a perceptive analysis of how steps that Jim Jones took in response to threats to his charismatic authority created new situations with elements that potentially undercut his authority, which in turn required new responses such that Jones and his community became locked into a spiraling process of increasing authoritarianism, anxiety, and volatility.

The responses that charismatic leaders make to perceived threats to their authority will often tend to embellish this authority and

extrapolate it in an increasingly authoritarian and absolutist direction. "Jim Jones required frequent tests of faith and commitment
from his core followers: signing false confessions, suffering public
humiliation, drinking unidentified fluids and then restraining
expressions of fear or hysteria on being told they were being poi-
soned" (Wallis 1984, 117). Ofshe (1980) describes various dramatic
and traumatic devices (e.g., male vasectomies, abortions, recoupling
of sexual dyads) whereby Chuck Dederich and the leadership of
Synanon was able "to force out members who were a potential threat
to the stability of the power structure" or had less intense commitment (p. 125; see also Wallis 1984, 117). In this way the followers of
a charismatic leader may be directly or indirectly prepared for future
violence as the leader consolidates a disciplined cadre of devotees
who have shed their inhibitions against taking extreme actions in
behalf of the prophet's vision.

The evolution of charismatic leadership too often operates to
embellish or intensify a basic definitional quality of charismatic
leadership: the absence of accountability and of inhibitions on the
impulsivity and freedom of the leader. This inhibition of restraint is
the other side of the precariousness of charismatic authority, that is,
both institutional *restraints* and institutional *supports* are lacking.
Both characteristics increase group volatility. Lacking both immediate restraints and long-term supports, a charismatic leader will be
tempted to use his authority to try to simplify the environment within the group by eliminating sources of dissension, normative diversity, and alternative leadership. This will attenuate the cross-pressures
that operate to inhibit followers from accepting extreme demands
made on them by an eccentric leader (Mills 1982).

These institutional (or anti-institutional) processes interact with
certain social-psychological patterns to enhance volatility. What
Lifton (1979) calls the "deification of idiosyncrasy" refers to the tendency for the devotees of charismatic leaders to interpret in deep and
legitimating terms actions on the part of a leader which might otherwise appear irresponsible, selfish, or destructive. Continual repeti-
tion of this dynamic may in effect condition the followers to accept
with enthusiasm increasingly bizarre behavior on the part of the
leader. It can also encourage such behavior on the part of the charismatic leader, who becomes freer to innovate and act in an eccentric
manner without eliciting disapprobation. The leader may also feel
increasingly impelled to act forcefully to meet the expectations of
the devotees.[7]

A key element of the precariousness of charisma is the uncertainty of succession, which cannot be routinized and institutionalized

without threatening the subjective basis of charisma. The result is continual factionalism within movements pervaded by charismatic authority and a looming threat of a crisis of succession when the erstwhile leader departs. As analyzed by Rocheford (1985), the failure of the Hare Krishna sect to institutionalize the charisma of the deceased founding prophet, Sri Prahupada, interfaced with financial difficulties to enhance factionalism and dissidence in the movement in the early 1980s. Escalating internal conflict led to the murder of a dissident in 1986 (Huber and Gruson 1987).

An additional threat to the authority of a charismatic leader derives from tendencies toward institutionalization, which may be promoted by the administrative staff, and which have the effect of isolating the leader, restraining his freedom of action, and sometimes leading to his actual deposition (Wallis 1984, 109-18; Johnson 1992). To resist such tendencies charismatic leaders may engage in continual crisis-mongering, whereby a movement is kept in such turmoil that stable institutional structures and routines cannot be consolidated (Bird 1993; Hiller 1975; Wallis and Bruce 1986a). "Routinization may be resisted by perpetual environmental change and the shifting of goals" (Hiller 1975, 344). Sudden policy shifts and a rapid succession of commitment rituals such as the vasectomies at Synanon are relevant here, as are grand upheavals such as the Maoist "Great Proletarian Cultural Revolution" in China (Hiller 1975) in the late 1960s, by means of which Mao Tse-tung undermined the institutionalized Communist party bureaucracy, but which ultimately degenerated into factional violence. Finally, a particularly precarious mode of crisis-mongering entails attempts to continually escalate tension between the movement and forces in the socio-organizational environment such that the external threat is continually thematized. The risk of this tactic may be illustrated by the lynching of the controversial Mormon prophet Joseph Smith, whose paramilitarist tendencies contributed significantly to the hostility his movement evoked in Missouri and Illinois.[8]

The nature and evolution of charisma can thus "provide opportunities for charismatic leaders to indulge the darker desires of their subconscious. Through effective resistance to the threat of institutionalization charismatic leaders may be able to render followers exclusively dependent upon them, eliminating constraints or inhibitions on their whims, leading to the possible emergence of unconventional sexual practices and violence" (Wallis and Bruce 1986a, 117).[9] The absence of institutional restraints on charismatic leaders combines with the lack of structural supports, to render charismatic leadership precarious and enhance volatility.

The late Roy Wallis was an outstanding contributor to the analysis of charismatic leadership in religious movements and its relation to apocalyptic worldviews and to violence (Wallis 1982, 1984, 1993; Wallis and Bruce 1986a, 1986b). Wallis developed a tripartite typology of religious movements in terms of world-rejecting, world-accepting and world-accommodating orientations (Wallis 1984). Millenarian and apocalyptic beliefs are said to be intrinsic to world-rejecting movements, which see "themselves as islands of sanity or righteousness in a hostile and degenerate world" (Wallis and Bruce 1986a, 122).[10] Yet, "so great a break with prevailing society can only be justified by the authority of someone perceived to be truly extraordinary. Thus such extremes of world-rejection are normally founded or fostered by a charismatic leader" (Wallis and Bruce 1986a, 122, emphasis in original), who may often resist institutionalization tendencies (which threaten to challenge his authority as well as mitigate the group's apocalyptic vision and world-rejecting stance) by continually shifting policies and practices within the movement and keeping the latter in turmoil. In the process the leader systematically "eliminates the sources of inhibition upon his translation of every new whim or inspiration into practice" (1986a, 123). The leader's power may thus become increasingly absolute. In increasing group volatility and the potential for violence, the defense of precarious charisma interfaces with the provocative quality of world-rejection. "Movements which sharply reject the world around them tend to provoke a reciprocal hostility which in turn creates anxiety, fear and paranoia and thus heightens the potential for violence as well as sex to be aspects of the leader's id which come to the fore" (Wallis and Bruce 1986a, 126).

It would appear logical that the tendencies described above will be more intense and strongly developed the more the leader exercises direct, personal control over a local, spatially concentrated community of believers (as opposed to a spatially dispersed or decentralized movement). Peoples Temple communities in San Francisco and Los Angeles did not suicidally self-destruct and initially denied reports that their vanguard community in Guyana, which was under Jim Jones's personal direction, had done so.[11] It also follows that the degree of institutionalization in a charismatically led movement may inhibit violence and volatility. In a comparison of the ill-fated Peoples Temple with the Unification Church, Galanter (1989, 121-25) notes that the latter, which experienced extreme conflict with forces in its environment in the early 1980s, was partly bureaucratized and spatially decentralized such that the individual devotee's relationship to the charismatic leader, "Father" Moon, was mediated by a "middle-management" strata that imparted to the movement some insulation against possible impulsive reactions on the part of the exalted leader. Smaller communities of believers may thus be most susceptible to any violent and antinomian proclivities of the charismatic leader (Bird 1993). Thus, in the period from 1969 to 1985 violent explosions took place in connection with movements led by Charles Manson, Lindberg "Black Jesus" Sanders[12] and Jim Jones. In contrast, "the larger charismatic groups of the 1970s, on the other hand, were relatively free from violence . . . they were usually run by a reasonably well-organized bureaucratic structure that served to mute the impact of their leaders' idiosyncrasies." They were also less isolated. "In addition, they had considerable visibility so that local and state authorities were fairly aggressive in scrutinizing potential areas of illegal activity and intervening when signs of violent behavior appeared" (Galanter 1989, 192).

Finally it is worth noting that charismatic authority tends to be volatile not only in consequence of its intrinsic precariousness but also in terms of its lack of legitimacy in American culture. As Bryan Wilson (1975, 1987) and others have noted, charismatic authority is viewed in the modern North American and European setting as legitimate exclusively in the "unserious" realms of entertainment and sports. In the area of religion, charismatic leaders are likely to be met with challenge and skepticism from the media.

Movement as Systems

Before concluding this paper we want to briefly explore some residual factors that are somewhat related to both apocalypticism and charisma. According to Marc Galanter (1989) a cult or charismatic group operates as a social system. It has a primary task or basic transformation function, which entails transforming input from the environment into a form that meets system needs, that is, converting and socializing recruits. A monitoring function monitors, regulates, and coordinates the action of component parts of the system. A feedback function enables the system to obtain information on how effectively it is carrying out its primary task. Negative feedback is vital to long-term self-regulation of the system but also poses a short-term threat to the system by undermining participants' morale and sometimes challenging group beliefs. The suppression of negative feedback is a constant temptation, which, however, may ultimately impair the system. Finally, charismatic social systems have a dimension of boundary control, protecting the systems from external threats.

Most outbreaks of violence associated with religious movements entail escalating boundary tension. This possibility is accentuated when communal systems turn in upon themselves such that recruitment is de-emphasized and the system's "energies now come to focus primarily on close monitoring of its members" (Galanter 1989, 121). This occurred at Jonestown and coincided with intensified demands for commitment to the leader's increasingly bizarre beliefs. The theme of apocalyptic doom became increasingly prominent among those beliefs and "soon became intertwined with the group's monitoring function" (Galanter 1989, 122). Negative feedback was suppressed, which, together with the attenuation of outreach, increasingly isolated the group from the outside community. In this context the imperative of preventing penetration of the system boundary was heightened. "The arrival of Congressman Ryan portended the imminent disruption of the group's control over its boundary, and thereby precipitated the final events at Jonestown" (Galanter 1989, 124). The integrity of the system was threatened in several ways: the threatened exodus of some defectors with Ryan "posed a challenge to the group's monitoring of the membership"; the intrusion of the U.S. state via Ryan "meant that the suppression of negative feedback could no longer be absolute." "Once it became apparent that his cult's boundary could no longer be secured, Jones chose to preserve its identity in spirit if not in living membership" (Galanter 1989, 124).

Galanter also applies his model to an analysis of the destructive confrontation of the Philadelphia police with MOVE, which culminated in authorities dropping a bomb on the house containing the group and inadvertently destroying a whole neighborhood. In the years preceding the final showdown with authorities, the anarchic ecology movement stopped actively recruiting "and its energies were channeled into monitoring its members" (Galanter 1989, 126). The group "increasingly cut back on the feedback it would accept from the surrounding community, shielding its members from opposing views" (p. 126). The group boarded up the house it occupied, electronically blasted obscenities at the neighborhood and refused to listen to the complaints of neighbors, which eventually elicited the intervention of the police, who tragically overreacted. Galanter concludes:

> MOVE and the Peoples Temple can show how a hostile confrontation can ensue at the boundary between a charismatic group and the surrounding community. Protective functions on both sides of the group's boundary may become intensified, leading to mutual provocation and paranoia. If neither party takes steps to defuse the situation, grave consequences can result. This vulnerability to

escalating destructiveness across the boundary of charismatic groups should not go unnoticed in dealing with terrorists and nations that have turned to religious fundamentalism with a vengeance. (Galanter 1989, 128)

An analysis of the tragedy of Waco in terms of Galanter's social system/boundary tension model cannot be undertaken here, but could be a fruitful enterprise.

Two other factors or realms of factors should be mentioned. Crusaders against cults have put forward analyses in terms of mind control (brainwashing, coercive persuasion, thought reform). Our objections to these orientations need not be repeated here (see Anthony and Robbins 1994). The best formulation along these anticult lines is by Anderson (1985), who discusses dimensions of deception and "psychological coercion" in "cultic systems." Groups that score high on the multidimensional variables of deception and coercion may not necessarily be dangerous or volatile, but the great power they exercise over the members renders them potentially destructive.

Finally it is worth considering whether certain kinds of movements—apocalyptic, militant, authoritarian—attract certain kinds of persons whose aggressiveness or submissiveness may accentuate the volatility of the group and the prerogatives of a wild leader. Recently the authors (Anthony and Robbins 1994) have re-evaluated the well-known work of Robert Lifton (1961), which is often considered to be an analysis formulated in terms of brainwashing. However, insomuch as Lifton is concerned with (voluntary or coerced) conversion to a totalist perspective and not simply forced behavioral compliance, he sees adoption of a totalist worldview as a product of the interaction of the content of a totalist ideological milieu and personality patterns that predispose certain persons to ideological absolutism (Anthony and Robbins 1994). "Ideological totalism" entails "the coming together of immoderate ideology with equally immoderate individual [totalist] character traits—an extremist meeting ground between people and ideas" (Lifton 1961, 419).

Lifton was strongly influenced by Erik Erikson's work on the constellation of psychological characteristics of people who convert to totalistic social movements, which Erikson had originally referred to as "totalism." Lifton's analysis of those few of his subjects who actually changed their attitudes significantly in a pro-Maoist direction when exposed to Maoist indoctrination is largely in terms of Erikson's totalism concept, which included notions of polarized identities and "negative external conscience" that Erikson had employed to analyze the psychological appeal of both fascism and communism (Anthony and Robbins 1994). To oversimplify radically, the protototalist personality escapes from an oppressively self-critical "negative identity" through immersion in an absolutist ideological totalism. His or her polarized identity is reconstructed in an absolutist manner such that the devotee identifies with the group, the cause, or the leader as the embodiment of the highest standard of heroic virtue and the foundation of the devotee's new idealized or grandiose self-image. Weaknesses and negative qualities, which the convert may once have condemned in himself, are projected onto "them," that is, the designated ideological scapegoats in an exemplary dualist worldview: Jews, counterrevolutionaries, occultists, or others (Anthony and Robbins 1978, 1994).[13] Persons with such identities are available for militant and even violent action against "them," or will readily approve of such actions taken by the leader and his close associates. A concentration of such totalistic types in the movement will reduce the inhibitions against extreme measures.[14]

To sum up, the endogenous potential for violence is likely to be enhanced when communal groups are energized by a fervent millenarian vision, and when the membership has totalist psychological characteristics, and when the group is under the direct personal control of a charismatic leader with an exalted messianic self-conception and a determination to resist any encroachments on his authority or constraints upon his freedom of action. A proselytizing outreach to the broader society may inhibit volatility and promote a stabilizing reality-testing. Conversely, an absence of open communication and interaction with outsiders may disinhibit violence and heighten volatility. Of course much will depend upon the specific content of the apocalyptic worldview, particularly if there is an expectation of persecution and violence against the group, and if the group views itself as the exclusive vanguard of a new order or saved remnant. Volatility may also be encouraged if political elements mitigate the otherworldly character of the apocalyptic scenario, if demonic qualities are attributed to sociopolitical or socioreligious forces or to opponents of the group, and if the unsaved or those bereft of grace are viewed as having sharply diminished claims to consideration. Much will also depend upon the particular personality of the leader, although his or her character might be expected to deteriorate somewhat over time to the degree that his authority is direct, absolute, and legitimated in grandiose millenarian terms.[15] The personality characteristics of members in these groups can also be important. Totalistic members who identify the grandiose elements of their polarized self-concepts with the personality of the leader, and who project their negative identities upon scapegoated contrast groups, tend to increase the volatility of the group. Finally the role of exogenous or environmental factors will always be crucial: many Branch Davidians might still be alive today if the BATF had initially exercised more restraint in dealing with a group which, notwithstanding its weapons stockpile, had no history of nonintramural violence.

Postscript

Dangerous confrontations and "cult-related violence" are likely to continue in the future. As the year 2000 approaches, apocalyptic excitation may be expected to intensify. Returning from a conference at which an earlier draft of this paper was presented, the senior author, while making a connection at O'Hare Airport, read the following on the first page of the "Evening Update" to the late edition of the *Chicago Tribune* (November 2, 1993):

> FIVE HUNDRED IN SUICIDE SECT ARE DETAINED:
> Ukrainian police have detained some 500 young followers of a religious sect in Kiev in a bid to prevent any possible suicides. The detentions were necessary, police said, because the sect, The White Brotherhood, which claims the world will come to an end Nov. 24, had called on its followers to take their own lives. The followers were in Kiev for a meeting of the sect led by former communist official, Marina Krivonogova-Zvigun, who now calls herself Maria Devi Christos. The sect members were detained for violations of passport and residency regulations. Many of them have rendered their identification papers illegible and defaced their photographs. Following orders from sect leaders, the detainees are refusing to tell police their names, ages and residence.

Notes

1. In this report we will focus primarily on *confrontational* violence involving conflict between factions within movements or more particularly, tension between a group and individuals, other groups, and authorities in the group's environment. Other modes of "cult-related" violence, such as child abuse through corporal punishment or the withholding of modern medical treatment, have specialized concomitants (e.g., "faith healing" doctrines or biblical literalism applied to corporal punishment). We will neglect these specialized subtypes of cult-related violence and probe instead the factors pertinent to violent *confrontations*, particularly violent actions which are seemingly perpetrated by a religious movement or its leadership.

2. This is particularly the case when a violent episode culminates a spiraling process of mutual antagonism and recrimination between a religious group and the broader community. The concept of "deviance amplification," which was developed by British sociologists to analyze the spi-

raling process of mutual escalation of conflict between deviants and authorities, was applied to conflicts involving the Church of Scientology by Wallis (1977) and has been critically evaluated as a tool for understanding sectarian tensions by Hammond and Beckford (1983). Deviance amplification entails feedback processes between societal labeling and increased endogenous deviance. It can be applied in terms of both the short-term unfolding of violent confrontation (Palmer 1994) and the long-term escalation of conflict ultimately leading to violence (Robbins 1986).

3. The Russian "Old Believers," who experienced mass suicides through immolation at the end of the seventeenth century, thought that purification by fire would open the seventh seal (Robbins 1986, 1989).

4. Knox discusses the doctrine, which was articulated by John Wycliffe but which can be identified in later groups such as the Hussites, Anabaptists, and early Quakers, that *dominion is founded on grace* (Knox 1950, 88, 108–9, 123–24, 133, 147–49, 585). The exercise of rule as well as rights to property and other values is legitimately vouchsafed only to the saints. Knox argues that the early Quaker principle of nonresistance, which condemns the bearing of arms, was grounded in the Anabaptist view of dominion. The doctrine of the latter "was not that nobody has a right to take the sword, but that no worldly person has a right to take the sword. Dominion is founded on grace; if you are not in a state of grace, you have, strictly speaking, no rights and therefore no authority either to govern or to make war—least of all on the saints" (Knox 1950, 148). But "dominion" can refer to a number of things including the right to rule, to property, to possess women, or to properly conduct sexual liaisons, and even to continue to live. Thus the sinister underside of the doctrine that dominion proceeds from grace is that "the worldling has no rights" (Knox 1950, 585). The principle thus converges with Robert Lifton's formulation of "the dispensing of existence" as a key element of "ideological totalism" whereby "those who have not seen the light, have not embraced the truth, are in some way in the shadows—bound up with evil, tainted—and do not have a right to exist as full equals" (Lifton 1985, 64; see also Lifton 1961, 433–34). Finally, some recent examples of the principle that dominion presupposes grace might be found in the idea, imputed to the Unification Church, that all property rightfully belongs to Father Moon and must be emancipated from the realm of sin (Bromley 1985), or the reported revelation to David Koresh that all marriages and couplings except his were adulterous.

5. Robbins (1986, 1989) attempts to disentangle the interrelationship of apocalyptic fanaticism and fierce persecution in the deviance amplification process which produced immolative mass suicides in settlements of Old Believers in Russia at the end of the seventeenth century.

6. Sharot (1982, 13–14) defines millenarianism as an orientation which "seeks the destruction of the natural and social orders as a prelude to a perfect society and state of being." He reproduces a typology of millenarian variations initially formulated by Talmon (1962, 125–48; 1966, 159–200). On a partly a priori basis we can speculate that volatility is

enhanced when a millenarian movement sees itself as surviving to enjoy (or rule) the millennium and, moreover, having a part in bringing about the millennium, and when there is an expectation that the advent of the millennium will be preceded by an apocalypse of upheavals, calamities, and wars. Wessinger (1994) identifies "pre-millennial" movements, which purvey the expectation that "collective terrestrial salvation will be accomplished in a catastrophic manner," as particularly prone to volatile authoritarian leadership. Wessinger has generalized the concept of pre-millennialism beyond the specific Protestant fundamentalist tradition of dispensational pre-millennialism, which envisions a Great Tribulation under the auspices of Antichrist preceding the second coming of the messiah. The dominant "pre-tribulationist" variation expects true Christians to be "raptured" and spared the Tribulation. In contrast, "post-tribulationist" perspectives expect Christians to have to survive the rigors of the Tribulation. Post-tribulationist groups, which include Aryan supremacist groups associated with the Christian Identity movement, may be particularly susceptible to becoming involved in violent confrontations because their emphasis on emerging chaos and persecution "sometimes leads them toward a 'survivalist' lifestyle—retreat into defendable, self-sufficient rural settlements where they can, they believe, wait out the coming upheavals" (Barkun 1994, 47).

7. According to FBI advisor, psychiatrist Murray Miron, "The adulation of this confined group [the Waco Davidian community] works on this charismatic leader [Koresh] so that he in turn spirals into greater and greater paranoia . . . He's playing a role that his followers have cast him in" (quoted in *Time*, May 3, 1993, 35).

8. Moore (1986) argues that Joseph Smith pursued a risky strategy of advertising Mormon deviance and eliciting hostility and persecution in order to build commitment and solidarity within the Mormon movement.

9. An important analysis of sex, violence, and religion in religious movements has been published by Wallis and Bruce (1986a). The analysis is based on four groups: the Manson Family, Synanon, the Peoples Temple (Jonestown) and the Children of God, all of which have been associated with deviant sexual patterns and implicated (except the Children of God) in violent events (see also Wallis 1982a). The authors conclude that deviant sexual practices and violence are often concomitant in religious movements because they are indirectly interrelated as consequences of the lack of institutional restraint on charismatic leaders. In attempting to prevent the emergence of rationalized structures and routines which would challenge inherently precarious charismatic authority, "the leader eliminates the sources of inhibition upon his translation of every new whim or inspiration into practice" (Wallis and Bruce 1986a, 123). According to Wallis, charisma is an essentially descriptive concept that can, however, be employed as an *explanatory* factor in the analysis of the development of deviant patterns in groups and in analyzing the actions of leaders (Wallis 1993).

10. Wallis (1993) refers to Wallis and Bruce (1986a) as "Wallis 1986a," although the article appears as a chapter in a volume by Wallis and Bruce (1986c).

11. In the late seventeenth century Russian Old Believers, who were divided between extremists and antisuicidal moderates, were organized in terms of separate quasi-monastic communities (Crummey 1970). The dynamics of charismatic leadership within each community was probably a factor in determining which settlements experienced suicidal events. As the extremists were consumed by their own lethal frenzy, the moderates ultimately came to dominate the movement (Robbins 1986, 1989).

12. A small (six-person) quasi-Christian group met a cataclysmic end in Memphis in 1983. Led by Lindberg Sanders, self-proclaimed "Black Jesus," "the group had come to believe that an imminent lunar eclipse would lead to an Armageddon, and they acted on this deluded shared belief" (Galanter 1989, 192). They took a local police official hostage and barricaded themselves in a small house, ultimately murdering the hostage and perishing to the last man in a shoot-out with police. Sanders had nearly been committed to a mental hospital a few days prior to the shoot-out (Galanter 1989).

13. Erikson's theory of totalism both influenced and was influenced by the better known work *The Authoritarian Personality* (Adorno et al. 1950), which still inspires research in which "authoritarian traits are correlated with religious fundamentalism and other variables (Altemeyer 1988).

14. The leaders of totalistic apocalyptic movements may be disproportionately recruited from persons exhibiting such traits.

15. These characteristics are likely indicators not only of intrinsic volatility and violent proclivities on the part of movements but also of those properties which make certain religious movements appear particularly objectionable in the view of observers and which are thus most likely to elicit hostile reactions.

References

Adorno, Theodore, Else Frenkel-Brunswick, Daniel Levinson, and R. Nevett Sanford. 1950. *The Authoritarian Personality*. New York: Norton.

Altemeyer, Bob. 1988. *Enemies of Freedom*. New York: Jossey-Bass.

Anderson, Susan. 1985. "Identifying Coercion and Deception in Social Systems." In *Scientific Research on New Religions*, edited by Brock Kilbourne, pp. 12–23. Proceedings of the Annual Meetings of the Pacific Division of the American Association of the Advancement of Science meeting jointly with the Rocky Mountain Division. San Francisco: AAAS.

Anthony, Dick, and Thomas Robbins. 1978. "The Effect of Detente on the Growth of New Religions: Reverend Moon and the Unification

Church." In *Understanding the New Religions*, edited by Jacob Needleman and George Baker, pp. 80–100. New York: Seabury.

———. 1994. "Brainwashing and Totalitarian Influence." In *Encyclopedia of Human Behavior*, edited by V. S. Ramchandran. San Diego: Academic Press.

Barkun, Michael. 1994. "Reflections after Waco: Millennialists and the State." In *From the Ashes: Making Sense of Waco*, edited by James Lewis, pp. 41–50. Lanham, MD: Rowman and Littlefield.

Bird, Frederick. 1993. "Charisma and Leadership in New Religious Movements." In *Handbook of Cults and Sects in America*, vol. 3A, *Religion and the Social Order*, edited by David Bromley and Jeffrey Hadden, pp. 75–92. Greenwich, CT: JAI Press.

Boyer, Paul. 1992. *When Time Shall Be No More: Prophecy Belief in Modern America.* Cambridge: Belknap/Harvard University.

———. 1993. "A Brief History of the End of Time." *New Republic* (May 17): 30–33.

Bromley, David. 1985. "Financing the Millennium: The Economic Structure of the Unificationist Movement." *Journal for the Scientific Study of Religion* 24 (3): 253–75.

Cherniavsky, Michael. 1970. "The Old Believers and the New Religion." In *The Structure of Russian History*, edited by M. Cherniavsky, pp. 140–88. New York: Random House.

Cohn, Norman. 1961. *Pursuit of the Millennium.* New York: Oxford.

Crummey, Richard. 1970. *The Old Believers and the World of Antichrist.* Madison: University of Wisconsin.

Frend, W. C. 1950. *The Donatist Church.* London: Oxford.

Fogarty, Robert. 1993. "Sects and Violence: 'Cults,' Guns, and the Kingdom." *Nation* (April 12): 485–87.

Galanter, Marc. 1989. *Cults: Faith, Healing, and Coercion.* New York: Oxford.

Hall, John. 1987. *Gone From the Promised Land.* New Brunswick, NJ: Transaction.

———. 1989. "Jonestown and Bishop Hill." In *New Religious Movements, Mass Suicide, and the Peoples Temple*, edited by Rebecca Moore and Fielding McGehee III, pp. 77–92. Lewiston, NY: Edwin Mellen.

———. 1990. "The Apocalypse at Jonestown." In *In Gods We Trust*, edited by Thomas Robbins and Dick Anthony, pp. 269–94. New Brunswick, NJ: Transaction.

Hammond, Annette, and James Beckford. 1983. "Religious Sects and the Concept of Deviance." *British Journal of Sociology* 34 (2): 208–9.

Hiller, Harry. 1975. "A Reconceptualization of the Dynamics of Social Movement Development." *Pacific Sociological Review* 17 (3): 342–59.

Huber, John, and Lindsay Gruson. 1987. "Dial OM for Murder." *Rolling Stone* 497: 53–59.

Johnson, Benton. 1992. "Of Founders and Followers." *Sociological Analysis* 53 (S): S1–S15.

Johnson, Doyle Paul. 1979. "Dilemmas of Charismatic Leadership: The Case of the Peoples Temple." *Sociological Analysis* 40 (4): 315–23.

Jones, Constance. 1989. "Exemplary Dualism and Authoritarianism at Jonestown." In *New Religious Movements, Mass Suicide, and the Peoples Temple,* edited by Rebecca Moore and Fielding McGehee, pp. 209–30. Lewiston, NY: Edwin Mellen.

Knox, Ronald. 1950. *Enthusiasm.* London: Oxford. Reprinted London: Collins Press.

Levi, Kenneth, ed. 1982. *Violence and Religious Commitment: Implications of Jim Jones' Peoples Temple Movement.* University Park, PA: Penn State.

Lewis, James. 1994. *From the Ashes: Making Sense of Waco.* Lanham, MD: Rowman and Littlefield.

Lifton, Robert. 1961. *Chinese Thought Reform and the Psychology of Totalism.* New York: Norton.

———. 1968. *Revolutionary Immortality.* New York: Norton.

———. 1979. "The Appeal of the Death Trip." *New York Times,* January 7.

———. 1985. "Cult Processes, Religious Totalism, and Civil Liberties." In *Cults, Culture, and the Law,* edited by Thomas Robbins, William Shepherd, and James McBride. Chico, CA: Scholars Press.

McGee, Jim, and William Clairborne. 1993. "The Waco Messiah." *Washington Post, National Weekly Edition.* May 17–23, 10–11.

Melton, J. Gordon. 1985. "Violence and the Cults." *Nebraska Humanist* 8 (2): 51–61.

———. 1992. *Encyclopedic Handbook of Cults in America.* Rev. ed. New York: Garland Press.

Mills, Edgar. 1982. "Cult Extremism: The Reduction of Normative Dissonance." In *Violence and Religious Commitment,* edited by Kenneth Levi, pp. 75–102. University Park: Penn State University Press.

Moore, R. Laurence. 1986. *Religious Outsiders.* New York: Oxford University Press.

Ofshe, Richard. 1980. "The Social Development of the Synanon Cult." *Sociological Analysis* 41 (2): 109–27.

Palmer, Susan. 1994. "Excavating Waco." In *From the Ashes: Making Sense of Waco,* edited by James Lewis, pp. 99–111. Lanham, MD: Rowman and Littlefield.

Richardson, James. 1985. The 'Deformation' of New Religions." In *Cults, Culture, and Charisma,* edited by Thomas Robbins, William Shepherd, and James McBride, pp. 163–75. Chico, CA: Scholars Press.

Robbins, Thomas, 1986. "Religious Mass Suicide before Jonestown." *Sociological Analysis* 41 (1): 1–20.

———. 1989. "The Historical Antecedents of Jonestown." In *New Religious Movements, Mass Suicide, and the Peoples Temple,* edited by Rebecca Moore and Fielding McGehee, pp. 51–77. Lewiston, NY: Edwin Mellen.

Rocheford, E. Burke. 1985. *Hare Krsna in America.* New Brunswick, NJ: Rutgers University Press.

Sharot, Stephen. 1982. *Messianism, Mysticism, and Magic.* Chapel Hill: University of North Carolina.

Talmon, Yonina. 1962. "Pursuit of the Millennium: The Relationship between Religious and Social Change." *Archives Européens de Sociologie* 3: 125–48.

———. 1966. "Millenarian Movements." *Archives Européens de Sociologie* 7: 159–200.

Wallis, Roy. 1977. *The Road to Total Freedom: A Sociological Analysis of Scientology.* New York: Columbia.

———. 1982. "Charisma, Commitment, and Control in a New Religious Movement." In *Millennialism and Charisma,* edited by Roy Wallis, pp. 73–140. Belfast: Queens University.

———. 1984. *The Elementary Forms of the New Religious Life.* London: Routledge and Kegan Paul.

———. 1993. "Charisma and Explanation." In *Secularism, Rationalism, and Sectarianism,* edited by Eileen Barker, James Beckford, and Karel Dobbelaere, pp. 167–79. Oxford: Clarendon Press.

Wallis, Roy, and Steven Bruce. 1986a. "Sex, Violence, and Religion." In *Sociological Theory, Religion, and Collective Actions,* edited by Roy Wallis and Steven Bruce, pp. 115–27. Belfast: Queens University.

———. 1986b. *Sociological Theory, Religion, and Collective Actions.* Belfast: Queens University.

Wessinger, Catherine. 1994. "Varieties of Millenarianism and the Issue of Authority." In *From the Ashes: Making Sense of Waco,* edited by James Lewis, pp. 55–73. Lanham, MD: Rowman and Littlefield.

Wilson, Bryan. 1975. *The Noble Savage: The Primitive Origins of Charisma.* Berkeley: University of California.

———. 1987. "Factors in the Failure of the New Religious Movements." In *The Future of New Religious Movements,* edited by David Bromley and Phillip Hammond, pp. 30–35. Macon GA: Mercer University.

Part Five

SCHOLARS, EXPERTS,
AND LAW ENFORCEMENT

11

JAMES D. TABOR

Religious Discourse and Failed Negotiations

The Dynamics of Biblical Apocalypticism at Waco

The very evening of the initial BATF raid on the Mt. Carmel Center outside Waco, on Sunday, February 28, 1993, the wounded leader of the Branch Davidian group, David Koresh, spoke several times by live telephone hookup over Dallas radio station KRLD and CNN cable television. Koresh began, in those initial gripping interviews, the first of hundreds of hours of explanations, based on his understanding of the biblical apocalyptic significance of the situation in which he found himself. His last live public communication was given over KRLD at 1.50 that Monday morning.[1] It is ironic, but true, that in those initial live interviews Koresh offered the basic clues to an understanding of the perspective of the Branch Davidians,[2] which had it been properly grasped, could very likely have led to a peaceful resolution of the standoff. Unfortunately, neither the FBI agents in charge, nor the myriad of advisors upon whom they relied, were prepared to comprehend the religious dynamics of the situation from such a perspective.

By Monday morning, March 1, the FBI had already been summoned and was in the process of taking over operations from the BATF. FBI Special Agent Jeffrey Jamar, from San Antonio, Texas, had taken command of the situation. The FBI's fifty-person Hostage Rescue Team (HRT), a counterterrorist unit, was preparing to arrive. The standoff had already been classified by the FBI, even at that early date, as a Complex Hostage Barricade Rescue Situation. Negotiators and tactical personnel were put in place, and a method of interchange with the Branch Davidians was initiated. One can hardly expect that the federal agents called to the area that day would think to pack their Bibles, or have had time to brush up on the book of Revelation, the last book of the New Testament. But from those initial live interviews with David Koresh over KRLD and CNN, one who knew the biblical texts and listened carefully to what the Davidian leader said would have been able to understand the predicament from a wholly different perspective than that of the government's "Hostage Rescue" approach. For the Branch Davidians, no one was a hostage, and these same federal agents represented an evil governmental system, referred to in the book of Revelation as "Babylonian." Given this understanding, the idea of "surrendering to proper authority," as the government demanded throughout the next seven weeks, was absolutely out of the question. As they saw it, their group had been wantonly attacked and slaughtered by government agents whom they understood to be in opposition to both God and his anointed prophet.

As I have argued elsewhere (Tabor 1993, 1994), the Waco situation could have been handled differently, and resolved peacefully. This is not unfounded speculation or wishful thinking; it is also the considered opinion of many others trained in the academic study of religion who understand the dynamics of such biblical apocalyptic belief systems as that of the Branch Davidians (see Ammerman 1993; Arnold 1994; Lewis 1994; Sullivan 1993). There was a proper and clear way to communicate with these religious people, but it had nothing to do with hostage rescue or counterterrorist tactics. Indeed, a peaceful strategy was being pursued, with FBI cooperation, by Phillip Arnold of the Reunion Institute in Houston and by me, in concert with lawyers Dick DeGuerin and Jack Zimmerman (who spent twenty hours inside the Mt. Carmel Center directly communicating with David Koresh) and Koresh's main spokesperson, Steve Schneider. Unfortunately, it came too late, and by the time it began to produce results, decisions had already been made in Washington to end the siege by force.

In the KRLD conversations Koresh was urged repeatedly by the station manager to surrender and get medical attention, and he was continually asked whether he would allow more children to come out. Koresh, in response, launched into a detailed exposition of his message, quoting biblical passages and trying to explain his view of the situation. What he tried to communicate obviously went over the head of the station manager, and one would presume it was largely incomprehensible to much of the radio audience. Koresh was a master at his own form of biblical exegesis. His message was systematic, consistent, and internally logical when understood within the theological perspective of the Branch Davidians. However, to one untutored in the details of the prophetic portions of the Bible, this message, delivered in his typical nonstop style, with lengthy quotations from the King James Version, would appear nonsensical. Among the many points he made in those initial conversations on KRLD, two stand out as vital for understanding the standoff from his perspective. First, he told his live audience, "We are now in the fifth seal," and second, he said that Psalm 2, and potentially, Psalm 89, were about to be fulfilled. If anyone at that point had been able to converse intelligently with Koresh about these two topics, much needless frustration and perhaps further deaths could have been avoided.

According to FBI records, during the fifty-one-day period negotiators spoke with fifty-four individuals inside Mt. Carmel for a total of 215 hours. There were 459 conversations with Steve Schneider, which consumed ninety-six hours. Koresh spoke with authorities 117 times—a total of sixty hours (U.S. Department of Justice 1993, 10–11). The Justice Department's report indicates that the conversations with Koresh were, as often as not, monologues in which he preached nonstop, sometimes for as long as two or three hours at a time. Although the tapes of these "negotiations" have not been made public, the Justice Department's report provides liberal samples of the style and content of Koresh's attempts to communicate with authorities. For example, on March 7 Koresh was on the phone with them from 12:11 A.M. until 3:15 A.M., just over three hours. The FBI notes that his delivery of "religious rhetoric was so strong that they could hardly interrupt him to discuss possible surrender" (U.S. Department of Justice 1993, 57–58). The report laments that Koresh "refused to discuss any matters of substance" and merely insisted on "preaching" to negotiators (U.S. Department of Justice 1993, 54–55). What the authorities never perceived was that Koresh's preaching was precisely such to him, the only matter of substance and means through which to work out a "surrender." One detects, in reading through the Justice Department's log of events, an increasing level of frustration in dealing with Koresh by the second week of March (see Stone 1993). On March 9, a series of pressure tactics were initiated, beginning with the temporary, and later permanent, cutoff of electricity to Mt. Carmel. These tactics were intensified over the next few weeks, and fell into a pattern of FBI demands followed by punitive measures. The FBI saw the situation as stalemated. They had little hope that Koresh would allow more children out. Those who were inside apparently intended to stay inside. All the while Koresh insisted that he would not exit until he received his "word from God." On March 15 the FBI formulated a "modified negotiation strategy," which urged negotiators to be firm, insist on peaceful surrender, but sharply refuse to listen any longer to what they were now calling Koresh's "Bible babble" (U.S. Department of Justice 1993, 70). Although there was never any effective flow of communication between the government negotiators and David Koresh which reflected an understanding of his biblical worldview and the situation, this strategy shift effectively sealed off even the possibility of such.

"Bible Babble" Deconstructed: Making Sense of the Seven Seals

What Koresh talked about incessantly in his lengthy scriptural expositions, whether delivered to friend or foe, were the "seven seals" of the book of Revelation. Absolutely and inseparably intertwined with his view of the seven seals was an understanding of himself as the unique one, sent by God, to reveal the mystery of the seals. This was clearly Koresh's primary theme. He routinely challenged anyone, particularly Adventist ministers and preachers who might claim to speak for God or to understand the Bible, to "prove him wrong" on the seven seals, or to match him in expounding their hidden meaning. Interviews with surviving members of the Branch Davidians confirm this point. Time and time again, both publicly and privately, they report that their attachment to Koresh hinged on his understanding of the Scriptures, particularly, his unlocking of the mysteries of the seven seals. More than one declared, "If the Bible is true, then David is who he says he is," reducing the entire question to a matter of the veracity of the Bible itself.[3] Furthermore, an examination of Koresh's beliefs suggests insights that clearly would have benefited authorities in their negotiations with the sect leader, had they not conveniently dismissed the religious discourse as "Bible-babble." Let us examine these briefly.

In chapter 5 of the book of Revelation the seven seals are introduced. The author John is taken to heaven, appearing before the Throne of God. In the right hand of God is a book or scroll, sealed with seven seals. Ancient scrolls were written on parchment or papyrus, rolled up and sealed with twine and wax. Obviously one could not read the contents without loosing the seal. This particular book is sealed seven times. The number seven, which appears often in the Bible, indicates completion or thoroughness. In other words, the contents of this book are totally and completely hidden from view. This idea of sealing up a prophetic book comes from Daniel 12:9, where the prophet is told that the words of his prophecy are "closed up and sealed till the time of the end." The contents of the book of Daniel and that of the book of Revelation are closely interrelated. Indeed, the book of Revelation is just that, a final revealing of the prophetic mysteries of the Bible, prior to the end. The question that dominates Revelation chapter 5, where the scene of the sealed book is introduced, is in verse 2: "Who is worthy to open the book, and to loose the seals thereof?" The text says that no one, in heaven or on earth, was found worthy. The apostle John weeps at this news, but is then told, "Weep not": the Lion of the Tribe of Judah, the Root of David, who is pictured before the Throne as a wounded Lamb, is declared worthy to open the sealed book. Traditional Christian interpreters would, of course, understand this Lamb to be none other than Jesus of Nazareth.

This is where Koresh's unique and unprecedented interpretation, based not only on the book of Revelation but on many hundreds of other prophetic passages from the Hebrew Scriptures, is significant.[4] Koresh had demonstrated to the satisfaction of his followers, that this particular figure, this Lamb, could not be Jesus of Nazareth, the first-century Messiah. He claimed he could prove from the Bible that another "Christ" figure was pictured here. Koresh argued that the book of Revelation, although written in the first century A.D., was intended primarily for the end time. The introduction to the book says it reveals "things which must shortly come to pass," for "the time is at hand" (Rev. 1:1,3). The book concludes with Jesus Christ saying, "Surely I come quickly." He argued that such statements would be patently false if applied to the first century. In other words, it is a book that could be understood only shortly before the end, when such statements about an imminent finale would make literal sense. As Koresh read things, Jesus Christ revealed the book in the first century, but it was not to be opened until our own time. David Koresh claimed to be the "seventh messenger" mentioned in Revelation 10:7: "But in the days of the voice of the seventh angel, when he shall begin to sound [his trumpet], the mystery of God should be finished, as he hath declared to his servants the prophets."[5]

According to Revelation 11:15 this seventh messenger appears on the scene shortly before the end, preparing the way for the return of Christ. These verses were in turn linked to Daniel 12:9, which spoke of the prophetic mysteries as "sealed" or hidden until the time of the end. As the Branch Davidians understood it, this final messenger would "open the seals" of prophetic and biblical truth. So, although Koresh did not claim to be Jesus Christ per se, he did claim to come in the power and spirit of Christ, as Jesus of Nazareth had come in his own generation, and he claimed to have received the final revelation of all the mysteries of the prophets. He often talked of this revelation he received. Prior to that time he was a gifted and diligent student and teacher of the Scriptures, but made no extraordinary claims to prophetic revelation. Like other Adventists he accepted the view that Ellen G. White, who died in 1915, was the last prophetic voice the people of God had been given. The revelation came to him dramatically and suddenly in 1985 while he was living in Israel. He describes it as a voice which began to reveal to him, through the Scriptures, all the intertwined levels of meaning contained in the entire Bible. As a high-school dropout, he often fondly quoted the passage in Isaiah: "The Lord GOD has given me the tongue of the learned, that I should know how to speak a word in season to him that is weary; he wakeneth morning by morning, he wakeneth mine ear to hear as the learned" (Isa. 50:4).

According to Koresh, after receiving this revelation he came to "understand it all," from Genesis through Revelation. He often said that he did not study the Bible, but that insights and understanding were given to him, day by day, poured out like a flood in his ear.[6]

Koresh as a Final Christ Figure

This claim obviously led to endless confusion. It was widely reported by virtually all the media, and certainly the FBI shared this perception, that Koresh claimed to be Jesus Christ returned to earth. However, this is a misreading of Koresh's teachings. For the record,

Koresh's view of himself is much more complex, and had been carefully worked out based on many dozens of texts in the Old and New
Testaments.

The Branch Davidians were a Christian sect, with roots in the
Millerite Advent movement which gave rise to the Seventh-Day
Adventists and other lesser known groups (see Nichol 1944; Boyer
1992). Like all Christian churches, they clearly believed that Jesus of
Nazareth was the Christ or Messiah, as well as Son of God and Sav-
ior.[7] David Koresh placed himself within a long history of mainstream Christian theological and prophetic interpretation. He often
referred to the seven stages of restoration of biblical truth since the
Reformation, each of which had been heralded by a dominant
reformer: Luther, John Knox, Wesley, Alexander Campbell, William
Miller, Ellen G. White, and last of all, the series of truths now
revealed to him and his immediate Branch Davidian predecessors.[8]
He believed that he was the seventh and final messenger, who would
restore all things before the return of Christ. This seventh stage of
reformation was inaugurated by Victor Houteff, who broke with the
Seventh-Day Adventists in the 1930s, and involved the establishment of a literal kingdom in Palestine, prior to the second coming of
Christ, thus fulfilling Isaiah 2:2–4 and 11. This kingdom would be
opposed by the political powers of the world, led by the United
States. According to Daniel 11:40–45 these "Babylonian" powers
would invade the Middle East, and march into Jerusalem, taking control in a "peace-keeping" operation against the Israelis. The Branch
Davidians expected to be living in Israel at the time and would be
allied with the Jews against these Western forces. David Koresh often
said that Daniel 11 was the most important prophecy in the Bible for
understanding his entire prophetic role.

The confusion over Koresh's understanding of himself arises from
his use of the term "Christ." Koresh knew a bit of Hebrew and Greek
and had worked out an understanding of the term "christ," or "messiah," which is biblically and historically correct from a linguistic
point of view, but quite understandably confusing to his general
Christian audience. The word "christ," in Hebrew and in Greek,
means one who is "anointed" or "chosen." It is not the proper name
of Jesus, but a title or designation. The Bible uses the term "christ"
or "messiah" for a variety of figures, including all of the high priests
and kings of ancient Israel. Koresh claimed to be the specific "christ"
mentioned in Isaiah 45:1, who is called "Cyrus" (or "Koresh," in
Hebrew), and is addressed as a messiah/christ, or anointed one. This
Cyrus/Koresh, ancient ruler of Persia, had conquered the Babylonian
empire in the year 539 B.C. However, since the book of Revelation is

about the final defeat of a spiritual kingdom of Babylon, shortly before the end time, Koresh understood Isaiah to be talking also about a spiritual Cyrus/Koresh, who would bring it to defeat. He had studied very carefully the text through Isaiah 40–61 and found this very figure mentioned repeatedly. For example in Isaiah 46:11, God says he would call "a ravenous bird from the east, the man that executeth my counsel from a far country." Koresh often referred to himself as this bird from the east, when he talked about his revelation in the land of Israel. In Isaiah 48:14 we read, "The LORD has loved him: he will do his pleasure on Babylon, and his arm shall be on the Chaldeans." Koresh would ask, who is the "him," here, who is the "arm of Yahweh" who is to destroy Babylon? The text goes on to say, "I, even I, have spoken, yea, I have called him: I have brought him, and he shall make his way prosperous . . . and now the Lord GOD, and his Spirit hath sent me." Psalm 80:17 states "Let thy hand be upon the man of thy right hand, upon the son of man whom thou madest strong for thyself." Who is this man of God's right hand?, Koresh would ask. He would painstakingly take his followers through these and other related sections of Scripture, repeatedly asserting that this mysterious figure could not have been Jesus of Nazareth, who fulfilled none of these prophecies. For example, he argued that the figure mentioned in Psalms 40 and 45 was a sinner like any human being, that he was married to more than one wife, that he would personally confront the "King of the North" in Daniel 11, and many other things that no Christian would claim about Jesus of Nazareth.

The Dynamics of Biblical Apocalypticism

David Koresh said on March 1, the morning after the initial BATF raid, that "we are now in the fifth seal" and that Psalm 2 was taking place, with Psalm 89 poised for potential fulfillment. What is operating here is a series of interpretive dynamics, well known to scholars of Jewish and Christian apocalypticism, which have played themselves out countless times in the past 2,500 years.[9] An understanding of these dynamics offered the most promising hope for a peaceful resolution of the Waco situation. Biblical apocalypticism involves the interplay of three basic elements: (1) The *sacred text*, which is fixed and inviolate; (2) The inspired *interpreter*, who is involved in both transmitting and effecting the meaning of the text; and (3) the fluid *context*, in which the interpreter or group finds itself. The text functions as a kind of map of things to come, setting forth an apocalyptic scenario of end-time events. Koresh's text was of course, the entire

Bible, but particularly the books of Daniel, Revelation, Psalms, Isaiah 40–61, and the Minor Prophets. The prophetic scenario that he had worked out was highly complex, but surprisingly concrete and specific, clearly set forth in all his expositions, to both his followers and any outsiders who would listen.

Although the text itself is fixed and unchanging, mirroring in advance an almost fatalistic reflection of what must happen, there are two variables in this scheme of things, allowing for a high degree of flexibility. First, the interpreter is doing just that, interpreting, both the text and sociohistorical events. And the sociohistorical milieu—the context—is always changing and changeable. This was the key to effective negotiations during the entire fifty-one-day standoff at Mt. Carmel. The government largely controlled the context, or outside situation. Given this dynamic, *this means that the FBI actually held within its control the ability to influence Koresh's interpretation, and thus, his actions.* Unfortunately, everything the government agents did for fifty-one days, following the standard negotiation strategies and tactical maneuvers associated with Hostage Rescue Barricade situations, simply confirmed Koresh's initial perception of the confrontation on February 28—that they were "in the fifth seal," and that Psalm 89 would likely be fulfilled. In other words, the FBI inadvertently played the part of the Babylonian forces throughout, validating in every detail, to both Koresh and his followers, this chiliastic interpretation of the standoff.

The fifth seal of the book of Revelation is chilling in its potential implications for the situation at Waco:

> And when he had opened the fifth seal, I saw under the altar the souls of them that were slain for the word of God, and for the testimony which they held; and they cried out with a loud voice, saying, How long, O Lord, holy and true, does thou not judge and avenge our blood on them that dwell on the earth? And white robes were given unto every one of them; and it was said unto them, that they should rest yet for a little season, until their fellow-servants also and their brethren, that should be killed as they were, should be fulfilled. (Rev. 6:9–11)

The opening of the fifth seal takes place shortly prior to the cosmic judgment of God, the Great Day of the Lord's Wrath, which is to be revealed by a massive earthquake and various heavenly signs, introduced by the sixth seal (Rev. 6:12–17). It is the last major event leading up to the end. The text speaks of a group of the faithful being slain, followed by a waiting period, prior to the slaughter of the rest of the saints. Koresh linked this event with Psalm 2, which describes

a final confrontation between the "kings of the earth" and an anointed one of God. On February 28 the killing had begun. From the
Branch Davidian point of view, the six who were killed died for no
other reason than their intense religious devotion, defamed and
branded as part of a "cult." In biblical terms, they gave their lives
"for the word of God, and for the testimony which they held." The
group is then told to wait for a "little season" until the rest would
also be slain. Their martyrdom would lead to the sixth seal, which
evokes the judgment of God on the world. As long as Koresh and his
followers believed the fulfillment of this fifth seal was upon them, it
appeared that the deaths of the entire community were inevitable.

The Consequences of Misinterpreting Koresh

The FBI accused Koresh of being a manipulating con man erratically
making up and changing the rules as things unfolded, and they
offered as evidence a pattern of broken promises. Curiously, no link
was made here between Koresh's so-called erratic behavior and the
FBI's psychological-warfare method of alternating gestures of coercion and conciliation. In any case, after March 2, Koresh stuck irrev-
ocably to his position: God had told him to wait. No matter how
hard the authorities pressed Koresh or his followers, demanding surrender, they were consistently given a single reply. The group
refused to leave until Koresh received his "word from God." The
potential horror of the impasse, since the group perceived itself to be
in the fifth seal, was that they might unwittingly or even willfully
orchestrate their own deaths, in order to become the final martyrs of
prophecy.

It is obvious that David Koresh himself was confused by the
events which had transpired. It is true that his prophetic scenario did
call for a final fulfillment of this fifth seal. However, based on Daniel
11:40–12:13, which he often said was the most important prophecy
for the end time, this was all supposed to happen at a later time and
in another place. The setting was supposed to be in Jerusalem, in the
Land of Israel, not in Waco, Texas. Also, the group was expecting the
final confrontation to come in 1995, not in 1993, based on their
understanding of a final ten-year period mentioned in Psalm 90.
According to Koresh's understanding, he would be inevitably
required, at some point in the future, as this final Koresh/Christ, to
die in a battle. The latter verses of Psalm 89, which Koresh mentioned on the day of the initial BATF raid, predict just such a fate for
this Davidic figure.

It was this uncertainty which offered the best hope for a peaceful resolution of the conflict. At one point in the KRLD conversation, Koresh was asked by that station manager how he felt about the BATF agents who were wounded. He answered with emphatic passion, "My friend, it was *unnecessary.*" He further stated that the whole thing was regrettable, that innocent lives had been lost, and that he would have peacefully submitted to any governmental investigation of the weapons he had purchased. This suggests that Koresh did not see the February 28 confrontation as some inevitable fulfillment of the final prophetic scenario that he had proclaimed to his followers in such detail. Too many things did not match. Nonetheless, he had been wounded, people had been killed, and he was now confronted by official agents of the United States government, whom Adventists have historically identified as representatives of the Babylon system which Christ defeats in the book of Revelation (chapters 17–18). It is clear from conversations with surviving Branch Davidians who were inside Mt. Carmel that they feared the overwhelming government forces and believed they might be slaughtered at any moment. Given these ambiguities, Koresh was not absolutely convinced that the events of February 28 had precipitated the final sequence of the book of Revelation. He was uncertain of what he was to do. So, although the text was fixed, like a script written in advance, the interpretation and the precise context were variable. Koresh was waiting for two reasons: because he understood that to be required by the fifth seal, but also because he was seeking his word from God, which would clarify for him the ambiguities and uncertainties of the situation.

Phillip Arnold and I offered our services to the FBI on March 7. As biblical scholars we had specialized in the history of apocalyptic interpretation. Our intentions were twofold. First, we offered to help interpret the rather bizarre complexities of books like Daniel and Revelation, as understood by the Branch Davidians. But even more important, we wanted to communicate with Koresh directly, offering him sympathetic and informed response to his apocalyptic interpretations. Our goal would be to build upon the ambiguity that we knew Koresh already felt about the situation. We intended to stress the point that given his interpretation of the Bible, right or wrong, one might not necessarily understand the standoff at Waco as a fulfillment of the end-time scenario. Koresh persisted in speaking only about his prophetic message with FBI negotiators. It was clear that he desperately wanted them to recognize his message and that the reason he was compelled to preach in monologue fashion was that none of the agents were equipped to discuss the many texts to which Koresh referred. There was no one to engage him in dialogue, so no substantive discussion ever ensued. Unfortunately, Arnold and I were never allowed to communicate directly with David Koresh. Also, our expertise was enlisted only in a very peripheral way in the few conversations that Phillip Arnold had with several mid-level FBI negotiators. In early March, Arnold was interviewed over Dallas radio stations KRLD and KGBS, discussing the book of Revelation. These broadcasts attracted the attention of Koresh and Schneider. On March 16, the Davidians made a formal request that they be allowed to discuss the Bible with Phillip Arnold. The FBI denied their request, but allowed tapes of these radio programs to be sent into Mt. Carmel (U.S. Department of Justice 1993, 186). Encouraged by the positive response, Arnold and I began to formulate a more carefully worked out plan to communicate with Koresh. Ron Engelman, host of a daily talk show over station KGBS, had shown sympathy toward the Branch Davidians from the day of the initial BATF raid. His program was faithfully followed by those inside Mt. Carmel on battery-powered transistor radios.[10] On April 1, Arnold and I appeared on the Ron Engelman show and discussed in some detail the prophetic technicalities of the Waco situation as it might be viewed by the Branch Davidians. Although this program took the form of a dialogue between us, it was deliberately pitched for the ears of Koresh and his followers and was designed to show that someone outside was listening and capable of discussing the book of Revelation on a level the Davidians could appreciate. David Thibodeau, and other surviving Branch Davidians who were inside at the time, report that this program created a very favorable response inside.[11] Around this time Arnold was in contact with Dick DeGuerin, Koresh's attorney, helping him to understand the religious framework of his client. On April 4, just before Passover, the FBI allowed a tape of our radio discussion to be taken into Mt. Carmel by DeGuerin and given directly to David Koresh. This was the last face-to-face contact anyone from the outside had with those inside the facility.

On April 14, just four days before the FBI assault and resulting fire, David Koresh received his long awaited word from God. According to survivors who were inside, he had spent the prior Passover week in devout prayer and meditation, seeking a divine answer to the crisis. On Wednesday, Koresh released what turned out to be his final communication with the outside world. It was a letter addressed to DeGuerin. He reported enthusiastically that the group would come out as soon as he finished his interpretation of the seven seals and was assured of its safe delivery to Phillip Arnold and me. In part the letter read:

I am presently being permitted to document, in structured form, the decoded messages of the Seven Seals. Upon completion of this task, I will be free of my "waiting period." I hope to finish this as soon as possible and to stand before man to answer any and all questions regarding my actions. This written Revelation of the Seven Seals will not be sold, but is to be available to all who wish to know the Truth. The Four Angels of Revelation are here, now ready to punish foolish mankind; but, the writing of these Seals will cause the winds of God's wrath to be held back a little longer. I have been praying so long for this opportunity; to put the Seal in written form. Speaking the Truth seems to have very little effect on man. I was shown that as soon as I am given over into the hands of man, I will be made a spectacle of, and people will not be concerned about the truth of God, but just the bizarrity of me in the flesh. I want the people of this generation to be saved. I am working night and day to complete my final work of the writing out of these Seals. I thank my Father, He has finally granted me the chance to do this. It will bring New Light and hope for many and they will not have to deal with me the person.

I will demand the first manuscript of the Seals be given to you [Dick DeGuerin]. Many scholars and religious leaders will wish to have copies for examination. I will keep a copy with me. As soon as I can see that people like Jim Tabor and Phil Arnold have a copy I will come out and then you can do your thing with this beast. We are standing on the threshold of Great Events! The Seven Seals, in written form are the most sacred information ever!

This letter offers invaluable insights into Koresh's apocalyptic theology. He spoke of receiving "permission" to write out his rendering of the seven seals. In Koresh's understanding of things, this is a central point. Indeed, as he envisioned it, the time had arrived, at long last, for the mysteries of the book of Revelation to be given to the world. In Revelation 10, an angelic figure is told to "seal up" and "write not" the mysteries of seven "thunders," which are equivalent to the events of the seven seals. Yet the figure has in his hand a "little book," and is given all the "mystery of God as declared to the prophets." He is subsequently told, "You must prophesy again before many people, nations, and tongues, and kings." Arnold and I analyzed this passage in detail in our taped discussion which was sent in to Koresh. We knew that he claimed to be this very figure in Revelation 10. We pointed out to him that although his name was now a household word—that he had been on the cover of *Time* and *Newsweek*, and was the subject of hourly CNN news reports—all the public knew about him were charges of child abuse, sexual molestation of minors, and a myriad of other bizarre practices widely reported in the media. The figure in Revelation 10 possessed a "little book," which apparently contained the sealed message, yet at some point this messenger is told to go to the world at large with the message. Arnold and I pressed the point that no one outside Mt. Carmel had any idea or comprehension of his principal claim—the revelation of the seven seals. His letter clearly responded to the major points we raised with him on the tape. He described, in a concessionary tone, his intent to separate the personality ("bizarrity of me in the flesh") from the message.

What the FBI tragically failed to recognize was that according to this letter, Koresh had received his long-awaited signal. The Davidian leader clearly stated that his waiting period would end upon completion of his written manuscript. Publicly, FBI agents ridiculed this latest development as one more "delay tactic" in Koresh's attempt to prolong the agony of the siege for his own twisted purposes. The chronology in the Justice Department's report fails even to mention the letter of April 14. It merely records that "David had established a new precondition for his coming out." Unfortunately no one in the FBI's inner circles of advisors was capable of understanding the most basic elements of the religious, apocalyptic mind-set of David Koresh, or the most elementary aspects of his prophetic system.

To compound matters, the FBI asked Murray Miron of Syracuse University to examine this and four other letters sent out the previous week. Miron, a psychologist and prominent member of CAN (Cult Awareness Network), concluded that the letters bore "all the hallmarks of rampant, morbidly virulent paranoia." In point of fact, the other four letters consisted mostly of scriptural quotations related to Koresh's understanding of the situation. Had Miron any training in theology or in church history of apocalypticism, he would have recognized that those texts were a kind of code, mapping out the perspectives of the group in biblical language. Miron so dreadfully misunderstood this vital April 14 letter that he apparently thought the reference to Arnold and me was concerning book rights, casting us as literary agents attempting to cut a deal with Koresh. Miron reported his analysis of the letters to the FBI on April 15, just three days before the fire, concluding that Koresh was "a determined and hardened adversary who [had] no intention of delivering himself" (U.S. Department of Justice 1993, 175). It should be obvious to those trained in religious studies that Miron lacked the expertise to judge or evaluate this type of material. Given Koresh's worldview, the April 14 letter was internally "rational" (in Weber's terms, *wertrational*), reflecting a cohesive set of principles and beliefs—logic—relative to an absolute value. For fifty days David Koresh consistently stated that he would not come out until he received his "word from God." Yet, he effectively communicated his intentions to leave to his attorneys, who had prepared the legal conditions related to a surrender.

What is doubly tragic is that apparently Attorney General Janet Reno was never told about the April 14 breakthrough, or shown the letter. The Justice Department report reveals that meetings were held in Washington all that week, prior to the Monday, April 19, assault on Mt. Carmel (U.S. Department of Justice 1993, 263–79). The FBI was pressing for permission to exercise force, and Reno was notably hesitant, asking whether there were alternatives. She repeatedly intoned, "What are arguments for waiting?" Indeed, the Justice Department report indicates that a crucial meeting was held with the attorney general on that very day, April 14, to discuss the effects of CS gas on children. However, no mention was made about the most significant development in the entire seven-week standoff. Toward the end of that week, as deliberations in Washington continued, Reno decided to proceed with the FBI's tactical plan, but then reversed herself, asking for more information. Not only did the FBI supply her with Miron's ill-informed analysis, but on April 17, just two days before the fire, officials presented her with a memorandum from Dr. Park Dietz of the UCLA School of Medicine, which also concluded that (1) Koresh was a manipulating con man, (2) further negotiations were hopeless, (3) he was not coming out, and (4) he would likely continue [sic] to sexually abuse the children inside. Reno was finally persuaded and gave permission for the CS gas operation. This memorandum appears to be the origin of Attorney General Reno's infamous *faux pas* regarding child abuse as a justification for the assault on April 19. Later that week the Justice Department issued a "clarification" stating that in point of fact they had no evidence of child abuse during the fifty-one-day siege.

On April 19, the day of the fire, Jeffrey Jamar, the FBI agent in charge at Waco, emphatically stated on CNN's *Larry King Show* and ABC's *Nightline* that the FBI had incontrovertible evidence, based on classified government surveillance techniques, that Koresh had not begun his manuscript on the seven seals and had no plans to do so. He was specifically questioned about the April 14 letter and Koresh's promise to surrender. He repeated that the government had hard evidence that this latest claim of Koresh was merely a further attempt to delay and manipulate the standoff. The Justice Department report, however, makes it clear that the FBI had already decided in advance to deploy the CS gas assault. In their view, Koresh was a dangerous sociopath who would respond only to force. When attorney DeGuerin told Jeffrey Jamar about the April 14 letter, Jamar was apparently concerned about not tipping him off regarding the upcoming plan. DeGuerin was told, "We've got all the time it takes," yet Jamar was fully aware of the meetings in Washington planning the Monday assault (Maas 1994, 6).

We now know that David Koresh was hard at work on his manuscript, which he considered to be his most important life accomplishment. He worked on it as late as Sunday evening, the night before the April 19 assault, completing his exposition of the first seal. Ruth Riddle, one of the surviving Branch Davidians, served as his stenographer and typist that weekend. On the day of the fire she carried out in her jacket pocket a computer disk containing what Koresh had written up to that point. It is a substantial piece of work, running about twenty manuscript pages, quintessentially Koresh in style, content, and passion. At the end of this document we have the last recorded words of David Koresh, dictated the evening before the fire. He quotes the book of Joel and then makes the following comment:

> Blow the trumpet in Zion, sanctify a fast, call a solemn assembly. Gather the people, sanctify the congregation, assemble the elders, gather the children, and those that nurse at the breast; let the bridegroom go forth from his chamber, and the bride out of her closet (Joel 2:15–16). Yes, the bride is definitely to be revealed for we know that Christ is in the Heavenly Sanctuary anticipating His Marriage of which God has spoken. Should we not eagerly ourselves be ready to accept this truth and *come out of our closet and be revealed to the world* as those who love Christ in truth and in righteousness. (From the unfinished manuscript of David Koresh. Emphasis added.)

Koresh had found his text for the situation at hand; the group was to come out and be revealed to the world. This does not mean he had abandoned the overarching apocalyptic scenario, or the view of himself as the Koresh/Christ who would finally confront and defeat Babylon. It is clear, even within the manuscript itself, that he expected this to unfold at a later time.

Conclusion

It is not an unreasonable assertion to suggest that effective communication with David Koresh would have required knowledge of the biblically based, apocalyptic world he inhabited. It is equally reasonable to assert that apocalyptic sects and their leaders are not tied to a fixed agenda. The dynamics of apocalypticism allow for considerable flexibility and variation. Indeed, apocalyptic religious movements have a long, rich history dating back over two millennia with varying degrees of tension with or accommodation to surrounding cultures. Yet to the FBI in 1993, the outcome of the Waco standoff was inevitable, predetermined by Koresh's beliefs, engendering a rigid, inflexible, and military posturing in the conflict. Koresh was reduced to a stereotype, a tabloid persona bent on self-destruction. To a few selected psychiatrists, he was psychopathic, suffering from delusional paranoia. Such perceptions, whether valid or not, certainly obscured the most constructive means of dealing with Koresh and his followers. (Indeed, what insights or advantages were gained by these secondhand psychiatric profiles?) Although the FBI charged that Koresh was erratic, contradicting himself and breaking promises at will, the Justice Department's highly detailed log of events reveals otherwise. The indelible impression one gets in reviewing these documents is how utterly consistent both Koresh and his followers were from March 2 to April 19. They had been told to wait by God, and no amount of pressure or abuse would divert them from their path. The final and insufferable tragedy is that when Koresh finally received his "word" on April 14, the decision to launch a second assault by authorities in Washington was made without the informed advice of professionally trained scholars in religion, who were either excluded or ignored, and who most likely could have helped them avert the deaths of seventy-four men, women, and children.

Notes

1. Koresh had spoken over CNN with anchorman David French at 7:25 p.m. on Sunday, the day of the raid. He subsequently called in and spoke with KRLD at 10:05 p.m. for about twenty minutes and then again at 1:50 a.m. for about twenty-five minutes.

2. The followers of David Koresh do not actually call themselves Branch Davidians, but merely "Bible students" or "students of the Seven Seals." It appears that at least for some of the newer converts, there were only loose ties with this tradition (see Bromley and Silver, this volume); and most had come to study with David Koresh. In this chapter I use the term "Branch Davidians" for convenience, with this explanation in mind.

3. This was consistently reported to me in interviews with some of the more articulate members of the group. It is also confirmed by tapes in my possession, most of them made in 1987, in which Koresh is teaching his doctrines to initiates. One can clearly see from these tapes that Koresh's power of persuasion rested upon his ability to clarify and explain the Bible in the greatest detail, particularly the mysteries of books of Haggai, Nahum, Habakkuk, Zechariah, Isaiah, and of course, the book of Revelation.

4. My exposition of Koresh's teachings is based primarily on three sources: tapes made in the late 1980s of his detailed Bible studies with his students, interviews with surviving Branch Davidians who studied under him, and Koresh's own expositions in his manuscript on the Seven Seals, which survived the fire on computer disc.

5. "Angel" in Greek, the word *angelos,* means "messenger," and is often used in the Bible for a human being, not necessarily a celestial being.

6. Branch Davidians described Koresh as not really "studying" the Bible, as one generally understands the term. In other words, he did not constantly pore over the text, with commentary and concordance, trying to figure out this or that point or doctrine. They also said he did not read much, or study other materials. They saw him rather as one who simply opened the Bible and expounded this or that insight, as it would come to him. They had an impression that he simply "knew things," without study. He often made fun of those who "wasted thousands of dollars" on biblical studies in college, and yet could not tell you the first thing about the complexities of the prophetic texts he expounded. It was this knowledge of the scriptures which riveted Koresh's followers to him. They tended to come from biblically oriented backgrounds in which the veracity of the Bible was an inviolate assumption. Accordingly, when Koresh showed them "what the Bible truly meant" they felt they had little choice but to follow. The surviving tapes of Koresh teaching his students in private sessions, some of which cover every verse in Isaiah 40–61, a most complex and difficult section of the Bible, demonstrate his amazing ability.

7. Sometimes Koresh would say he did not believe in "Jesus," meaning the paganized figure of apostate Christianity, whom he would distinguish from the historical "Yeshua," the Nazarene. The perspective is common among the more radical reformers and restorationists.

8. According to this belief, each figure is associated with a key step or insight that brought the people of God closer to the original, primitive truth of the early Church: Luther (faith), Knox (spirit), Wesley (grace), Campbell (baptism), Miller (second coming), White (sabbath), Houteff (Davidic kingdom on earth), Ben Roden (Jewish feast days), Lois Roden (feminine nature of God).

9. I am using "apocalypticism" here to refer to the view that the end of time is imminent, with signs of the end unfolding according to an interpretive scenario revealed in the prophetic texts of Scripture.

10. At one point, early in March, Engelman asked the Branch Davidians to move their satellite dish to a specific position if they were listening. They responded a few minutes later. Also, David Thibodeau, one of those who survived the fire, reports that Engleman's show was avidly followed by the group each day.

11. I conducted these interviews on November 15, 1993, in Washington, DC.

References

Ammerman, Nancy T. 1993. "Report to the Justice and Treasury Departments Regarding Law Enforcement Interaction with the Branch Davidians in Waco, Texas." In *Recommendations of Experts for Improvements in Federal Law Enforcement after Waco*. U.S. Department of Justice. Washington, DC: Government Printing Office.

Arnold, J. Phillip. 1994. "The Davidian Dilemma: To Obey God or Man?" In *From the Ashes: Making Sense of Waco*, edited by James R. Lewis, pp. 23–32. Lanham, MD: Rowman and Littlefield.

Boyer, Paul. 1992. *When Time Shall Be No More*. Cambridge, MA: Harvard University.

Lewis, James R. 1994. *From the Ashes: Making Sense of Waco*. Lanham, MD: Rowman and Littlefield.

Maas, Peter. 1994. "None of This Had to Happen." Interview with Dick DeGuerin. *Parade Magazine*, February 27, 4–6.

Nichol, Frances. 1944. *The Midnight Cry*. Washington, DC: Review and Herald.

Stone, Alan A. 1993. "Report and Recommendations Concerning the Handling of Incidents Such as the Branch Davidian Standoff in Waco, Texas." Washington, DC: U.S. Department of Justice.

Sullivan, Lawrence E. 1993. "Recommendations Concerning Incidents Such as the Branch Davidian Standoff in Waco, Texas, between February 28, 1993, and April 19, 1993." In *Recommendations of Experts for Improvements in Federal Law Enforcement after Waco*. Washington, DC: U.S. Justice Department.

Tabor, James D. 1993. "Apocalypse at Waco." *Bible Review* 9.5 (October): 24–33.

———. 1994. "The Waco Tragedy: An Autobiographical Account of One Attempt to Avert Disaster." In *From the Ashes: Making Sense of Waco*, edited by James R. Lewis, pp. 13–21. Lanham, MD: Rowman and Littlefield.

U.S. Department of Justice. 1993. *Report to the Deputy Attorney General on the Events at Waco, Texas: February 28 to April 19, 1993*. Washington, DC: U.S. Government Printing Office.

12

NANCY T. AMMERMAN

Waco, Federal Law Enforcement, and Scholars of Religion

After the disastrous BATF raid on the home of the Branch Davidians, as the FBI settled into their long siege and the world's news organizations created a small village outside the perimeter, scholars of religion—with near unanimity—shook their collective heads in disbelief at the strategies being adopted by federal law enforcement. Did they not know that a group was more likely to rally behind its charismatic leader than to surrender to his enemies? Did they not know that apocalyptic beliefs should be taken seriously, that they were playing the role of the enemies of Christ? Did they not know that any course of action that did not seem to come from the Bible would be unacceptable to these students of Scripture? Did they really believe they were dealing with hostages? I have yet to encounter a single sociologist or religious studies scholar who has the slightest doubt that the strategies adopted by the FBI were destined for tragic failure.[1]

So the question arises, how could the FBI proceed with a strategy of increasing psychological and tactical pressure, if there was such a large body of expert opinion that would have advised against such a strategy? That is the primary question with which I undertook advising the Justice and Treasury Departments on future dealings with "persons whose motivations and thought processes are unconventional" (the language of our charge from Deputy Attorney General Philip Heymann and Assistant Secretary of the Treasury Ron Noble). During the summer of 1993, after the tragic end of the siege in Waco, officials in both Justice and Treasury had concluded that mistakes had been made, that the situation was not one that could be dealt with like a normal "hostage/barricade" situation, and that such "unconventional thinking" was likely to present itself to federal law enforcement again. They decided they needed advice.

But they still did not know who to call. Through their usual "old boy" networks (which evidently needed to include at least one girl), a group was assembled and designated the "behavioral science experts." We were to be "non-compensated temporary government employees" until such time as we had each delivered a report to the deputy attorney general. Each of us had some experience in studying religious persons and groups that might be called by many in "mainstream" America unconventional, but none of us came from the well-recognized group of scholars who specialize in new religious movements. Professor Lawrence Sullivan, of Harvard Divinity School, had studied millennial movements in Brazil. Professor Alan Stone of Harvard Law School and Professor Robert Cancro of NYU Medical School had both studied and written on the intersection of law, psychiatry, and religion. And I had conducted research on fundamentalists, including those in the Southern Baptist Convention. I decided that one of my basic goals would be to introduce federal law enforcement officials to relevant scholars and scholarly literature.

The data-gathering for this project began with oral briefings conducted at the Justice Department by the investigative teams Justice and Treasury had put in place to find out what happened in Waco,

and continued with group interviews with the people in charge of
negotiations and tactical strategy in Waco. A second round of brief
ings, at the Treasury Department and at the FBI Training Academy
at Quantico, introduced the behavioral science experts to the people
behind the scenes for BATF and the FBI, respectively. In addition, I
had access to a number of other sources. I was supplied with a list of
the experts consulted by the FBI during the affair. I also spoke with
Glenn Hilburn, professor of religion at Baylor (who was one of those
experts), and I made a second trip to Quantico to talk with agents
Pete Smerick and Gregg McCrary at the FBI Academy.

During our first round of briefings, especially in our conversations
with the hostage negotiators who had been involved in Waco, the
most striking finding was the FBI's near total dismissal of the religious beliefs of the Branch Davidians. For these men, David Koresh
was a sociopath, and his followers were hostages. Religion was a convenient cover for Koresh's desire to control his followers and monop-
olize all the rewards for himself. They saw no reason to try to understand his religious beliefs, indeed thought them so bizarre as to be
incomprehensible by normal people.[2] The negotiators expressed deep
regret at this state of affairs, but could see no alternatives to the way
they had come to understand the situation. The tactical commanders
had no real regret, seeing the final outcome as unavoidable.

Why Religion Was Ignored

In those conversations, and in subsequent ones, four reasons for this
dismissal of religion can be seen. First, for at least some of those
involved, religion is itself a foreign category. They have little experience with religion themselves, and they do not really understand
how anyone could believe in a reality not readily provable by empirical means. They are what Max Weber would call "religiously unmu-
sical" (in Weber 1946, 25). The level of religious unmusicality in this
case is evident in the investigative and evaluative reports compiled
by the Justice Department's own staff. A small, but telling example:
throughout those reports, the last book in the Bible is incorrectly
identified as "Revelations" (rather than the book of Revelation). People in positions of public service have perhaps come to believe that
religion is not a part of the culture about which they have any need
to be conversant, whether or not they themselves are believers. Sullivan's report to the Justice and Treasury Departments concentrates
very effectively on this aspect of the problem. At least for a significant segment of those involved in Waco, the "culture of disbelief"
(Carter 1993) was a tragic fact.

Within the law enforcement community, this skepticism about religion has a particular flavor. Given a history of encounters with manipulative conversions of convenience, many officers are inclined to dismiss the validity of religion as an independent variable. When a criminal "gets religion," that person is still—to their minds—fundamentally a criminal. This reason for dismissing religion's impact is closely related to a second factor at work in the federal officials whom I observed.[3] At least some of those officials had significant religious upbringing, but now reject that past as benighted. They were not ignorant of religion or of its power to shape a way of life. They simply did not think that any rational person would choose to be religious. At best, they had a "live and let live" attitude about religion. Their history did not make them tone-deaf so much as it made them unsympathetic.

Still a third group of agents was thoroughly attuned to the power of religion. As people of deep faith themselves, they knew that beliefs mattered. However, the depth of their own faith sometimes made it difficult for them to identify with someone whose faith was so different. Because Koresh practiced many things their faith forbade, they could only see his group as heretical or perhaps as a "cult." They could not see the functional similarities between their own experience and the experiences of the Branch Davidians.

Fourth, overlapping all the other causes for law enforcement's failure to understand the religious dynamics of the Branch Davidian standoff, everyone involved fell victim to the images inherent in the label "cult." Others have addressed this problem in more detail elsewhere (see Lewis, this volume). Here it will suffice to note that when religious categories were invoked at all, they were categories derived from the definitions of cult leadership and behavior promulgated by the news media over the last two decades. A "cult leader," according to these images, can be easily seen as a sociopath, and "brainwashed" members can be defined as hostages. By defining a "destructive cult" as a group with an egomaniacal leader and ego-deficient followers, one need not attend closely to the particular religious beliefs and practices of the group. All that matters is the psychological control being exercised by the leader over unwitting followers.

For the four reasons I have suggested, those directing the federal law enforcement effort in Waco were unable or unwilling to see that they should take seriously the religious nature of the social system they had entered. But they were also blinded by the structures of their own agencies and their own standard operating procedures.

Why Good Advice Was Ignored

In the months that led up to the February 28 attempted "dynamic entry" at the Branch Davidians' home, the Bureau of Alcohol, Tobacco, and Firearms (BATF) apparently failed to solicit any social science background information about the nature of the group with which they were dealing.[4] BATF has no internal behavioral science division and did not consult with any other behavioral science persons within the government. Nor did they consult with outside persons in religious studies, sociology of religion, or psychology of religion. There were, for instance, persons in the Baylor University Department of Religion who had studied this particular group for much of its history; they were not consulted. The agency viewed this operation exclusively through strategic and political lenses, with no attempt to ascertain why this group had guns, what they might want to do with them, and how the larger citizenry might be assured that no harm would result from the weapons that had been purchased. In that atmosphere, I believe, it became easy to lose sight of the human dynamics of the group involved, to plan as if the group were indeed a military target. It also discouraged the BATF from seeking other forms of intervention in the group. Quite simply, the agency pursued the line of action—armed assault—for which they were best equipped (and that not very well, as it turned out). If they had been better equipped to pursue interventions based on human science advice, they might have acted differently.

In their attempt to build a case against the Branch Davidians, the BATF concentrated on informants who could presumably provide the strategic information they needed to plan their assault. They interviewed persons who were former members of the group and at least one person, Rick Ross, who had "deprogrammed" a group member. Ross has been quoted as saying that he was "consulted" by the BATF, and their records include accounts of multiple interviews with him. He supplied them, according to BATF records, with "all information he had regarding the Branch Davidian cult," including the name of a former member whom he believed would have important strategic information. At the same time, he and Cult Awareness Network affiliates seem to have been among the sources for the series of stories run by the Waco newspaper, beginning February 27. At the very least, Ross and any former members he was associated with should have been seen as questionable sources of information, but no such caution seems to have been present in BATF dealings with him. Having no access to information from the larger social science community, BATF had no way to put in perspective what they heard from angry former members and an eager deprogrammer.

Unlike the BATF, the Federal Bureau of Investigation did have an extensive system of internal and external expertise on which to call. After the failed raid, handling of the crisis passed to the FBI. Although they had a much broader array of information available, they still failed to consult a single person who might be recognized by the social science community as an expert on the Branch Davidians or on other new, marginal, or apocalyptic religious movements. The official list of outside experts consulted, compiled by the investigative team, includes three persons in the field of psychiatry who have been regular consultants to the FBI on other cases (Murray Myron, Syracuse University, a member of the Cult Awareness Network; Joseph Krofcheck, Yarrow Associates; and Park Dietz, University of California–Los Angeles). From my conversations with the persons in the National Center for the Analysis of Violent Crime (NCAVC) who worked with the negotiators at Waco, I believe that these three persons were the most frequently consulted experts throughout the siege. Dietz assisted in writing the profile of Koresh. Others apparently assisted in recommending strategies to the negotiators and tacticians.

It is unclear which of these consultants (if any) recommended the psychological warfare tactics (Tibetan chants, sounds of rabbits dying, rock music, floodlights, helicopters hovering, etc.). None of the persons associated with NCAVC with whom I have talked claims to have favored these tactics, but no one was willing to say who recommended them or how the decision was made to use them.

Three other persons were apparently called in for specific, limited consultations. Because he was examining the children who were leaving the ranch, Bruce Perry, a Baylor Medical School psychiatrist, was consulted. A pastor in Virginia (Douglas Kittredge) was consulted on one occasion, offering assistance in interpreting the scriptural references being used by Koresh. And CBN talk show host Craig Smith was consulted regarding the airing of the Koresh tape. With the possible exception of Perry, these persons clearly had no effect on the strategy in Waco. Kittredge was evidently the pastor of the church attended by one of the agents, and Craig Smith happened into the drama when Koresh wanted his teachings to receive a wide and sympathetic hearing.

On the official list of outside experts consulted, one person in religious studies is listed—Glenn Hilburn, chair of the Religion department at Baylor. He was contacted about one week after the initial raid and was asked especially for help in interpreting Koresh's ideas about the seven seals. He offered the negotiators basic tools for interpreting scripture (a set of commentaries and concordances) and consulted with them on a number of occasions about various biblical interpretations. While Hilburn is a reputable scholar in church history, he would never claim to be an expert on the Davidians or on other marginal religious movements. He often offered to help the FBI get in touch with others who might offer such expertise, but he was not asked to do so. For instance, Professor Bill Pitts, also of the Baylor faculty, had studied the history of the Davidians, but was not consulted by the FBI. Nor did they seek Hilburn's help in locating others, outside the Baylor faculty, who might help.

In my judgment, the FBI's list of outside consultants is sorely wanting. The psychiatrists who were most intimately involved are undoubtedly experienced in helping the FBI understand "the criminal mind." This however, was a very different situation, and we have no evidence that any of these men had background or experience in dealing with a high-commitment religious group. Both of the psychiatrists who later offered reports to Justice and Treasury—Cancro and Stone—were highly critical of the assessments and strategies that resulted from failing to take the religious and social situation into account. The only experts in religion who were consulted lacked the kinds of expertise necessary for understanding the dynamics of an ostracized religious movement. They tended to be religious leaders who had developed their own views on the meaning of the Bible, but had little comparative perspective with which to offer insight.

In addition to the experts sought out by the FBI, many others were eager to offer their help, and one of the problems faced by the Waco negotiators was that of assessing the potential helpfulness of such outside experts. Agents on the scene in Waco described their situation as "information overload." One person referred to the threat of "fax meltdown." Not only were they receiving constant information about the situation as it unfolded, they were also being bombarded with offers of help from all sorts of unknown sources. Many of these were judged to be "crackpots." Others were probably legitimate and potentially helpful persons. However, the persons on the scene had no way to evaluate this information. With no one in the scholarly community at their disposal to help evaluate the credentials and experience of these persons, their impulse was to discount everything they received.

Over the course of the siege, agents on the scene received communication from several persons who claimed biblical expertise and urged the negotiators to take Koresh's beliefs seriously. In all cases, it appears, the information was taken down, passed along, and ignored. For instance, the logs from March 17 make clear that agents on the scene did not take seriously the possibility that Philip

Arnold's broadcast discussion of biblical prophecy might be useful to their negotiations.[5] They evidently recognized that Arnold is a reputable scholar, but had apparently not talked with him or listened to the broadcast themselves.

Some of the theologians who got through to Waco were of doubtful credentials, but they were uniform in their suggestions that successful negotiations would require meeting Koresh on his own biblical ground. Talking about the Bible, however, was proving frustrating to the negotiators. In the log of March 15, negotiators reported that they would start being "more firm with the group—no more Bible babble."

Although the negotiators were apparently discounting the efforts of theologians, biblical scholars, and others, they were still listening to Rick Ross. The FBI's interview transcripts document that Ross was, in fact, closely involved with the BATF and the FBI. He talked with the FBI both in early March and in late March. He apparently had the most extensive access to both agencies of any person on the "cult expert" list and was listened to more attentively. The BATF interviewed the persons he directed them to and evidently used information from those interviews in planning their February 28 raid. In late March, Ross recommended that agents attempt to humiliate Koresh, hoping to drive a wedge between him and his followers. While Ross's suggestions may not have been followed to the letter, FBI agents apparently believed that their attempts to embarrass Koresh (talking about his inconsistencies, lack of education, failures as a prophet, and the like) would produce the kind of internal dissension Ross predicted. Because Ross had been successful in using such tactics on isolated and beleaguered members during deprogramming, he must have assumed that they would work en masse. Any student of group psychology could have dispelled that misapprehension. But the FBI was evidently listening more closely to these deprogramming-related strategies than to the counsel of scholars who might have explained the dynamics of a group under siege.

The FBI interview report includes the note that Ross "has a personal hatred for all religious cults" and would willingly aid law enforcement in an attempt to "destroy a cult." Significantly, the FBI report does not include any mention of the numerous legal challenges to the tactics employed by Ross in extricating members from the groups he hates.[6] Both the seriousness with which agents treated Ross and the lack of seriousness with which they treated various religion scholars and theologians demonstrate again the inability of agents on the scene to make informed judgments about the information to which they had access and their inability to seek out better information. It also demonstrates the preference given to anticult psychological tactics over strategies that would meet the group on grounds that took faith seriously.

While all this advice was coming in from the outside, the FBI was also relying on its own internal Behavioral Science Unit. The Behavioral Science Services Unit, especially its Investigative Support Unit, at the NCAVC, houses a number of people with considerable working knowledge of marginal religious groups. For instance, Gregg McCrary, in the Criminal Investigative Analysis subunit, is well informed in this area and was on the scene in Waco throughout much of the siege. While no one there would be considered an expert by the usual standards of scholarship (academic credentials and publication, that is), several have done sufficient reading to have a good basic knowledge of the nature of religious groups. They know that religious beliefs have to be taken seriously, and they know that it takes more than understanding an individual personality to understand the dynamics of a group. They could benefit from additional training and from access to reliable outside experts, but they had the basic social science knowledge they needed to analyze this situation.

In the early days of the siege, Pete Smerick, along with outside consultant Park Dietz, put together a profile of David Koresh and of the group. They used materials gathered by the BATF, but knew they should weigh carefully the reports from former members. Based on that assessment, Smerick (with Special Agent Mark Young) wrote on March 5, in a memo to his superiors (the Special Agents in Charge, or SACs, at Waco and people in headquarters in Washington),

> For years he [Koresh] has been brainwashing his followers for this battle [between his church and his enemies], and on February 28, 1993, his prophesy came true. As of March 5, 1993, Koresh is still able to convince his followers that the end is near and, as he predicted, their enemies will surround them and kill them. In traditional hostage situations, a strategy which has been successful has been negotiations coupled with ever increasing tactical presence. In this situation, however, it is believed this strategy, if carried to excess, could eventually be counterproductive and could result in loss of life. Every time his followers sense movement of tactical personnel, Koresh validates his prophetic warnings that an attack is forthcoming and they are going to have to defend themselves. According to his teachings, if they die defending their faith, they will be saved.

On March 7, Smerick and Young listed the psychological warfare tactics available to the FBI, but cautioned that these options "would also succeed in shutting down negotiations and convince Koresh and his followers that the end is near."

On March 8, the same pair cautioned that the Mt. Carmel compound was for the Davidians sacred ground, something they were likely to defend against the intrusions of people they considered evil (the federal government). Summarizing the arguments of people using primarily criminal or psychological categories to explain Koresh, they wrote,

> It has been speculated that Koresh's religious beliefs are nothing more than a con, in order to get power, money, women, etc., and that a strong show of force (tanks, APC's, weapons, etc.) will crumble that resolve, causing him to surrender. In fact, the opposite very well may also occur, whereby the presence of that show of force will draw David Koresh and his followers closer together in the "bunker mentality," and they would rather die than surrender.

They go on to detail the way in which FBI actions were playing into the prophetic scheme of Koresh, warning that "we may unintentionally make his prophesy [death, or the "fourth seal"] come true, if we take what he perceives to be hostile or aggressive action." They note that "mass suicide ordered by Koresh cannot be discounted." Then, following their logic through to its conclusion, they point out that "one way to take control away from him is to do the opposite of what he is expecting. Instead of moving towards him, we consider moving back. This may appear to be appeasement to his wishes, but in reality, it is taking power away from him. He has told his followers that an attack is imminent, and this will show them that he was wrong."

It is my belief that this understanding of Koresh's ideas was basically accurate and that their assessment of his likely behavior was on target. While outside experts might have refined this picture and added nuance to the assessment, the basic direction of the FBI's own behavioral analysts was sound.

Clearly the advice of these agents was not heeded. Why? The answer to that question takes us first to the structure of command and second to the culture and training of the FBI itself. Most basically, people representing the Behavioral Sciences Unit were outranked and outnumbered. Within the command structure, people from the Hostage Rescue Team carried more weight than people who were negotiators. In addition, it is evident that people from the tactical side were simply trusted more and were more at home with the SACs in Waco.

As I understand it, the SACs for this operation were chosen on the

basis of proximity, not on the basis of any special training or experience for an operation like this. Understandably, their primary skills
are in the apprehension of criminals and in the management of personnel. Under normal circumstances, they can count on key assistance in apprehension of criminals from their SWAT teams and from
Hostage Rescue Teams (HRTs), and predictably they listened most
closely to people who spoke the language of forceful tactics. This
was the territory in which they were most comfortable, possibly the
direction in which they perceived the most potential rewards. There
was an understandable desire among many agents in Waco to make
Koresh and the Davidians pay for the harm they had caused. Arguments for patience or unconventional tactics fell on deaf ears.[7]

Those ears were deaf for a number of reasons, many of which have
to do with the training and culture of the FBI. In all likelihood, these
SACs had had no behavioral science training since their very early
training as agents. And then, they were very unlikely to have heard
anything about religious belief systems or group dynamics. Their
entire professional world has been constructed (understandably)
around comprehending and outmaneuvering criminals. They think
(again, understandably) in terms of individual behavior (hence the
near exclusive focus on Koresh, rather than on the group) and on
criminal wrongdoing (hence the label "sociopath" for someone seen
as dangerously at odds with society's norms). Little, if anything, in
their previous experience prepared them for the kind of situation Mt.
Carmel presented them.

The tendency to discount the influence of religious beliefs and to
evaluate situations largely in terms of a leader's individual criminal
or psychological motives is, I believe, very widespread in the FBI. In
our initial briefings with negotiators and tacticians, the consensus
around the table was that when they encountered people with religious beliefs, those beliefs were usually a convenient cover for criminal activity. While they were willing to consider that this case might
have been different, they were still not convinced that Koresh was
anything other than a sociopath who had duped some people into
helping him carry out aggressive criminal activity. They continued
to refer to the members of the group as hostages, failing to recognize
the free choice those people had made in following Koresh.

Behavioral science advice, then, failed to get an adequate hearing.
In the culture of the law enforcement community, neither training
nor experience prepares agents for taking behavioral scientists seriously. And in the crisis situation, behavioral scientists are outranked and out-numbered. As a result, those in charge approached
this situation as if it were one more familiar to them—a criminal

committing illegal acts for personal gain for whom the threat of force is a significant deterrent.

What Can Be Done?

To alter that basic pattern of action and response, a number of changes in law enforcement practice are essential. In my report to the Justice and Treasury Departments, I recommended the following.

1. *Basic training.* The training for all agents should include units in the behavioral sciences and units that give attention to the nature of political and religious groups. These units should emphasize both the rights of such groups to exist unhindered and the characteristics of high-commitment groups that may be relevant to future efforts at law enforcement. Such units should be aimed not so much at making every agent an expert as at sensitizing agents to the complex human dimensions of the situations in which they may find themselves. When they hear behavioral scientists advising them later, it will not be the first time they have heard such voices in the law enforcement community.

2. *Advanced training.* Incidents like Waco are, fortunately, relatively rare. Not everyone in federal law enforcement needs to be an expert on such situations. However, it appears that there is a need for a standing group of specialists in managing this sort of crisis. Rather than turning to whomever happens to be the local SAC, the FBI (and similar federal agencies) should have a small corps of crisis managers available. These persons should have received advanced training both in the various tactical measures at their disposal and in the insights available to them from the behavioral sciences.

3. *Training and expertise for other federal agencies.* An expanded Behavioral Sciences Unit, perhaps not lodged in a single agency, might make a broader pool of behavioral science information available on a regular basis to all federal law enforcement agencies. I was particularly struck by the fact that BATF has no such unit. No one ever had the responsibility of imagining what the people at Mt. Carmel were like, or how they might be thinking. With dozens of federal law enforcement agencies, it would not be cost-effective to set up behavioral science units in each one, but such expertise should be available to all of them.

4. *A broader pool of experts who can be consulted.* Not all sorts of expertise are needed all the time. But agencies should not be caught in a moment of crisis wondering who to call and how to assess the credentials of those who call them. It is essential that behavioral scientists inside federal law enforcement and behavioral

scientists in the academic community forge expanded working ties. People in law enforcement have for too long distrusted the "ivory tower" position of academics who do not have to make "real world" decisions. They have too long insisted that only someone who is really an insider to law enforcement can give them advice. For their part, academics have for too long discounted the experience and wisdom of persons working in law enforcement because it did not come in standard academic packages. It is my sense that this incident provides an opportune moment for overcoming both those problems. Law enforcement people are more aware than ever of the need for additional insight and training, and academics are more aware of their obligation to the public.

That new cooperation might take a number of forms. The various training facilities for federal law enforcement might host a series of consultations in which a small group of academics and a small group of agents work together for two or three days on problems and potential problems facing law enforcement. Academics, for their part, might organize sessions at annual professional meetings at which such questions are raised and to which law enforcement people are invited. In addition, people teaching in the various academies should be encouraged to read more widely and to draw in outside experts for both routine and specialized training whenever possible. Such ongoing collaboration would have the benefit of acquainting the two communities with each other so that each would be better prepared for cooperation in a time of crisis.

Most concretely, it is essential that federal law enforcement develop an expanded list of experts on whom it can call. These people need not be on contract. They simply need to be people the agencies already know to be legitimate, reliable, and willing to cooperate with them. The sorts of activities I am suggesting above would aid in the development of such a list. In addition, the various professional associations—the American Sociological Association, the American Psychological Association, the American Psychiatric Association—could also be helpful. It is essential that persons in federal law enforcement use this occasion to think proactively about the kinds of situations they are likely to encounter in the future and to seek out now the expertise they will need in confronting groups who may have broken the law not for personal gain, but out of ideological and religious conviction.

The siege in Waco provided dramatic and tragic proof both that religion remains a potent motivating force for many in American society and that most of those who serve as the watchdogs and interpreters of American society have little ability to understand the religious forces they encounter. The explanations offered by anticult groups comport well with this culture of disbelief. They offer us "psychological disturbance" and "brainwashing" to account for the life paths of committed believers whose practices put them at odds with materialist, secular pursuits. But those explanations neither made sense of the actions of the Branch Davidians nor provided sound guidance to federal law enforcement. It is time for the rest of the social science community to abandon its silence and to be heard at least as loudly and often as are the voices of the "experts" who have gained their expertise by seeking to destroy the groups they purport to understand.

Notes

1. It is interesting to note that the four behavioral science experts asked to review the Waco affair arrived at similar conclusions. Although we had never worked together before and came from very different backgrounds, we were unanimous in our assessment that FBI strategies had been misguided.

2. I was sufficiently influenced by this widespread assessment of Koresh as incomprehensible that I was surprised when I first began to listen to and read his teachings. They are but a variant on what could be found in many fundamentalist and millennialist churches. The methods of study and exegesis he used would be familiar to many conservative students of the Bible, even if they would disagree with his particular interpretations. The assessment of these beliefs as "incomprehensible" reflects both the biblical ignorance of many public officials and news reporters and the power of the term "cult" to render all other attempts at understanding unnecessary.

3. This assessment of the reasons for law enforcement's dismissal of religious motives is based on conversations with the principals involved in Waco, as well as with people involved in training law enforcement persons at the FBI Academy at Quantico.

4. Much of the remainder of this essay is based closely on the report I wrote for the Justice and Treasury Departments.

5. Indeed the efforts by Arnold and James Tabor represented probably the best hope for a peaceful end to the siege. By working within Koresh's biblical system, they had suggested to him an alternative reading of critical passages in the book of Revelation. By this reading, Koresh should have written or recorded his explanation of the seven seals. The prophesied destruction of the true believers would not have taken place, in this reading, for a long time. The Davidians would have been free to leave their settlement and deal with the government to resolve their differences. Koresh evidently took this teaching and began his interpretive writing. In his last letter, written the week before the fiery end, he stated that he intended to come out when it was complete. The FBI, howev-

er, did not take this scenario seriously or believe that Koresh would actually write the document (see Tabor 1994, this volume).

6. Ross was recently under indictment in the state of Washington for the kidnaping of a young man whose membership in a United Pentecostal Church had become worrisome to the young man's mother. Since the victim was legally an adult, his forcible removal from the church earned Ross the kidnaping charge. Minors can sometimes be legally removed, at the behest of their parents, but even this tactic has become less defensible in the courts (see Bromley and Robbins 1992).

7. *Editor's note:* Pete Smerick, who retired immediately after Waco, later stated publicly that "bureau officials pressured him into changing his advice on how to resolve the situation without bloodshed" (*Washington Times,* May 1, 1995). Smerick said that he had advised a cautious, nonconfrontational approach to Koresh in four memos written for senior FBI officials between March 3 and 8. But he was "pressured from above" when writing the fifth memo on March 9. "As a result, that memo contained subtle changes in tone and emphasis that amounted to an endorsement of a more aggressive approach against the Branch Davidians."

References

Ammerman, Nancy T. 1993. "Report to the Justice and Treasury Departments Regarding Law Enforcement Interaction with the Branch Davidians in Waco, Texas." In *Recommendations of Experts for Improvements in Federal Law Enforcement after Waco.* Washington, DC: U.S. Department of Justice.

Bromley, David G., and Thomas Robbins. 1992. "The Role of Government in Regulating New and Nonconventional Religions." In *The Role of Government in Monitoring and Regulating Religion in Public Life,* edited by James Wood and Derek Davis, pp. 205–41. Waco: Baylor University.

Carter, Stephen L. 1993. *The Culture of Disbelief: How American Law and Politics Trivialize Religious Devotion.* New York: Basic Books.

Tabor, James D. 1994. "The Waco Tragedy: An Autobiographical Account of One Attempt to Avert Disaster." In *From the Ashes: Making Sense of Waco,* edited by James R. Lewis, pp. 13–22. Lanham, MD: Rowman and Littlefield.

Weber, Max. 1946. *Max Weber: Essays in Sociology,* edited by Hans Gerth and C. Wright Mills. New York: Oxford University.

Part Six

13

RHYS H. WILLIAMS

Breaching

the "Wall of

Separation"

*The Balance between
Religious Freedom and
Social Order*

The violent resolution to the standoff between the Federal Bureau of Investigation, the Bureau of Alcohol, Tobacco, and Firearms, and the Branch Davidian religious group in their Mt. Carmel compound outside Waco, Texas, left approximately seventy-four dead. As law enforcement officials debated the tactical effectiveness of various military-style options, main-

Conversations with Derek Davis, Chris Ellison, Katherine Jahnige, Thomas Robbins, and Stuart Wright sharpened the arguments in this paper; of course, I remain responsible for the resulting interpretations.

stream media representatives painted lurid portraits of sexual
license, and antioult activists generated hystorical concerns about
cultic "mind control," the voices of legal and historical scholars
knowledgeable about the relations between the government and
marginal religious groups were absent. Among the questions lost in
the hoopla were those regarding the fundamental legality of the government's campaign against the Branch Davidians. From the initial
attempts to infiltrate the Mt. Carmel group with undercover BATF
officers, to the warrants sworn out against David Koresh, to the decision to take the compound forcibly, to the media accounts of the
standoff, to the congressional hearings afterward, issues of religious
freedom seem never to have arisen. This paper raises those questions
by focusing on the legal and social issues at stake in the balance
between religious freedom and social order.

United States society is committed on one hand to a generally
laissez-faire attitude toward the regulation of social relationships
and, on the other hand, to enforcing harmony within civil society.
That is, Americans generally think that what goes on between private citizens is none of the government's business, but also expect
the government to intervene when disruptive persons, groups, or
behaviors threaten tranquility. And in recent years Americans have
turned increasingly to the government, particularly the courts, for
protection from harm resulting from social relationships. This has
been especially the case when relationships involve money and some
sort of "consumer" relationship. There has also been an increased
call for governmental protection for people unable to protect themselves, such as children, the elderly, and the disabled. Yet, American
society has a history of religious diversity and pluralism, and a legal
tradition that grants special status to religion as a social activity. The
balance of liberty and order is especially difficult when considering
religion, since ultimate values and deep commitments are at stake.
Support for the freedom of religious expression is offset by the government's duty to maintain the public welfare, including the public's
increasing expectations that it do so.

Were the events in Waco an example of the state interfering with
religious liberty, or were government agencies following their mandate to "provide for the common welfare?" One aspect of that question concerns the Branch Davidians' status as a "cult": was the conventional wisdom about unconventional religious groups a factor in
prompting the government to act? If indeed an issue of religious liberty was involved, did the state have a compelling interest that justified its actions? Was the government's intervention necessary to
preserve civil order or protect persons who could not otherwise pro-

tect themselves? Or was this another example of the persecution of marginal religious groups that extends back to America's founding?

This chapter examines aspects of contemporary church-state law and the legal balance between religious freedom and social order as it was manifest in issues surrounding the Branch Davidians. First I offer a sociological account of societal repression—including governmental action—against unconventional religious groups in the United States. Second, I discuss aspects of relevant church-state constitutional law concerning the "free exercise" clause of the First Amendment. Finally, I examine concerns for religious liberty focused on issues surrounding the Branch Davidians. Contemporary religious and social pluralism have increased the difficulty of the modern nation-state's regulation of civil society. Can American society currently afford to protect conceptions of religious liberty with the idealistic vigilance some call for? Alternatively, can modern society afford *not* to protect religious liberty with such jealously? The Waco conflagration provides a tragic setting for questions about the nature of religious freedom and social order.

Society, the State, and Marginal Religions

In his important book *Religious Outsiders and the Making of Americans,* Laurence Moore (1986) argues that "outsiderness" is more than just a common feature of religious minorities in United States history. Rather, he maintains that outsiderness has been a necessary aspect of the struggle to establish new religions in this country. Moore argues that outsiderness has often been promoted by the groups themselves, eager to maintain a distinct identity even as they try to find a niche in American society. Moreover, this "self-stigmatization" has been so common that it is part of what it means to be an American; the often uneasy balance between group distinctiveness and social accommodation defines American religion.

Moore's thesis is persuasive, even though he understates the role of dominant-group discrimination in order to make his point. But his insights into the functions of outsiderness are particularly useful in light of the religious vitality that has accompanied American religion's legal disestablishment and cultural voluntarism. Religious pluralism and an ideology of religious liberty came early to England's North American colonies, and as a result outsiderness has been a cultural distinction more often than a legal category.

Wilson (1990) examines the social context of the Constitution's ratification and notes how the legal disestablishment of religion for the federal government solved a number of difficult political problems. It left state governments free to continue their colonial practices regarding religion, which ranged from fairly open tolerance (Rhode Island, Pennsylvania) to established state churches (Connecticut, Massachusetts, New Hampshire). Disestablishment ratified extant arrangements; religious pluralism as a social fact made disestablishment a legal necessity and hopes for re-establishing a religious "center" a pipe dream (cf. Wood 1988). Had the Constitution's framers wanted to establish a national religion, they would have jeopardized the chances for ratification; religious identification was too diverse and too divisive to do other than disestablish the fledgling federal system.

Nonetheless, the legal disestablishment that formalized religious freedom did not necessarily produce religious equality (Commager 1983, 46). An informal cultural establishment, centered in the "mainline" Protestant groups, dominated politics and most of civil society's major institutions. Even as these groups celebrated the separation of church and state as the key to American religious liberty, they participated in actions and ideas that maintained discrimination against outsider religions. The idea of the United States as a Protestant nation died—if the past tense is in fact accurate—only with great difficulty (see Handy 1984).

In the twentieth century the informal cultural establishment of mainstream Protestant Christianity gave way. This second disestablishment opened American society to a degree of religious pluralism—and equality—previously unknown (Demerath and Williams 1987). With these social structural changes came a more pronounced sense of voluntarism regarding church membership; indeed, church involvement itself came to be seen as more and more optional (see Roof and McKinney 1987). Concomitantly, the courts have often held that disestablishment means that religion cannot be favored over nonreligion; predictably, this is a point of great political dispute (Demerath and Williams 1987, 1992).

Noting that the religious center has not been maintained is not to say that there were not attempts to do so. Much of the hostility directed against marginal religious groups in the United States came from other groups within civil society, rather than the state. For example, anti-Catholic sentiment (often mixed with anti-immigrant nativism) was often endorsed—and sometimes organized—by Protestant churches (see, e.g., Bennett 1988, 51–53). Similarly, the anticult movement today is headed by family members and professional deprogrammers, not government officials (Beckford 1985).

The state, however, has often played a significant role in maintaining religious conformity. Even after disestablishment was firmly recognized as a legal principle, both federal and state governments moved against churches deemed too far from the boundaries of "legitimate" religious expression. For example, after the Mormons fled persecution first in New York and then in Illinois to create their Zion in what is now Utah, the federal government made attempts at controlling them. President Buchanan dispatched military forces to Salt Lake City in the 1850s (Lewis 1989) and a federal "reconstruction" of Utah was threatened in the 1880s and 1890s (Mauss and Bradford 1988). Both federal and state laws prohibited the Mormon practice of polygamy, the most salient symbol of the group's outsiderness (Moore 1986). And the Supreme Court upheld as constitutional several measures directed against Mormons.

The American state also applied military force in order to squelch religious revival among Native Americans in the late nineteenth century. In the 1870s and 1890s the "Ghost Dance" swept through tribes and reservations on the Great Plains, many of whom, such as the Lakota, had been only recently "pacified." The dance was seen as both a direct threat to white control of the west and as a symbol of continued Indian rejection of proper Christian religious practices. While the concern that the Ghost Dance was a rallying cry for violent rebellion was unfounded, the army launched a campaign against it and stopped holy men from traveling among reservations, disrupted or prohibited dances, and had a hand in killing several of the dance's symbolic leaders, one of whom was Sitting Bull (Bailey 1970; Utley 1993).

While the twentieth century has seen fewer cases of violent state repression against marginal religious groups, there are still a number of examples to point to. There have been shoot-outs with polygamous Mormons and with white supremacist and survivalist groups that consider themselves to be engaged in a religious crusade. One of the most dramatic confrontations was between the Philadelphia police and the urban communalist group MOVE in 1985. The group was literally destroyed when the police firebombed the building in which they lived, eventually burning an entire city block. Direct challenges to the main agents of state coercion provoke violent responses.

However, as society has become more regulated by governments at all levels (Demerath and Williams 1987), governmental repression of marginal religious groups is increasingly manifested as administrative harassment. It is perhaps more indicative of the bureaucratized character of contemporary society that the preeminent threat to unconventional religions is the challenge to their tax-exempt status. In several well-known cases prominent religious leaders such as Rev. Sun Myung Moon of the Unification Church (or even Jim Bakker of the PTL Club) have been jailed on tax-related charges.

Tax exemption has more subtle effects on unconventional religions as well. Tax exemption requires particular structural forms and organizational practices, and has the effect of "channeling" movements into "organizations" (McCarthy, Britt, and Wolfson 1991 offer an account of this process for secular social movement organizations). Stark suggests (1987, 19), with customary hyperbole, that the Internal Revenue Service may be the United States' functional equivalent of the Holy Inquisition in that it represents the primary institutional attempt at enforcing religious conformity. Several commentators on new religious movements have observed how administrative regulations force many groups to take on particular organizational forms and practices for legal and administrative, rather than theological, reasons (see Richardson 1985, 1988; Bromley and Robbins 1993).

Bureaucratic regulation goes well beyond the tax code and the IRS. Robertson and Chirico (1985), Cochran (1990), and Robbins (1993), among others, have noted that the contemporary state has expanded its decision-making power into "telic" areas such as the definition of human life and the conditions of death. These are not just boundary areas of religious concern; they speak to some of the core tenets of religious belief. These are the home domain of religious organizations' expertise; they inject public institutions into areas that are often considered the most private and intimate. But the public politics of morality, so common now in the United States, have made the public-private distinctions of liberal capitalist society increasingly problematic, and religio-government conflict increasingly widespread and frequent.

It is important to note that church-state conflict is more significant to religious groups than to the state. Beckford (1985) argues that modern states have bigger problems to worry about than small religious movements; most state action against marginal religious movements is a by-product, not the intent, of governmental purposes.

Religious organizations are often forced into contradictory positions regarding the division between public and private life in modern society. On one hand, preserving the private sphere from the incursions of public authority is often necessary for religious groups to operate the institutions, such as schools, that will preserve their subculture. Religious groups facing a hostile majority or an indifferent secular culture assert their right to structure their collective life free from interference. Yet, religious organizations often lead attempts to hold public institutions (particularly the state) accountable to moral standards, and see this as a religiously mandated duty (cf. Williams 1994).

Both the coercive and administrative burdens of the state have fallen harder on some religious groups than on others. These burdens are more likely to lead to violence with some groups than with others. In this volume Robbins and Anthony offer an insightful analysis about the *internal* factors within marginal religious movements (MRMs) that can lead to volatility and violence. There are also *external* factors that increase the potential for violent repression, particularly regarding the nature of the contemporary state and the types of challenges MRMs present to the boundary between social legitimacy and deviance.

Harper and Le Beau (1993) offer a conceptual scheme for understanding the adaptation or "problematization" of MRMs. They focus on the "interaction pattern" between MRMs and their dominant society: movements must interact with their environment, and the direction of the interaction may defuse or amplify tensions. For example, deviant doctrines can be constructed as either eccentric but benign, or dangerous; which interpretation gains prominence depends more on the course of events than any intrinsic properties of the doctrine.

However, some doctrines and structures are easier to construct as dangerous than others. Boyer's (1992) recent work on apocalyptic belief in the United States demonstrates how volatile it can be as a belief system. People convinced that the end of time is approaching, and that their immortal souls depend upon their actions during the final struggles, can be a powerfully motivated enemy. Further, believers in such a transcendent meaning and purpose to history tend to interpret current events as signs of impending Armageddon between absolute good and evil. They demonize the forces of the social status quo even as it ostracizes them. The rationale of compromise politics is distinctly foreign to millennialist ideology.

Bromley and Busching (1988) highlight the fundamental incompatibility between many MRMs and "straight" society through an analysis of contemporary social relations as they are embodied in "contractual" and "covenantal" worldviews. Modern industrial society is increasingly dominated by social relationships modeled on the contract—rational agreements specifying the exchange of products or services between fully autonomous individuals. On the other hand, covenantal relationships are marked by mutual commitments to a holistic "integrality" where the other person or group, not the exchange, is the focus. "Communalist" social organization, whether in the family, clan, or religious group, is marked by the salience of covenantal relations. The potential for conflict between government—legitimated in the United States with "social contract" ideology—and covenantally organized communalist religious groups is clear.

A particularly telling point is that from the perspective of a contractual ideology, covenantal relationships are ipso facto irrational. They are not "good deals" in exchange terms, and often pledge away aspects of individual autonomy, something no rational calculator would do.

Communalist or corporatist groups provoke societal response with their oppositional stances on matters of values and ideology. But there are also oppositional interests embedded in what are clashing social structures. Corporatist organizations go farthest in providing substitute societies for their members (see Lofland and Richardson 1984). That is, the more corporate an organization, the more it provides all the physical, social, and emotional services members require. Correspondingly, the less likely members are to maintain their ties with people, groups, and institutions in straight society. Thus communalist groups such as the Branch Davidians present challenges, either direct or indirect, to a wider assortment of groups within society. They challenge established churches as inadequate, offer an explicit affront to members' families and former friends, and undermine the control of businesses that employ members. As groups expand their control of members' lives, they challenge more of straight society's institutions and thus make more enemies. At some point in their development, it seems almost inevitable that communalist movement organizations will challenge government agencies or standing laws.

As noted above, encounters between the state and MRMs usually involve the regulatory functions of government agencies. We live in a "society of organizations" (Perrow 1991) in which formal organizations, and particular bureaucratic forms of organization, dominate ever more aspects of social life. As society becomes increasingly regulated, the state assumes responsibility for more steering functions. Government regulations require greater conformity in both structure and function—and greater financial outlays from societal groups attempting to meet those standards. For example, health and safety inspections of buildings, religious schools, group kitchens, and the like are frequent points of church-state contention (see Emory and Zelenak 1985; Robbins 1993).

As Bromley and Robbins (1993) note, these burdens are greater on

MRMs, many of which are poorly funded and organizationally precarious. Further, government inspectors, as representatives of the state, may be particularly demanding of groups perceived as deviant. In many communities local government officials display a certain deference to culturally legitimate religious groups and organizations, regulating them less strictly (see, e.g., Demerath and Williams 1992, chap. 4). But it is easy to imagine that such deference is less likely when the group in question is marginal or new.

Few marginal movements themselves seek open conflict with state authorities, even if they use a rhetoric of opposition. Rather, Harper and Le Beau (1993, 185) posit the "nature and power of opposition, combinations, and coalitions mobilized" against marginal movements as the most important factor leading to violence between movements and the state. In other words, violence is as much a product of the forces arrayed against an MRM as it is the characteristics of the movement itself. In the case of the Mt. Carmel Branch Davidians, this seems to be clearly true.

The reports generated by the government in the aftermath of the final confrontation at Waco give the distinct impression that the Bureau of Alcohol, Tobacco, and Firearms picked a fight with the Branch Davidians. For whatever reason—incompetence, interagency competition, and the need to justify the BATF budget have all been suggested—the BATF pursued a course seemingly designed to amplify rather than diffuse the potential for confrontation. No attempt was made to serve the initial search and arrest warrants before the February 28 "surprise"[1] raid. After that raid left four BATF agents dead, government forces then became locked into a cycle of increasing tension seemingly predicated on each side showing the other who was in control of the situation. Each step of the ensuing interaction functioned as a self-fulfilling prophesy of the agencies' initial misunderstandings.

Even without questioning the motives or competence of BATF and FBI agents, the ingredients for a violent confrontation with the Branch Davidians were all there. First, of course, was the compound's arsenal of weapons, Koresh's belief system with its elements of apocalyptic paranoia, and a regional culture that makes issues of manhood, gun ownership, and violent confrontation salient. In addition, the increasingly corporatist character of the Mt. Carmel compound played a role in isolating the Davidians from straight society. The isolation wove a web of secrecy around the group that lent an aura of plausibility to charges made against them. The allegations of child abuse, sexual perversity, and mind control were difficult to dispel. Indeed, the affidavit for the search warrant cites the secrecy of the compound as evidence for the BATF's suspicions that illegal weapons were being produced.

The communalist sense of outsiderness was thus an important element in the Davidians' group identity as well as the government's actions; it was strengthened rather than weakened by the pressure tactics used in the fifty-one-day standoff. Neither the FBI nor the BATF had any in-house behavioral science advisors with expertise on religious groups; rather, their agency resources were geared toward dealing with criminals pursuing self-interest. This perspective no doubt contributed to the government's image of the Davidians as irrational and unpredictable. Agents came to think of Koresh as a con man using religion as a cover and his followers as hostages; the agents failed to believe that any authentic religious sentiment might animate such an unconventional group. As a result, the Davidians were regarded increasingly as a threat by law enforcement agents impatient for those inside to act in ways they could understand, predict, and control.

In addition to the fundamentally incompatible worldviews of the Branch Davidians and the law enforcement forces, the latter were under intense pressure from the media and organized anticult activists to "do something." Mainstream media accounts of controversies about MRMs—quickly labeled "cults"—tend toward sensational accounts of violence and sexual deviance (van Driel and Richardson 1988; Richardson 1993); the Waco standoff was no exception in that regard. "Doing something" was also a major component of the FBI/BATF cultures. The state began the interaction pattern in the form of a violent confrontation, and it came to seem inexorable that it should end that way as well.[2]

Postevent evaluations done at the behest of the Justice Department make it clear that the strategy for dealing with the Branch Davidians once the standoff began changed from negotiation to pressure tactics and confrontation (Ammerman 1993; Stone 1993). The course of events in Waco provides dramatic confirmation of Harper and Le Beau's (1993) contention that the character of an MRM's secular opposition and the interaction pattern between the group and its opponents are the most significant factors in determining whether violence erupts. Both the history of American religious movements and the sociology of communalist religious organizations suggest that, far from being unique, the Branch Davidians offer yet another example of the difficulty American society has had with religious deviance.

The Constitutional Protection of Religious Freedom

The legal framework of church-state interactions in the United States is grounded in the Constitution's First Amendment:[3] "Congress shall make no law respecting an establishment of religion or prohibiting the free exercise thereof." The phrase has been generally interpreted as containing two clauses: the "establishment" clause prohibiting official sponsorship; and the "free exercise" clause prohibiting interference with religious expression. While on one hand complementary, as an official religion would restrict dissenters' religious freedom, there is a certain amount of logical tension between the two clauses. Thoroughly secularizing all aspects of government is often claimed to impinge upon the free exercise of religion itself, while providing special recognition to religious groups because of their religion can be construed as verging on an impermissible establishment (Demerath and Williams 1987). Historically, the free exercise clause has not been litigated as often as its companion establishment clause.

While plumbing the intentions of the framers is a tricky business, it is doubtful that their support for the free exercise of religion was meant to guarantee libertarian practices. It is most likely that the legal guarantee that government would not mandate religious belief or affiliation existed alongside the cultural assumption that the American populace was—and probably would remain—overwhelmingly Christian and generally Protestant. Certainly the courts, for the most part, have not understood the free exercise clause in terms expansive enough to cover the religious diversity existing today. However, they have often considered religion as particularly "privileged" by its mention in the First Amendment.

Davis (1993) notes that the lack of a clear definition of religion in the Constitution left the matter to later generations to contest within changing historical circumstances. One of the Supreme Court's first attempts to provide a definition of religion, and significantly, an early restriction on free exercise, was *Reynolds v. U.S.* (1878). *Reynolds* and a later case (*Davis v. Beason* [1890]) both upheld antipolygamy statutes. Though the laws were clearly aimed at the Mormons, the court ruled that the absolute freedom of religious belief did not extend to religious practices, particularly religious practices "inimical to the peace, good order and morals of society" (quoted in Davis 1993, 93).

It was not until the twentieth century that church-state law began to take up much room on the Supreme Court's docket,[4] and it is doubtful whether the *Reynolds* case would be decided today as it was in 1878. Constitutional law regarding free exercise since World War II has developed what is generally known as the "Sherbert-Yoder" test (*Sherbert v. Verner* [1963]; *Wisconsin v. Yoder* [1972]). The test calls for a "compelling state interest" standard; that is, the government is burdened to demonstrate that any abridgment of the right to free religious expression is justified by a compelling state interest. Considerations of the "centrality" of any contested practice to the religion in question, and whether the government's infringement is "substantial" and the "least restrictive" possible, all constrain state action (Robbins [1993] and Wood [1993a] offer fuller reviews).

The balance between religious free expression and state-supervised social order struck by the Sherbert-Yoder rationale has resulted in a number of practical compromises in social policy areas. For example, while adults cannot be forced to seek medical treatment that conflicts with their religious beliefs, children can be; the state has a compelling interest in guaranteeing children's health before they reach an age of consent. Consequently, Christian Scientists and Jehovah's Witnesses have been prosecuted for failing to consult medical science-based health care for their children.[5] Parental rights to religious beliefs and practices are counterbalanced by the societal consensus on the most effective form of health care. Similarly, schools and daycare centers run by churches are generally held to the health and safety standards applicable to secular organizations.

The state's "compelling interest" has fallen harder upon some religious groups than it has on others. Rarely are groups in the religious and cultural mainstream restrained from their central religious practices, whereas members of sects and "cults" have a long history of experiencing governmental intervention, including coercion, and having it upheld as constitutional. This pattern has been pervasive enough so that the history of the nation's religion-government interactions is less one of "church versus state" than it is "state versus sects," with mainstream churches often on the side of civil authorities (Demerath and Williams 1987, 81).

A recent Supreme Court decision, *Employment Division of Oregon v. Smith* (1990), has changed the ground rules governing free exercise decisions by severely constraining the grounds upon which religious groups and persons can claim impermissible state infringement on religious expression. In effect, the burden has shifted from the government to the religion group, forcing religious groups to demonstrate that governmental action is impermissible because it is directed at specific religious practices or groups with clear discriminatory intent (Robbins 1993). This in effect guts the free exercise provision, since any government action directed at a specific religious group could be decided on "establishment" grounds—such an action would unconstitutionally favor one religion over another. This is a significant broadening of the justificatory rationale the state may use for intervention and may be a powerful tool for future cases of government intervention and control. Indeed, approximately fifty church-state cases (federal and state) since 1990 have made references to *Smith* (Wood 1993b, 719).

Carmella (1992; 1993) offers analyses of free exercise litigation with a particular focus on the *Smith* decision and the changes it portends. She makes the shrewd point that the association of free exercise claims with marginal groups and "deviant" practices served to undermine general legal and political support for free exercise claims. In the 1960s and 1970s the proportion of marginal religious groups successfully pressing free exercise claims increased (see Way and Burt 1983). Carmella argues that the public now associates free exercise claims primarily with marginal or deviant groups; as a result, free exercise claims may be interpreted by many as a cynical dodge by con artists using religion to get around the law. Certainly, there are enough scams in American society to give that suspicion credibility.

A result of the weakening support for free exercise has been the government's ability to infringe upon "acculturated" religious practices without serious challenge. Acculturated religious practices are those practices that resemble secular activities—such as running schools or businesses—but are religiously motivated. Carmella (1992) notes that many such practices arise from a religious group's active engagement with its social world. Withdrawal from the world into monastic communities is clearly viewed as a religious activity. But engagement with the world, and participation in secular activities for religious reasons, are less clearly recognized. If individuals' motivations for actions are not recognized as relevant to whether the action is "religious" (as the *Smith* decision implies) determination of what is religious and what is secular must be made by "objective" means by outsiders. The decision effectively forces state authorities to decide what is authentically religious and therefore entitled to protection.

Carmella's argument is persuasive, with the addendum that acculturated religious practices arc associated not only with acculturated or mainstream religious groups. Marginal religious groups may be more likely to engage in acculturated practices as part of their efforts to construct the institutions that will keep an alien world at bay. Marginal movements may compensate for smaller memberships (and thus smaller donation resources) by running commercial activities; these may be "businesses," but they may be essential for a religious group—particularly a communalist group—to survive (Bromley and Robbins 1993; Robbins 1993).

Marginal religious groups in particular are likely to be committed to living communally. The groups often claim that this is religiously motivated—a religious duty similar to praying or holding services. The courts have generally been unsympathetic to this claim, holding that providing for members' necessities of life is not a tax-exempt purpose of the group (Emory and Zelenak 1985; Richardson 1988). Thus marginal groups, particularly corporatist ones, are most likely to have their acculturated practices infringed upon by state agencies who claim that their practices are secular activities seeking protection under a religious disguise. And as corporatist groups try to provide for all of their members' needs they are more likely to have more of the state's regulatory powers infringe upon them.

While Way and Burt (1983) demonstrated that marginal religions were more likely to press free exercise claims successfully in the 1960s and 1970s, that tide has clearly turned. The *Smith* decision marks a clear turn away from tolerance of those on the margins. *Smith* shifts power back to the government; coupled with other actions by the Reagan and Bush administrations, the course of church-state relations in the 1980s was "statist" (see Robbins 1987). The courts have allowed the government increasing latitude in fostering or participating in religious observances that might be perceived as sponsorship in establishment terms; simultaneously, the courts have given the state and its agencies increasing capacity to regulate religious practices in free exercise terms.

Increasing state control of religious life has benefited those groups closest to the cultural center. The separation of church and state is being construed in increasingly "majoritarian" terms (Williams and Demerath 1991). That is, the state is seen as properly keeping deviant groups out of the public sphere, or at least controlling their less conventional practices, while expressions of majoritarian religion are supported as fostering a public benefit or representing a nondivisive "culture" religion. In the *Smith* decision Justice Antonin Scalia notes, without apparent irony, that minority religions may have to turn to the legislative process for protection of their practices (Carmella 1993; Robbins 1993); it was precisely because the political process could not be counted on to prevent majoritarian discrimination that judicial protections were first developed.

Smith reverses the implicit definition of religion developed in free exercise cases over the past three decades. In a series of cases the court constructed an image of religion that was individualist rather than institutional, and functional rather than substantive (Gleason 1977). That is, what counted as authentic religion was the sincerity of the individual's beliefs, not membership or identification with an institution or group. Further, those beliefs need not have any particular substantive content (such as a doctrine of a supernatural god); what was important was that the relevant beliefs *function in the individual's conscience* as religious beliefs do. Two cases dealing with conscientious objection to military service (*United States v. Seeger* [1965]; *Welsh v. United States* [1970]) make this implicit definition most clear (Davis 1993). *Smith* obviously reverses this view, substituting an external standard of majoritarian legitimacy for subjective sincerity when assessing religion deserving free exercise protection.

The *Smith* decision caused an uproar among many scholars of church-state law and representatives of both marginal and mainstream religious groups. With almost unprecedented unity, a coalition of religious groups pressured Congress to pass legislation to restore the "compelling interest" test. As a result, in November 1993, the Religious Freedom Restoration Act (RFRA) became law, explicitly reinstating pre-*Smith* standards. Passed overwhelmingly by both chambers of Congress (its Senate sponsors were Catholic Democrat Edward Kennedy and Mormon Republican Orrin Hatch), RFRA is a clear expression of legislative intent to protect free exercise as it had been understood (Wood 1993b). Given *Smith*'s rationale of deference to the political process, RFRA may well succeed in undoing *Smith*'s changes. However, it is too early to document any effects of RFRA; also, any potential constitutional challenges to the act itself have not yet surfaced.

The social history of religious movements in the United States demonstrates that the boundaries of the culturally legitimate may change, but at any one time they push minority groups firmly to the margins. The dynamics of marginalization have been reflected in the changing fortunes of free religious expression in Constitutional law. These two themes come together in the government's actions against the Mt. Carmel Branch Davidians. It demonstrates that the difficult balance of social order and religious liberty can be fatal, even in the relatively tolerant climate of contemporary America.

Social Order and Religious Liberty: The Waco Case

In the wake of the disastrous ending to the confrontation with David Koresh and the Branch Davidians, the government has produced a variety of rationales for its actions. The two primary justifications for governmental action have been Koresh's weapons supply and allegations of child abuse. These rationales were used in varying proportions to start the initial BATF investigation, decide on the February raid, proceed with the April CS gas and tank assault, and justify the actions to the media and Congress.

Whether the government's actions against the Branch Davidians were violations of free exercise protection is to some extent a moot question. But considering the question is instructive for future situations in which a marginal religious group faces state action. In this section I consider each of the government's rationales in turn, beginning from the assumption that the Branch Davidian's status as a religious group entitled them to particular protection from government intervention and that any such intervention must be justified by the state's compelling interest in social order.

Certainly the prevalence and distribution of firearms in society are relevant to the state's interest in maintaining social order. If the weapons were purchased, owned, or operated illegally, the Branch Davidians' religion would not have entitled them to special protection. Further, an accumulation of weapons could at some point threaten the safety of people outside the group itself; that would be a clear case of a threat to public order.

The preponderance of evidence indicates that the Branch Davidian's weapons were acquired legally. Many were acquired in unassembled parts that were legal until assembled. Some of the guns had been adapted for automatic fire, but again the kits for doing that adaptation were also purchased legally. The primary issue in the search warrant affidavit was that many of the weapons were unregistered, thus making them illegal.

In any case, the Branch Davidians had a significant arsenal. Whether the weapons were perceived as a threat by their neighbors is a matter of some dispute. A neighbor had complained about hearing automatic weapons' fire on the Davidian compound. Some reports indicate that the report was investigated and not substantiated, but other reports claim that the local sheriff's frustration with trying to investigate the compound led him to approach the BATF. The search warrant affidavit claims that tips from parcel service and post office personnel first raised suspicions. Making the circumstances of the initial investigation even murkier are reports that Koresh had a good relationship with the sheriff, but viewed the BATF in apocalyptic terms as a representative of evil. There are also allegations that the BATF deliberately held automatic weapons practice sessions within the hearing range of the compound.

In any case, there is little evidence indicating widespread concern around Waco that the Branch Davidians were a significant threat; journalistic accounts record several of their neighbors responding favorably about the group (Solotaroff 1993). This was, after all, Texas; gun control is anathema, and military and weapon fascination is deeply ingrained in the culture. Koresh's arsenal was undoubtedly not the largest private collection in the state. While large numbers of weapons in private hands do not necessarily improve public safety, there is no firm evidence that the Branch Davidian's arsenal had directly threatened anyone outside the Mt. Carmel compound.

Thus this justification for targeting the Branch Davidians for investigation seems a bit strained. It seems doubtful that the BATF was deliberately targeting a religious group for investigation. Weapons, not deviant religion, drew the government's attention. But there is evidence that law enforcement officers tend to have basic suspicions of sectarian religious movements; for example, the search warrant affidavit is filled with pejorative references to the "cult" and doubts as to Koresh's religious sincerity. Also, the focus of law enforcement officials on Koresh's sex life demonstrates the ease with which the government saw the Branch Davidians primarily as elements of the lunatic fringe. These factors may have influenced the BATF's decision to investigate Mt. Carmel. The Branch Davidians were seen as irrational, unpredictable, and potentially dangerous. The members had, it seemed, voluntarily relinquished personal autonomy to a charismatic leader—an action "irrational" by definition according to a "contractual" worldview (Bromley and Busching 1988). Also, an isolated and marginal religious group was unlikely to have powerful political allies coming to its defense if the agency pressed its investigation. Thus the Davidians' status as a marginal religious group no doubt contributed to the BATF's decision to investigate. An MRM is an easy target for persecution even if there is doubt as to whether there is a genuine threat to public safety.

A post-*Smith* interpretation of the free exercise clause, however, would have little trouble rationalizing the BATF's concern for weapons. One could claim that despite Koresh's apocalyptic beliefs the weapons themselves were not integral to the group's religious mission in theological terms and were thus not protected. Controlling firearms is part of government's secular task for providing public safety and any harm to the religious group's sense of mission or purpose would be incidental. Since firearm laws are "religion neutral"—they do not specify religious groups for any special treatment with regard to weapons—the government's attempt at regulation is not an infringement on the Davidians' First Amendment guarantees.

Indeed, even before the court's recent contraction of free exercise protection one could make a case that the state's compelling interest in a peaceful civic order allows the government to regulate large collections of weapons in civil society. Whether the Branch Davidians had the largest arsenal in the state was irrelevant; securing social order requires that the state maintain its monopoly on force.

Such reasoning has some appeal, particularly to those who doubt that society benefits from individuals owning machine guns and hand grenades. However, one must still wonder why a small religious group living in a rural setting—whose weapons were generally legal—was the subject of intervention. There was a history of guns and violence at the compound—Koresh and several followers were acquitted in a 1987 shooting incident with the group's former leader George Roden. But Koresh and his codefendants surrendered peacefully after that situation. In fact, that incident raises more questions about the BATF's decision to investigate and their mode of serving the warrants.

While the regulation of weapons is not necessarily a constitutional infringement of religious liberty, certainly this particular enforcement of that regulatory power seems motivated (or at least abetted) by the group's status as a "cult," and thus facilitated by religious prejudice. That the group had no history of threatening nonmembers may be relevant in this regard. The government seems reluctant to regulate weapons in many other contexts. If religious groups are not accorded any special First Amendment protection for a weapons arsenal, neither are they subject to particular restrictions based on assumptions of irrationality.

The issue of child abuse is more difficult in both conceptual and moral terms. An ongoing debate in American politics concerns whether representatives of the public should intervene in private relationships that are exploitative or abusive. Once that question is answered, the line differentiating an "exploitative" from a "committed" relationship must be defined. Historically, Americans have believed that most freely chosen relationships between adults should be free from governmental interference.[6] It is neither unusual nor peculiar to religion for adults to subject themselves to rigorous physical discipline and extreme emotional demands. In social-psychological terms, there are similarities between the Branch Davidians' religious discipline and some of the training experienced by police or Marines, experiences said to "build character." And it can be persuasively argued that the right to individual autonomy is substantially undermined if one is prevented from forfeiting one's autonomy to a goal or cause considered worthy. As Bromley and Busching (1988) point out, covenantal social relationships often require demonstrations of commitment and sacrifice that attenuate individual autonomy.

Opponents of communal religious groups claim that the relationships found within "cults" are so psychologically dangerous that they cannot be voluntary. That is the crux of the controversy over "brainwashing": those who charge MRMs with mind control practices assume that some beliefs and practices are so deviant and damaging they cannot be freely held. Thus members of MRMs have not made a choice under conditions in which they simultaneously had the knowledge of what they were doing and the capacity to act otherwise (see Bromley and Robbins 1993). The judiciary has generally sided against charges of mind control. While unconventional religions continue to elicit controversy, the courts have generally been unwilling to negate decisions about religious commitments made by adults when there is no sign of physical coercion.

The protection of religious free expression does not, however, automatically extend to activities that jeopardize the safety or health (physical or emotional) of children. While adults have the right to accept a variety of commitments for themselves, parents have limited rights to impose such discipline on their children. The difficult constitutional debate is whether the free exercise clause enlarges parental prerogatives to raise their children as they see fit. On one hand, religious liberty is severely constricted if one is not free to pass on one's religious beliefs and heritage to one's children. This was the essence of the *Yoder* decision. On the other hand, children cannot be said to assume such commitments voluntarily, and it is in society's larger interest—and a matter of the child's rights—that children be free from abuse, religiously motivated or not.

Concern for children's welfare is close to the top of American society's social agenda (see Best 1990); allegations of abuse are now often investigated from the perspective that they must be disproven rather than proven. Religion has not been spared from recent accusations of abuse. Revelations of sexual abuse by Roman Catholic priests have not produced state-directed action against the entire organization, but criminal cases have been brought against individuals and civil cases have held the Church culpable. Similar cases have been made against other religious providers of social services for young people. As with other situations of abuse, the long history of denial and societal coverups of the exploitation of children has produced good reasons for taking allegations seriously. The courts have become increasingly protective of children, even from their parents.

However, it is easy to view the government's concern with child abuse at Mt. Carmel cynically. The original affidavit requesting a search warrant mentions the child abuse allegations—but neglects to note that they had been investigated and not substantiated. It is curious that the Bureau of Alcohol, Tobacco, and Firearms would discuss child abuse allegations at all when constructing a rationale for a search for weapons. Koresh's arrest warrant was solely on weapons charges. Further, while Attorney General Janet Reno cited child welfare concerns as a primary concern for the April assault, it was admitted that there was no hard evidence that abuse was occurring. The children released from the compound during the standoff did not show clear signs of abuse. And a CS gas assault on an enclosed building that was housing children hardly seems calculated to keep their health and safety uppermost.

Further, allegations of child abuse in cults is widespread. Certainly it has historical pedigree going back to the anti-Catholic and anti-Mormon literatures of the nineteenth century (Lewis 1989). Many of the stories now circulating have deep structures almost identical to that earlier literature. Further, anticult activists have increasingly turned to allegations of child abuse in order to prompt government agencies to investigate unconventional religious movements. The anticult movement's brainwashing charge is waning in its effectiveness. Not only is mind control a difficult charge to prove, it does not lend itself to "medicalization" as well as child abuse charges do.[7] Many conservative religious groups advocate corporal punishment for children, including the Davidians. Advocacy alone may be grounds for investigation, but this investigation had not produced hard evidence. Again, the Davidians' marginal status seemed to leave them open to governmental inquiry, an issue on the boundary of violating their constitutional protections.

In sum, whether the government's particular justifications for investigating the Mt. Carmel compound were violations of the Branch Davidians' rights to religious liberty is not a clear issue. The Davidians' status as a religious group offers them some privileged constitutional protections from government interference. Amassing weapons and abusing children, however, are grounds upon which the state can argue justifiably that it has a compelling interest in regulation. Yet, the manner in which the government pressed these claims seemed to give scant regard to issues of religious liberty; the Davidians' status as a marginal religious group living in a communal setting seemed to make them a more likely target for investigation. Thus there was the unfortunate but not unusual irony that a group of religious nonconformists—exactly the people for whom constitutional protections were developed—were subject to harassment and investigation from representatives of the government that guaranteed religious liberty.

While there is no easy or clear answer as to whether the Branch Davidians were illegally persecuted by the government, there are still questions as to whether the state should have intervened at Mt. Carmel. These are matters of values and politics as much as law. More crucial than constitutionality is the question as to whether prejudice toward marginal religion led the government to focus on the Branch Davidians in the first place. And once the interactions started, and the failed raid led to a prolonged standoff, a complete lack of understanding of communalist religious groups led law enforcement agencies into the mistakes that took so many lives.

As several of the Justice Department's evaluative reports state, the FBI and BATF need to improve their knowledge of religion and its dynamics. In retrospect, perhaps the only real surprise of the Waco conflagration is that the government confronted an apocalyptic communalist group led by a charismatic leader with paranoid tendencies and a $200,000 arsenal—and was then "surprised" that it ended violently.

But beyond tactical considerations, law enforcement agencies need to acquaint themselves with some of the social realities of religious diversity and the subtleties of the constitutional protection of religious liberty. As with many aspects of America's legal system, the presumption for liberty means that some charlatans and con artists will benefit from protection. Such is the price of a free society. Large collections of weapons and child abuse are serious matters. Religious groups do not forfeit their status from suspicions and allegations.

Religious pluralism is on the rise; if religious liberty and equality are to keep pace with it, considerations of free expression must not get lost in moral panics or knee-jerk law-and-order reactions.

Notes

1. The eleven Branch Davidians who survived the siege stood trial in San Antonio, Texas, on murder and conspiracy charges stemming from the events of February 28—not for preraid activities.

2. I am also firmly convinced that aspects of law enforcement's organizational culture pushed the FBI toward a confrontational final solution. Fellow cops lay dead; their killers could not go unpunished. Any backing off would be disrespectful and a sign of weakness.

3. Wilson (1990) makes a persuasive argument that Article VI's prohibition of "religious tests" for public office is more indicative of the framers' intentions toward religion and government than are the clauses of the First Amendment.

4. Of course, it was not until mid-century that the religion clauses of the First Amendment were even deemed applicable to state governments.

5. However, Christian Scientists have won in five out of six cases.

6. Interracial and same-sex romantic relationships, of course, have been and continue to be publicly regulated or even criminalized.

7. Also, the antidote for cultic mind control—deprogramming—is of dubious legality itself and thus has diminished as an effective ideological weapon.

References

Ammerman, Nancy T. 1993. "Report to the Justice and Treasury Departments Regarding Law Enforcement Interaction with the Branch Davidians in Waco, Texas." Washington, DC: U.S. Department of Justice.

Bailey, Paul. 1970. *Ghost Dance Messiah.* Los Angeles: Westernlore Press.

Beckford, James A. 1985. *Cult Controversies.* London: Tavistock.

Bennett, David H. 1988. *The Party of Fear.* Chapel Hill: University of North Carolina Press.

Best, Joel. 1990. *Threatened Children.* Chicago: University of Chicago Press.

Boyer, Paul. 1992. *When Time Shall Be No More.* Cambridge: Harvard Belknap Press.

Bromley, David G., and Bruce C. Busching. 1988. "Understanding the Structure of Contractual and Covenantal Social Relations: Implications for the Sociology of Religion." *Sociological Analysis* 49 (S): 15–32.

Bromley, David G., and Thomas Robbins. 1993. "The Role of Government in Regulating New and Nonconventional Religions." In *The Role of Government in Monitoring and Regulating Religion in Public Life,* edited by J. E. Wood, Jr., and D. Davis, pp. 205–40. Waco, TX: Dawson Institute for Church-State Studies, Baylor University.

Carmella, Angela C. 1992. "A Theological Critique of Free Exercise Jurisprudence." *George Washington Law Review* 60: 782–808.

———. 1993. "The Religion Clauses and Acculturated Religious Conduct: Boundaries for the Regulation of Religion." In *The Role of Government in Monitoring and Regulating Religion in Public Life,* edited by J. E. Wood, Jr., and D. Davis, pp. 21–49. Waco, TX: Dawson Institute for Church-State Studies, Baylor University.

Cochran, Clarke E. 1990. *Religion in Public and Private Life.* New York: Routledge Press.

Commager, Henry Steele. 1983. "Religion and Politics in American History." In *Religion and Politics,* edited by J. E. Wood, Jr., pp. 37–56. Waco, TX: Dawson Institute for Church-State Studies, Baylor University.

Davis, Derek. 1993. "The Courts and the Constitutional Meaning of

'Religion': A History and Critique." In *The Role of Government in Monitoring and Regulating Religion in Public Life,* edited by J. E. Wood, Jr., and D. Davis, pp. 89–119. Waco, TX: Dawson Institute for Church-State Studies, Baylor University.

Demerath, N. J., III, and Rhys H. Williams. 1987. "A Mystical Past and an Uncertain Future?" In *Church-State Relations: Tensions and Transitions,* edited by T. Robbins and R. Robertson, pp. 77–90. New Brunswick, NJ: Transaction.

———. 1992. *A Bridging of Faiths: Religion and Politics in a New England City.* Princeton: Princeton University Press.

Emory, Meade, and Lawrence Zelenak. 1985. "The Tax Exempt Status of Communitarian Religious Organizations: An Unnecessary Controversy?" In *Cults, Culture, and the Law,* edited by T. Robbins, W. C. Shepherd, and J. McBride, pp. 177–201. Chico, CA: Scholars Press.

Gleason, Phillip. 1977. "Blurring the Line of Separation: Education, Civil Religion, and Teaching about Religion." *Journal of Church and State* 19: 517–38.

Handy, Robert T. 1984. *A Christian America: Protestant Hopes and Historical Realities.* 2d ed. New York: Oxford University Press.

Harper, Charles L., and Bryan F. Le Beau. 1993. "The Social Adaptation of Marginal Religious Movements in America." *Sociology of Religion* 54: 171–92.

Lewis, James R. 1989. "Apostates and the Legitimation of Repression: Some Historical and Empirical Perspectives on the Cult Controversy." *Sociological Analysis* 49: 386–96.

Lofland, John, and James T. Richardson. 1984. "Religious Movement Organizations: Elemental Forms and Dynamics." *Research in Social Movements, Conflicts, and Change* 7: 29–51.

Mauss, Armand L., and M. Gerald Bradford. 1988. "Mormon Assimilation and Politics: Toward a Theory of Mormon Church Involvement in National U.S. Politics." In *The Politics of Religion and Social Change,* edited by A. Shupe and J. Hadden, pp. 40–66. New York: Paragon.

McCarthy, John D., David W. Britt, and Mark Wolfson. 1991. "The Institutional Channeling of Social Movements by the State in the United States." *Research in Social Movements, Conflicts, and Change* 13: 45–76.

Moore, R. Laurence. 1986. *Religious Outsiders and the Making of Americans.* New York: Oxford University Press.

Perrow, Charles. 1991. "A Society of Organizations." *Theory and Society* 20: 725–62.

Richardson, James T. 1985. "The 'Deformation' of New Religions: Impacts of Societal and Organizational Factors." In *Cults, Culture, and the Law,* edited by T. Robbins, W. C. Shepherd, and J. McBride, pp. 163–76. Chico, CA: Scholars Press.

———. 1988. "Changing Times: Religion, Economics, and the Law in Contemporary America." *Sociological Analysis* 49 (S): 1–14.

———. 1993. "Definitions of Cult: From Sociological-Technical to Popular-Negative." *Review of Religious Research* 34: 348–56.

Robbins, Thomas. 1987. "Church-State Tension in the United States." In *Church-State Relations: Tensions and Transitions*, edited by T. Robbins and R. Robertson, pp. 67–76. New Brunswick, NJ: Transaction.

———. 1993. "The Intensification of Church-State Conflict in the United States." *Social Compass* 40: 505–27.

Robertson, Roland, and JoAnn Chirico. 1985. "Humanity, Globalization, and Worldwide Religious Resurgence: A Theoretical Explanation." *Sociological Analysis* 46 (3): 219–42.

Roof, Wade Clark, and William McKinney. 1987. *American Mainline Religion*. New Brunswick, NJ: Rutgers University Press.

Solotaroff, Ivan. 1993. "The Last Revelation from Waco." *Esquire*, July.

Stark, Rodney. 1987. "How New Religions Succeed: A Theoretical Model." In *The Future of New Religious Movements*, edited by D. Bromley and P. Hammond, pp. 11–29. Macon, GA: Mercer University Press.

Stone, Alan A. 1993. "Report and Recommendations Concerning the Handling of Incidents Such as the Branch Davidian Standoff in Waco, Texas." Washington, DC: U.S. Department of Justice.

Utley, Robert M. 1993. *The Lance and the Shield: The Life and Times of Sitting Bull*. New York: Henry Holt and Co.

van Driel, Barend, and James T. Richardson. 1988. "Categorization of New Religious Movements in American Print Media." *Sociological Analysis* 49: 171–83.

Way, Frank, and Barbara Burt. 1983. "Religious Marginality and the Free Exercise Clause." *American Political Science Review* 77: 654–65.

Williams, Rhys H. 1994. "Movement Dynamics and Social Change: Transforming Fundamentalist Ideology and Organizations." In *Accounting for Fundamentalisms: The Dynamics of Movements*, edited by M. E. Marty and R. S. Appleby, pp. 783–831. Chicago: University of Chicago Press.

Williams, Rhys H., and N. J. Demerath III. 1991. "Religion and Political Process in an American City." *American Sociological Review* 56: 417–31.

Wilson, John F. 1990. "Religion, Government, and Power in the New American Nation." In *Religion and American Politics*, edited by M. A. Noll, pp. 77–91. New York: Oxford University Press.

Wood, James E., Jr. 1988. "Religious Pluralism and American Society." In *Ecumenical Perspectives on Church and State*, edited by J. E. Wood, Jr., pp. 1–18. Waco, TX: Dawson Institute for Church-State Studies, Baylor University.

———. 1993a. "Government Intervention in Religious Affairs: An Introduction." In *The Role of Government in Monitoring and Regulating Religion in Public Life*, edited by J. E. Wood, Jr., and D. Davis, pp. 1–20. Waco, TX: Dawson Institute for Church-State Studies, Baylor University.

———. 1993b. "The Restoration of the Free Exercise Clause." *Journal of Church and State* 35 (4): 715–22.

14

EDWARD MCGLYNN GAFFNEY, JR.

The

Waco

Tragedy

*Constitutional Concerns
and Policy Perspectives*

Introduction: On Second-Guessing

I candidly acknowledge that this essay is an attempt to second-guess the acts and omissions of the federal officials responsible for the Waco tragedy. Since second-guessing is normally thought inappropriate, I offer some

I am grateful to Steven R. Williams for research assistance, and I would like to acknowledge the friendly criticism of several colleagues who reviewed an earlier draft of this essay: Richard Baepler, Bruce Berner, Stephen Carter, Jesse Choper, John Garvey, Mary Ann Glendon, Stanley Hauerwas, Dean M. Kelley, Wayne La Fave, Douglas Laycock, Martin Marty, Michael McConnell, Mark Tushnet, Richard Parker, Alan Stone, Cass Sunstein, David Vandercoy, and John Howard Yoder. I, of course, accept responsibility for the views expressed here.

comments at the end of the essay explaining why I regard it a legitimate exercise in a democracy that has established important constitutional limits on governmental authority.

Suffice it for now to observe that President Clinton ordered a
"vigorous and thorough investigation" of the events at Waco, and
that on September 30, 1993, Treasury Secretary Lloyd Bentsen submitted to President Clinton the *Report of Department of the Treasury on the Bureau of Alcohol, Tobacco, and Firearms Investigation of Vernon Wayne Howell, Also Known as David Koresh* (U.S.
Department of Treasury 1993); and on October 8, 1993, Attorney
General Janet Reno released the *Evaluation of the Handling of the
Branch Davidian Stand-Off in Waco, Texas, February 28 to April
19, 1993* (U.S. Department of Justice 1993). A month later the Justice Department released a paper by Harvard University psychiatrist Dr. Alan Stone (1993), *Report and Recommendations Concerning the Handling of Incidents Such as the Branch Davidian
Standoff in Waco, Texas.* Thus both the Treasury Department and
the Justice Department have also undertaken their own forms of
second-guessing, which appear in these two reports. In both
instances, moreover, Treasury and Justice urged external reviewers,
including peace officers such as Los Angeles Police Chief Willie
Williams, and scholars such as Nancy Ammerman (who has contributed an essay to this volume), to look over their shoulders and
evaluate their work.

My addition to the second-guessing is a reflection that the Constitution did not serve to inform the discretion of the government,
either in planning the raid on the Branch Davidians in the first place
or in bringing it to its tragic end. Frequently issues of constitutional law are framed in lawsuits to determine whether a governmental
official has violated rights secured under the federal Constitution or
under some federal statute. On March 22, 1994, the children, parents, and siblings of eleven members of the Branch Davidian community who died in Waco filed a civil lawsuit in the federal court in
Houston, charging various officials within the Treasury Department's Bureau of Alcohol, Tobacco, and Firearms (BATF) and the FBI
with violation of their constitutional rights.[1] This essay does not
hazard a guess as to the outcome of this litigation. It focuses instead
on the power of the Constitution to inform the discretion of officials who have undertaken a sworn duty to uphold it. In my view,
that duty is sturdier than that which courts acknowledge as a governmental obligation in lawsuits in which the government is a

defendant. Thus the Constitution ought constantly to serve as a reminder to governmental officials of strong limits on their authority, long before they are haled into court. Second-guessing by an alert citizenry is especially needful when, as I illustrate in this essay, the government does not tell the truth to the public about its misconduct.

A Brief Narrative of the Facts

The facts in the Waco episode are complicated. As the Treasury report acknowledges, moreover, the public reception of the event was not made easier by the intentional distortion of important facts by government officials at several turns. My purpose here is not to "set the record straight," a task that would require much more space than this essay allows, but simply to lay out a detached statement of the facts essential to the discussion that follows.

The history of the Branch Davidian community[2] is set forth in the essays by Pitts and Bromley and Silver in this volume and is not repeated here. It is enough to note that Vernon Wayne Howell became the leader of the Branch Davidians in 1987 after an armed struggle at the community's compound with George Roden, who had emerged as the leader of the community in 1985. Howell was acquitted of the criminal charges stemming from this incident.

In 1992 two difficulties arose for the community. The first involved allegations of child abuse by former members of the community. Joyce Sparks, a caseworker with the Child Protective Services (CPS), a division of the State of Texas Department of Protective and Regulatory Services, later reported to the BATF that in the course of investigating the complaints about child abuse, she heard Koresh say: "My time is coming. When I reveal myself as the messenger and my time comes, what happens will make the riots in L.A. [after the first acquittal of LAPD officers who beat Rodney King] pale in comparison" (U.S. Department of Treasury 1993, 30). The Treasury report clarifies that this statement was made to Sparks on April 30, 1992, the day after the L.A. riots (1993, 126), but the report nowhere mentions that the CPS had concluded that there was no evidence to support the allegations about child abuse and dismissed the complaint. Although the federal government has no jurisdiction over such matters, Attorney General Reno, who has an otherwise commendable concern about the welfare of children and its relation to crime, repeatedly referred to this allegation as a justification for her order to attack the community compound, including the children within it at the time, on April 19, 1993

The second major difficulty for the community, which ultimately led to its destruction, concerned the amassing of weapons at the compound. In May 1992 Daniel Weyenberg of the McLennan County Sheriff's Department informed the BATF office in Austin that a United Parcel Service (UPS) agent had informed him that members of the Branch Davidian community had received shipments of firearms worth more than $10,000, inert grenade casings, and a substantial quantity of an explosive known as black powder. On June 9, a neighbor reported to the sheriff's office that he heard a noise that sounded like machine-gun fire at the Mt. Carmel compound. The sheriff also notified the BATF of this report.

BATF Special Agent Davy Aguilera formally initiated an investigation into potential violations of federal gun laws by Koresh and his followers. This investigation was identified as "sensitive" within the bureau, meaning that it required supervision by the regional and national offices. Aguilera first followed the paper trail of the purchases of weapons identified in the invoices for UPS shipments. He then interviewed as many former members of the community as he could identify, including Isabel and Guillermo Andrade, and Jeannine Bunds and her daughter, Robyn, and son, David. Aguilera gathered (unsworn) testimony about Koresh's sexual abuse from Poia Vaega, a former member of the community living in New Zealand. He secured an affidavit from Marc Breault, a former member of the community living in Australia; Breault's sworn testimony refers to child abuse by Koresh (paddling of children), to the presence of firearms, including AK-47s, and to Koresh's disdain for gun control laws, including his desire to manufacture machine guns. In January 1993, Aguilera interviewed David Block, another former Branch Davidian, who reported that two members of the community were using a metal milling machine and a metal lathe to produce weapons, that Koresh was amassing an arsenal of weapons, including fifteen AR-15s, twenty-five AK-47s, and three "streetsweepers" (12-gauge shotguns which rotate the magazine to position the next shot for firing), and that Koresh posted armed guards at the compound every night (U.S. Department of Treasury 1993, 27–33).

On January 11, 1993, BATF established an undercover house near the compound, from which BATF agents posing as college students maintained surveillance of the members of the community. BATF Special Agent Robert Rodriguez established contact with Koresh on January 28, feigning interest in purchasing a horse walker on the compound. Koresh invited Rodriguez to join the community's Bible study group, which he did. Rodriguez gained Koresh's confidence swiftly, and continued to interact as a neighbor.

On February 25, Aguilera secured from United States Magistrate Judge Dennis G. Green a warrant for the arrest of David Koresh, and a warrant to search the premises of the Mt. Carmel compound for illegal weapons. Some of the information in the affidavit submitted by Aguilera in support of his application for warrants was based on the recollection of former community members about the situation in the compound as it was while they were still members, that is, over a year before their testimony.

On February 26, the afternoon of the day on which the World Trade Center had been bombed, with a devastating impact on the Secret Service, Acting Secretary of the Treasury for Enforcement John P. Simpson directed that the raid be called off, because of "grave reservations" over the adequacy of precautions to ensure the safety of BATF agents and those inside the compound (U.S. Department of Treasury 1993, 75–76, 177–79). Ronald Noble, who was then acting as a consultant to the BATF pending confirmation of his appointment as assistant secretary of the Treasury for enforcement, concurred with this view. BATF Director Stephen Higgins offered no objection at the time of Simpson's decision, but later called back to urge Simpson to reconsider his order, arguing that the warrants had to be executed forcefully because Koresh was not likely to surrender voluntarily, and assuring both Simpson and Noble that "those directing the raid were instructed to cancel the operation if they learned that its secrecy had been compromised" (U.S. Department of Treasury Report 1993, 179). On these understandings, Simpson revoked his earlier decision and let the raid go forward.

On February 27, Higgins informed Simpson that the first in a series of articles about Koresh entitled "The Sinful Messiah" had appeared in a local newspaper, but that it did not contain any suggestion that law enforcement was imminent. Higgins remained confident that the raid could proceed as scheduled, and stressed that the raid needed to go forward on Sunday because Koresh would eventually conclude from the newspaper stories that he was the subject of a federal investigation.

Early on the morning of February 28, BATF agents heavily armed with semiautomatic handguns, AR-15s, and MP-5 submachine guns, set out in a convoy a mile long to conduct a "dynamic entry" of the Branch Davidian compound in an effort to execute the arrest and search warrants.

As it turns out, the decision by the government to seek some free publicity of its efforts to enforce the law proved to be a fatal flaw in the execution of the warrants. A television cameraman named Jim Peeler who had been notified by the government about the raid, and who had apparently lost his way, inadvertently tipped off a member of the Branch Davidian community named David Jones, when asking Jones for directions to Mt. Carmel. Agent Robert Rodriguez was inside the compound when Jones reported to Koresh the news of the impending raid. Rodriguez was understandably concerned that he might not be able to extricate himself from the compound, but an agitated Koresh shook hands with him and let him go. Rodriguez promptly notified the Deputy Tactical Coordinator, Jim Cavanaugh, that the element of surprise had been lost and that Koresh was expecting a raid. Cavanaugh then brought this information to the tactical coordinator, Chuck Sarabyn, who decided to go forward with the armed attack anyway. In explanations to the media after the raid, BATF officials repeatedly lied about these facts, suggesting that the raid would never have been carried out had the government realized that the element of surprise had been lost (U.S. Department of Treasury 1993, 193–210).

During the gun battle, Branch Davidian Wayne Martin called the Waco authorities on the emergency 911 line and repeatedly pleaded that the attack be called off, in part because of the presence of innocent children within the compound. After ninety minutes of gunfire, in which confusion reigned both within the compound and within the BATF, a cease-fire was eventually arranged, but not before four BATF agents (Conway LeBleu, Todd McKeehan, Robert Williams, and Steven Willis) had lost their lives, as had six of the Branch Davidians (Winston Blake, Peter Hipsman, Perry Jones, Peter Gent, Michael Schroeder, and Jaydean Wendell).

On the evening of February 28, the command over the situation passed to the FBI, which at first exercised remarkable restraint by mounting a standoff and attempting to negotiate with Koresh and his followers. Some progress was made in this phase. For example, some adults and children came out of the compound. After a few days, however, the patience of the FBI officials evidently wore thin. They switched roles, from that of a "conciliatory, trust-building negotiator to that of a "more demanding and intimidating negotiator" (Stone 1993, 41), and the FBI began concentrating on tactical pressure, by using "all-out psycho-physiological warfare intended to stress and intimidate the Branch Davidians . . . and by 'tightening the noose' with a circle of armored vehicles" (p. 10).

Finally, on April 19, on the order of the new attorney general, the government attacked the compound with tanks in order to breach the community's walls and put an end to the siege by placing canisters of

CS gas throughout the compound. CS gas has the effect of producing choking, chest pain, gagging, and nausea in healthy adults; Dr. Stone expressed the view that "It is difficult to believe that the U.S. government would deliberately plan to expose twenty-five children, most of them infants and toddlers, to C.S. gas for forty-eight hours. . . . It is difficult to understand why a person whose primary concern was the safety of the children would agree to the FBI's plan" (1993, 29, 39). Military use of this gas was banned by the Chemical Weapons Convention, an international covenant to which 100 nations, including the United States, joined as high contracting parties in 1993. Amnesty International declares the gas "particularly dangerous when launched directly into homes or other buildings" (Wood 1993, 233–34). No federal officials lost their lives on this occasion, but the overwhelming majority of the Branch Davidians remaining within the compound were consumed in the flames that erupted shortly after the government's final assault on the compound.

Some Difficulties with the Official Reports

To the extent that I disagree with some of the conclusions reached in the two official reports referred to above, a decent respect for the role of these federal officials—to paraphrase Thomas Jefferson—compels me "to state the causes for the separation," or for my disagreement with the government.

First, it is not inconsequential that the Treasury report refers to the events of February 28 as an "ambush" (p. 1). On the government's theory, the first shots were fired by the Branch Davidians who lay in wait to "murder" the federal agents. This theory, however, was roundly rejected not only by Dr. Stone, who filed an independent report with the Justice Department (Stone 1993, 18–21), but also by the jurors in San Antonio who rendered verdicts on February 26, 1994, in the subsequent criminal trial of the Branch Davidians who survived the events at Waco. Although it remains unclear who fired the first shots, the jury acquitted all the defendants of the charge of murder.

Second, it is not a small quibble that the Treasury report is dedicated to the memory of the "four courageous ATF special agents" named above (pp. iii, v), while the six Branch Davidians killed in the same event are relegated to anonymity. This mentality is all too reminiscent of the approach to recent American foreign wars, such as the Vietnam War and the Gulf War, in which attention is focused exclusively on the body count of dead American soldiers. At least with the

Civil War and with World War I, historians recall the terrible carnage on both sides of those conflicts, and with World War II we at least continue to be horrified by the victims of the Holocaust. So why be insensitive to the fallen on either side at Waco?

Third, the BATF planned to surprise the Davidians, but did not call off the raid when the element of surprise was lost through the inadvertent contact with a member of the Branch Davidian community by a television journalist who had lost his way to the "dynamic entry" at Mt. Carmel. The Treasury report exposes and criticizes the official lies repeatedly issued to the media shortly after the events of February 28 about the fact that BATF officials knew they had lost the element of surprise, but decided to go forward anyway (pp. 165–75; 193–210). The Justice Department report is completely silent on this matter, perhaps because the department wished to pursue vigorously the ambush theory in the subsequent criminal trial against the holocaust survivors.

Fourth, the Treasury report criticized the lack of a control agent as a serious flaw in the planning decision to go forward with the raid (p. 167). This flaw was rectified from the government's perspective by the prompt decision to transfer authority over the operation to the FBI. I would, however, go further than this criticism. Although the FBI was better equipped as an institution than the BATF to comprehend the complex nature of the religious community the government had surrounded, even this advantage remained only notional or theoretical, for the command post established at the site ignored the perspectives of the FBI behavioral science experts at Waco who appreciated the community's intense religious convictions and who were offering a different interpretation of the events that were unfolding (Ammerman, this volume; Stone 1993, 12). In short, the ones who had most to contribute were isolated from the decision-making process. Thus in the siege that lasted for fifty-one days, the tactical approach that prevailed was premised on an evaluation of the situation as one involving a mission to rescue "hostages" held under the sway and control of David Koresh.

Three Constitutional Values That Should Inform Federal Policy

The usual criticism of second-guessing is that it is anachronistic; replaying the game on Monday morning, for example. I think I avoid this problem here because the normative judgments that have led me into disagreement with the government surely could have been known at the time of the events. These judgments are widely shared perspectives arising from the high regard in our society for the right of the people to live out their religious convictions without governmental interference, the right of the people to keep and bear arms, and the right of the people to be secure in their homes from unreasonable searches and seizures. None of these three constitutional guarantees is an absolute bar to governmental involvement in the lives of the people. For example, the government may stop a religious practice that threatens the public safety without violating the First Amendment. It may regulate the possession of at least some kinds of weapons without violating the Second Amendment. And by the very terms of the Fourth Amendment, it may conduct warranted or reasonable searches and seizures. But these three freedoms are secured in the Bill of Rights precisely to set limits on governmental power, and that rather elementary fact appears to have been neglected by the federal policymakers who planned and executed the events at Waco.

In this chapter I explore each of these competing constitutional considerations, concluding that the Waco tragedy could and should have been avoided if the considerable discretion of the policymakers in these events had been more carefully informed by the underlying commitment of our society to privacy in our home environment, to possession of weapons by the people, and to religious freedom. Although all three of these constitutional principles were interrelated in this episode, each merits separate comment. The narrative flow of the events can unfold more easily and the issues can be analyzed more sharply by exploring them in the following order: (1) the ineffectiveness of this raid as a means of ensuring compliance with federal law limiting gun ownership (the Second Amendment issue), (2) the defective process of executing the arrest and search warrants (the Fourth Amendment issue), and (3) the availability of meaningful alternative mechanisms of enforcing the federal interest in gun control in a manner less restrictive of the religious freedom of the Branch Davidians (the First Amendment issue).

I. The Ineffectiveness of the Waco Raid as a Means of Ensuring Compliance with Federal Restraints on Gun Ownership

The first ground for questioning the legitimacy of the government raid on the religious community at Mt. Carmel is found in the command of the Second Amendment: "A well regulated militia, being necessary to the security of a free State, the right of the people to keep and bear Arms shall not be infringed." The full text of this provision clearly discloses that the framers had in mind some functional relation between the people's right to keep and bear arms and the need for common defense reflected in the ability to raise a militia at short notice.

The important previous question, of course, is: "Who gets to raise the militia, the people or the prince?" First, one must note the different historical responses to this question that lay behind the Second Amendment. For example, James I and Charles I with their notions of the divine rights of kings answered the question very differently from the way that Charles Cromwell and the Parliamentarians did. In Stuart England the phenomenon of the standing army was viewed as a potent weapon of royal prerogative, an "instrument of fear intended to preserve the prince" (Friedman 1969).

Exploring the purpose of the Second Amendment against the background of Stuart England and the eighteenth-century debates over popular sovereignty, Vandercoy argues that the original intent of this provision was not only to protect each individual's right to keep and bear arms, but also to "guarantee that individuals acting collectively could throw off the yokes of any oppressive government which might arise. Thus, the right envisioned was not only the right to be armed, but to be armed at a level equal to the government" (1994, 1009). Other scholars have also suggested an insurrectionist theory of the Second Amendment, according to which citizens have a constitutional right to engage in armed insurrection against tyrannical governmental authority, whether state or federal (Halbrook 1984, 1991; Levinson 1989). Needless to say, this view is not without vigorous opponents (Henigan 1991). There is no scholarly consensus over whether the Second Amendment was enacted at least in part to preserve an individual right to keep and bear arms (Caplan 1976; Vandercoy 1994) or whether it was designed only to assure that the states would retain the right to an organized and effective militia (Ehrman and Henigan 1989; Feller and Gotting 1966).

The Supreme Court has not decided many cases in this area, but has inclined to the second view. In the leading case on the Second Amendment, *United States v. Miller* (1939) the court sustained a federal regulation of interstate transportation of sawed-off shotguns, noting that the "obvious purpose" of the Second Amendment was "to assure the continuation and render possible the effectiveness of [the State militias]" (178).[3]

Second, the conflict over the historical meaning of the "embarrassing Second Amendment" (Levinson 1989) spills over into contemporary political debate. At one extreme, there is the absolutist approach that relies upon the text of this provision to oppose all forms of governmental regulation of the ownership of virtually all forms of weapons. This view, in effect, reads out of the text the reference to the "well regulated militia" and its relation to the necessity for "the security of a free State." It is no accident, for example, that the version of the Second Amendment emblazoned on the wall of the headquarters of the National Rifle Association, reads simply (that is, without elisions): "THE RIGHT OF THE PEOPLE TO KEEP AND BEAR ARMS SHALL NOT BE INFRINGED."

At the other end of the spectrum of current interpretations, some gun-control advocates place such emphasis upon the historical connection between gun ownership and the ability to raise a militia on short notice that they truncate the significance of the principal clause of the Second Amendment referred to in uppercase above, and they tend to ignore its connection to the dependent clause, which suggests that the amendment is designed to preserve the people's right to a "free State." Among these advocates is the American Civil Liberties Union (Kates 1983, 207), a group otherwise ready to champion the view that the Bill of Rights was enacted to protect individuals and communities from abusive governmental power. As Vandercoy notes, "In the context of the Second Amendment, civil libertarian instincts are overcome by our fear of one another" (1994, 1008).

An intermediate position on the Second Amendment would acknowledge the legitimacy of popular ownership of some kinds of guns. For example, adherents to this position have no difficulty conceding that it is permissible to shoot ducks for sport, or—better yet—for the consumption of *canard à l'orange,* leaving to the several states such regulatory matters as hunting licenses and seasons. On the other hand, the same view would acknowledge the legitimacy of governmental efforts to regulate and in some instances to prohibit the manufacture, sale, and possession of other types of weapons. For example, first-graders may be prohibited from bringing guns to school. None of us has a constitutional right to own a bazooka. And—Tom Lehrer to the contrary notwithstanding—the Teamsters and Alabama may be forbidden to get an atomic bomb. Regrettably, the first of these seemingly ludicrous hypotheticals is becoming an alarmingly difficult problem for school administrators. To offer a fresh example of a gun regulation that most would regard as reasonable, the recently enacted Brady Law does not offend against this understanding of the Second Amendment merely by requiring persons seeking to buy a gun to register and to wait until a background check is performed before they may lawfully possess that weapon.

My own view of the Second Amendment is the one I have described above as the middle position. I thus readily acknowledge the legitimacy of a federal interest in regulation of weapons, especially the sort of automatic weapons that the BATF investigation disclosed to be in the possession of Koresh and his community. But that does not end the inquiry for me; it only begins it.

Even if we are prepared to concede that the government may place some reasonable limits upon our ability to own weapons, the Waco affair should be giving all of us some second thoughts about the disarray into which the enforcement of this federal interest has fallen. As one South Texan puts this point: "What were the Davidians doing to provoke [the raid]? Probably they were converting semiautomatic rifles to full auto. That is certainly a crime; even possessing the capability to convert them is a crime. But down here in the Fifty-Caliber Belt this particular crime is usually treated as seriously as spitting on the sidewalk" (Wattenberg 1993, 37).

In my view, the real problem is that Koresh was but one, lone owner of automatic weapons in this country. On any given Saturday, illegal transactions are openly carried on at gun shows at hundreds of locations throughout the country. I would have preferred that the scarce resources allocated to BATF efforts to enforce the law be spent on regular interdiction of such massive violations of federal laws.

The Treasury report sets forth an elaborate justification of the propriety of its investigation of Koresh and its efforts to enforce federal firearms laws against him and his community (pp. 119–32). Although it seems clear to me that the government had a prima facie case against Koresh and others in his community, that still does not mean that the government needed to proceed in the way that it did. For example, the Government Accounting Office has prepared a comprehensive analysis of the priorities that BATF has established for recommending cases for federal prosecution (*Firearms and Explosives* 1993). Koresh and his followers actually fell pretty low on this list of the BATF's priorities, for no narcotics were involved, Koresh was not a career or violent criminal, and he was not using the firearms for other federal offenses such as bank robbery or acts of organized crime or terrorism. Koresh gained the attention of BATF through the contact of local law enforcement personnel. It is, of course, one of the many goals of the BATF to assist local law enforcement officers, but it seems equally clear that the BATF had bigger fish to fry in Texas.

What, then, prompted the decision to go after Koresh in a big way, that is, with "the largest law enforcement effort ever mounted by BATF and one of the largest in the history of civilian law enforcement" (U.S. Department of Treasury 1993, 13)? One suggestion is that the BATF investigation disclosed that Koresh derided in general a policy that makes it illegal to transform legal automatic weapons into illegal machine guns. Koresh did so in part because of his awareness both of the widespread existence of legal automatic weapons in our society, such as the Soviet bloc AK-47 assault rifle, and of the ease of access to conversion kits to transform these weapons into machine guns. More particularly, Koresh regarded the BATF as an "evil agency that threatened the liberty of U.S. citizens" (U.S. Department of Treasury 1993, 35).

Another suggestion is that the BATF, which had been threatened with merger into the FBI, needed a splashy event to illustrate to Congress its need for continued independent existence. If this rationale was ever in play after Vice President Gore's proposal to redefine government, it seems that the BATF shot itself in the foot at Waco.

A third rationale, which I discuss below, is both more speculative and more sinister: that the BATF was happy to go after Koresh and his community precisely because they were so vulnerable as religious "crazies." Even if the Branch Davidians were not intentionally targeted in this case, the net effect of the BATF and FBI actions was the destruction of a religious community. That should give pause to all of us. As I suggest hereafter, this is a subtle matter not easily resolved by stark bipolar alternatives, either total immunity for religious communities that arm themselves or all-out war on such communities that literally takes no captives.

Inserting the free exercise clause more deeply into the policy planning of the BATF would, of course, result in limiting the government's ability to enforce the law. But that was the very purpose of the Bill of Rights in the first place. Greater care (that is, greater humility and patience) by the government in instances such as the Waco episode would, in my view, substantially improve the government's performance in law enforcement. Rather than rush into dynamic entries and big gunfights, the government would then have to focus its limited resources on winnable battles in the "war on violence." Ironically, this war may ultimately be won only when the government abandons its almost exclusive reliance on violence to combat violence, and becomes a little shrewder and a little more nonviolent itself. I turn now to the manner of the execution of the warrants.

II. The Defective Process of Executing the Arrest and Search Warrants

Even if one were to agree with the BATF as to the effectiveness of the means they chose to enforce the federal interest in gun control, there is a second reason why the government should have stayed its hand at Waco: the Fourth Amendment's commitment that "the right of the people to be secure in their persons, houses, papers, and effects, against unreasonable searches and seizures, shall not be violated, and no Warrants shall issue, but upon probable cause, supported by Oath or affirmation, and particularly describing the place to be searched, and the persons or things to be seized."

Under the rubric of the Fourth Amendment, I discuss three issues: the government's reliance upon cult-bashers to help shape its case against Koresh, the staleness of the government's information, and the manner of executing the warrants. I conclude that the government had performed extensive investigation that supports a finding of probable cause that violations of federal gun regulations were occurring at Mt. Carmel, but that the raid was an improper exercise of governmental authority.

First, there is the problem of reliance by the government upon biased witnesses, that is, upon former members of the Branch Davidian community. Several of the essays in this volume have pressed this claim. I am generally very sympathetic to the view that all of us need to be more comprehending and tolerant of diverse religious convictions. Indeed, I have repeatedly urged that mere toleration of religious diversity is not enough, that genuine respect for religious difference is what is called for in our society. On the other hand, against the background of the extensive investigation of the Branch Davidians conducted by the government, I would not want to push the argument against the cult-bashers very far in this instance, for the government had cured whatever defects arose from its reliance upon biased witnesses (are there any other kinds of witnesses?) by independent corroboration of the facts to ground a finding of probable cause that violations of federal firearms laws were occurring at Mt. Carmel. As *Time* magazine put it in its May 3, 1993, issue, the government had "plenty of justification for entering the Waco compound" (33). This account refers to the UPS deliveryman who dropped off two cases of hand grenades; and the cash outlays in excess of $200,000 on weapons in the seventeen months before the BATF raid. A search, of course, is not made good by what it turns up, but it seems pedantic to me to object to lack of probable cause to issue an arrest warrant or a search warrant in this instance.

To be sure, there was at least one difficulty with the affidavit that BATF Special Agent Aguilera submitted in support of his application for these warrants. The affidavit attributes to David Koresh a quotation by CPS caseworker Joyce Sparks to the effect that when his time came, it would make the riots in L.A. "pale in comparison." Daniel Wattenberg noted a difficulty in giving any credence to this statement, since the affidavit states that Sparks's visit occurred on April 6 (1993, 32). The Treasury report tidies up this matter by clarifying that Sparks made another visit to Koresh on April 30, 1992, which Aguilera forgot to include in the affidavit. Conveniently, April 30 is the day after the L.A. riots (U.S. Department of Treasury 1993, 126). Even with this tidier account, I am inclined to view the Koresh quotation as an invention, although with or without Sparks's citation of Koresh, the government still had probable cause.

Second, there is the staleness problem. This is related to the reliance upon former members of the community, whose recollections of life at Mt. Carmel went back months or even years before the time of the search warrant. This problem arises only with respect to a search warrant, not with respect to an arrest warrant. The general rule is that information submitted to a magistrate must be based on recent information that supports the conclusion that the item sought in a search warrant is probably still in the place to be searched (*Sgro v. United States* 1932).

Information is regarded as stale to the extent that it is not reliable. In making this determination, courts not only look to the number of days between the date on which the information in the affidavit was gathered and the date of application for a warrant; they also take into consideration other relevant factors such as the nature of the criminal activity at issue, the length of the activity, and the nature of the property to be seized. In *Andresen v. Maryland* (1976) the court offered a series of questions illustrating these factors. Is the character of the crime a chance encounter (with the affiant) or a regenerating conspiracy? Is the criminal a nomad or entrenched in the place where the search will occur? Is the thing to be seized perishable or of enduring utility to its holder? Is the place to be searched merely a forum of convenience or a secure operational base for the criminal activity? Even though there was a three-month delay between the completion of the real-estate transactions on which the warrants and ensuing searches in *Andresen* were based, the court rejected the staleness claim because "the business records sought were prepared in the ordinary course of . . . business . . . [and] it is eminently reasonable to expect that such records would be maintained in [Andresen's] offices for a period of time and surely as long as the three months required for the investigation of a complex real estate scheme."

An example where the nature of the property to be sought in the search made a difference involved a case where the informant's observation of hand grenades thirty days before the search supported an inference that the hand grenades would still be at the defendant's apartment. The court in this case reasoned: "Hand grenades are not, to the best of our knowledge, in great demand even by the criminal element in our society; and they do not lend themselves to rapid disposition in the market place" (*United States v. Dauphinee* 1976). This case is closely analogous to the BATF investigation of the

Branch Davidians, who were alleged to have received all the raw ingredients for manufacturing hand grenades, evidently for the purpose of adding these explosives to their arsenal, not for the purpose of selling them on the market that is far more open than the *Dauphinee* court seems to realize. Thus a warrant is valid when the property sought is likely to remain at the same place for a long time, even though there was a substantial delay in the application for the warrant (*United States v. Shomo* 1986). Similarly, probable cause to search for incriminating objects that are not easily moved, such as traces of heroin allegedly spilled on a rug (*United States v. Beltempo* 1982), is likely to grow stale less quickly than probable cause to search for evanescent evidence or for evidence that can be easily disposed of, such as a single handgun sought in the defendant's home where the affidavit recites that the gun was allegedly used to commit a murder (*United States v. Charest* 1979).

A warrant will not be rejected for staleness, moreover, when the government has corroborated older information by means of an ongoing investigation that discloses the continuous nature of the criminal conduct being investigated (*United States v. Henson* 1988). Once again, the BATF had a precedent for its application for a search warrant in the Waco case that is closely analogous, for it did not merely rely on the older information it gathered from former members of the Branch Davidian community, but conducted its own undercover investigation of Koresh and his followers.

A final point needs to be made about the search warrant: that there was one. Under *United States v. Leon* (1984), police officers are allowed to rely in good faith on a warrant even if it is later found invalid because it was not supported by probable cause. My own view is that probable cause for a search existed, but even if I am mistaken on this point, no one has contended that Magistrate Judge Green was merely rubber-stamping Agent Aguilera's application for a warrant. Since Green was acting as a "neutral and detached magistrate," the BATF was entitled to rely on the warrant, and the government did in fact introduce evidence seized at the compound at the subsequent criminal trial of the survivors.

Third, there is the problem of the manner of executing the warrants. I can be brief here, for this is the real brunt of my criticism of the government based on the Fourth Amendment. Even when a neutral and detached magistrate issues a valid warrant, that does not mean that the government may use excessive force in executing the warrant.

The issue of excessive force has not been dealt with comprehensively by the Supreme Court. Its precedents are murky. On the one hand, the court has invalidated a search that violated a federal statute requiring arresting officers to knock and announce their identity and purpose (*Miller v. United States* 1958), but in *Ker v. California* (1963) the court was unwilling to construe the Fourth Amendment to require this rule. More recently, relying on its procedural doctrine relating to mootness, the court declined to enjoin an egregiously excessive use of force—the often lethal chokehold—by the Los Angeles Police Department (*City of Los Angeles v. Lyons* 1983). These precedents may have sent the wrong signal to the LAPD, which relies frequently on the use of an armored vehicle with battering rams to crash into crack houses (*Langford v. Superior Court* 1987). Whether or not cases like *Ker* and *Lyons* actually had these effects with local police, the court's permissive line of cases did little to guide or shape the discretion of the federal officials at Waco relating to limits on their use of force.

On the other hand, in another line of cases the Supreme Court has repeatedly condemned lawless police brutality. For example, in *Screws v. United States* (1943), Justice Douglas described as a "shocking and revolting episode in law enforcement" a case in which Georgia state officers beat a young black man to death after arresting him on suspicion of stealing a tire. The court held the officers liable for their acts under a federal civil rights statute that governs action under "color of law." In *Tennessee v. Garner* (1985) the court ruled that the use of deadly force to stop an unarmed, nondangerous fleeing suspect violates the Fourth Amendment; the court clarified that deadly force may be used only when an officer has probable cause to believe that a suspect poses a significant threat of death or serious physical injury to the officer or others. And in *Brower v. County of Inyo* (1989) the court again clarified that the Fourth Amendment limits the use of force in apprehending suspected criminals; the court would not allow the police to end a high-speed chase by placing an eighteen-wheel truck completely across a highway in the path of the fleeing automobile, behind a curve, with a police cruiser's headlights aimed in such a way as to blind the fleeing suspect on the approach.

One can, in short, piece together at least some clear indications that the courts are not prepared to vest in the police complete discretion as to the level of force used in carrying out their difficult and often dangerous work. Thus an objective reasonableness standard would mean that law enforcement officials must gauge the level of their own use of force according to the degree of force that they reasonably anticipate will be necessary. Precisely because a rule of reason admits of few bright lines and lots of blurred boundaries, it is imperative that an alert citizenry discuss openly the sorts of restraints on the use of force that the people believe their police must live with.

The term of art among law enforcement agencies to describe the raid at Mt. Carmel on February 28 is "dynamic entry." Increasingly familiar through film and television depictions of police activity, this method of arrest has been sustained in some instances by appellate courts as an appropriate use of force. On the facts in the Waco events, where the subject sought by the arrest warrant routinely jogged outside the compound and where law enforcement authorities were well aware of the presence of small children, the dynamic entries resorted to by the government on February 28 and April 19 strike me as excessive in both instances. The circumstances at Waco were different from those in *Garner*, where the fleeing suspect was unarmed and nondangerous. Even so, it was not necessary to execute the warrant at Mt. Carmel on February 28 with hordes of BATF agents heavily armed with semiautomatic handguns, AR-15s, and MP-5 submachineguns. And the facts at Waco are not identical to those in *Brower*, where the suspect was fleeing at high speed. But the result in *Brower* suggests that the new attorney general probably exceeded the limits of the Fourth Amendment when she ordered the government attack on the compound on April 19 with tanks in order to breach the community's walls and put an end to the siege by placing canisters of CS gas throughout the compound.[4]

The Treasury report clearly acknowledges that there was insufficient caution for the safety either of the BATF agents or of the members of the Branch Davidian community. Ronald Noble knew this in his heart of hearts on the Friday afternoon before the raid, a day when he was otherwise preoccupied with the bombing of the World Trade Center (U.S. Department of Treasury 1993, 178–79). He later changed his mind, and went along with Director Higgins, who insisted that the raid was necessary. My hope is not that Noble repents of his own second guess on Friday, February 26, 1993, but that for the duration of his service as assistant secretary of the treasury for enforcement, he will always be more skeptical of the likelihood of success of flashy shoot-outs between the Eliot Ness types and the desperadoes they try to gun down.

Almost two years after the events in Waco, it is still difficult to get past the grief over the loss of those who died there, on both sides of the wall at Mt. Carmel that was thought to separate church and state. This grief stems in part from the failure of the government to pay enough attention to the reasons why the sanctities of the private home and of the religious community require the government to be careful when they contemplate entering either, especially with such destructive force as they did at Mt. Carmel. I turn now to the concern about the religious character of the community that was destroyed at Waco.

III. The Inadequacy of the Commitment to Religious Freedom as a Restraint on Governmental Power

Even if the policy objectives of the BATF were completely flawless from the perspective of the Second Amendment and even if the process of application for a search warrant was itself completely in conformity with the requirements of the Fourth Amendment, there is yet another reason why the government should have stayed its hand at Waco: the First Amendment's commitment that "Congress shall make no law respecting an establishment of religion or prohibiting the free exercise thereof."

In the jurisprudence of the past fifty years or so, this provision is commonly misunderstood to have two independent clauses, with competing criteria for application to various situations. In this view, the first provision banning a federal establishment of religion is thought to be in tension with the provision securing the free exercise of religion. In my own view, one that is shared by a growing number of scholars, the two provisions should be construed more harmoniously, with free exercise understood as the purpose of nonestablishment (Esbeck 1990; Gaffney 1993; Glendon and Yanes 1991; Laycock 1990; McConnell 1985; Neuhaus 1990). In the words of the Williamsburg Charter, a bicentennial document that exalted the achievement of the First Amendment: "the mutually reinforcing provisions [of the First Amendment] act as a double guarantee of religious liberty" (1990, 6).

Before turning to judicial interpretation of the religion clause, I briefly explore some legal history, in an effort to uncover what our heritage discloses about federal power over religious minorities. The Williamsburg Charter states: "The right to freedom of conscience is premised not upon science, nor upon social utility, nor upon pride of species. Rather, it is premised upon the inviolable dignity of the human person. It is the *foundation of, and is integrally related to, all other rights and freedoms secured by the Constitution.* This basic civil liberty is clearly acknowledged in the Declaration of Independence and is ineradicable from the long tradition of rights and liberties from which the Revolution sprang" (1990, 8). In this perspective the free exercise of religion is the first of our civil liberties, giving meaning to all of our other civil liberties. This perspective also recognizes the historic contribution of religion in America to the struggle for more adequate protection of civil rights and civil liberties, especially for racial minorities and for women (Gaffney 1990; Kelley 1990). As the charter puts it: "Many of the most dynamic social movements in American history, including that of civil rights, were legitimately inspired and shaped by religious motivation" (p. 20).

But to tell the plain truth, America has had a spotty history on religious freedom. This land was a safe haven for the Pilgrims, who escaped persecution by the established order in Stuart England only to impose a rigid establishment of their own faith in New England, complete with the execution of "witches" in Salem (Starkey 1949) and the hanging of Quakers in Boston (Ahlstrom 1972, 178; Littell 1971, 26–32; Stokes 1950, 184).

Religious persecution did not die with the enactment of the First Amendment. By its terms this provision is aimed at governmental acts ("*Congress* shall make no law"), not acts of private citizens. Thus the First Amendment did nothing to inhibit the outrageous violence against Roman Catholics committed by members of the American Protective Association, the Nativists, and the Knights of the Ku Klux Klan at various periods of the nineteenth century (Myers 1940; Laycock 1986, 416–17).

The First Amendment was equally powerless to stop the highly effective attack on one of the religious groups that sprang up in this soil, the Mormons, an attack that was embodied in the official policies of the national government in the same period. In *Reynolds v. United States* (1879), the Supreme Court imposed criminal sanctions on orthodox Mormons because of conduct relating to plural marriages.[5] In *Davis v. Beason* (1890) the court sustained a test oath prohibiting orthodox Mormons from voting in federal territory because of their beliefs about plural marriages. And in *The Late Corporation of Church of Jesus Christ of Latter-Day Saints v. United States* (1890), the court upheld the seizing of the assets of the church until it changed its religious convictions (Myers 1940, 158–62; Laycock 1986, 416–17; Noonan 1992, 571).

Although the First Amendment to the federal Constitution and the Bills of Rights of the several states enshrine a deep national commitment to religious freedom, America is still no safe haven for new religious movements (Shepherd 1985). It should be noted, moreover, that some of these movements are "new" only in the sense of being introduced to these shores recently despite the antiquity of the faith. For example, the International Society for Krishna Consciousness, also known as the Hare Krishnas, were recently threatened with their elimination as a religious movement in this country through the device of a tort action for emotional injuries allegedly suffered by the parents of a young woman who voluntarily embraced the religious tenets of this community (*International Society for Krishna Consciousness v. George* [1990]).

The civil lawsuits filed against government officials by survivors of the Branch Davidians will subject the government's claims about the reasonableness of its conduct to the rigors of constitutional litigation. But even if no such suits were ever filed, it would be necessary to put the events at Waco under the scrutiny of the religion clause. As I noted above, this provision of the First Amendment was utterly useless as a check against a federal campaign targeted against the Mormons. In the modern period, however, the Supreme Court fashioned an interpretation of the free exercise provision of the religion clause that put teeth into this provision. In 1963 the court ruled in *Sherbert v. Verner* that the government could not penalize the free exercise of religion by requiring religious adherents to pay a higher price for their faith than their secular counterparts. *Sherbert* marked a departure from a series of cases involving Sunday closing laws that had been decided adversely to Jews only two years before (*Braunfeld v. Brown* 1961).

In *Sherbert* Justice William Brennan tried to give religious freedom more effective protection than it had previously enjoyed. To achieve this end, he imported from equal protection analysis in cases involving racial discrimination the standard requiring the government to show that its interest in a racial classification was truly compelling. After the breakthrough decision in *Brown v. Board of Education* (1954), in case after case in the race area, the court had repeatedly told the government that no interest that it might articulate on behalf of apartheid (or its American cousin, Jim Crow) could match this strict standard of review (see, e.g., *Loving v. Virginia* 1967).

The requirement of a compelling governmental interest is more necessary in our period of the republic than in the founding period precisely because government at all levels is now far more intrusive than it was at the time of the founding. As one commentator has noted, "The style and scope of twentieth century government has led to its involvement with ends and values of varying importance" (Giannella 1967, 1388). Similarly, McConnell has argued that religious exemptions are more necessary after the New Deal than in the founding period since "the growth of the modern welfare-regulatory state has vastly increased the occasions for conflict between government and religion" (1985, 23).

In addition, Justice Brennan reached out in *Sherbert* to commerce clause cases such as *Dean Milk Co. v. City of Madison* (1951) to require further that the government must use the "least restrictive alternative" to achieve its "compelling interest." In *Dean Milk* the court had ruled that the City of Madison had a powerful interest in the purity of milk sold to its inhabitants, but that this goal could be achieved by requiring pasteurization of milk in Illinois as easily as requiring that the milk be transported in raw state up to Wisconsin for pasteurization and inspection, then be transported back down to Illinois for packaging, and then be transported up to Wisconsin for sale. The court correctly intuited that the imposition of additional transportation costs on the out-of-state farmers was a none too subtle way of discriminating against them in favor of local merchants.

By combining these two standards—compelling state interest and least restrictive alternative—into one new test for the adjudication of free exercise claims, the *Sherbert* court sent a signal to lower courts and governmental agencies that religious freedom was to be given the same favored status accorded to the national commitments to racial equality and to the elimination of tariff barriers in a national common market.

From *Sherbert v. Verner* (1963) to *Employment Division v. Smith* (1990), these two standards were embedded, however precariously, in Supreme Court precedents construing the free exercise provision of the First Amendment religion clause. When the court diminished the protection afforded to free exercise claims in *Smith*, Congress responded with legislation that restored the "compelling governmental interest" standard and the "least restrictive alternative" standard to their position before *Smith*. President Clinton signed the Religious Freedom Restoration Act on November 16, 1993.

Whether found in a judicial interpretation of the Constitution or in a federal statute that seeks to promote constitutional values, these standards should be applied to the conduct of the government in the Branch Davidian case. When I do so, it is not difficult to understand why the BATF initiated the investigation of this group in the first place. To be sure, government attorneys will be swift in any case to assert that the federal interest is always "compelling." I regret, moreover, that the courts have sometimes made it too easy for the government to demonstrate the relative significance of its interest over a sincere religious claim. But in the case of the Waco community, I am prepared to acknowledge that the federal interest in gun control was a significant one that probably outweighed the claim of a religious community to arm itself.

This argument works, however, only if the governmental interest is stated in terms as general and universal as I have just done. Suppose that, although the government has a vague general interest in gun control, it does not in fact enforce this policy very vigorously. And suppose the government waits until it gets a case with a group like the Branch Davidians to hold up to the nation as a bunch of religious crazies who deserve whatever grief they get. That raises the awful specter of selective prosecution that is biased because of religious beliefs, an evil the Supreme Court has roundly condemned.

Even if the government has a compelling justification for refusing to accommodate a religious concern, the First Amendment absolutely prohibits the government from targeting vulnerable and unpopular religious minorities in a manner that it would never contemplate doing to dominant religious communities. In *Larson v. Valente* (1982), the Supreme Court taught that courts should scrutinize most carefully any policy that has the effect of granting a denominational preference to mainstream religions while imposing special burdens on fringe groups, such as the Unification Church, or "Moonies," who were targeted by the statute at issue in *Larson*. Justice Brennan wrote: "The clearest command of the Establishment Clause is that one religious denomination cannot be officially preferred over another" (*Larson* 244). As recently as 1993 the court again clarified this point in *Church of the Lukumi Babalu Aye, Inc. v. City of Hialeah*. In this case Justice Anthony Kennedy wrote for a unanimous court that the ordinances in question were not of general applicability, but "had as their object the suppression of religion" (2231; see also *Lamb's Chapel v. Center Moriches Union Free School District* 1993).

Carter has written tellingly of the trivialization of religion in America (1993a), and he writes that the decision in *Lukumi Babalu Aye* does not mean that "religious freedom is now alive and healthy, least of all in a legal and political system that often seems to see religion as more in need of suppression than liberation. Rather, religious freedom is still terribly ill, and our national dabbling in the homeopathic magic of kicking and kicking and kicking may yet lead to its death—at least, to the death of the sort of religious freedom that allows us to offend or infuriate our fellow citizens because of the content of our beliefs. Unless the court and the society it serves broaden the vision of what it means for religion to be exercised freely, we will very likely end up in a society in which the mainline religions flourish, protecting themselves through political clout, and the sparkling diversity of religious life at the margins is snuffed out" (Carter 1993b, 142). Carter was not writing consciously about the Branch Davidians, but his conclusion has an eerie echo with the tragedy in Waco. The Treasury report gives short shrift to the claim that the BATF had targeted the Branch Davidians for special adverse treatment (p. 120), but the government has not persuaded me on this score. To quote again from the Williamsburg Charter, "Religious liberty finally depends on neither the favors of the state and its officials nor the vagaries of tyrants or majorities. Religious liberty in a democracy is a right that may not be submitted to vote and depends on the outcome of no election. A society is only as just and free as it is respectful of this right, especially toward the beliefs of its smallest minorities and least popular communities" (1990, 8).

My principal concern in this essay, however, is not with the formal requirement of federal law that government attorneys must justify an intrusion into religious life by demonstrating that the governmental interest is compelling. Several scholars have noted the distressing ease with which this standard is met (Carter 1993a; McConnell 1989). For example, McConnell lists the following government "victories" over religious claimants in recent years: "Orthodox Jews have been expelled from the military for wearing yarmulkes; a religious community in which all members worked for the church and believed that acceptance of wages would be an affront to God has been forced to yield to the minimum wage; religious colleges have been denied tax exemptions for enforcing what they regard to be religiously compelled moral regulations; Amish farmers who refuse Social Security benefits have been forced to pay Social Security taxes; and Muslim prisoners have been denied the right to challenge prison regulations that conflict with their worship schedule" (McConnell 1989, 46).

In the light of these precedents, it seems probable that a court would defer to the government's assertion that its interest in regulation of automatic weapons was substantial or compelling. Once the four federal agents were killed in the gun battle, moreover, the ante surely went up, whether the gun battle was provoked by the government or was—as the Treasury report implausibly suggests—an "ambush" of government agents.

For these reasons, I focus my criticism on the too often neglected standard that requires the government to refrain from action injurious to religious freedom if the government may achieve its legitimate objective in a *manner that is less restrictive of religious freedom*. For example, this standard has been used to inform federal policy relating to the uniform enforcement of tax collection. Religious communities are not afforded a wholesale immunity from federal investigation of their income, but through a federal statute inspired by the "less restrictive alternative" standard, the Internal Revenue Service is required under the terms of the Church Audit Procedure Act to proceed cautiously when seeking to review the tax records of an exempt religious organization.

Analogously, I do not suggest that there is or ought to be an exemption from gun control laws grounded in the free exercise provision of the religion clause that would allow religious adherents special license to amass an arsenal as they await the end of the world. No serious First Amendment scholar would argue that the government must sit by idle if there is credible evidence that a religious community believes it has a duty to kill others and is likely to carry out that goal imminently (*Brandenburg v. Ohio* 1969). But I am insisting that there is no evidence whatever to support the notion that the Branch Davidians ever thought of using their weapons to kill innocent civilians. Koresh and his followers relied heavily on the apocalyptic vision of the book of Revelation. In this vision the dead are the saints, or members of the community of the Lamb who are persecuted by the Roman emperor, not the emperor's other subjects or even his imperial army. And I am suggesting that the government could have achieved its legitimate objectives in a far less destructive manner.

This criticism, moreover, is not Monday morning quarterbacking. It was offered at the time of the standoff at Waco. On March 11, 1993, while the Branch Davidians were still under siege, sober religious leaders like Dean Kelley, the Counselor on Religious Liberty of the National Council of Churches of Christ, and James Dunn, the Executive Director of the Baptist Joint Committee on Public Affairs, wrote to President Clinton, urging him to "demilitarize the confrontation in Waco." "To invade a center of energy (like Mt. Carmel)," they wrote, "is like sticking a finger in a dynamo. Whether it explodes or implodes, the result will be tragic for all." It is sad that no one in the government paid much heed to this voice at the time it was raised.

When measured against the "less restrictive alternative" standard, the government's actions at Waco fall far short of the mark. For example, as I mentioned above in part II of this essay, the government could have presented its concerns directly to David Koresh, who responded to an earlier complaint about his conduct in 1987 by subjecting himself to a criminal trial, at which he was acquitted of the charges pressed against him. Koresh himself proposed a less restrictive alternative when he asked, "Why don't they just try to talk to me about it?"

If the government insisted on arresting Koresh, it could have done so during one of his routine jogs outside the Mt. Carmel compound. I am assuming that the government knew this fact at the time because of its extensive surveillance of the Mt. Carmel compound by BATF agents hidden in the undercover house.

And once the cease-fire was arranged, the government could have pursued much more diligently the path of mediation and negotiation of a nonviolent settlement. As James Tabor's chapter in this volume illustrates, this path was a reasonable alternative even in the tense situation after the fatal raid. Dr. Alan Stone regards the failure of the FBI "to involve as a third-party negotiator/intermediary a person of religious stature familiar with the unconventional belief system of the Branch Davidians" as "a significant omission at Waco" (1993, 42). Tabor had gained the confidence of Koresh, and had already worked out a satisfactory solution to the dilemma of the standoff. According to this plan, Koresh would work out the details of his own interpretation of key passages in the book of Revelation, and then turn himself in, leaving his followers unharmed.

Despite the excellent prospect of success in Tabor's plan, the government went forward with the raid that Attorney General Reno personally ordered on April 19. I do not believe the assertion of Byron Sage, the lead special agent for the FBI in the Waco "negotiations," who stated, "We had moved heaven and earth to try to resolve this situation." The tanks moved the earth all right, but the federal "mediators" surely did not move the heavens.

To be sure, there were some potent forces out there on the plains of Texas militating against the calmer counsel of the less restrictive alternative standard. For example, it probably did not help that the media swiftly turned a possession of firearms case into a crisis of huge proportion, with increasing difficulty for the parties to find some face-saving way out through mediation. In addition, the crisis was perceived in starkly apocalyptic terms within the Mt. Carmel community. The amazing thing is that the government did not seem to grasp the seriousness of the convictions of the Branch Davidians about the end of time. Neither did it help that those policing the siege had evidently reached a stage of severe fatigue.

As for the views of the Branch Davidians about the end of the world, they may seem quite odd to the vast majority of Americans, but beliefs alone do not justify a government raid. Assume for a moment that Koresh and his company were, as the media regularly suggested, pathological case studies of paranoia or some other mental abnormality readily diagnosed and labeled according to one or more of the categories in the *Diagnostic and Statistical Manual.* What follows? Perhaps treatment, or maybe leaving them alone. But not the provocative, intrusive behavior that the government engaged in for nearly two months. Even if the Branch Davidians were "nuts," as they were frequently characterized in the media, their kind of nuttiness did not merit the end that came to them. The better part of prudence would have been to leave the Davidians alone. Especially with respect to those who believe that the end time is coming soon, it behooves our government to take a wait-and-see attitude rather than to rush in with the sound effects and the military power that only confirm that the end of the world is indeed nigh.

In our society, after all, the government has no duty to protect us from eccentric ideas, whether secular or religious. This point has been made repeatedly in cases involving secular ideologies such as communism (*Dennis v. United States* 1951) and the views of the Ku Klux Klan (*Brandenburg v. Ohio* 1969). When ideas get translated into illegal conduct, the government may, of course, take prompt and appropriate action both to prevent and to stop the conduct. But no one has yet adduced credible evidence that Koresh's community was likely to have come out of their compound with guns blazing against their fellow Texans. Until that is demonstrated, it seems plausible that the same standards that protect the Communist party and the Klan ought minimally to have governed the case of the Branch Davidians. In *Brandenburg*, for example, the court ruled that the First Amendment protects even "advocacy of the use of force or of law violation except where such advocacy is directed to inciting or producing imminent lawless action and is likely to incite or produce such action." Although there may be reliable evidence that the Branch Davidians possessed illegal firearms—which are not protected under the First Amendment, but might be under the Second Amendment— all the evidence of "inciting or producing imminent lawless action" points to the BATF and the FBI, not to the Branch Davidians.

It bears repeating that the criticism about the failure of the government to seek the path of less restrictive alternatives is not based on facts that only later came to mind. These genuinely alternative ways of proceeding were entirely plausible in this case, and were urged upon the government at the time of the events. None of these alternatives would have resulted in the tragic loss of life on February 28 or in the all-consuming holocaust that ensued on April 19.

Conclusion: In Defense of Second-Guessing

At the outset I acknowledged that this essay is a second guess. Indeed, all of the essays in this volume might be regarded as second guesses. I offer now a few words in defense of the enterprise of second-guessing the government. No less astute an observer of the American scene than Martin E. Marty suggested as much when he described America as a "nation of second-guessers" in an op-ed piece shortly after the time of the Waco tragedy (Marty 1993). As usual, Marty made several telling observations in the brief space of his article. On this occasion, however, the normally decisive Marty waffled. On the one hand, he suggested that there are reasons to be "nervous about seeing the government define the limits . . . on activities of the religiously dangerous." On the other hand, Marty also concluded that "there are still good reasons to assert that the government had the right to make its moves in the Branch Davidian case," but he did not identify what those reasons were.

As it turns out, I agree with Marty's nervousness about governmental limits on the "religiously dangerous," but disagree with his conclusion that the government made the right moves at Waco. There are other differences between Marty's approach to the Waco question and my own. For example, Marty left to one side "questions about the wisdom of the federal moves" and focused only on the "more enduring and, in the long run, more troubling if not finally insoluble issue of rights." I have chosen a different path, exploring the policy wisdom of the government's tactics at Waco, and leaving for others an analysis based on rights discourse.

More to the point, I am puzzled by Marty's implicit criticism of second-guessing the government. For all of our differences, Marty's column and my essay are both instances of second-guessing. And as the readers of this volume evaluate the reasons offered here to determine whether they are valid, each person who does so will be second-guessing the government, irrespective of the judgments about Waco that we reach. Hence I thought it might be well to conclude this essay with a brief defense of the whole enterprise of second-guessing that lies at least implicitly at the heart of this volume.

First, it should be remembered that second-guessing has a distinguished constitutional pedigree. For example, judicial review of the constitutionality of congressional legislation has been secure since *Marbury v. Madison* (1803). Similarly, federal review of state action has been fundamental to our federalism since *Cohens v. Virginia* (1821). Judicial review, moreover, routinely involves the second-guessing of judicial acts at the trial court level by at least one panel of appellate judges.

In his recent volume, *The Partial Constitution*, Sunstein gives new meaning and power to the function of judicial review. He argues skillfully against what he calls "status quo neutrality," that is, the mistaken belief that all current arrangements and practices are "neutral" and may not be set aside without disrupting the basic trust that our republican form of government reposes in elected representatives of the people. Instead, he calls for a method of constitutional interpretation that takes into account the crucial distinction between "a system in which representatives try to offer some reasons for their decisions, and a system in which political power is the only thing at work" (Sunstein 1993, 28). Thus when someone is aggrieved by action of the government, Sunstein would have the courts require the government to articulate real reasons for its policies, not feigned ones invented by the judiciary to mask commitments to the status quo. For their part, judges should offer publicly accessible justifications of their constitutional interpretations. The criticisms of the government's actions at Waco offered in this volume seem to me to partake of the very form of critical discourse which Sunstein and others have commended for the enlivening of our democracy.

Furthermore, the task of review of administrative policy or actions is not limited to judges. Congress regularly second-guesses the executive branch through its investigative agency, the General Accounting Office; indeed, the GAO issued a report on BATF law enforcement operations in 1993 (*Firearms and Explosives* 1993). It also does so through its oversight committees. In this instance, the House Judiciary Committee promptly held hearings to bring the attorney general to account for herself. Regrettably, the committee has delayed the publication of these hearings for over two years. Immediately after the tank attack on the Mt. Carmel compound, President Clinton asked the right question: "Why are we taking this action now, after seven weeks?" But once it became clear that his new attorney general was getting praised, not blamed, on Capitol Hill, then the commander-in-chief wanted his fair share of the praise and started talking as though he had known all along where the buck stops.

Review of agency determinations regularly occurs within the executive branch as well. To his credit, President Clinton ordered a "vigorous and thorough investigation" of the events at Waco, which resulted in the detailed and voluminous reports critical of at least some of the actions of governmental officials within the Treasury and Justice Departments. Why should the second-guessing stop there?[6]

In short, there are important constitutional reasons for the task of second-guessing. It is especially appropriate in a democracy that the people are free to pass their own judgments about the legitimacy of acts of the government, which in our constitutional order makes the government accountable to the sovereign people who created it. The second-guessing in this volume corresponds to a view of our republic which maintains that constitutional interpretation is far too important to be left to judges and lawyers. In this view, all serious citizens are to reflect about the critical connection between the limits that our Constitution places on governmental power and the quality of our democracy (Parker 1993; Sunstein 1993; Tushnet 1992).

Several essays in this volume, including my own, have noted specific constitutional limits on the authority that the government exerts on our behalf. Maybe Marty was right in suggesting that "there are still good reasons to assert that the government had the right to make its moves in the Branch Davidian case." But in my view there are still better reasons for concluding that the raid on Mt. Carmel was violative of the First Amendment principle about less restrictive alternatives to burdening religious freedom, that it was at least an unwise allocation of resources to enforce the federal interest in gun control, and that it was flawed as a matter of Fourth Amendment law governing excess force in the execution of a warrant.

In effect, the government got it wrong at Waco by trying to make the case look much too easy. Far from agreeing with Attorney General Reno that "we need a plan to protect us from people like [the Branch Davidians] doing this to us again," I think that after Waco what we need in the federal government is a rededication to the original plan of the First Amendment that severely limits federal authority over religious groups and that absolutely prohibits the targeting of vulnerable and unpopular religious minorities.

Far from agreeing with former BATF Director Stephen Higgins that what we needed was a paramilitary attack on Mt. Carmel in order to reduce the number of guns in Texas, I think that it would be far more effective for the BATF to work within the perimeters of the Second Amendment to interdict the sales of illegal weapons of mass destruction at the wholesale distribution level.

And far from agreeing with the idea that the raid was justified by the nature of the offense for which the BATF had concluded there was probable cause, I think that mounting the biggest law enforcement effort in American history was itself a blunder that backfired, and that the BATF and other federal agencies need to review their policies on "dynamic entry" in light of the Fourth Amendment commitment to keep the government from invading the privacy and sanctity of the people's homes in the manner that the government did at Mt. Carmel.

Precisely because there will probably be no meaningful judicial review of any of these constitutional issues in the Waco case, it is all the more imperative in our democracy that we, the people, think critically about what the government did at Waco, lest the raid on the Branch Davidians become by our silence or our complicity a precedent for doing it again to some other marginalized religious group of which the government disapproves. I hope that the tragic end of the Branch Davidians serves not as a precedent for more paramilitary operations against the strongholds of religious and secular "crazies," but as the basis for tougher federal restriction on access to automatic weapons at the wholesale end. If a federal policy of this sort takes shape, then perhaps these dead—the BATF agents and the Branch Davidians—may not have died in vain.

Notes

1. For example, the Ku Klux Klan Act of 1871, as amended in 1979, provides: "Every person who, under color of any statute, ordinance, regulation, custom or usage, of any State or Territory or the District of Columbia, subjects, or causes to be subjected, any citizen of the United States or other person within the jurisdiction thereof to the deprivation of any right, privileges, or immunities secured by the Constitution and laws, shall be liable to the party injured in an action at law, suit in equity, or other proper proceeding for redress" (42 U.S.C. 1983). This provision has been the chief instrument of vindicating people whose federal constitutional or statutory rights have been violated by state officials. In *Bivens vs. Six Unknown Named Agents* (1971), the Supreme Court likewise implied a cause of action against federal officials, such as the BATF agents involved in the raid on February 28 and the FBI agents involved in the attack on April 19, which resulted in the deaths of many Branch Davidians.

2. Throughout the Treasury report, the Branch Davidians were referred to as a "cult." On the one hand, the editors of this report state: "The Review is quite aware that 'cult' has pejorative connotations, and that outsiders—particularly those in the government—should avoid casting aspersions on those whose religious beliefs are different from their own." On the other hand, the editors cite a dictionary definition of the term "cult" as "a religion regarded as unorthodox or spurious," and conclude that "in light of the evidence of the conduct of Koresh and his followers set out in this report, the Review finds 'cult' to be an apt characterization" (1993, 1, n. 2). Rather than further the pejorative connotation that the Treasury review finds "apt," I have chosen to use the more neutral term "community" throughout this essay.

3. The court could not detect any evidence that possession or use of a sawed-off shotgun had any "reasonable relationship to the preservation or efficiency of a well regulated militia," and it doubted that "this weapon is any part of the ordinary military equipment or that its use could contribute to the common defense." In 1943 a federal appeals court upheld a similar provision of the federal Firearms Act on the view that *Miller* means that "the federal government can limit the keeping and bearing of arms by a single individual or a group of individuals, but it cannot prohibit the possession or use of any weapon which has any reasonable relationship to the preservation or efficiency of a well-regulated militia." *Cases v. United States* (1942): 922.

4. Although there may be some circumstances in which dynamic entries may truly be the only way of enforcing the law, the Waco event should serve to prompt further review of the manner of executing valid search warrants. This review should take note of the literature docu-

menting examples of mistaken, surprise, unannounced raids by federal, state, and local law enforcement agents, including ones in which no in Waco—police officers have died as a result of these raids (Malcolm 1973). Not only Zen spirituality, but also the events of Waco teach that less can be more. There is indeed a jungle out there in which government agents have to work, but serious enforcement of federal firearms laws is going to have to get a lot shrewder and probably a lot less violent before it is going to get much better.

5. Although many commentators doubt the ongoing vitality of this case, it should be noted that "the extraordinary discipline that Koresh imposed on his followers" (U.S. Department of Treasury 1993, 127), as well as the sexual conduct of Koresh, were factors leading the federal government to take action against him.

6. Both the president and the attorney general made public and dramatic declarations that each took full responsibility for the events at Waco. One corollary of these declarations is that the full measure of this responsibility should be determined by an independent counsel. Congress has already invoked the process of appointing an independent counsel to investigate the details of the financial interests of the president and the first lady in the Whitewater matter. Both the president and the first lady have assured the public that a full investigation would disclose that neither of them has ever engaged in any illegal or improper activities relating to this matter. The Whitewater independent counsel, Kenneth W. Starr, seems nonetheless determined to press a full investigation in the federal grand jury, as does Senator Alfons D'Amato before a select committee of the Senate. Whatever one thinks of Whitewater, its investigation seems far less critical to the well-being of the republic than an inquiry into the massive loss of life that occurred at Waco.

One counterargument to appointing an independent prosecutor to investigate the Waco matter is that full cabinet-level reviews of the matter have already been undertaken with the Justice and the Treasury Departments. The chief difficulty with this counterargument, however, is that the review at Justice took place under an attorney general who testified before the House Judiciary that there should be no "recrimination" for any of the official acts that took place at Waco, including the apparently reckless endangerment of life that some commentators believe was entailed in the raid on April 19 authorized by the attorney general. For example, in his TRB column in The *New Republic*, Mickey Kaus compared Reno's reply to Congressman John Conyers with Henry Kissinger's plea that the country should avoid an "orgy of recrimination" at the time of the Watergate scandal. Kaus makes the case for recrimination, "even orgies of it," as the only way for the full truth about Waco to be disclosed. If, for example, the attorney general was misled about the likelihood of success of the path she ultimately chose, should not all of her colleagues at Justice know that there is a very high price to pay for that? The truth about Watergate did not begin to emerge until the full investigation of the matter by both the Senate select committee and the special prosecutor, when all sorts of middle-management bureaucrats started pointing the finger at one another and at higher-ups. As the essays in this volume suggest, reasonable people still have substantial doubts about the "full responsibility" for the events at Waco. Under these circumstances, recrimination may be exactly what is necessary to find out the full truth of who ordered what, when, and why.

References

Ahlstrom, Sydney E. 1972. *A Religious History of the American People.* New Haven: Yale University Press.

Caplan, David I. 1976. "Restoring the Balance: The Second Amendment Revisited." *Fordham Urban Law Journal* 5: 31–~~53.

Carter, Stephen. 1987. "Evolutionism, Creationism, and Treating Religion as a Hobby." *Duke Law Journal* (1987): 977–1001.

———. 1993a. *The Culture of Disbelief.* New York: Basic Books.

———. 1993b. "The Resurrection of Religious Freedom?" *Harvard Law Review* 107: 118–42.

Dennis, Edward, S. G., Jr. 1993. *Evaluation of the Handling of the Branch Davidian Stand-Off in Waco, Texas, February 28 to April 19, 1993.* Washington, DC: U.S. Department of Justice.

Ehrman, Keith A., and Henigan, Dennis A. 1989. "The Second Amendment in the Twentieth Century: Have You Seen Your Militia Lately?" *University of Dayton Law Review* 15: 5–58.

Esbeck, Carl. 1990. "Three Criteria for Constitutional Interpretation: Predictability, Flexibility, and Intelligibility." *Notre Dame Journal of Law, Ethics, and Public Policy* 4: 549–58.

Feller, Peter B., and Gotting, Karl L. 1966. "The Second Amendment: A Second Look." *Northwestern University Law Review* 61: 46–70.

Firearms and Explosives: Information and Observations on ATF Law Enforcement Operations. 1993. Washington, DC: U.S. General Accounting Office.

Friedman, Leon. 1969. "Conscription and the Constitution: The Original Understanding," *Michigan Law Review* 67: 1493–1552.

Gaffney, Edward McGlynn, Jr. 1990. "Politics without Brackets on Religious Convictions: Michael Perry and Bruce Ackerman on Neutrality." *Tulane Law Review* 64: 1143–94.

———. 1992. "Hostility to Religion, American Style." *DePaul Law Review* 42: 263–304.

———. 1993. "The Religion Clause: A Double Guarantee of Religious Liberty." *Brigham Young University Law Review* 36: 189–220.

Glendon, Mary Ann, and Yanes, Raul F. 1991. "Structural Free Exercise." *Michigan Law Review* 90: 477–550.

Giannella, Donald. 1967. "Religious Liberty, Nonestablishment, and Doctrinal Development: Part I. The Religious Liberty Guarantee." *Harvard Law Review* 80: 1381–1431.

Halbrook, Stephen P. 1984. *That Every Man Be Armed: The Evolution of a Constitutional Right.* San Francisco: Liberty Press.

———. 1991. "The Right of the People or the Power of the State: Bearing Arms, Arming Militias, and the Second Amendment." *Valparaiso University Law Review* 26: 131–207.

Henigan, Dennis A. 1991. "Arms, Anarchy, and the Second Amendment." *Valparaiso University Law Review* 26: 107–29.

Heymann, Philip B. 1993. *Lessons of Waco: Proposed Changes in Federal Law Enforcement.* Washington, DC: U.S. Department of Justice.

Kates, Don P. 1983. "Handgun Prohibition and the Original Meaning of the Second Amendment." *Michigan Law Review* 82: 204–73.

Kaus, Mickey. 1993. "TRB from Washington: Local Hero." *New Republic* 208, no. 21 (May 24): 4.

Kelley, Dean M. 1990. "The Intermeddling Manifesto, Or the Role of Religious Bodies in Affecting Religious Policy in the United States." *Journal of Law and Religion* 8: 85–98.

———. 1994."Was Religious Liberty Violated at Waco?" *ACRM INFO* (April).

Laycock, Douglas. 1986. "A Survey of Religious Liberty in the United States." *Ohio State Law Journal* 47: 409–51.

———. 1990. "Formal, Substantive, and Disaggregated Neutrality toward Religion." *DePaul Law Review* 39: 993–1018.

Levinson, Sanford. 1989. "The Embarrassing Second Amendment." *Yale Law Journal* 99: 637-59.

Littell, Franklin H. 1971. *From State Church to Pluralism: A Protestant Interpretation of Religion in American History.* 2d ed. New York: Macmillan.

Malcolm, Andrew H. 1973. "Violent Drug Raids against the Innocent Found Widespread." *New York Times.* June 25, p. A1.

Marty, Martin E. 1993. "Drawing the Line on Religious Freedom: Should Government Set Limits to Prevent Another Waco?" *St. Louis Post-Dispatch,* 27 April, p. 3C.

McConnell, Michael W. 1985. "Accommodation of Religion." *Supreme Court Review* 47: 1–59.

———. 1989. "Why 'Separation' Is Not the Key to Church-State Relations." *Christian Century* 107 (January 18): 43–46.

———. 1990. "Free Exercise Revisionism and the *Smith* Decision," *University of Chicago Law Review* 57: 1109–53.

Myers, Gustavus. 1940. *History of Bigotry in the United States.* New York: Capricorn.

Neuhaus, Richard John. 1990. "Contending for the Future: Overcoming the Pfefferian Inversion." *Journal of Law and Religion* 8: 115–29.

———. 1992. "A New Order of Religious Freedom." *George Washington Law Review* 60: 620–32.

Noonan, John T., Jr. 1992. "The End of Free Exercise?" *DePaul Law Review* 42: 567–82.

Parker, Richard D. 1993. "'Here the People Rule': A Constitutional Populist Manifesto." *Valparaiso University Law Review* 27: 531–84.

Shepherd, William C. 1985. *To Secure the Blessings of Liberty: American*

Constitutional Law and the New Religious Movements. New York: Crossroads.

Starkey, Marion L. 1949. *The Devil in Massachusetts: A Modern Inquiry into Salem Witch Trials.* New York: Knopf.

Stokes, Anson Phelps. 1950. *Church and State in the United States.* 3 vols. New York: Harper.

Stone, Alan. 1993. *Report and Recommendations Concerning the Handling of Incidents Such as the Branch Davidian Standoff in Waco, Texas.* Washington, DC: United States Department of Justice.

Sunstein, Cass R. 1993. *The Partial Constitution.* Cambridge, MA: Harvard University Press.

Tushnet, Mark. 1992. "The Constitution Outside the Courts: A Preliminary Inquiry." *Valparaiso University Law Review* 26: 437–63.

U.S. Department of Justice. 1993. *Recommendations of Experts for Improvements in Federal Law Enforcement after Waco.* Washington, DC: Government Printing Office.

———. 1993. *Report to the Deputy Attorney General on the Events at Waco, Texas, February 28 to April 19, 1993.* Washington, DC: Government Printing Office.

U.S. Department of Treasury. 1993. *Report of Department of the Treasury on the Bureau of Alcohol, Tobacco, and Firearms Investigation of Vernon Wayne Howell, Also Known as David Koresh.* Washington, DC: Government Printing Office.

Vandercoy, David. 1994. "The History of the Second Amendment." *Valparaiso University Law Review* 28: 1007–39.

Wattenberg, Daniel. 1993. "Gunning for Koresh." *American Spectator* (August): 31–40.

"The Williamsburg Charter." 1990. *Journal of Law and Religion* 8: 5–22.

Wood, James E., Jr. 1993. "The Branch Davidian Standoff: An American Tragedy." *Journal of Church and State* 35: 233–40.

Cases

Andresen v. Maryland, 427 U.S. 463 (1976).

Bivens v. Six Unknown Named Agents, 403 U.S. 388 (1971).

Brandenburg v. Ohio, 395 U.S. 444 (1969).

Braunfeld v. Brown, 366 U.S. 599 (1961).

Brower v. County of Inyo, 489 U.S. 593 (1989).

Brown v. Board of Education, 347 U.S. 483 (1954).

Cases v. United States, 131 F.2d 916 (1st Cir. 1942), cert. denied, 319 U.S. 770 (1943).

Church of the Lukumi Babalu Aye, Inc. v. City of Hialeah, 113 S.Ct. 2217 (1993).

City of Los Angeles v. Lyons, 461 U.S. 95 (1983).

Cohens v. Virginia, 19 U.S. 264 (1821).

Davis v. Beason, 133 U.S. 333 (1890).

Dean Milk Co. v. City of Madison, 340 U.S. 349 (1951).

Dennis v. United States, 341 U.S. 494 (1951).

Employment Division v. Smith, *494 U.S. 872 (1990).*

International Society for Krishna Consciousness v. George, cert granted and vacated, *495 U.S. 930 (1990).*

Ker v. California, *374 U.S. 23 (1963).*

Lamb's Chapel v. Center Moriches Union Free School District, *113 S.Ct. 2141 (1993).*

Langford v. Superior Court, *43 Cal. 3d 21, 729 P.2d 822 (1987).*

Larson v. Valente, *456 U.S. 228 (1982).*

The Late Corporation of Church of Jesus Christ of Latter-Day Saints v. United States, *136 U.S. 1 (1890).*

Loving v. Virginia, *388 U.S. 1 (1967).*

Marbury v. Madison, *5 U.S. 137 (1803).*

Miller v. United States, *357 U.S. 301 (1958).*

Reynolds v. United States, *98 U.S. 145 (1879).*

Screws v. United States, *325 U.S. 91 (1943).*

Sgro v. United States, *287 U.S. 206 (1932).*

Sherbert v. Verner, *374 U.S. 398 (1963).*

Tennessee v. Garner, *471 U.S. 1 (1985).*

United States v. Beltempo, *675 F.2d 472 (2d Cir.),* cert. denied, *457 U.S. 1135 (1982).*

United States v. Charest, *602 F.2d 1015 (1st Cir. 1979).*

United States v. Dauphinee, *538 F.2d 1 (1st Cir. 1976).*

United States v. Henson, *848 F.2d 1374 (6th Cir. 1988).*

United States v. Leon, *468 U.S. 897 (1984).*

United States v. Miller, *307 U.S. 174 (1939).*

United States v. Shomo, *786 F.2d 981 (10th Cir. 1986).*

Statutes

Church Audit Procedure Act, 26 U.S.C. 7611.

Ku Klux Klan Act, 42 U.S.C. 1983.

Religious Freedom Restoration Act, 42 U.S.C. 2000a.

15

DEAN M. KELLEY

The Implosion of Mt. Carmel and Its Aftermath

Is It All Over Yet?

The text of this essay is taken from mocking phrases blasted out over the FBI loudspeaker during the CS-gas assault on the home of a religious community near Waco, Texas, on April 19, 1993: "You've had your fifteen minutes of fame, Vernon; you're not a messiah any more; it's all over now!" Later that day seventy-four members of the religious group perished in fire, and a few weeks later the charred ruins of their residence were bulldozed into rubble "for health reasons," burying the remains of a bad scene.

Is it all over now? Many people would like to think so, including citizens of Waco, whose city has become noted—or notorious—all over the world for events they did not cause and could not control. Many a bureaucrat and law enforcement official in Texas and in Washington, DC, also hopes that we have "put behind us"—as the saying goes in Washington—the mistakes of the past and can go on to other things. But, as a baseball notable once remarked, "The game ain't over 'til it's *over*"; and Ella Wheeler Wilcox wrote, "No question is ever settled/Until it is settled right." To some reflections on that theme this essay is devoted.

Unpacking "Implosion"

First a clarification of the energies at work in the religious community of Mt. Carmel is in order—a complete misunderstanding of which was the central error of the governmental agencies involved. Edward Gaffney, in his contribution to this volume, referred to a letter sent to the president of the United States on March 11, 1993, in the second week of the siege of Mt. Carmel, by James Dunn, Executive Director of the Baptist Joint Committee on Public Affairs, and this writer. A copy of that letter follows:

> Dear Mr. President:
> *Please demilitarize the confrontation in Waco, Texas.* It does not call for hundreds of heavily-armed federal employees and Abrams tanks waiting for a showdown.
> We are concerned that more people will be killed before the protracted encounter in Waco is over. Is there not some way to stand down from this stand-off without throwing more lives after those already lost? We are reluctant to judge from a distance the tactics of law-enforcement personnel who have been asked to risk their lives in line of duty, since we are informed only by sensationalized media coverage, but we wish to urge a different way of thinking about this problem.
> The law-enforcement agencies are not being helped to understand this situation by the many anti-cultists on the scene uttering their shrill cries about "destructive cults" and "hostages" being held in "captivity" by a "cult leader" using "mind control." Neither they nor the officers seem to have any real understanding of what is involved in a high-energy religious movement, where the members are drawn into a tight circle of devotion and commitment to a charismatic leader whose spiritual insight and guidance they value more than life itself. The leader may seem eccentric or egotistical to outsiders, but there is no law against that.
> Threats of vengeance and the mustering of troops and tanks are

but proof to the "faithful" that the powers of the world are arrayed against them, evidence of their importance in the cosmic struggle—confirmation of their worst fears and validation of their fondest prophecies. Their level of commitment to their faith is higher than most other people give to anything and is therefore very threatening to others. *To invade a center of energy of that kind is like sticking a finger in a dynamo. Whether it explodes or implodes, the result will be tragic for all.*[1] The ordinary strategic calculus of physical combat is as useless here as it was in understanding how the followers of the Ayatolla Khomeini could overthrow the Shah of Iran.

According to the press, some anti-cultists are claiming that they have been working for months on the Davidian "problem" with the federal agency that mounted the attack, which suggests that they helped to shape the conceptualization that led to the scenario of disaster. Central to their definition of the situation is the notion of "mind control"—that there is a technique for controlling the human will at a distance without use of force or threat of force, and that "cult" leaders have this power (though no one else seems to) and can use it to gain and keep and manipulate followers.

This hypothesis is not generally accepted in the relevant disciplines of psychology and sociology (see the rejection of "expert" testimony to this effect for this reason by the federal district court of the Northern District of California when it was offered by the defense as justification for criminal conduct, *U.S. vs. Fishman*, 745 F.Supp. 713, 719 [1990]), and it ill prepares those whose lives are at stake to understand what they are up against.

We are deeply distressed to suspect that an approach that should—at most—have been a last resort was used as the first resort. What opportunity were the members of the religious group given to surrender peaceably or to accede to arrest—if that was what was required—without violence? (A former prosecutor is quoted as saying that they did not resist an earlier investigation and arrest—*N.Y. Times*, March 9, 1993.) This situation is not a problem that can be handled either with force or with arguments over biblical interpretation. It is better let alone as much as possible until it either runs down or stabilizes as a more conventional religion (as did the Mormon movement and the Christian faith itself, both of which began with a small group of faithful followers whose leader was killed by the authorities—in Joseph's Smith's case by a band of militia after his arrest and jailing in Carthage, Illinois).

It would be even more tragic if the government has invested so much money and credibility in this no-win situation that it cannot be satisfied with less than a total eradication of the offending sect (without ever explaining what offense justified the assault in the first place[2]). And if there must be a "victory" to save face for the government, can it not be brought about in a humane way? Surely there are technological means of immobilizing resisters without slaughtering them—and others—in the process. In any event, the public that is paying for all of this deserves a fair and objective post mortem on how this debacle ever developed.

Yours sincerely,

Dean M. Kelley, Counselor on Religious Liberty,
National Council of Churches
James Dunn, Executive Director, Baptist Joint Committee

In order to compress this argument within a couple of pages, it was necessary to telescope a chain of exposition that may have left some readers perplexed, perhaps including the president (if he ever saw it). Casting the equation in terms of "energy" may have seemed obscure, especially since hundreds of heavily armed and armored law enforcement agents, with Bradley personnel carriers, Abrams tanks, and heavy Combat Engineering Vehicles represented a seemingly overpowering array of energy on the government's side. But that is precisely the misconception that afflicted the government's (mis)understanding of the situation. The Shah of Iran had all that going for him—and more—and couldn't hold onto his throne.

Measuring Energy on a Human Scale

The appropriate measure of energy in human affairs is not horsepower or firepower or kilowatts or British Thermal Units, but human commitment of human effort, time, thought, argumentation, loyalty, imagination, patience, anguish, even the dedication of the whole self. The cause that can mobilize the highest level of this kind of energy will prevail over lesser causes, and will attract others to its company because it seems so much more alive than the rest. Few people enlist themselves fully in anything, even the attainment of their own fondest ambitions. But religious movements—at their inception—can often attract and retain higher levels of human energy in devotion to their spiritual vision than any other form of human endeavor. They try to harness every waking thought and action of their adherents for the advancement and enhancement of their cause. That is one reason why members of such groups often live together communally—to intensify and reinforce their common grasp of, and allegience to, their faith.

The steep energy-gradient between such a group and the rest of "the world" can be very threatening to the latter. The neighbors call them "enthusiasts," "obsessed," "fanatics," "over-intense," "cultists," and other terms of opprobrium that tend to downgrade and dehumanize. In addition to the energy-gradient, the communal group may develop distinctive modes of dress, a coded in-house language, unconventional domestic arrangements, and other peculiar traits, and the result between them and others can be mutual dislike, suspicion, fear, and stereotyping. This growing antipathy serves to increase the religious group's alienation and distrust to a degree approaching paranoia.

Nevertheless, the highly structured, high-energy group can be very attractive to people with intense needs for ultimate meaning in their lives. During the siege several people tried to make their way in through the federal perimeter to join the Mt. Carmel community, and two of them made it—Louis Alaniz and Jesse Amen—though they left before the end, and were arrested (U.S. Department of Justice 1993, chronology for March 24, 27, 28). At least one convert has joined the survivors since the holocaust, a young man named Ron Cole. For those who hunger and thirst for a faith that gives meaning to life, no price is too high. If they find it, they may invest their lives in it, not to mention their fortunes, for in this market money is cheap.

As new, high-energy religious movements grow and age, their energy gradually subsides until, after several generations, it reaches the relaxed, avocational level of the large, conventional, "respectable" religious bodies to which we are more accustomed, in which religion has ceased to be a central preoccupation of the members and has become peripheral and attenuated for most of them. Since the adherents of these large bodies are far more numerous, we tend to think that they provide the norm for religious behavior. Instead, they are but vestiges of the more intense and purer forms of the religious enterprise seen at its high-energy beginning. Most major historic religions began in this way, and it is the main means by which new impartations of ultimate meaning come into the world.

Looking back over the centuries, one sees a few scattered peaks of investment of human energy. They mark not migrations, empires, or industries, but the inceptions of the great religions, when a handful of unprepossessing followers of a charismatic prophet or guru or revelator were lifted up by their shared commitment to their vision until the rest of society sloped down from them. They often had a profound effect on their times, reshaping old cultures, revitalizing tired economies, raising the level of people's moral expectations of one another. Not all new religious movements reached these heights. Some failed along the way. Others were suppressed by their older rivals or by disquieted rulers, for the way of the religious innovator is hard (see Fogarty, this volume).

No one knows how these infusions of high energy are injected into the ordinary stream of life. Whether initiated by divine inspiration or human, they attain a remarkable head of power, energizing succeeding generations of the movement and even to some degree the rest of society. No one could *pay* people to put in the kind of time and energy and enthusiasm and investment of self that these devotees give to their all-absorbing vision. Eric Hoffer considered the fanatical mass movement (of which religious movements are the preeminent form) "a miraculous instrument for raising societies and nations from the dead—an instrument of resurrection" (1951, 166). They can have a formative and reformative effect on whole cultures.

They are a rare and valuable resource for the society in which they occur, however dissonant and uncongenial they may seem at the time. Precisely because they offer a critique and corrective to the status quo, they run great risk at the hands of those who embrace and benefit from it. These high-energy movements are the forms of religious behavior at the same time most in need of legal protection and least likely to receive it. Instead, the governmental powers that should protect them are often the very ones embarked against them, usually in the name of maintaining order and enforcing the law.

Flaws of the Hostage Model

In the case of Mt. Carmel, the federal agencies were working out of a "hostage" model that was seriously flawed, as Nancy Ammerman and others have pointed out (U.S. Department of Justice 1993). They saw David Koresh as a "sociopath," a "con man," who had gulled a bunch of weak-willed victims into according him dominance over their lives for his own aggrandizement and the gratification of his sexual appetites. Once his hold on them was loosed, it was supposed, his followers would welcome rescue and release from psychological bondage. He was conceded to have a glib command of memorized passages from Scripture that he wove into a mandate for his hegemony, but it was construed by perplexed officers to be but a facile facade for control and exploitation of his hapless minions.

The tactics developed over the past few years by the FBI for use in hostage situations involve patient persuasion combined with encirclement, isolation, and gradual increase of pressure, characterized as "tightening the noose." Measures are taken to protect the innocent hostages and to loosen the leader's control over them. If they are duped into believing he is entitled to control them, then by discrediting him in their eyes that control can be weakened. Eventually there may come an opportunity to break the circle, release the captives, and seize the hostage-holder. The FBI's Hostage Rescue Team (HRT) was operating out of this model, and it is a vast improvement over the "dynamic entry" approach undertaken at the outset by the Bureau of Alcohol, Tobacco, and Firearms, which was apparently designed to surprise and intimidate the target with their masked hoods and dark commando outfits, heavy firepower, and overwhelming numbers. (Unfortunately for them, it didn't work; they lost the element of surprise and were outnumbered and outgunned. The targets did not even seem to be awed by the Batman costumes.)

The hostage model was seriously at fault because it focused almost exclusively on Koresh as the miscreant and viewed the rest as—at best—unwitting puppets. It discounted the commitment of the members of the religious group to their shared vision and its envisioner. The hostage model disregarded the articulation of that vision in biblical language, calling it "Bible babble" without fathoming its meaning to its believers or realizing that it was the key to the conundrum and the only tongue in which they could be reached. And the hostage model belied the cohesion within the group, the reservoir of human energy their common devotion had built up, such that they were jointly and mutually attached to their cause, prepared to prevail in its defense or to go down with the ship if it failed. In fact, their apocalyptic faith convinced them that the powers of the world were mobilized against them, that they were encircled by the hosts of darkness, and that their fate indeed was to be martyrs in the final battle of Armageddon that would bring on the end of the age. Virtually everything the agencies of law enforcement did, whether under the dynamic entry model or the hostage model, served to reinforce this conviction and to fortify the believers' spirits for the approaching end.

That end must have appeared to have arrived on the morning of April 19, 1993, when the government's tanks were crushing in the walls of their home and the poisonous clouds of CS gas were enveloping them. One can imagine them, in that hour of the Last Trump, accepting with one accord the way out that they had seen approaching for fateful days and weeks.

> No, we will not come out, laying down our arms in abject surrender to the Babylonians, to be paraded in chains before the unbelieving public, suffering their mockery and scorn—not just for a day, but for months and years. We are not going to play the role they want us to play—of cowed thugs or failed rebels. We are not awed by their iron chariots and brazen trumpets prating of their petty authority by night and day. When they believe they have at last conquered us, we will not come out to them with our hands

up, begging for mercy. Like the defenders of Masada, rather than capitulate to the powers of darkness, we will go out all together, with our loved ones, go out through the Other Door into the radiance of the Realms of Glory, where we will be welcomed with praise and honor and understanding, and will be exalted in the sight of the Most High and seated on the thrones that have been prepared for us.

To those who believe it, that is not a scenario of defeat but of transfiguration.

A Federal Conspiracy to End It?

It was a scenario that the federal agencies apparently were not expecting. Working out of the hostage model, they expected the puppets to break loose from their strings and come hurrying out to escape the CS gas. Though they weighed the possibility of mass suicide, they had discounted it on the advice of psychologists who thought in terms of hostages and on the basis of assurances by Koresh and others that they were not contemplating suicide. But, as Dr. Stone pointed out, those assurances were not given in the context of a "show of overwhelming force, and using CS gas" to force an end to the protracted confrontation (Stone 1993, 21). The survivors have maintained that mass suicide was not committed by the group, and there are outsiders who give credence to this claim (Oliver 1994, 79–83) and blame the holocaust on the tanks that pushed in the walls, disabled doors and stairways, crushed propane tanks, and knocked over Coleman lanterns (used for heat and light because the FBI had cut off the electricity).

Whether the victims of the final conflagration set it themselves seems a bit beside the point. It would not have happened if the government forces had not decided to "tighten the noose." And there are some troubling indications that the government itself was determined to bring things to an end. According to a nurse interviewed on the Waco radio station, someone from the FBI dropped by the local hospital at 5:00 on the morning of April 19 to find out if it was equipped to handle burn victims (Lewis 1994, 115). Yet the FBI did not arrange for fire-fighting equipment to be at hand. When the fire broke out, fire trucks were not summoned from Waco for ten minutes. They seemed to be waiting to go—to judge by a 911 call recorded by the sheriff's office—but were in no rush to get there. When they finally approached Mt. Carmel, they were held at the checkpoint by the FBI for another sixteen minutes, while the flames, driven by thirty-mile-an-hour winds, reduced the flimsy frame buildings to charred rubble (Lewis 1994, 118–19). People around the area were told by the FBI that "it was going to end today" (Oliver 1994, 80). Back on March 2, according to the *Houston Chronicle*, former McLennan County [Waco] District Attorney Vic Feazell predicted, "The feds are preparing to kill them. That way they can bury their mistakes" (Bragg 1993, 7A).

Being congenitally suspicious of conspiracy theories, the present writer is not yet prepared to accept this analysis of governmental culticide. It would require greater purposiveness, secretiveness, meticulousness, and internal coordination than the federal agencies displayed in other aspects of this ill-fated enterprise.[3] Instead, it appears that the FBI and the Department of Justice were trying to resolve this difficult situation with a minimum of bloodshed. They took great pride in reporting that "after February 28, no weapons of any kind were fired [at Mt. Carmel] by any law enforcement officer, whether state, local or federal" (U.S. Department of Justice 1993, 9). Apparently this claim did not count "flash-bangs" (grenade-type projectiles causing a loud report and bright flash of light fired on several occasions by the FBI to dissuade Koreshians from going outside their buildings) or "ferret rounds" (cannisters of CS gas fired through the windows of the buildings) as "weapons of any type." However, it seems likely that either side could have massacred the other if it had wanted to do so, but both withheld the full force of their firepower.[4]

Until greater evidence is adduced to the contrary—which may yet happen—this writer concludes that the FBI and Justice Department officials were doing what they thought should be done, according to their lights at the time (which this analysis suggests were seriously mistaken). They had a tiger by the tail that they did not want to kill, could not hold onto indefinitely (at immense expense) and could not let go without incurring accusations of having wasted four agents' lives and millions of dollars, as well as leaving the government liable for huge damages (which still may be levied in the civil suits brought by survivors). That they should have done otherwise, or better, is easy for outside observers to say in hindsight, or even for those of us who warned of a tragic outcome in advance but bore no responsibility for dealing with it. That they have learned from their errors is less clear. One defense attorney, Douglas Tinker, remarked after the trial in San Antonio, "They'll be kicking down doors tomorrow just like they did at the Mount Carmel center" (*New York Times* February 28, 1994, A14).

Religious Communities Should Be Left Alone

In view of the danger of implosion, it is the contention of this writer that *religious communities that pose no clear and present danger to others should be left alone.* Such a contention will immediately evoke the response that religious groups should not be above the law. Just because they claim to be religious, it is said, members of such groups are not entitled to disobey laws that everyone else has to obey. That is perhaps true in the abstract, but other considerations should apply as well. Everyone is bound by the laws that protect and regulate the social relations in society. But not all laws are equally enforced. In fact, few laws are fully enforced. Police and prosecutors (rightfully) enjoy considerable discretion in focusing on particular targets for enforcement to the neglect of others because they could not possibly enforce all laws fully all the time. Indeed, when police employees undertake a job action, one of the ways they show displeasure with their working conditions is to enforce all laws aggressively on everyone, thereby virtually bringing the workings of society to a grinding halt. Since the laws are underenforced or differentially enforced, the decisions of enforcement are necessarily related to questions of priority. Which of the many greater or lesser threats to peace and order should be the targets of limited law enforcement resources and the burdens of an overburdened criminal justice system and overcrowded prisons?

Presumably a rational law enforcement policy would be to go after the most serious threats to peace and safety first, and to leave the lesser for later (or for never). That is a policy followed by most law enforcement agencies (subject to political crosspressures and the calculus of risk). On that scale, most religious groups would normally not be in the top range of priorities because normally they do not have the *mens rea*, or criminal intent, that is—or should be—an essential element in an offense punishable by the criminal law. That is, they are not outlaws, out to rip off the public or to victimize their neighbors for their own aggrandizement, like a drug-running gang or a racketeering mob. They are at most "nonlaws," in the sense of being preoccupied with their religious vision to the exclusion of everything else (as Tom Robbins and Dick Anthony have so well explained in their contribution to this volume).

This visionary obsession may sometimes need to be reined in for the sake of others, but only if others are actually and immediately at risk. If in actual fact (not mere supposition) such a group does pose a genuine threat to others, its specific malefactors (rather than the group as an undifferentiated whole) should be proceeded against by law enforcement, using the least intrusive means, for the protection of the public. The followers of David Koresh were not remotely such a group. They were seeking mainly to be left alone and fortifying their community only in defense against imagined (or all too real?) threats. Some will take issue with this assertion. For example, in an effort to show Koresh as a threat to the public, the federal reports quote several idiomatic and jingoistic threats attributed (at second or third hand) to him, but they seem weak reeds to support a major para-military onslaught when less catastrophic means might have suf-ficed and certainly should have been tried.

Rescue the Dupes and Captives?

Some will contend that law enforcement also has an obligation to protect the members of such groups from themselves or their lead-ers. That supposition is part of the hostage model that so clearly mis-defined the situation at Mt. Carmel. The Mt. Carmel community sent out a videotape on March 9 showing interviews with members of the community who asserted that they did not want to come out. Even the Justice Department report (in hindsight) admitted, "Each person on the video—male and female, young and old—spoke in a calm, assured tone of their desire to remain inside, even after the experience of the ATF raid only a few days earlier. . . . The abiding impression is not of a bunch of 'lunatics,' but rather of a group of peo-ple who . . . believed so strongly in Koresh that the notion of leaving the squalid compound was unthinkable" (1993, 205). In the absence of very strong proof to the contrary deriving directly from the state-ments of the persons themselves—not just from outsiders' supposi-tions—the presumption should be that the members of a religious group have freely and knowingly chosen to belong to the group and to remain in it. To presume otherwise and to act against them on such a presumption is a gross and arrogant violation of their personal reli-gious liberty.

There is a literature that runs to the contrary (cf. Delgado, 1977, 1984), claiming that some members of religious communities have been duped into joining while in a condition of diminished capacity. That is, they are deceived into thinking that it is not a "cult" they are joining until it is too late. After their faculties are weakened by loss of sleep, overwork, chanting, and malnutrition, they may discover what they have gotten into, but then they no longer have the strength of will to get out. That ingenious rationale is belied by the immense natural turnover in membership in most groups the antic-ultists consider "cults" without anyone's having to be "rescued" by outsiders (Barker 1984, 1988; Wright 1984, 1987). Joining such groups meets certain personal needs, and when those needs are no longer acute and the group experience becomes unsatisfactory, many members drift away and go on to other things.

Furthermore, the "diminished capacity" argument is not new; it and many of the other anticult accusations, such as deceptive recruiting, exploitation of cheap labor for aggrandizement of cult leaders, authoritarian discipline, and sexual irregularities, were trotted out in a long line of cases in the nineteenth and early twentieth centuries in which disaffected members of communal religious groups or heirs of deceased members tried to break the collective covenant that bound such groups together and get a share of the communal property. These cases are virtually unknown today, but are the only precedents in the case law of the Supreme Court of the United States and several state supreme courts on this subject (See *Waite v. Merrill*, Maine, 1826 [member leaving Shakers cannot claim share of common property]; *Gass and Bonta v. Wilhite*, Kentucky, 1834 [same]; *Schriber v. Rapp*, Pennsylvania, 1836 [claim of entrapment will not compel recovery of share of common property of Harmony Society]; *Goesele v. Bimeler*, U.S. Supreme Court, 1852 [heirs of Society of Separatists of Zoar cannot recover from group property]; *Gasely v. Separatists of Zoar*, Ohio, 1862 [same]; *Baker v. Nachtrieb*, U.S. Supreme Court, 1856 [defecting member of Harmony Society cannot recover share of property from the society]; *Speidel v. Henrici*, U.S. Supreme Court, 1887 [same]; *Burt v. Oneida Community*, New York, 1893 [same]; *Schwartz v. Duss*, U.S. Supreme Court, 1902 [Society of Economy not shown to have been dissolved, so property not subject to distribution]; *Iowa v. Amana Society*, Iowa Supreme Court, 1906 [economic pursuits not outside charter of religious corporation]; *Order of St. Benedict v. Steinhauser*, U.S. Supreme Court, 1914 [member of religious order cannot erect a personal estate independent of order]). In every instance, the courts rejected the arguments and left the religious organization to go its own chosen way. The only state supreme court giving any credence to the anticult farrago was Minnesota, in *Peterson v. Sorlien*, 1980, which a federal district court in that state refused to follow (*Eilers v. Coy*, 1984).

The religious community at Mt. Carmel presented a situation where "probable cause" (to believe that a crime was committed) was at least debatable (Gaffney to the contrary notwithstanding). Even the handpicked firearms experts asked by the Treasury Department to evaluate the validity of the warrants said there was no illegal smoking gun in the inventories of UPS shipments given them for analysis. They had to rely on a concatenation of conjectures to reach the expected conclusion: if the Koreshians had the necessary milling machine and lathe, and if they had someone willing and able to use them, and if they had a sample "drop-in sear" to clone, they could have turned legal semiautomatic weapons into illegal automatic ones (U.S. Department of Treasury 1993, B-166, 183). That may satisfy all-too-cooperative magistrates, but it is not necessarily what the Founders meant by "probable cause" in the Fourth Amendment.

In such marginal cases, where suspicion is diffuse and tentative, the religious group should be left alone unless or until there is unambiguous evidence of actual and imminent danger to the public. There is no dearth of drug gangs unambiguously shooting innocent bystanders with assault rifles on the streets of major cities to which the federal agencies could devote their attention without expending millions of dollars of taxpayers' money to quell a supposed threat from a reclusive millennialist sect out on the dusty Texas prairie. The BATF and FBI could occupy themselves for years with far more obvious and dire threats to public peace and safety before they reached the minor threat (if it was even that) of Mt. Carmel. But that would be more dangerous for federal agents than the Waco community was thought to be when the BATF zeroed in on it as a promising site for an Eliot Ness-type raid and consequent favorable media coverage.

Does the counsel that religious groups in ambiguous cases be left alone mean that they should be allowed to think they are not bound by the laws that bind others? Such groups usually are not purposing to break the law as an end in itself. But if the law interferes with what they believe to be their religious duty, they will often take the stance historically characteristic of religious rebels and reformers. As Peter and the apostles said to the legal authorities of their time, "We must obey God rather than men" (Acts of the Apostles 5:29). Martin Luther is reported to have said something to that effect to the Holy Roman Emperor, Charles V, and the Imperial Diet when they demanded his submission and recantation, "Here I stand; God help me, I can do no other." If those are "outlaws," the world needs more of them.

Religious Groups Are Not Above the Law; They Are in It

The law of the United States, at its best, has tried to avoid such confrontations with religious duty by exempting persons acting out of conscience from the full rigors of the law impinging upon it (See McConnell 1990), as in the statutory exemption for conscientious objectors to military service—a provision that may cost someone else's life in place of the objector's. Certainly many lesser accommodations can and should be made that do not displace such costs onto others. If Mt. Carmelites are not sent to jail for trafficking in illegal firearms, no one else has to go to jail in their stead.

After all, it is not correct to say that religious groups are *above* the law; they are *in* it. Religion is a unique and clearly identified entity expressly recognized and protected in the fundamental law of the United States: "Congress shall make no law . . . prohibiting the free exercise [of religion]." That was one of the monumental achievements of the Founders of this nation: to try to spare believers the civil burdens and disabilities that had befallen them at the hands of governments in earlier times and other places and to make the pursuit of religious visions by every person as free as possible of government regulation or imposition. That consideration has even been extended—though somewhat grudgingly and unevenly—to groups of believers whose autonomy is to a considerable degree recognized and respected by law. That is a basic right for which we should all be forever grateful and which we should sedulously maintain and defend for everyone, even new and unconventional religious movements like the followers of Koresh. It is more than justified for its own sake, as one of the highest provisions for one of the most precious of human rights.

Some people, however, seem to think that—while no doubt laudable—this solicitude for religious rights is essentially an indulgence of individual idiosyncracy that may need to be abrogated or attenuated in the interest of more pressing public needs. That line of thought seems to have infected the Supreme Court of the United States—or a bare majority thereof—several years ago, when it cut back on the protection afforded by the Free Exercise Clause of the First Amendment to a level common to lesser interests that are not specified in the Bill of Rights. For almost three decades the court had held that governmental burdening of religious practice must be justified by a "compelling state interest" that could be served in no less burdensome way (since *Sherbert v. Verner*, 1963). But in *Employment Division of Oregon v. Smith* (1990), Justice Antonin Scalia announced that this level of "strict scrutiny" was a "luxury" the nation could no longer afford, and that henceforth the claim of free exercise of religion would not exempt believers from laws of general application (such as the convoluted federal firearms statutes?) that did not expressly target religion or religious practice. That holding was supplanted by the Religious Freedom Restoraton Act of 1993, reinstating the compelling interest test for free exercise of religion, which was signed into law by President Clinton on November 16, 1993, seven months too late to do the Mt. Carmelites any good.

The Supreme Court in *Smith* seemed to have forgotten its obligation to protect and enforce the guarantees of the Bill of Rights, without which there might well not have been a United States of America. The Constitution would probably have failed of ratification in 1788 if Washington and other leading Federalists had not assured the five states that insisted on an explicit guarantee of religious freedom that a Bill of Rights would be enacted by the First Congress (Stokes 1950, 606), as it indeed was, with ratification following in 1791.

Those who think that other pressing public needs take precedence over freedom of religion fail to realize that the key covenant on which adoption of the nation's fundamental law turned, the First Amendment, *defines* the free exercise of religion as *preeminent among all pressing public needs.* That priority is entirely consonant with the human-energy analysis set forth above. Such a dynamo of energy can be a valuable resource for society if allowed to mature and stabilize itself over time, or it can be a colossal source of turbulence and trouble if invaded, as the tragedy of Mt. Carmel demonstrated.

That lesson should have been learned from the nineteenth-century experience with the Church of Jesus Christ of Latter-day Saints, which was hounded from Ohio to Missouri to Illinois to Utah, legislated against by Congress, prosecuted by the courts, and harassed by the cavalry—all at great expense in money, time, energy, and turmoil. Eventually the church capitulated on plural marriage, and its people have become staunch and stable pillars of society. Much trauma on both sides could have been avoided and much human energy conserved if they had been left alone to go their own way in the land of the Great Salt Lake until they found a peaceable modus vivendi with the rest of the country, as they eventually would have. Indeed, plural marriage in time might even have been peaceably acceptable, or dispensable, and by the mid-twentieth century era of sexual "liberation" would have seemed a rather strait-laced and pedestrian arrangement.

A Jury Rejects the Government's Charge of "Ambush"

The flames that consumed Mt. Carmel have died down; the embers have cooled. The corpses have been autopsied and the site bulldozed. The Treasury and Justice Departments have pored over the events and issued their apologias, but not apologies. At long last a court heard the charges against eleven survivors of the Mt. Carmel community. The jury weighed the evidence against them and acquitted all the defendants of the most serious counts: conspiring to murder, and aiding and abetting murder of four federal agents who were killed in the raid. They acquitted four defendants of all charges. They convicted five defendants of aiding and abetting voluntary manslaughter, which the judge defined as "acting in the sudden heat of passion caused by adequate provocation." And they convicted one defendant of possession of a grenade and one (who was not present at Mt. Carmel during the entire siege) of conspiracy to manufacture and possess a machine gun and aiding and abetting possession of a machine gun (*New York Times*, Feb. 27, 1994).[5]

At least two things can be said about the verdicts: (1) the jury rejected the government's oft-repeated allegations of "ambush." Perhaps the jury had seen enough Western movies in which the settlers pull their wagons into a circle to defend against an Indian attack to know that the settlers are not said to be trying to ambush the Indians. The Treasury report had voiced this allegation repeatedly, and its attempt to define the situation as the victimization of federal officers was epitomized by the claim that "On February 28, Koresh and his followers knew ATF agents were coming and *decided to kill them*" (U.S. Department of Treasury 1993, 165, emphasis added). A more accurate description would have been "decided to *fend them off.*" That description is more consistent with the jury's verdict, with the characterization by Dr. Alan Stone (one of the Justice Department's outside behavioral experts) that the followers of Koresh were "willing to kill but not cold-blooded killers" (Stone 1993, 18), and with the fact that much of the firing at BATF agents was through walls and roofs, where those firing could not see who they were shooting at, but mainly wanted to make the vicinity untenable for intruders.

(2) The most serious charges—both those resulting in acquittals and those resulting in convictions—arose out of reaction to governmental action. There is a medically recognized category of *iatrogenic illness*—illness caused by the physician. Likewise there is—or should be—a category of *constabulogenic crime*—crime caused by the police.[6] Sophisticated grand jurors (who are rare), confronted by a suspect who is disabled and bandaged and charged with "resisting arrest," "interfering with a police officer in the performance of his duty," or "attempting escape," but with no substantive charge to justify the arrest in the first place, may discern "police brutality," in the sense of punishment of a supposed offender without evidence to substantiate a preexisting offense. In the case of the Mt. Carmel verdicts, there were only two defendants convicted on three minor charges of firearms violations (and of no other charges) to justify the whole sorry performance. Of course, it could be claimed that the real culprits died

in the fire, and only minor offenders were left. But that argument would apply equally to the heavy counts that the prosecutors did not hesitate to pin on all eleven defendants. They were expected to pay for all the sins of the community, of which firearms offenses were the least. All the other offenses occurred after and as a result of the federal intervention. That does not justify firing at the *federales*, but helps explain it, and renders the jury's verdict more proportionate to the actual events than were the prosecutors' allegations.

The judge set aside one count against seven defendants—using and carrying a firearm in commission of a violent crime, but reinstated it a few weeks later and sentenced those convicted under it to thirty years each in addition to the ten-year sentences for voluntary manslaughter. Three were given lesser sentences, and three had been acquitted of all charges. The foreman of the jury claimed that the jury had not intended such heavy penalties and wished they had acquitted them all. Appeals will be taken on several issues, which could prolong matters for months or even years. And some day the convicted defendants may come out of prison (if they live so long) to resume their private lives and perhaps a public mission.

A few other loose ends are still unresolved. Several congressional committees held hearings on the Waco debacle in April, May, and June of 1993 Ramsey Clark, former U.S. attorney general, filed a $900,000,000 lawsuit against the government on behalf of survivors and relatives of the deceased. That civil suit may produce some interesting information through discovery. Newt Gingrich, Speaker of the House, announced in January 1995 that there will be hearings on the Waco disaster. A curious confluence of firearms enthusiasts and libertarians with progressive activists and apprehensive new religious movements—afraid they may be next—has been trying to keep the pot boiling. But no federal agents have been put on trial, civil or criminal, although the three top officers of the BATF have resigned. Two federal officers, Phillip Chojnacki and Chuck Sarabyn, who led the raid, were suspended from the BATF for nearly a year, but were reinstated on December 24, 1994, with full back pay and benefits, presumably because they have "suffered enough." No riots have broken out on the streets of Waco or anywhere else. One commentator, Paul Roberts, wrote in the *Washington Times*, referring to the videotaped police assault on Rodney King, "If a billy club is excessive force, what is a tank?" (Oliver 1994, 80). The television talk shows have long since turned to more current outrages and more engaging perversions. When these last ripples of turbulence die out, will it all at last be over?

Is It All Over Yet?

Maybe the FBI fellow on the loud-hailer was right. Maybe Koresh's messiahship is at an end, and it is all over. Maybe not. If there is one thing governments are not very good at, it is terminating messiahships. Messiahs they may kill, but their reigns are less manageable. One thinks of another messiah of about thirty years of age who was executed by the law enforcement agencies of his time and place (who doubtless thought his theological assertions pretentious nonsense, if they were even aware of them). He left behind a disheartened handful of leaderless followers who had believed he was God's Chosen One. Only after the attention of the law had turned elsewhere did they recover their zeal, convinced that God had raised him from the dead and that they were to spread his word and his reign throughout the world. He was probably looked upon by the provincial powers of his time as the guru of a ragtag cult, a small-time con man stirring up trouble in the sacred precincts and disrupting the sacrifice trade. He was put down almost casually as a brief bother in the course of the routine running of a small outpost of a mighty empire. But he did not stay down.

Suppose that history should repeat itself, and the followers of Koresh should spread abroad the gospel of their messiah, who was put down by the massed might of the greatest power on earth in full view (albeit at a distance) of hundreds of observers from the press of the world—a much larger scene than Golgotha! And suppose that, given this larger launching pad, they were comparably successful in their cause. In another millennium or two, how might history view this seeming debacle? Will it have become the clumsy but futile effort by the modern Babylon to snuff out the Lamb of God, the divinely anointed Messenger bringing salvation to millions? In those times, will one President Clinton and one Attorney General Reno and their minions be seen in retrospect as spear-carriers in the glorious Drama of Redemption, unwitting but necessary tools of destiny playing the bit parts once played by Herod Antipas and Pontius Pilate?

And who would the heroes of the sacred tale be then? St. David Jones, who brought the warning of the BATF attack? St. Perry Jones, his father, who carried the warning to the Lamb, and was one of the first to die at the hands of the Assyrians? St. Wayne Martin, the Harvard-trained attorney who called the sheriff's 911 number and arranged the cease-fire? St. Steve Schneider, the Lamb's lieutenant, who negotiated with the hosts of darkness during the siege? The Mighty Men, who were his chief aides and disciples? The women who were his spiritual wives, and their children, the bearers of the prophet's genes? They are all dead now, but that does not necessarily mean it's "over." That only history will decide.

Notes

1. First emphasis in original; second emphasis added to indicate the material quoted by Gaffney.

2. The search and arrest warrants were not available to the public at the time of writing—not that they necessarily resolve the problem, since their sufficiency has been widely challenged.

3. The trial transcript indicated that the defense attorneys believed that the FBI got wind the day before of a plan to fight any invading tanks with fire, perhaps from electronic bugs planted on milk cartons sent in by the FBI, and this led to preparations for fire, including the unusual arrangement for Forward-Looking Infra-Red (FLIR) photography in a circling helicopter. But the FBI took no steps to prevent or put out the fire.

4. "If [the Davidians] were militants determined to ambush and kill as many ATF agents as possible, it seems to me that given their firepower, the devastation would have been even worse. . . . The ATF agents brought to the compound in cattle cars could have been cattle going to slaughter if the Branch Davidians had taken full advantage of their tactical superiority. They apparently did not maximize the kill of ATF agents" (Stone 1993, 19).

5. Nowhere do the federal reports mention that the Branch Davidians, like many other Texans, relied on a lucrative trade in guns and ammunition as a source of revenue.

6. I am sorry for the clumsy coinage; the Greeks did not have a word for it because they did not have police (in the sense of an occupation devoted to apprehending criminals); the closest approximations are "assistants," "guards," "(night) watchmen," more akin to bailiffs or wardens than constables.

References

Barker, Eileen. 1984. *The Making of a Moonie: Choice or Brainwashing?* Oxford: Blackwell.

———. 1988. "Defection from the Unification Church: Some Statistics and Distinctions." In *Falling from the Faith,* edited by David G. Bromley, pp. 166–84. Newbury Park, CA: Sage.

Bragg, Roy. 1993. "Ex-Prosecutor Laments Agent's 'Storm Trooper' Tactics." *Houston Chronicle.* March 2, 7A.

Delgado, Richard. 1977. "Religious Totalism: Gentle and Ungentle Persuasion." *Southern California Law Review* 51: 1–100.

———. 1984. "When Religious Exercise Is Not Free." *Vanderbilt Law Review* 37 (5).

Hoffer, Eric. 1951. *The True Believer.* New York: Harper.

Lewis, James R. 1994. "Fanning the Flames of Suspicion." In *From the*

Ashes: Making Sense of Waco, edited by James R. Lewis, pp. 115–20. Lanham MD: Rowman and Littlefield.

McConnell, Michael. 1990. "The Origins and Historical Understanding of Free Exercise of Religion." *Harvard Law Review* 103: 1410–1517.

Oliver, Moorman. 1994. "Killed by Semantics." In *From the Ashes: Making Sense of Waco,* edited by James R. Lewis, pp. 71–86. Lanham, MD: Rowman and Littlefield.

Stokes, A. P. 1950. *Church and State in the United States.* 3 vols. New York: Harper.

Stone, Alan. 1993. "Report and Recommendations Concerning the Handling of Incidents Such as the Branch Davidian Standoff in Waco, Texas." Washington, DC: U.S. Department of Justice.

U.S. Department of Justice. 1993. *Report to the Deputy Attorney General on the Events at Waco, Texas: February 28 to April 19, 1993.* Redacted version, October 8. Washington, DC: U.S. Government Printing Office.

U.S. Department of Treasury. 1993. Report of the Department of Treasury on the Bureau of Alcohol, Tobacco, and Firearms Investigation of Vernon Wayne Howell, Also Known as David Koresh. Washington, DC: U.S. Government Printing Office.

Wright, Stuart A. 1984. "Post-Involvement Attitudes of Voluntary Defectors from Controversial New Religious Movements." *Journal for the Scientific Study of Religion* 23 (2): 172–82.

———. 1987. *Leaving Cults: The Dynamics of Defection.* Washington, DC: Society for the Scientific Study of Religion.

Cases

Baker v. Nachtrieb, 19 Howard 126 (1856).
Burt v. Oneida Community, 137 N.Y. 346, 33 NE 307 (1893).
Eilers v. Coy, 582 F. Supp. 1093 (D.Minn. 1984).
Employment Division of Oregon v. Smith, 494 U.S. 872 (1990).
Gasely v. Separatists of Zoar, 13 Ohio 144 (1862).
Gass and Bonta v. Wilhite, 2 Dana (Ky.) 170 (1834).
Goesele v. Bimeler, 14 Howard 589 (1852).
Iowa v. Amana Society, 132 Ia. 894 (1906).
Order of St. Benedict v. Steinhauser, 234 U.S. 640 (1914).
Peterson v. Sorlien, 299 N.W.2d 123 (1980).
Schriber v. Rapp, 5 Watts (Pa.) 351 (1836).
Schwartz v. Duss, 187 U.S. 8 (1902).
Sherbert v. Verner, 374 U.S. 398 (1963).
Speidel v. Henrici, 120 U.S. 377 (1887).
U.S. v. Fishman, 745 F.Supp. 713 (1990).
Waite v. Merrill, 4 Greenleaf (Maine) 102 (1826).

Other Authorities

U.S. Constitution, Amendment I.
U.S. Constitution, Amendment IV.
Religious Freedom Restoration Act, 42 U.S.C. 2000a.

Appendix

Branch Davidians Who Died at Mt. Carmel

Adults (N=59)	Age	Citizenship	Race/Ethnicity
Katherine Andrade	24	Canada	White
Jennifer Andrade	20	Canada	White
Winston Blake	28	U.S.	Black
Alrick George Bennett	35	Great Britain	Black
Susan Benta	31	Great Britain	Black
Mary Jean Borst	49	U.S.	White
Pablo Cohen	28	Israel	White
Abedowalo Davis	30	Great Britain	Black
Shari Doyle	18	U.S.	White
Beverly Elliot	31	Great Britain	Black
Doris Fagan	60	Great Britain	Black
Evette Fagan	30	Great Britain	Black
Lisa Farris	24	U.S.	Black
Raymond Friesen	76	U.S.	White
Nicole Gent	23	Australia	White
Peter Gent	24	Australia	White
Aisha Gyarfas	17	Australia	White
Sandra Hardial	26	Great Britain	Black
Diana Henry	28	Great Britain	Black
Pauline Henry	24	Great Britain	Black
Philip Henry	23	Great Britain	Black
Stephen Henry	20	Great Britain	Black
Vanessa Henry	19	Great Britain	Black
Zilla Henry	55	Great Britain	Black
Novellette Hipsman	36	U.S.	White
Peter Hipsman	27	U.S.	White
Floyd Houtman	61	U.S.	White

Sherri Jewell	43	U.S.	White
David Michael Jones	00	U.S.	White
Michele Jones	18	U.S.	White
Perry Jones	64	U.S.	White
Rachel Jones Howell	23	U.S.	White
David Koresh (Howell)	33	U.S.	White
Jeffery Little	31	U.S.	White
Livingstone Malcolm	26	Great Britain	Black
Anita Martin	18	U.S.	Black
Diane Martin	41	Great Britain	Black
Douglas Wayne Martin	42	U.S.	Black
Wayne Martin, Jr.	20	U.S.	Black
Juliet Santoyo Martinez	30	U.S.	Hispanic
John Mark McBean	27	Great Britain	Black
Allison Monbelly	31	Great Britain	Black
Rosemary Morrison	29	Great Britain	Black
Sonia Murray	31	U.S.	Black
Theresa Nobriega	48	Great Britain	Black
James Riddle	32	U.S.	White
Rebecca Saipaia	24	Phillipines	Asian
Judy Schneider	41	U.S.	White
Steve Schneider	41	U.S.	White
Michael Schroeder	29	U.S.	White
Cliff Sellers	33	Great Britain	White
Floracita Sonobe	32	Phillipines	Asian
Scott Sonobe	34	Phillipines	Asian
Greg Summers	28	U.S.	White
Lorraine Sylvia	47	U.S.	White
Margarida Joann Vaega	50	New Zealand	White
Neil Vaega	37	New Zealand	White
Jaydean Wendell	34	U.S.	Asian
Mark Wendell	37	U.S.	Asian

Children (N=21)

Chanel Andrade	14 mos	U.S.	White
Cyrus Howell	8	U.S.	White
Star Howell	6	U.S.	White
Bobbie Lane Koresh	2	U.S.	White
Dayland Gent	3	Australia	White
Paige Gent	1	Australia	White
Chica Jones	22 mos	U.S.	White
Latwan Jones	22 mos	U.S.	White
Serenity Jones	4	U.S.	White
Lisa Martin	13	U.S.	Black
Sheila Martin	15	U.S.	Black
Abigail Martinez	11	U.S.	Hispanic
Audrey Martinez	13	U.S.	Hispanic
Crystal Martinez	3	U.S.	Hispanic

Isaiah Martinez	4	U.S.	Hispanic
Joseph Martinez	8	U.S.	Hispanic
Melissa Morrison	4	Great Britain	Black
Mayanah Schneider	2	U.S.	White
Startle Summers	1	U.S.	White
Hollywood Sylvia	2	U.S.	White
Rachel Sylvia	13	U.S.	White

Contributors

NANCY T. AMMERMAN received the Ph.D. degree from Yale University in 1983 and taught at Candler School of Theology at Emory University from 1984 through 1995. She will join the faculty of Hartford Seminary's Center for Social and Religious Research in 1995. She has written extensively on conservative religious movements. Her books include *Bible Believers: Fundamentalists in the Modern World* (1987), and *Baptist Battles: Social Change and Religious Conflict in the Southern Baptist Convention* (1990). She has also written essays published in various volumes of the Fundamentalism Project of the American Academy of Arts and Sciences. In 1993, she was asked by the U.S. Justice and Treasury Departments to serve on a panel of experts commissioned to evaluate the government's role in the Branch Davidian encounter.

DICK ANTHONY is an advanced doctoral candidate in the religion and psychology program at the Graduate Theological Union in Berkeley, California. He is senior author-editor of *Spiritual Choices* (1988) and coeditor of *In Gods We Trust: New Patterns of American Pluralism* (1981, 1990). He has published numerous articles on religious movements which have appeared in a variety of social science and psychology journals. A critic of brainwashing theories of conversion processes in religious movements, he has recently coauthored "Brainwashing and Totalitarian Influence," which appeared in the new *Encyclopedia of Human Behavior* (Academic Press, 1994). He also works as a consultant to attorneys contending with varieties of mind-control claims.

JOHN P. BARTKOWSKI is a Ph.D. candidate in the department of sociology at the University of Texas at Austin. He is currently conducting dissertation research on the construction of masculinity in conservative Protestant families. His work has appeared in *Sociology of Religion* and selected edited volumes. His substantive areas of interest include religion, gender, and the family.

DAVID G. BROMLEY is professor of sociology at Virginia Commonwealth University and visiting professor at the University of Virginia. He received a Ph.D. from Duke University in 1971. He is currently president of the Association for the Sociology of Religion (ASR) and past editor of the *Journal for the Scientific Study of Religion*. Bromley has authored or edited numerous scholarly books, the most recent including *New Perspectives in the Study of Religion* (1993), *The Handbook of Cults and Sects in America* (1993), and *The Satanism Scare* (1991). He is currently completing work on his latest book, *Strange Gods and Cult Scares*.

CHRISTOPHER G. ELLISON is associate professor of sociology at the University of Texas at Austin. He received his Ph.D. from Duke University in 1991. His current research focuses on religious differences in family ideology and practice, with particular attention to parent-child relations among conservative Protestants. Additional interests include the mental health implications of religious involvement, the contemporary Black Church, and the persistence of regionalism in the United States. His work has appeared in numerous professional journals, including *American Sociological Review, Social Forces, Journal of Health and Social Behavior*, and *Review of Religious Research*, as well as edited volumes.

ROBERT S. FOGARTY is professor of history at Antioch College and he is currently editor of the *Antioch Review*. A noted historian of religious and communal movements, he has published several books on the subject, including *Special Love/Special Sex: An Oneida Community Diary* (1994), *All Things New: Communal and Utopian Movements, 1865–1914* (1990), *The Righteous Remnant: The House of David* (1981), *Dictionary of American Communal and Utopian History* (1980), and *American Utopianism* (1972). He has been a visiting fellow at All Souls College, Oxford, and the New York University Humanities Institute, as well as the Lloyd Lewis Fellow at the Newberry Library, Chicago.

EDWARD M. GAFFNEY, JR. is dean and professor of law at the Valparaiso University School of Law. He studied theology at the Gregorian University in Rome, received his law degree and M.A. in legal history from Catholic University of America, and earned the LL.M. degree from Harvard Law School. He was scholar-in-residence at Stanford Law School, held the James P. Bradley Chair in Constitutional Law at Loyola Law School, Los Angeles, and was director of the Center for Constitutional Studies at Notre Dame Law School. Gaffney has written extensively on issues of interpretation of constitutional law, principally on matters involving religious freedom. He has also participated in litigation involving religious liberty issues in many of the federal appellate courts, as well as the U.S. Supreme Court.

JEFFREY K. HADDEN is professor of sociology at the University of Virginia. He is past president of the Southern Sociological Society, the Association for the Sociology of Religion, and the Society for the Scientific Study of Religion, and is currently book review editor for *Journal for the Scientific Study of Religion*. Hadden has published extensively in the field of sociology of religion. His recent books include the coedited *Handbook of Cults and Sects in America* (1993) with David Bromley, as well as *Secularization and Fundamentalism Reconsidered* (1989), and *Televangelism: Power and Politics on God's Frontier* (1988), both with Anson Shupe.

JOHN R. HALL is professor of sociology at the University of California, Davis. He is the author of a scholarly work on religious communes and sects, *The Ways Out: Utopian Communal Groups in an Age of Babylon* (1981), and has written a sociological and cultural history of Peoples Temple, *Gone From the Promised Land: Jonestown in American Cultural History* (1987). Hall has also written on a variety of other sociology topics, including *Culture: Sociological Perspectives* (1993), coauthored with Mary Jo Neitz.

DEAN M. KELLEY is an ordained Methodist minister who has been the staff executive of the National Council of Churches in the field of religious liberty since 1960. He is author of *Why Conservative Churches are Growing* (1972), and *Why Churches Should Not Pay Taxes* (1977), and editor of *Government Intervention in Religious Affairs I & II* (1982, 1986). He is currently living in semiretirement in New Hampshire and completing a five-volume treatise, *The Law of Church and State in America*, for Greenwood Press. He serves as secretary to the National Council's Committee on Religious Liberty, which has taken a strong interest in the Waco disaster.

JAMES R. LEWIS is senior editor for the Center for Academic Publication and editor of *Syzygy: Journal of Alternative Religion and Culture*. He has authored a number of works in the reference book field, including the recently published *Encyclopedia of Afterlife Beliefs and Phenomena* (1994), and the forthcoming *Encyclopedia of Sects, Cults, and New Religions*. He has published extensively in the field of new religious movements, and is the editor of several recent volumes: *From the Ashes: Making Sense of Waco* (1994), *Sex, Salvation, and Slander* (1994), and *The Gods Have Landed: New Religions from Other Worlds* (1995).

WILLIAM L. PITTS, Jr. is professor of church history at Baylor University, where he has served as director of graduate studies in religion since 1988. Pitts received the Ph.D. in church history at Vanderbilt University in 1969. He has published in professional journals on alternative religions, spirituality, and ecumenics. Recent publications include "Holiness as Spirituality: The Religious Quest of A. B. Simpson," in *Modern Christian Spirituality: Methodological and Historical Essays* (1990), and "Letters from Waco: Millennial Spirituality of the Branch Davidians," in *Christian Spirituality Bulletin* (1993). He is one of the few scholars to gather data and conduct research on the Branch Davidians prior to their recent notoriety. He gave more than two hundred interviews with the media during and after the fifty-one-day standoff in Waco.

JAMES T. RICHARDSON is professor of sociology and judicial studies at the University of Nevada, Reno, where he directs the Master of Judicial Studies Program. He received his Ph.D. from Washington State University in 1968. He has written or edited six books and over 100 articles and chapters in journals and edited volumes on the subject of new religions. His most recent books include *The Satanism Scare* (1992) and *Money and Power in New Religions* (1988).

THOMAS ROBBINS is an independent scholar. He received his Ph.D. from the University of North Carolina and has taught or held research appointments at Yale University, Queens College of the City of New York, Central Michigan University, the Graduate Theological Union, and the New School of Social Research. He has published extensively on the topic of new religious movements. Some of his works include *In Gods We Trust: New Patterns of Religious Pluralism in America* (1990), *Cults, Converts, and Charisma* (1988), and *Cults, Culture, and the Law* (1985).

ANSON SHUPE is professor of sociology and anthropology at the joint campus of Indiana University–Purdue University. He received his Ph.D. from Indiana University in 1975. His research interests include the sociology of religious movements and family violence. His most recent books include his coedited volume (with Bronislaw Misztal), *Religion and Politics in Comparative Perspective: Revival of Religious Fundamentalism in East and West* (1992), and *In the Name of All That's Holy: A Theory of Clergy Malfeasance* (1995).

EDWARD SILVER is a graduate student in the Ph.D. program in sociology at the University of Virginia. His interests are in the sociology of religion, social movements, and deviance.

JAMES D. TABOR is associate professor of religious studies at the University of North Carolina, Charlotte. His field is ancient Judaism and Christian origins with a special interest in apocalyptic movements, both past and present. He is coauthor (with Arthur J. Droge) of *A Noble Death: Suicide and Martyrdom among Christians and Jews in Antiquity* (1992), and has just completed a book on the Branch Davidian confrontation (with Eugene V. Gallagher) titled *Why Waco? The War against Cults and Religious Freedom in America* (1995).

RHYS H. WILLIAMS is associate professor of sociology at Southern Illinois University. During the 1992–94 academic years, he was a visiting fellow at Yale University's Program on Non-Profit Organizations and department of sociology. He is coauthor (with N. J. Demerath III) of *A Bridging of Faiths: Religion and Politics in a New England City* (1992) and author of numerous scholarly articles, including "Movement Dynamics and Social Change: Transforming Fundamentalist Ideology and Organizations," in *Accounting for Fundamentalism* (1994), edited by Martin R. Marty and R. Scott Appleby. His interests include the interactions among religion, politics, and culture.

STUART A. WRIGHT is associate professor of sociology at Lamar University in Texas. He received his Ph.D. from the University of Connecticut in 1983. Wright was a postdoctoral fellow and lecturer in 1984–85 at Yale University, where he received an NIMH grant to study the social and psychological effects of participation in new religions. He has published a monograph on the subject, *Leaving Cults: The Dynamics of Defection* (1987), as well as numerous articles and book chapters in edited volumes. Recent contributions include "Reconceptualizing Cult Coercion and Withdrawal," in *Social Forces* (1991); "Leaving New Religions" (with Helen R. Ebaugh) and "Families and New Religions" (with William V. D'Antonio), both in *The Handbook of Cults and Sects in America* (1993), edited by David G. Bromley and Jeffrey K. Hadden.

Index